Fullerton's Rangers

John F. Fullerton, first captain of the New Mexico Mounted Police
(near the Fullerton Ranch corrals, spring 1905; Irene Fullerton's photograph album)

Fullerton's Rangers

A History of the New Mexico Territorial Mounted Police

Chuck Hornung

FOREWORD BY FRED LAMBERT

McFarland & Company, Inc., Publishers
Jefferson, North Carolina, and London

The present work is a reprint of the illustrated case bound edition of Fullerton's Rangers: A History of the New Mexico Territorial Mounted Police, *first published in 2005 by McFarland.*

LIBRARY OF CONGRESS CATALOGUING-IN-PUBLICATION DATA

Hornung, Chuck, 1943–
Fullerton's Rangers : a history of the New Mexico Territorial Mounted Police / Chuck Hornung ; foreword by Fred Lambert.
p.   cm.
Includes bibliographical references and index.

ISBN 978-0-7864-6426-5
softcover : 50# alkaline paper ∞

1. Fullerton, John Ferguson, d. 1928.
2. New Mexico. Mounted Police — History.
3. Mounted police — New Mexico — Biography.
4. Mounted police — New Mexico — History.   I. Title.
HV7911.F85H67   2011   363.2'09789 — dc22   2005017521

BRITISH LIBRARY CATALOGUING DATA ARE AVAILABLE

© 2005 Chuck Hornung. All rights reserved

No part of this book may be reproduced or transmitted in any form or by any means, electronic or mechanical, including photocopying or recording, or by any information storage and retrieval system, without permission in writing from the publisher.

On the cover: John Ferguson Fullerton (Irene Fullerton's photograph album); a Mounted Police mountain scout on horseback (Fred Lambert collection); a New Mexico Mounted Police badge

Manufactured in the United States of America

*McFarland & Company, Inc., Publishers
Box 611, Jefferson, North Carolina 28640
www.mcfarlandpub.com*

To my son Wyatt,
who would like to have lived the adventure
of being one of Fullerton's Rangers,
and to the
men and women of the New Mexico State Police

Acknowledgments

I am indebted to many people for the facts, insights and encouragements that finally made this book a reality. I received assistance from three main sources: personal memories of those who lived the adventure, reminiscences of those who knew the principal characters, and the official records and the newspaper archives.

My grandfather-grandson friendship with the late Charles Fredrick "Fred" Lambert was the focal point that sparked my desire to record the deeds of the New Mexico Mounted Police. When I first met Lambert, in the summer of 1967, he was the last living member of the territorial rangers and over the last four years of his life we spent many wonderful days reliving his adventures. One day, Fred suggested that I write an account of the mounted police and he even recorded comments to be used as the foreword for that book. I promised him that I would undertake the project, and this book is the first step in my plan to record the complete history of the New Mexico Mounted Police.

Two very gracious ladies, the late Mrs. Elmer (Irene) Fullerton and Mrs. Susan Fullerton Leverett, with her husband Bill, opened their Albuquerque home to the author and shared their family memories of Capt. John F. Fullerton. These ladies are the daughter-in-law and granddaughter of the captain. This book would have been more difficult to write without their gracious help and encouragement. I hope I have captured the essence of the man they both loved.

I am deeply indebted, as history should be, for the personal recollections of family members of many of the men who served in the mounted police. Thank you: Mrs. Cipriana Baca Randolph and Mrs. Florentino (Louise) Baca; Tom McGrath; Mrs. I. B. Singer, Steve Meyer, and Jessie B. Meyer; Frank Shofner; Mrs. Jettie Avant Sullenger; Chandler Elkins and Fred and Lois Fornoff, Jr., Virginia Brunner, Sheriff J. B. McNeil, C. E. MacConnell, M. T. Everhart and Persy Sickles. Each shared with me their recollections of members of Fullerton's Rangers. Unfortunately, some of these lovely individuals will not see this volume, because they have been called home to their final reward.

Howard Bryan, retired columnist for the Albuquerque *Tribune* and western history writer, spent many hours discussing the men who had been in the mountie service. As a young reporter, Howard had known and interviewed a few of these former mounties and he made these interviews available to me, including one with Bob Lewis during the late 1940s and the early 1950s. Howard also offered encouragement on this project.

A special thank-you is due to the late Katherine McMahon, who served notably as the head of the Southwest Room at the Albuquerque Public Library (the present day Special Collections Division). During my early years of tracking Fullerton's Rangers she made constant suggestions of places to look for information. Katherine, we miss your ready smile and your encouragement. Special help was also provided me by Dr. Myra Ellen Jenkins and J. Richard Salazar and the staff at the New Mexico State Records Center and Archives in Santa Fe. Assistance was also given by the special collection staff of the old Coronado Room (now the vastly expanded Center for Southwest Research) of the Zimmerman Library at the University of New Mexico in Albuquerque. The research staffs at the Haley Memorial Library and History Center, Midland, Texas; the Rio Grande Historical Collection, New Mexico State University, Las Cruses; New Mexico Tech Library, Socorro; and the Texas State Archives, Austin, were especially helpful. The Genealogical Research Center at the Midland County Public Library, Midland, and the Southwest History Room at the Ector County Public Library, Odessa, Texas, each contain valuable research collections and helpful staff and volunteers.

Ron and Pat Fuss, and their family of friendly cats, have made their Albuquerque home a welcome place for me and my wife to hang our hats during hundreds of trips to the Duke City for fun and research. We love you both and enjoy our always too-short times together.

Thank you to Leon C. Metz and Robert K. DeArment, first-rate western historians and friends, for their encouragement during the difficult early days of discovery. Pat Jones, my retired secretary, always told me "you can do it." Thank you for the encouragement.

The words "thank you" seem so small a reward for my wife. This special lady, like me, loved Fred Lambert, and he became the namesake and godfather for our oldest son. V. J. has shared my dream of completing the needed research and finally writing this volume. She has also lived with the ghosts of Fullerton's Rangers for over three decades.

During their school years, our sons Scott and Wyatt spent many summer vacations helping their father search for hidden graves in forgotten cemeteries. Many times they waited, sometimes under duress, for Dad to finish looking at one more faded newspaper or musty document. Thank you, guys, for letting the mounted police become "living" members of our family.

I cannot end this acknowledgment without mention of my constant companion during those long, lonesome early years of compiling the data and drafting and reworking the format of this volume. Little Cat was always in my lap, on my desk or asleep at my feet. I miss you, little friend.

Table of Contents

Acknowledgments	vii
Foreword by Fred Lambert	1
Introduction: The Legend Begins	5
1. New Mexico: The Land of Enchantment`	9
2. Lawmakers at Santa Fe, 1899	13
3. The Arizona Rangers: The New Mexico Mounted Police's "Grandpa"	22
4. Lawmakers at Santa Fe, 1905	29
5. John Ferguson Fullerton: The Journey Begins	37
6. The Men of Fullerton's Rangers	50
7. "The Governor Shall … Organize a Corps of Mounted Police"	67
8. "The Mounted Police … Shall Have Full Power to Make Arrests"	98
9. Fullerton's Personnel Problems	163
10. The New Mexico Mounted Police Fund	172
11. Road to Oblivion: The Removal of Capt. John F. Fullerton	181
12. From Fullerton's Rangers to Fornoff's Boys	196
13. John Ferguson Fullerton: The Final Years	198
Epilogue	206
Appendix: Cover Route Sheet and Text of Greer Mounted Police Bill	207
Notes	221
Bibliography	245
Index	253

Foreword

by Fred Lambert
The Last Living Territorial Mounted Policeman
29 June 1969

I was a teenager when the Territorial Legislative Assembly created the Mounted Police, but I remember the excitement among the local ranchers; even father. Colfax County was range country and we had recently experienced a rash of cattle rustling. We all knew about the Texas Rangers and their reputation concerning catching stock thieves, and the newly formed Arizona Rangers was having an effect on their mountain outlaws. Our local ranchers supported the need for a New Mexico ranger force.

My older brother Bill wanted to be one of these rangers real bad, but he never made it. Little did I know that I would become one of the Mounted Police instead of Bill. When I received my territorial commission [in 1911] from Governor [William J.] Mills, I was the youngest man ever appointed to the Mountie Service. I was 24 years old when I started working for Captain Fornoff, and I sure had no way to know that I would outlive the rest of the boys.

I served with the Mountie Service until the state legislature refused to fund the police. So, with no money to run the service the Mounties were disbanded in December 1913, except for me. Governors [William] McDonald, [Ezequiel Cabeza] DeBaca and [Washington E.] Lindsey each renewed my commission and kept me on the job and paid me with funds from their office. I worked as the only paid Mounted Police from 1914 until 1917 and took my orders from the governor. I was appointed to the reorganized state police in the summer of 1918, but I choose not to accept the appointment because I had taken a good paying job out of state working for Katie's brother [a brother-in-law] in the Kansas City stock commission business. We later returned home to Cimarron.

I knew some of Fullerton's Rangers from later days and I liked most of the ones I knew. I never knew Captain Fullerton. I knew Cipriano Baca by reputation, but I can't recall having seen him. Bob Lewis I knew; he was a big man. I knew him when he was working up the Vermejo [River] as a range foreman for a big cattle company. I was in the police then and we talked some about the old horse back days before we had automobiles that could reach into the backcountry. I had no idea that I would be riding a motorcycle a few years later when I was in the U.S. Indian Service. Bob had a bad case of rheumatism and couldn't stand the cold mountain air, so he went back to the Magdalena country.

Will Dudley also came up in the north country in later years. He was the marshal at Dawson when I knew him. He was a leader in KPs [Knights of Pythias, a fraternal organization] and I was in the CMA [Coming Men of America, an early version of the Jaycees], but I know that he was a heavy drinker and a ladies' man. He was a big man with a wide waistline, and he was the boss enforcer among the miners. Will had a little bit of a wife, a headstrong woman who kept him in tow, and two teenage daughters, as I recall.

I had some dealings with Herb McGrath when he was the sheriff of Grant County. I was on an undercover mission [for the mounted police] and got arrested by the Silver City marshal, and I got McGrath to get me out of jail. I completed the case and returned home only to be called back south to work with McGrath again. He was a well mannered gentleman. A widower if I remember right; well liked by the people in Grant County. He had a ranch just outside of town, but McGrath lived in a big brick house in town.

Dick Huber was an old-timer who loved to spin tall tales of the old days; Indian raids, stagecoach robbers and his adventures. Made up most of them tales, but he could sure tell a story. I was in Santa Fe in them days working for the U.S. Indian Service, and Huber was known as a town character. If I remember right he worked for a moving company or something like that kind of work. Huber had a big droopy mustache and a head of white hair and a voice that boomed across a room. He drove the stagecoach in the Santa Fe parade each year; a real windy.

I knew Rafael Gomez best. He had been with Fullerton and then stayed on with Cap Fornoff. Gomez was among the best boys in the Mountie Service. He was a good officer and was respected by Anglos and the Mexicans. Ole Rafael and me had some good times together. I'll never forget the time we policed the big fight at Las Vegas [July 4, 1912] between John Johnson and "Fireman" Flynn for the world heavyweight championship. That was the time Cap Fornoff jumped into the ring to stop the fight. Rafael was a drinker, a gambler and a ladies' man, but he was a true gentleman and a good friend. Coulda been just yesterday we had that running shoot-out near the line [Mexican border] at El Paso [with some of Pancho Villa's Raiders] and I went down like a boxer had hit me when I got my boot-heel shot off. I weren't hurt none, but [it] sure is hard to run with no heel on your boot. Ole Gomez he stayed near and covered me. We had some times with Cap and the rest of the boys. The old Mountie Service was a grand life and Gomez was one of the best. He was a real practical joker; fun to be around. A true ace-high gentleman.

Julius Meyer was the sheriff of Torrance County when I knew him. He and Cap was business partners, so Meyer would sometimes come to Santa Fe to see the chief when I was working out of the office. I don't remember much about him, except that he had a droopy eye and was a big coffee drinker and he and the captain would flood the office with cigar smoke and tell jokes all day. Some of them jokes were not proper in mixed company or for them with a tender ear.

Law enforcement in my day was a tough business. Things could tighten up mighty fast and death was the final judgment. Being a lawman in the territorial days called not only for courage, good luck, and a quick trigger finger, but the ability to outwit the lawbreaker and sometimes even the letter of the law. I'm proud of having

Fred Lambert and friends photographed at the author's birthday celebration in June 1969, held at Lambert's home in Cimarron, N.M. Lambert is holding the author's son Scott Lambert Hornung, named in honor of the elderly lawman. Beside him is V. J. Hornung, the author's wife (NMMP/AC).

been a peace officer and to have been in New Mexico's Mountie Service. It was a great life and the Mounties that I worked with were all men with the right kind of steel.

Chuck, I want to give you some advice I learned over my lifetime. This is my birthday gift to you, not quite up to V.J.'s wonderful cake, but given with love just the same. Do right for right's sake and never do right from fear of punishment. Look every man in the eye and be able to tell him to go to hell if he even intimates he wants you to violate the law and in your last days you'll be glad. Do things right, not only on your own account, but on account of your loved ones, V.J. and little Scotty now. They will be honored to follow in your footsteps. My time's near up and I'll join Katie soon, but I hope to awaken in a much cooler climate than if I had wasted my life trying to evade the law. I see it in your eyes, and by your actions, you are a true lawman in your heart. You would have been one of us. Yep, you would have been with us for sure. Always serve justice, my friend.

You want to write a history of the Mounted Police? Well let me tell you, a book about we boys would be something that would make the angels and devils mingle their tears. Now son, if you tell this story about the Mountie Service you tell it right. Tell the truth, my friend. Tell it like it was with no dime novel heroics. It was a tough job that needed doing and we boys just done it. Nothing more; nothing less. We got paid to do a job and we done it.

Introduction: The Legend Begins

"The United States ought to declare war on Mexico and make it take back New Mexico."

Gen. William T. Sherman
1878 military dispatch

In his autobiography concerning his years as territorial governor, Miguel A. Otero declared, "Outlaws, train robbers, and other desperadoes furnish a rather picturesque element in the West of fiction and the scenario. However, in real life they gave the southwestern territories a reputation for crime and violence and insecurity of life and property which greatly retarded the coming of both immigration and capital [investment for business expansion]."[1] New Mexico Territory, at the turn of the century, had become the catch basin for the flotsam and jetsam of humanity.

In late August 1905, the *New York Times* carried an illustrated Sunday feature story on New Mexico Territory with a banner headline that proclaimed, "MOST UN-AMERICAN PART OF THE UNITED STATES." A subhead read, "Strange Stories of People and Things in New Mexico. A Large Proportion of the Population Ignorant of or Indifferent to Our Laws and Institutions." The author reported wild tales about Indians performing human sacrifice dances, Mexican officials who did not know or understand American law and a Mexican governor (M.A. Otero) who was "helpless" when it came to his duty to support law enforcement.

The last paragraph of the feature began, "Meantime New Mexico [Territory] is a whole lot of things that are good. It has even a thing or two that is absolutely the best in the world." In the end, the article devoted a couple of sentences to the scenic beauty and healthful climate of the Sunshine Territory. The closing comment speaks for itself. "And surely New Mexico is the strangest and most interesting corner of our country, inasmuch as when one gets there he must pinch himself to make himself really believe that he is not in a foreign land among a foreign people while still within the United States and still under the flag that Betsey [sic] Ross made."[2] Strange as it may seem today, the *New York Times* feature of so long ago is just a distant echo of feelings that linger and are often expressed, by many citizens of other states in the federal union. Many of these people have never been to New Mexico.

Not everyone was so limited in his view of New Mexico. In the spring of 1905, a geologist and civil engineer traveling the territory recorded his observations concerning scenery. "There is not a plain nor valley so wide in all New Mexico but that you can see mountains from any portion of it. The air is so clear and pure that the natural eye commands a view in every direction for many miles. The medical springs of New Mexico are truly wonderful. But few of them are known outside of their immediate neighborhood.... [However] there are few employers of labor."[3] New Mexico has always been a land of scenery. The area was once nicknamed the Sunshine Territory and after statehood it became the Turquoise State. Today, New Mexico is called the Land of Enchantment and the state's motto is "*Crescit Eundo*— It Grows As It Goes." To truly understand the state a person must first understand the land and its people. This may be why some call this multicultural paradise God's Country.

New Mexico is 121,666 square miles of mountains and deserts, and 78 million acres of timber, water, livestock range and farmland. The Enchanted Land is equal in size to the combined area of Connecticut, Delaware, Maine, Massachusetts, New Hampshire, New Jersey, Rhode Island, Vermont and New York. Much of this vast expanse of the southwest is publicly owned. The federal government controls over a third of New Mexico, the state controls about 12 percent of the land, and Indian reservations are allotted another 10 percent. Private land ownership accounts for about 38 million acres.

Over the centuries people from many nationalities have discovered the enchanting natural beauty that is New Mexico; piñon and ponderosa pine cover mountains that reach over 13,000 feet and a cavern sprawls for miles more than 800 feet underground. The state's large eastern plains, the Llano Estacado, and the rolling hill country with its sparse vegetation give way to plateaus and mesas and mountain or spring-fed waterways. The summer temperatures range from 50 to 100 degrees on the plains. Six of the seven life zones of North America exist within this land of God-given charm. New Mexico's crystal clear blue sky masks the fact that the land has less surface water than any state in the union. Water has been the focal point of life and death in New Mexico since the arrival of man during the Stone Age. The annual rainfall is 6 to 16 inches, and this lack of moisture is difficult for a nonresident to appreciate.[4]

New Mexico has never been a melting pot of culture or racial heritage. The native Indian, the Spanish or Mexican, the *nuevomexicano,* the Anglo and other ethnic groups have each clung to its social and political relationships. New Mexico has two official state songs; one is in English and the other is in Spanish. The Land of Enchantment is a cultural mosaic, and the wealth of New Mexico is its multicultural composition.[5] It is this mix that kept New Mexico a territory for over six decades and it was the conflicts of becoming an American people that finally led to the formation of the territorial police.

Time has clouded the remembrance of how conditions really were in New Mexico just before the formation of Fullerton's Rangers. The Sunshine Territory, at the turn of the twentieth century, was deeply divided by political factions that represented the large rancher and farmer and the small hand-to-mouth enterprises. The Hispanic population was fighting to remain in control of its lands and power. Cattlemen fought sheepmen over grazing rights. Miners and lumbermen struggled with conservationists over pollution, and farmers seemed to always have financial problems with bankers and merchants. In 1890, the federal government had declared that the frontier was settled and that the era of the Wild West was history, but the general impression in New Mexico was that crime knew no limit and that the gun was still the final answer to all problems. The territory's leaders understood that New Mexico's progress—self-government under statehood—hinged upon citizen safety and business security. Law and order had to be restored and maintained.

What remains of the old New Mexico Mounted Police records are stored away and almost forgotten by present-day historians. Contemporary newspapers are yellowed and crisp from age, and the youthful voices of a bygone era are stilled. The smell of gunpowder has been blown away by winds from a distant past; bitter feelings and happy dreams are faded memories. Those hard, lonely days of yesteryear have become glorified legends of the present, and with each new decade it becomes more difficult to separate the heroic western myth from the stark facts.

It was in a forge of civil crisis, upon an anvil of necessity that the New Mexico Mounted Police was hammered to life. This is the story of that birth. These are the tales of Capt. John F. Fullerton and his rangers.

1

New Mexico: The Land of Enchantment

> "We step upon the threshold of 1900 which leads to the new century facing a still brighter dawn of civilization."
> — *The New York Times*
> 31 December 1899

When the twentieth century dawned, 60 percent of the female population of the United States lived in rural areas, while in New Mexico Territory that figure was 86 percent. The median age of America's women was 24, while in New Mexico it was 19 years old. Nationally 72 percent of the women age 25 to 29 had been married. In the Sunshine Territory, the percentage reached 88. New Mexico was higher than the national average in its death rate per babies born. The national census showed that the average woman in New Mexico lived in a rural area, married young, had many children and lost a high percentage to childhood death. A woman living in New Mexico had a life expectancy of about 47 years and her babies were born at home.

In 1900, New Mexico had a female population of about 78,000. Most were native-born, and a large percentage of these women were Spanish speaking and Hispanic in their cultural heritage. Less than 1 percent of New Mexico's female population was of African American descent. These few black women were widely scattered throughout the territory.

Four-fifths of New Mexico's farm and ranch lands were controlled by about 3 percent of the families that made a living in this manner. The truth behind the homesteading myth is that the women worked the small farm while their men earned wages as day laborers on the larger farms, in the mines, on the large ranches or as railroad construction help. Most homesteading in New Mexico was done on the high plains in the northwestern part of the territory or in the central Estancia Valley. These small family enterprises raised chickens, hogs, turkeys or maybe a few dairy cows. Some homesteaders were able to sell eggs and vegetables to nearby city families, but most homestead farms failed within a few years because of the weather and the hard day-to-day life.

During the first decade of the twentieth century, Americans began to "modernize" their lifestyle. People in New Mexico Territory were no different from other Americans in the desire to make their life more enjoyable. The territory's newspapers and national magazines kept readers updated on the newest developments in creature comforts.

Quick breakfast foods were in their infancy, and among these early choices was boxed Cream of Wheat, Quaker Oats and Shredded Whole Wheat Biscuits. Another very popular breakfast food was the packaged flour mix for Aunt Jemima Pancakes with the new syrup from the tin can shaped like a log cabin. President Teddy Roosevelt had declared that the fresh ground coffee served at Nashville's Maxwell House was "good to the last drop" and now that same coffee was available, pre-ground, in cans. Even so, America's most popular coffee was Arbuckle's Ariosa with the Flying Angel trademark on the airtight canisters.

New Mexico's children learned moral principles, social graces, patriotism, and self-discipline from studying their *McGuffey's Eclectic Readers*. Each of these eight textbooks, one for each grade level, based its message upon passages from the Bible, great literature and the lives of historical heroes.[1] Over a third of the articles published in the *Ladies Home Journal, The Women's Home Companion* and *Good Housekeeping* magazines dealt with good character development, the importance of motherhood, the home and child rearing. In the decades around the turn of the century, mothers held a place of honor and respect in America's culture. Religion was a central focus of the family and the community in New Mexico. For centuries there had been a strong foundation for Indian nature ceremonies, but the Catholic Church soon held center ground. However, new settlers brought with them their own faith, and by 1905 most of the major protestant Christian denominations were represented in many of the territory's larger communities, while many small villages had a community house of worship. The Jewish faith was centered in Albuquerque and Las Vegas, and the Mormons had settlements along the Arizona border.

Ninety percent of America's physicians had no college education because a college degree was not required to attend a medical school in the United States. In most states and territories, a doctor was not required to be licensed, but only to have attended, but not necessarily have graduated from, a medical school. It should also be noted that the federal government considered many of the nation's medical schools to be substandard academically. America's health care situation was not all bleak. The average veterinarian was better educated, licensed, and earned more money than a family practice doctor. The leading causes of death in the United States were pneumonia and influenza. These were followed by tuberculosis, diarrhea, heart disease and stroke.

Marijuana, heroin and morphine were all sold over the counter at any well supplied apothecary. One national advertisement claimed, "Heroin clears the complexion, gives buoyancy to the mind, regulates the stomach and the bowels, and is, in fact, a perfect guardian of health." Coca-Cola, containing cocaine instead of caffeine like most other soft drinks, was sold at the soda fountain in most drugstores as a health drink. True health care remedies were slowly replacing the popular alcoholic or drug-based patent medications. Among the new packaged products were Smith Brothers' Cough Drops, Vaseline Petroleum Jelly, and Richardson's Croup and Pneumonia Cure Salve, today called Vick's VapoRub. Arnica Tooth Soap was sold for oral hygiene. Many women's personal hygiene and contraceptive products were not widely available in local general stores, so New Mexico's women bought these supplies mostly via mail order catalogs or on a trip to a big city drugstore.

A century ago, the health food industry was just a baby. C.W. Post was trying to market Sanka and Postum as coffee substitutes. Post also tried to sell a cornflake breakfast food he called Elijah's Manna, but conservative Jewish and Christian believers in the Bible Belt caused such an uproar over the name that the cereal was renamed Post Toasties. Eagle Brand condensed milk, marketed by a Texan named Gale Borden, was very popular on New Mexico's cattle and sheep ranges and remote farms areas because the milk needed no refrigeration and had a long shelf life. Van Camp's Pork and Beans, in a tin can, was popular on the Western range because the beans were presoaked and just needed heating. The progressive housewife with extra money would sometimes serve her family a quick dessert called Minute Tapioca, or maybe she bought a new easy-to-cook gelatin, sold in ten-cent boxes, called Jell-O.

Women who could afford the price washed their clothes with 20 Mule Team Borax powder and scrubbed their children with "99 & $^{44}/_{100}$ per cent pure" Ivory soap. Many New Mexico ranch folks still used homemade lye soap for both of these purposes. Beauty conscious women often used John H. Woodbury's facial soap, facial powder and facial cream for their complexion. Women could also wash their hair with his new "medicated scalp soap" and use his new "dental cream" to brush her teeth. Even with the new convenient hair care products available, most women still only washed their hair once a month, and then they used the old standard of borax, tar soap or egg yolks for shampoo. Sophisticated women used a new product called Coolene. It cost 50 cents per bottle and was advertised to stop "excessive perspiration" and "eliminate all offensive odor." Few country women used deodorant; most just used strong soap. For most rural men the idea of using a deodorant was unmanly; men were supposed to smell like men and even the Saturday night bath was taken under duress. Bathing is so commonplace today, it is often forgotten that in the early 1900s only 14 percent of America's homes contained a built-in bathtub.

New Mexico's tough working men puffed Genuine Durham Smoking Tobacco, but because of the steer logo on the cloth bag the brand was popularly called Bull Durham. In the cities, society gentlemen were smoking pre-rolled Chesterfield cigarettes. Men looked forward to a barber shop trip so they could read the latest issue of the *National Police Gazette, Popular Mechanics* and the *Farm Journal*. The daily barbershop shave or the straight razor nightmare was no longer necessary to the men who used King C. Gillette's new safety home razor and its interchangeable blade. In small towns, the neighborhood tavern was still in vogue and the men would stop by after work or for weekend drinks with the "boys" while the "women folk" stayed at home with the children.

Ready-made clothing manufacturers had a new gadget to assist with their trade because early in the century the zipper was patented; belt loops also started to appear on men's pants. It would be 50 years before the suspenders disappeared only to be rediscovered as a high society fashion statement in the late 1990s. Women still made household work dresses out of colorful grain sacks and men still wore their work pants with patched knees and flared cuffs well into the 1950s.

In an Albuquerque business office, the secretary could use an electric typewriter or the Y&E Quick Copier Machine. The 1900 federal census counters had, for the first time, used the new punch card data processing system to compile their results. This was an early predecessor of the computer. An accountant could use the self-adding machine and the large city newspapers could, because of advertising revenue, afford to print photographs instead of line cuts in their daily editions.

Major production motion pictures were "two reels" and told a simple story. On June 19, 1905, the first theater house devoted exclusively to presenting a program of motion pictures was opened in Pittsburgh. A single-line long distance telephone service was available, in at least one business, in many of New Mexico's remote areas. Train travel was the most popular mode of transportation in the territory, with the new gasoline motor coach a distant second. Cyanide had been discovered, the first vaporized fire extinguisher was manufactured and the theory of relativity was first presented to the scientific community.

In 1900, the nation had just over 144 miles of paved roads and a growing number of automobiles. Five years later the nation had over 161,000 miles of paved roads and that number was increasing daily. New Mexico saw more horseless carriages after the territory established a new road building and paving program across the countryside. The citizens of Santa Fe even became accustomed to seeing Governor Otero driving his motor car to and from his office on the dusty streets of the capital city.[2]

Fewer than 100 wild buffalo still roamed free in the western United States in 1905. New Mexico's gold and silver mining industry was still recovering from the 1893 depression, but copper, zinc, lead and especially coal were experiencing record production. New railroads were opening up vast undeveloped areas for livestock, agricultural, lumbering and recreational interests. Albuquerque was the territory's largest city, just ahead of the joint population of the two sister communities of Las Vegas. Santa Fe was next in size, followed by Las Lunas, Tierra Amarilla, Socorro and Silver City. New villages were developing in eastern New Mexico's homestead areas. Settlements were becoming towns and towns were becoming cities.[3]

Both the economy and the population of New Mexico Territory were experiencing annual growth. Governor Otero reported to Washington that "progress has been made in the establishment of new manufacturing industries or the expansion of those which have been established. Especially has this been the case in the manufacture of cement, of lumber and of the treatment of ores."[4]

The turn of the twentieth century saw New Mexico Territory in a growth mode and with that new growth came change. Economic development attracts all classes of people to a region, and these new people bring new opportunities and the need for more public safety. This set the climate for the birth of the New Mexico Territorial Mounted Police.

2

Lawmakers at Santa Fe, 1899

> "Anent [concerning] the organization of a [territorial] ranger company for the protection of the livestock interests, why wouldn't it be a good idea for the cattle sanitary board to take charge of the maintenance of such a company and levy a special tax on stockmen for the money necessary?"
>
> The (Socorro) *Chieftain*
> 10 February 1899

Early in January 1899, 12 men gathered in the Council Chamber of the Capitol in Santa Fe to conduct serious public business. They were the upper house of New Mexico Territory's Legislative Assembly, and one of the many pressing issues these men would debate dealt with the formation of a territorial police force.[1]

Once again law enforcement was a major issue before the territorial lawmakers. It seemed to be the same old dragon back for another joust with the champion of justice. Legislators made the laws and peace officers sometimes enforced them, but in either case the judicial system often followed local sentiment in the prosecution of lawbreakers.

In the 1870s the territorial lawmakers had made it illegal to wear pistols on the person while in a settlement, and in 1887 lawmakers enacted a heavy fine for the conviction of "carrying arms." Conviction, however, was predicated upon an arrest and a trial. In most parts of the territory enforcement was slow or nonexistent.

New Mexico had a Sunday closing law for saloons as early as 1876. Saloon owners just closed their front doors but conveniently left the side or back doors unlocked for self-service patrons. High license fees were enacted to control saloon operation during the 1880s and 1890s, and then local ordinances began to prohibit bars altogether. Territory-wide prohibition was supported by the Women's Christian Temperance Union and the Anti-Saloon League of America.

Gambling rooms were made illegal in the 1870s, but the fine for a violation of the law was considered more of a tax than a fine for committing a crime. In 1887, the territorial assembly reversed itself and made "gaming" legal wherever local ordinances did not prohibit it. Citizens of the newly settled southeastern section of the territory led the fight against gambling as they had led the fight to close the saloons. In March 1905, Artesia voters approved New Mexico's first local ordinance to close gaming halls. By December 31, 1907, gambling once again had become illegal everywhere in New Mexico Territory.

Firearms had been outlawed from public wear, saloons were closed on Sunday and gambling was only semi-legal across the territory. The only remaining sin was the "pleasure palace," and these centers for male amusement had been officially declared illegal in 1860, but the public still tolerated "red light" districts. In fact, many towns depended upon the fines imposed upon the brothels and the individual prostitutes to finance their local governments.

New Mexico's leading citizens knew that just making a law would not change a community's moral character. Many felt that moral values should be taught at home, in church and in the schoolhouse, so the almost entirely Spanish-American controlled territorial assembly, in 1878, enacted a law commonly called the Jesuit School Bill. This legislation incorporated the Jesuit Fathers as a New Mexico business with the right to establish educational institutions anywhere in the territory. The bill also gave the Jesuits the right to own property tax free in perpetuity. Territorial Gov. Samuel B. Axtell felt the bill crossed the line between freedom from state religion and the government's responsibility for public education, so he vetoed the act only to have the legislature override his objection and make the act law. Congress agreed with Axtell and annulled the Jesuit School Act on February 4, 1879, thus ending that attempt to set up a tax-supported, church-run public school system. The tragic result was that it took over a decade before public education again became a hotly debated issue with territorial lawmakers.

The 1891 Territorial Legislative Assembly passed a public school code that became the foundation for education in New Mexico. This act provided for a territorial superintendent of public instruction and a territorial board of education. It also authorized issuance of bonds to finance construction of buildings and gave local school trustees authority to levy a public school tax to support the educational program in their district.

A public school system had been created, but many districts struggled to maintain the mandated minimum three month school term. The hiring of a teacher, furnishing the school's firewood or coal, and the janitor's job became political plums that were awarded to "favored" individuals; bribes played a big part in this system. Wealthy families continued to send their children to private schools while tax-supported public education struggled to stay alive.

New Mexico, two decades after statehood, would still rank only forty-sixth among the 48 states in literacy. It would take more decades before the feeling that basic education for "common folk" was not a luxury. Slowly the concept that public education for all citizens was an investment in the state's future took root and in 1996 the state lottery began to fund college tuition for New Mexico high school graduates who would maintain a 2.5 grade point average while enrolled full-time in a New Mexico public college or university. Higher education was founded upon the creation of the University of New Mexico and the present day New Mexico State University in 1889. Several other higher level educational institutions were founded during the next decades.

The Southwest Frontier

New Mexico was a land for dreamers, and the lure of free or cheap land brought many homesteaders to settle on the land grants claimed by Mexican families.

Congress was finally forced to create a special Court of Private Land Claims to settle the four-decade-old legal fight over who held rightful ownership of the territory's Spanish and Mexican land grants. The *Gorras Blancas*, as the Mexican natives called the White Caps, had their own answer to the land grant problem. They would burn the Anglos' homes, kill their cattle and drive them off the "stolen" lands.

In New Mexico violence always seemed to be the answer to any disagreement. Raton, Las Vegas and Albuquerque were sites of demonstrations and railroad worker strikes during the 1894 national Pullman Coach Company troubles. Silver City lost a marshal in a street shooting because he and a local attorney disagreed on a point of law; another Silver City peace officer was killed because he tried to stop a fight between some cowboys. A cattle association special prosecutor and his young son were killed to stop his pursuit of cattle rustlers. The murder of Col. Albert J. Fountain and the boy in the vast White Sands shocked the territory and caused a 13-year hunt for the assassins. The trail ended when Pat Garrett, the manhunter, was also murdered.

Eddy County Sheriff Les Dow was murdered on the streets of Eddy, present-day Carlsbad, and his killers were freed at their trial. Cattle and horse rustlers took heart at the verdict. Train robbery was not deterred by the territorial law that made it a capital offense to hold up an iron-horse in New Mexico. The outbreak of the Spanish-American War did not even cause the outlaw gangs to take a second breath. When the outlaw's trail was followed death was often the reward. Three lawmen discovered this fact in a blazing ambush in May 1898.[2]

The federal government, by the mid–1890s, had withdrawn most of its military units from New Mexico's forts. The national Posse Comitatus Law hampered the use of the remaining federal troops to assist local peace officers; even federal marshals could not be used to help prevent non-federal crime.[3] New Mexico was in the midst of a crime wave that threatened to destroy the territory's improving economy. The Sunshine Territory's major business was stock raising, and many out-of-work Spanish War veterans had flocked to the western ranges in search of employment. Few jobs were available, so stock theft and other range crimes began to increase so quickly that stockmen felt the problem needed some swift action.[4] In the fall of 1898, one of the leading newspapers in New Mexico's sister territory of Arizona proclaimed, "When such conditions [livestock rustling] exist, a company of paid 'Rangers' are required to stamp out and destroy the characters that bring about such a state of affairs. Let us have a Territorial Ranger Service."[5]

By the time New Mexico's Thirty-Third Legislative Assembly convened, political assassination had become a better technique than ballet box stuffing to gain power. One leader so marked for death was Republican territorial boss Thomas B. Catron. To many people Catron was a pariah who lived off the misfortunes of others and was the worst of the land grant opportunists who took advantage of Native Americans and Hispanics. The bullets fired through Catron's Santa Fe law office window missed him, but did hit his friend J.H. Ancheta. The Silver City man was not badly injured, but the experience scarred him for life. Catron and Ancheta were both members of the newly elected Thirty-third Territorial Legislative Council and would deal with the problem of crime in the territory.[6]

Granville A. Richardson

In 1873, Canada's Northwest Territory had experienced problems similar to New Mexico's current breakdown of law and order. Sir John H. "Old Tomorrow" MacDonald, first prime minister of the Dominion of Canada, asked his parliament to create a force of police mounted and equipped like soldiers, but commissioned as civil guardians of the law. If the mounted police system had worked in the remote sections of Canada, would it not also work in rural New Mexico Territory? The very name New Mexico Mounted Police seemed to command respect for the law and civil order. It was this name and this concept of law enforcement that was championed by one of New Mexico's legislative councilmen.

Granville A. Richardson was a native of Hopedale, Ohio, and the youngest of three brothers who helped to settle the Lincoln County area that would become Chaves County. He was educated as a lawyer and became a Democrat. He married in 1893 and raised one son. His hometown paper said Richardson "is making a good record in the [1899] legislature and is receiving a great many well deserved compliments from the territorial press. He has presented a large number of bills in the Council, and is one of the most active, energetic members."[7] Later, Richardson served as commissioner for the 1905 Colorado-Kansas water dispute, mayor of Roswell, many terms as president of the Board of Regents for the present-day New Mexico State University, and as a delegate to the 1910 Constitutional Convention. He also spent two terms in the New Mexico legislature he helped to create. Richardson was a judge of the Fifth Judicial District Court, perhaps his greatest public service. The 66-year-old Richardson died in Boston in 1934.[8]

Granville Addison Richardson was a freshman and minority party member of the Thirty-third Legislative Council when he proposed his revolutionary mounted police concept in 1899.

The Mounted Police Bill

Councilman Richardson created a stir on the twelfth day of the 1899 legislative session when he proposed his mounted police idea. Council Bill 54, "An Act to Provide for the Protection of Property in the Territory of New Mexico and to Provide for the Organization and Maintenance of a Company of Mounted Police in the Territory of New Mexico and for Other Purposes," was introduced at the morning session on Monday, January 30. The bill was first read by title, then chamber rules were suspended and the bill was read in full. The Mounted Police Bill was ordered translated into Spanish, printed and referred to the Committee on Territorial Affairs for review. Richardson was one of the three members of that committee.[9]

Richardson's bill provided that the territorial police force would have a dual function as semi-guardsmen and semi-lawmen. The men would be enlisted for two years' service to the citizens of New Mexico. The mounted officers would serve under the authority of the territorial governor through the territorial adjutant general and these quasi–peace officers would have the power to arrest with or without warrants. The mounted police would be governed by the rules and regulations then in force for the army and would be authorized a uniform similar to the one worn by New Mexico's Rough Rider regiment during the Spanish-American War. The captain, to set him apart, was to wear a different style of hat than that worn by the enlisted men.

Richardson proposed a company of ten privates officered by a captain, a lieutenant and a sergeant. The bill provided for the main headquarters to be located at Santa Fe with a field office at Roswell when the company was not on "campaign work." The captain's monthly salary of $200 was slightly less than what the average public schoolteacher made annually. The lieutenant would earn $100, the sergeant $60 and each private $40 per month. The new territorial police force would cost the territorial treasury $1,520 per month or $9,120 per year in salaries.[10]

The Legislative Process

The Richardson Mounted Police Bill had strong support in the southern part of the territory and in fact this section even had a favored-son candidate to lead the territorial police.[11] He was veteran manhunter and Deputy U.S. Marshal George Scarborough.[12] The Santa Fe *New Mexican* said, "Mr. Scarborough has many friends who are morally certain that if he is made captain of the proposed troop of New Mexico rangers, he will clean out the foul roosts that have caused so much trouble."[13] One of the strongest supporters for both the creation of the mounted police and for Scarborough to lead the new lawmen was New Mexico's U.S. Marshal Creighton M. Foraker.[14]

Scarborough even traveled to Santa Fe on "legislative business" to add support to the Richardson Bill, but all the good wishes of friends and the dreams of command did not come true for Scarborough. It took less than two weeks before the Richardson Bill was in trouble. The Socorro *Chieftain* recorded the prevailing sentiment: "Businessmen object to paying for protection to other industries and cattlemen seem willing to stand the brunt of the matter." The major objection to Richardson's mounted police proposal was the generally perceived notion that only the livestock industry would benefit from the protection of a territorial ranger service.[15]

At 10 o'clock on Tuesday morning, March 14, 1899, Chairman T.D. Burns, who represented Taos, Rio Arriba and San Juan counties, presented the report of the Territorial Affairs Committee concerning Council Bill 54. The committee members had listened to citizen concerns and made some amendments. The two chief proposals provided that the mounted police would be funded by private business through the Cattle Sanitary Board and that the officers would limit their operation to the territory's southern counties. These eight counties were listed as Socorro, Grant, Sierra, Dona Ana, Otero, Lincoln, Chaves and Eddy, and it was assumed that stockman residing in these counties would provide the needed funding for the police's operation.[16]

Malaquies Martinez, representing the territory's north central counties, quickly moved that the committee's report be "laid upon the table indefinitely" because he felt that range law enforcement was a rightful duty of the stockmen's associations and was not a matter of territorial concern. A roll call vote was demanded by Councilman J.H. Ancheta of Grant and Dona Ana counties, and the resulting vote was cast along regional lines. The council's journal recorded, "The vote being six in the affirmative and six in the negative the motion is lost. Upon motion of Mr. Ancheta the bill was recommitted."[17] Council President Chaves ordered the bill sent back to committee for refinement, but it died in committee without any further action.[18]

Every two years Congress would authorize the funding for a 60-day legislative session to be held in New Mexico Territory. If the territorial business could not be completed during the allotted time, any unsettled issue must wait for the next session in two years, because the territorial governor had no authority to convene a special legislative session. The fate of Richardson's Mounted Police Bill was sealed when the Legislative Council suddenly adjourned on Thursday, March 16, 1899, 13 days short of a full session.

Governor Otero would later claim that Councilman T.B. Catron, a political rival within his own party, had called for the hasty final adjournment as a means to belittle the governor's office and show the new chief executive who was really the boss in New Mexico politics. Tradition called for the governor to notify the council that all territorial business was completed and the chamber could adjourn. Catron had promised to support the Mounted Police Bill if Councilman Richardson, a true friend of the new governor, would get Otero to sign a bill that Catron was especially interested in becoming a law. Otero signed the bill, but Catron double-crossed Richardson by calling for a quick adjournment. The governor later wrote, "Senator [Councilman] Richardson was heartbroken and cried when denouncing Senator Catron," but Otero and Richardson had their revenge when Otero "pocket vetoed" some other bills that Catron had championed.[19]

Richardson had lost his fight for the territorial police, as well as another law enforcement measure he had proposed. Council Bill 24 had been "An Act to Prohibit the Unlawful Carrying and Use of Deadly Weapons in the Territory of New Mexico." Conviction carried a fine of up to $300 or six months to two years in jail and the arresting officer would have received a third of the fine.[20]

Scarborough's Rangers

Since no agreement could be reached concerning a territorial police force, the lawmakers chose to provide a new mileage system to encourage better performance by sheriffs and their deputies. The new scale was 12½ cents per business mile and 50 cents per diem for feeding while transporting their prisoners.[21] The lawmakers also created a new stock detective law that authorized the governor to hire special manhunters to track down extra-troublesome criminals, but limited the annual cost of these manhunters to $1,000 per year.[22]

Lawmakers selected these methods to solve the territory's outlaw menace and the territorial coffers were also spared the expense of over $9,000 for the proposed mounted force. With the "manhunter law" the lawmakers could claim that they had dealt with the outlaw problem and also saved taxpayers money. In his first State of the Territory address, Governor Otero had reminded lawmakers that for the past 12 years territorial government had operated by red ink financing. Otero recommended a retrenchment plan and said that it "may seem a hardship to those sections immediately affected, it is, nevertheless necessary for the good name and financial standing of the territory."[23]

The Legislative Assembly had now forced New Mexico's long rider problem back upon the territory's regional stock grower's associations. The funding needed to hire professional manhunters to track down range thieves would have to be contributed by vested interest groups and one of the most active of these was the Southwestern New Mexico Cattle Protective Association. This organization quickly developed a plan to fund a corps of range detectives to police the pastures within the association's boundaries.

George Scarborough was the leader of the Southwestern New Mexico Cattle Protective Association's range riders.

In 1959, one of these association range riders remembered, "In 1899, when the New Mexico Cattle Raisers' [sic] Association decided to organize a force to combat the increasing activities of cattle rustlers, George Scarborough was called upon to head the force, and was allowed to select the men who were to work with him. This small force of only six or eight men made many arrests and put the rustlers on the run." J. Marvin Hunter added happily, "I was with that 'Ranger' force barely five weeks—or 33 days to be exact—and was glad to get release from such dangerous work. We were paid $75 a month." Hunter had served, in 1900, under Scarborough's successor,

> ### The Legislative Council Roll Call Vote to Table Council Bill 54
>
> AN ACT TO CREATE A COMPANY OF NEW MEXICO MOUNTED POLICE
> TUESDAY, 14 MARCH, 1899
>
> *Councilman's Name and the Area Represented   Vote to Table*
>
> | | | |
> |---|---|---|
> | 1. Jesus M. Valdez | Colfax/Mora/Union | N |
> | 2. James S. Duncan | San Miguel/Guadalupe | Y |
> | 3. Eugenito Romero | San Miguel/Guadalupe | N |
> | 4. T.D. Burns | Taos, Rio Arriba/San Juan | N |
>
> ### The Legislative Council Roll Call Vote (continued)
>
> | | | |
> |---|---|---|
> | 5. Malaquies Martinez | Taos /Rio Arriba/San Juan | Y |
> | 6. Thomas B. Catron | Santa Fe | N |
> | 7. Thomas A. Finical | Bernalillo | N |
> | 8. Thomas Hughes | Bernalillo | Y |
> | 9. J. Francisco Chaves | Valencia | Y |
> | 10. J.A. Ancheta | Grant/Dona Ana | N |
> | 11. Holm O. Bursum | Socorro/Sierra | Y |
> | 12. G.A. Richardson | Dona Ana/Lincoln/Chaves/Eddy | Y |
>
> The vote on tabling CB 54 was a referendum to kill the bill, but failed due to the tie vote. The council president returned the measure to the Committee on Territorial Affairs for further discussion and possible revision before another vote of the body. The early closing of the council session gave the committee no time to resubmit the bill for a vote, so the idea died in committee without a floor debate.

Frank M. McMahan. McMahan was Hunter's brother-in-law; he was also Scarborough's brother-in-law.[24]

This semi-official posse carried multiple deputy sheriff commissions that granted them police authority within the present day counties of Catron, Socorro, Sierra, Grant, Hidalgo, Luna and Dona Ana.[25] Some evidence would seem to indicate that this same association's range riders may have held limited police detective authority granted by the territorial governor under the provisions of Council Bill 81 passed by the 1899 Legislative Assembly.[26] This quasi-official posse, referred to in the press as "Scarborough's Rangers," was never a very large force. At various times the posse was composed of Ed Scarborough[27], George's son, and Dan Hataway. Walt Birchfield and men named Doak and Collier[28] also rode with Scarborough. These special detectives were captained by Frank McMahan for a short period following George Scarborough's death in April 1900.

Following the murder of George Scarborough, the need for the range riders came into question due to their high-handed tactics. Respect for these private police had quickly turned to resentment. It was this sentiment that caused New Mexico lawmakers to reject the territorial ranger concept in 1901 and again in 1903. Few official records survive to document the true activities of George Scarborough's controversial turn of the century cattlemen's posse, but it would seem that they had no long term effect upon the illegal activities of the range country criminals.[29]

Bringing law and order to the New Mexico frontier would prove to be a slow and painful process. The territory's rugged mountain terrain and proximity to Mexico made the area hard to police. Some of these mountain regions were even claimed as "robbers' roosts" and few lawmen ventured alone into these areas. Some local peace officers proved to be no better than the outlaws they were supposed to pursue.

The idea of a territorial police force was once again debated, in 1901, as Arizona lawmakers took note of New Mexico's mounted police concept and considered the idea their own. They authorized the formation of an 11-man corps of territorial police, called the Arizona Rangers, to handle their outlaw problem. In 1903, the Arizona Rangers were increased to a 26-man company that served until the spring of 1909, when lawmakers disbanded the service.[30]

New Mexico's outlaw problem was not destined to be solved by special range detectives or an increased mileage fee for sheriffs. The success of the Arizona Rangers combined with the efforts of the Texas Rangers proved that point. The simple fact was that New Mexico Territory needed its own ranger force.

3

The Arizona Rangers: The New Mexico Mounted Police's "Grandpa"

> "The personnel of the Arizona Rangers is not known to the general public, as secrecy is required in order that the most effective work may be done. Rangers are often operating in a community without the knowledge of the residents, and their presence is not known until they have completed their work."
>
> Alexander O. Brodie
> Governor of the Territory of Arizona
> *Report to the Secretary of the Interior*
> 1904

In 1901, the structure for a territorial police force was adopted by Arizona lawmakers who had taken note of New Mexico's aborted attempt to create a company of mounted police. These men liked the range rider concept and considered the idea their own, but they choose to call their territorial lawmen rangers instead of mounted policemen.

Thomas Harbro Rynning, the Arizona Rangers' second captain, talked about the police in his autobiography. "The story of the Arizona Rangers isn't just the record of a bunch of mounted police. They were as real a part of that Southwestern Territory as its hills and valleys and deserts; not only one of the biggest chapters in its history, but something without which it couldn't noways ever have become a state." Rynning believed his men were the best lawmen in history. No other body of peace officers "ever did more for civilization than that hard-working and fearless bunch of boys who served under me in Arizona [from 1902 to 1907]."[1] The ranger captain summed up the company when he said they were "there to stop the bad man, not to be one." He added an afterthought by saying an Arizona Ranger "had to slam the fear of Christ into thousands of the meanest outlaws that ever forked leather."[2]

Arizona's business leaders believed there was a real need for this type of territorial lawman. "Along about 1900, things had got so all-fired lawless that small cattlemen were going out of business fast, especially along the border," wrote Rynning. "The sheriffs and their deputies couldn't get nowheres. Half the deputy sheriffs was cattle thieves themselves, anyhow or had been." In the spring of 1901 the matter reached flash point. "Something had to be done if Arizona didn't want to give the killers and thieves a bill of sale to the dam' Territory."[3]

There where those who had a different view of the conditions in Arizona during the spring of 1901. One of these men was rancher-businessman Burton C. Mossman, who told a reporter, "The fact of the matter is that life and property in Arizona is safer than in many of the large eastern cities. The Ranger company was organized to prevent cattle stealing and to rid unsettled sections of the Territory from fugitives from justice who find refuge there."[4] In 1945, Mossman reflected further upon his days of yesteryear. "When I organized the Rangers there had been six sheriffs and deputy sheriffs killed in the past year; I think in the past six months by these goddamned outlaws."[5]

The real reason behind the formation of the Arizona Rangers was pure and simple economics. The territory's economic welfare was at issue. The Arizona Rangers were conceived in a time of turmoil, born during controversy, matured during continual strife and died unwanted and embattled eight years later. The old rangers' law enforcement legend has endured all these fates and in fact it continues to grow in a new era.

Money is a powerful force in the political world and in the Arizona Territory of 1901 the money was controlled by livestock interests, mining companies and railroad capitalists. It would seem that leaders of these groups silently supported the ranger concept. No Arizona newspaper promoted the ranger company idea and Governor Nathan Oakes Murphy made no public request for a territorial police force, yet the Territorial Assembly, in less than a week, enacted the Arizona Ranger Law with little opposition to the measure.

With only eight days left in the legislative session, House Bill 178 was introduced on Wednesday, March 13, and was assigned to the Committee on Appropriations. This bill authorized the governor to raise a 14 man company of rangers; one captain, one sergeant and 12 privates. These men would have "full power to make arrests of criminals in any part of the territory" and would enlist for a twelve month tour of duty "unless sooner discharged." The governor was the commander-in-chief of the rangers "for the purpose of carrying out any measure that may contribute to the better security of the frontier." Two days later the bill moved from committee to the floor with a "do pass" recommendation. The next day, a Saturday, the bill passed the full House with a nineteen to three vote, even with the powerful speaker of the House voting against the measure.[6]

The House sent its ranger bill to the council for their action on Monday morning, March 18. House Bill 178 was given to the Militia and Indian Affairs Committee for consideration. However, the next day the bill was reassigned to the County and County Boundaries Committee for faster action. On Thursday, March 21, the council approved House Bill 178 with a two-vote margin in a seven to five roll call vote.[7] Governor Murphy signed the act into law the same day and the Arizona Rangers were born.

The Rangers of Texas

"A Texas Ranger is the synonym for courage and vigilance," wrote Texas Adjutant General Woodford Mabry. "A bold rider, a quick eye, and a steady hand, he is the terror of the criminal and merely his presence had its moral effect and acts as a wholesome restraint." In 1874 the Texas Legislature had created two divisions of state police. The Special Force was established for duty along the south Texas boundary fighting Mexican bandits, while the Frontier Battalion was organized for service on the western plains fighting Indians and other "troublemakers." Both groups were commonly called rangers, but some historians have claimed that only the members of the Frontier Battalion were legally rangers and that has provided for lively discussions on the subject. Over the years the authority of the rangers had been questioned, so in the spring of 1900 Texas Attorney General Thomas S. Smith was asked to clarify the matter. The creation act said that "officers of the law had the power to make arrests." The question was, who was an "officer"? Most of the public had believed that all rangers had the authority to arrest a person accused of a crime, but Smith ruled that only "commissioned officers" held that authority. This narrow interpretation of the law severely limited the state police function for over a year.[8]

On March 29, 1901, the Twenty-seventh Texas State Legislature with the governor's approval abolished the Special Force and the Frontier Battalion and created the new Ranger Force of Texas commanded by the state adjutant general. Each of the four field companies was led by a captain, with a sergeant and up to 18 privates, but the force was only funded for eight privates per company. All the members were given "full power to make arrests" and were paid a dollar a day for their food and 50 cents per day per active duty horse. The captain earned $120 per month, sergeants earned $75 per month and privates were paid $55 per month. The Ranger Force law took effect on July 9, 1901.[9] The captain, sergeant and privates of the new Arizona Rangers were paid the same monthly salary and food per diem as the new Texas Rangers.

The author has long held the belief that the 1901 Arizona Ranger Bill was modeled after the 1899 New Mexico Mounted Police Bill. It is difficult to make a definitive judgment concerning that theory because the original copy of each of these bills is missing from the archives in their respective states. No copy of the 1899 Mounted Police Bill is known to exist and only newspaper reports of its proposals remain. No working drafts of the 1901 Arizona Rangers Bill have been located; however, the final signed copy is among the records of the Twenty-first Legislative Assembly. It is noteworthy that all of that session's bills that were passed and signed into law, except for the Arizona Ranger Bill, were handwritten and contained marked out revisions. The Arizona Ranger Bill stands alone; it is nicely typed on quality legal size paper and properly formatted in the legislative style.

One legend concerning the birth of the Arizona Rangers has Governor Murphy asking Burt Mossman and Frank Cox, chief attorney for the Southern Pacific Railroad in Phoenix, to draft a bill to create a territorial police force. This story has the two men sequestered in Phoenix's Adams Hotel while they created an outline for the Arizona Rangers. Did Mossman or Cox have a copy of the 1899 New Mexico Mounted Police Bill? Murphy and Otero were good friends, plus both Mossman and Cox had high placed friends in New Mexico's political framework.

The legend is that Mossman was to be the head of the new ranger force with a mission to clean up Arizona and make the territory safe for decent folk. So much for that part of the legend, because Mossman told a newspaper reporter that he had turned down the offer to be the ranger captain twice before he finally accepted the position on August 1.[10] Another tale even suggests that prominent New Mexico politician Albert Bacon Fall, attorney for Arizona's major mining interests, actively promoted fellow New Mexico rancher Burt Mossman for the captain's post.[11]

Another part of the legend claims that Arizona was in imminent danger of outlaw rule, yet over four months elapsed between the date that Governor Murphy signed the Arizona Rangers Act into law and when he finally appointed Mossman as the first captain. It was another month before Mossman had the ranger force ready for patrol duty around the territory.

At the time, no one seemed to have asked why a man who claimed he had made a thousand dollars a month the year before would suddenly accept so little pay, $125 per month, for such a dangerous job. One ranger historian has suggested that some of Mossman's wealthy business friends may have supplied him with additional funds as a bonus for this civic duty for one year.[12] In his twilight years, Burton Mossman gave his own answer to the money question: "An attorney at Flagstaff kept my money loaned out at a good rate of interest. I had been down to Phoenix and made pretty good wages there for several years, five or six hundred [dollars] per month, salary and fees, as [a] cattle inspector."[13]

Murphy and Otero

In mid–August 1901, Governor Murphy wrote his good friend New Mexico Governor Miguel Otero concerning the formation of the new Arizona Rangers. He said the rangers were "to patrol the border and mountain fastnesses [sic] of the Territory for the purpose of arresting and ridding the country of desperadoes and outlaws." Murphy continued, "I am informed that in the Mogollon mountains, along the Black River, and near the New Mexico line, these outlaws find refuge." Now Murphy made the tough request from one governor to another governor, one friend to another. Murphy needed a big favor.

"I have selected as Captain of the Ranger company a very capable and reliable man, who informs me that in hot pursuit of criminals very likely he will at times get into New Mexico; and he would like permission to pursue criminals over the line and make arrests without the formality of extradition proceedings." This is the same request still made by twenty-first century peace officers.

Murphy now qualifies his request. "Of course, if outlaws arrested in New Mexico appeal to the courts and a strict interpretation of the law is had, probably the regulations would have to be observed in the matter of obtaining their surrender for trial in this Territory." It was unspoken knowledge that a suspect could die in an escape effort if he resisted arrest in New Mexico.

"So far as you can, however, I earnestly request your co-operation in assisting in the arrest and destruction of desperadoes, train robbers and other outlaws who may seek refuge in your Territory when driven across the line; and I assure you that the rangers will faithfully arrest a known offender against the laws of New Mexico as they will against the laws of Arizona."[14] With that promise by Governor Murphy, the Arizona Rangers would not only be Arizona lawmen, but were pledged to also be "ex officio" policemen of their sister territory.

It was six weeks before Governor Otero was able to reply to Murphy's letter. Otero explained to his friend that his letter had arrived while he was on vacation and also attending the funeral of President William McKinley in Canton, Ohio. "I have only been back a few days and have just reached your letter regarding the organization of a company of range riders in Arizona."

Otero was quick to state the point of his letter. "I can assure you that I will heartily co-operate with you in assisting in the arrest, destruction of desperados, train-robbers and other outlaws, who may seek refuge in New Mexico. You may depend upon it that I will aid you in every way possible in securing the arrest of these people." Murphy had the support he was seeking, but Otero added a qualifier to that support. "While I do not feel authorized to give any direct permission in the matter [of arrests made in New Mexico] I will state that I will protect your men in every possible way, and will see that none of our officers obstruct the rangers in their desire to make arrests of this class of criminals." Otero told his friend, "I am pleased to note that Arizona has taken a lead in this direction. While a similar bill has been up before our legislature we have been unable to pass it."[15]

Tom Rynning sized up the Arizona Rangers as being fearless lawmen. "And when I say fearless, I mean fearless. No man who ever showed the white feather stayed with the Arizona rangers, for they had to take their lives in their hands every time they started a new day."[16] On October 7, 1901, that statement rang true when the infant territorial police force suffered a tragic loss. Ranger Carlos Tafolla, a New Mexico native, was killed in the line of duty on the Black River in northern Graham County. He had been trailing the Bill Smith rustler gang when they ambushed his posse.

An expense account request for Arizona Ranger George Ed Scarborough provides a clue as to how the Arizona Rangers worked in New Mexico. In November 1901, Scarborough filed two statements to cover the expense for his trip deep into eastern New Mexico Territory while trailing some of the Smith gang that had killed Ranger

Miguel A. Otero served as governor of New Mexico Territory for nine years, 1897–1906, making him the longest serving territorial chief executive. He was the first commander-in-chief of the New Mexico Mounted Police (courtesy of the John F. Fullerton Papers, NMMP/AC).

Tafolla. Scarborough said he visited Lava (on the Rio Grande in southern Socorro County), "Engel" (the ghost town of Engle is in Sierra County about eleven miles east of Elephant Butte Lake), Capitan (in Lincoln County) and Alamogordo (in Otero County) on his trip east. Scarborough requested $9.90 for forage for his horse and $13.40 for provisions for himself, for a one way trip total of $23.30 for his 20-day trip into the Sunshine Territory.[17] Even toward the end of his life Mossman still carried hard feelings toward Scarborough. "He was one of our rangers for awhile. I gave him a bob-tail discharge. He was a worthless kind, dangerous too, would kill a man."[18]

It is uncertain how many other semi-official Arizona Ranger expeditions were made into New Mexico Territory in search of outlaws before the formation of the mounted police in 1905. In 1903, the rangers were increased to a twenty-six man company that served Arizona Territory until they were unceremoniously disbanded in the spring of 1909.

Governors Murphy and Otero held a strategy meeting in January 1901 while they were both on a trip to Chicago. Otero later wrote of his relationship with Murphy, "I was a warm personal friend of Governor N.O. Murphy and his brother Frank."[19] In a Chicago hotel room, the two men made plans to work together to block Congress' attempt to join Arizona and New Mexico into one single state and they also agreed to lead a public relations effort to fight the measure with statehood conventions to be held that fall in both territories, with the two men speaking at each of the events.

On October 15, 1901, Murphy and Otero each addressed the Albuquerque convention held in the ballroom of the Commercial Club. The next week Otero was in Phoenix and the two governors lobbied the delegates assembled at the Opera House. Otero and Murphy seemed to genuinely enjoy each other's company and Otero believed that Murphy "was quite a wit" and a powerful speaker. Otero also seemed to have admired the company of Mrs. Sarah Murphy, a Phoenix socialite.[20] The Murphys were divorced in 1903 due to the former governor's alleged habitual drunkenness.[21] After he left the governor's office in 1906, Miguel Otero would spend some time in a sanitarium "drying out" due to his own abuse of alcohol; the Oteros, like the Murphys, also divorced.

Considering their friendship and at least two personal visits following the passage of the Arizona Ranger Act, had Otero experienced any problems with the actions of the Arizona Rangers he could have cleared up that matter quickly. The author has located no evidence to suggest that Governor Otero disapproved of any Arizona Ranger operations conducted near to or within the legal jurisdiction of New Mexico Territory.

The Legend

"After my day," wrote Captain Burton Mossman in 1935, "the Rangers were in distinctive garb; wore a conspicuous badge, bristled with weapons, and were so widely and systematically press agented, they soon achieved a dubious fame with old timers and passed on to a natural and inevitable Falstaffian reward."[22] Mossman was 89 when he died in September 1956. He did not live to witness the Arizona Rangers' greatest press kudos when a syndicated television series based upon the lawmen's factual and fictional adventures premiered in October 1957.

The *26 Men* television show was produced by veteran western movie actor Russell Hayden and was filmed at a location studio near Phoenix using local actors for many background parts. Hayden's birth name was Pate Lucid and he had been the sidekick Romeo character "Lucky" in the Hopalong Cassidy motion picture series.[23] The 78 episodes of *26 Men* were filmed in black and white and stared Tris Coffin as Captain Tom Rynning and Kelo Henderson as a rookie fictional ranger who led the action. These half hour adventures were tailored for "adult western" drama, but they also contained some historical facts taken from the rangers' case files.

At least seven of the 107 men who had served as an Arizona Ranger were still alive when *26 Men* was first broadcast. During the first season three of the real former Arizona Rangers, Clarence Beaty, Oliver Parmer and John McK Redmond, were employed to do short historical introductions to at least a third of these episodes. The on-screen appearances of these old rangers gave an air of authenticity to the story being told.[24] The last living Arizona Ranger, John R. Clarke, died on May 5, 1982, at his small home in Rosemead, Calif. He was 97 years old and is buried in Whittier.[25]

Ninety-three years after the Arizona Rangers were disbanded, the legacy of these territorial police has been re-established with a volunteer group that wear a modern day cowboy uniform complete with a silver Arizona Ranger star. These men and women contribute thousands of man-hours a year as an "unpaid, noncommissioned civilian auxiliary" to help local law enforcement officers keep the state of Arizona a safe and peaceful place to raise a family.[26]

Early in January 1902, Captain Mossman returned to Arizona from a Christmas visit to his parents in Las Cruces, New Mexico. The captain spoke with a Tucson reporter concerning his rangers: "Our company is patterned after the Texas rangers and we only wish that the territorial government of New Mexico would organize a Ranger troop to cooperate with us in this work. With their aid we could soon clear both territories of the fugitives from justice who have sought refuge here and continue to carry on their depredations. A New Mexico company would make work in Arizona much more effective."[27]

4

Lawmakers at Santa Fe, 1905

> "I have been urged by stockmen to recommend the passage of a Ranger Law, whose duty it shall be to patrol the ranges, to prevent the theft of stock and to aid in the apprehension of criminals. The suggestion seems to me a good one, if such a ranger force can be provided for at the expense of the special interests to be served and will not impose any additional burden upon the general taxpayer. A law of that kind is reported to be working very satisfactory in the neighboring Territory of Arizona."
>
> Governor Miguel A. Otero
> Message to the 36th Legislative Assembly
> 16 January 1905

Representatives of the citizens of New Mexico gathered at Santa Fe for the thirty-sixth time since the formation of the territorial government in 1850. January 1905 was cold in the northern New Mexico mountains and snow was seen on the streets of the capital city as men of strong conviction and loyalties gathered to make new laws designed to drag the Sunshine Territory into full partnership in the federal union. But as always, a few opposition voices were heard. Money and power have always been a moving force in the history of mankind and it was no different that winter in the legislative chambers in the Ancient City of Holy Faith.

A few years earlier, the Nogal *Republican* had published an editorial about "the man with a gun." The paper demanded action. "The cowardly habit of carrying a gun to make other people think he is a 'bad man from Bitter Creek' has led to many a murder, and this is true of 'peace officers' as well as others. There are a half a dozen deputy sheriffs and 2 X 4 special officers and constables in Lincoln county who carry guns so long that they have to get on house tops to pull them out of their pistol pockets. There is a strict law against this and it should be enforced. New Mexico is too far advanced in civilization to harbor these kind of men. It is time for the 'man from Bitter Creek' to either pull off his gun or move on to the uncivilized country."[1]

The economic survival of the territory was also a major concern to the lawmakers.[2] The Santa Fe *New Mexican* touched the heart of this issue when it reported that the territory "is overrun with stock thieves and other outlaws including murderers from Arizona and Texas." The answer to the problem was simple. "Not only the stock interest but every other interest in New Mexico would be protected by a ranger force."[3]

During their first 12 months of operation the Arizona Rangers had put 125 major hard cases in jail and killed one other. By the end of the 1904 fiscal year, the rangers' arrest record had grown to 1,052. In January 1905 Arizona Ranger Captain Tom Rynning reported to Governor A.O. Brodie that cattle rustling was practically wiped out in the Arizona Territory.[4]

The successful operation of the Arizona Rangers, the Republic of Mexico's Frontier *Rurales* and the unequalled record of the Texas Rangers spelled trouble for New Mexico. This three pronged attack combined to provide a vice grip effect on outlaws, and it compressed the undesirable elements east, north and west into the Sunshine Territory.[5] New Mexico's outlaws were a special class of hard cases; even behind prison walls they continued to cause trouble. Two penitentiary riots cost the lives of inmates and guards and one escape attempt was stopped only after the prison warden shot and killed one of the escapees. Holm Bursum, the prison chief, was dressed in his night shirt and had been on his way to bed when the escape attempt began.[6]

Early in the spring of 1904, Governor M.A. Otero wrote, "We are in the midst of a drought such as the great Southwest has never before seen or experienced. Conditions never have been as bad nor could they possibly be much worse."[7] Conditions did get worse. In late spring the rains came and the dry land could not contain the moisture. The flooding was massive across the New Mexico Territory. When summer was in full bloom the rustlers came back in force. The gangs became so reckless that they murdered some ranchers who vainly tried to protect their property. No one was safe. A territorial councilman's home was broken into and robbed in August. September 1904 brought a new reign of crime into New Mexico. The postmaster at the mining town of Golden was murdered during a holdup and the Wells Fargo Express office at Magdalena was robbed. A train near Tularosa and another near Logan were held up. Taos County was once again home to the fence cutting rustler gang called the White Caps and another Grant County peace officer gave his life defending the law.

New Mexico next suffered the loss of two territorial officials when the solicitor general and the superintendent of public instruction were each murdered. The assassination of Col. J. Francisco Chaves in November 1904 caused as much reaction as the murder of Albert J. Fountain had generated eight years earlier. Rustlers had killed again to protect themselves from prosecution. Tucumcari's police force was "treed" by a mob of drunken railroad section hands in December 1904. To the causal observer it appeared as if all manner and form of misdemeanor crime was on the increase in all sections of the territory.[8] Stores were not safe and neither were banks. In 1905, the Sierra County Bank at Hillsboro was robbed, and the bandits were never caught. Many Indian bands disregarded the territorial game hunting laws as they killed deer and other animals out of season. Hunting parties rode across private range land or the national forests whenever the mood struck them. The Indian outlaw known as the Apache Kid made raids upon isolated homes in the Western mountains along the Arizona–New Mexico line and the Kid held no fear of the law.

Miguel A. Otero, the 45-year-old governor of the territory, was starting his ninth year as the chief executive. He had been governor less then two years when the territorial lawmakers first debated the concept of a mounted police unit. Now in 1905, Governor Otero joined with the legislative leadership in requesting a territorial police force. Cattlemen, sheepmen and horse breeders had been joined by railroad executives, bankers and merchants in a common voice to demand that a corps of rangers be organized to rid New Mexico Territory of hard cases and non–law abiding citizens.[9] This time when a mounted police bill was introduced in the Council of the Territorial Legislative Assembly, the Las Vegas *Daily Optic* commented that "the chances for its passage at this session are brighter than ever before." The newspaper then added, "There is no longer the general opposition from the sheep interest and strong influences are at work to secure the passage of the bill."[10]

Young Mr. Greer

The Cattle Sanitary Board took the lead in spearheading the ranger movement and this group selected one of their members to introduce the new mounted police legislation.[11] Col. William Hugh Greer, a former board director, was a very popular and shrewd businessman who understood both territorial politics and the mechanics of making money in a variety of business enterprises. He was tall, handsome, and a well spoken gentleman. Greer was born in Waterloo, Iowa, in 1872. His early youth was spent in Michigan and California, but Greer's law degree was from the University of Chicago. His graceful and charming wife, Mary Jastro, was born into a wealthy Bakersfield, California, family and she enjoyed her husband's passion for travel. Greer and his brothers, A.J. and George, were well versed in world and national affairs.

Greer's chief occupation after moving to New Mexico was as general manager of the vast Victor Land and Cattle Company, but cattle raising was only one of his concerns. He and his business partner, D.K.B. Sellers, either financed or managed eight Albuquerque area businesses. The two men headed an investment company, a local telephone system, a brick manufacturing company, a land development company, a printing company, an entertainment house and substantial rental property. Greer and Sellers were also the principal owners of the Duke City's rail-bus transit system.

Will Greer's prominence in the

William H. Greer. This pencil drawing is taken from a photograph published in the Albuquerque *Morning Journal* in 1905. This is the only known picture of the multi-talented Mr. Greer (NMMP/AC).

business community of the territory prompted Governor Otero to appoint him a colonel of the New Mexico National Guard. Greer's cattle interests were served by his being a director of the Territorial Sanitary Board while his civic duty was fulfilled as the president of the Territorial Fair Association. Col. Greer represented his political party as a delegate to the 1904 Republican National Convention. Greer seemed to always be in the forefront of community service. Once he donated some steel cable to Silver City to help that town rebuild its suspension bridge, destroyed by flood waters, because the crossover was a lifeline in the bustling community. Greer's generous gift was a godsend in the days before federal government disaster relief funds were available to help communities with their rebuilding programs.

In November 1904, Greer was elected to a seat in the council chamber for the Thirty-sixth Legislative Assembly. It was his first try at elective office and he represented the Fifth Council District composed of Bernalillo, Sandoval, and McKinley counties. Greer resigned his commission on the governor's military staff and his seat as a director of the Territorial Cattle Sanitary Board because he had not wished to project a pro-administrative position or seem to have a conflict of interest.

The novice lawmaker sponsored bills to prohibit cattle roping exhibitions, sale of liquor near railroad construction camps and his pet project — a territorial police force. Greer knew how to use friendships and collect on past and future favors so that each of his bills would pass and be signed into law. It should be noted that Greer's political mentor and good friend, Nestor Montoya, had served as speaker of the Territorial House of Representatives. During the 1905 lawmaking session councilmen Greer and Montoya had adjoining rooms at the Palace Hotel in Santa Fe.[12]

Greer reached the height of his glory during the spring of 1905 when the passage of the Mounted Police Bill made him a first-rate hero among all classes of leadership in the territory. The *New Mexican* was strong in its praise. "Councilman Greer has worked assiduously and strenuously for passage of the measure and those who will be benefited by its provisions should thank him as its author and as a member of the assembly who did his best to have it enacted into law."[13]

During February 1906, when the nation's press was debating the value of joint statehood for Arizona and New Mexico, William Greer was suggested as a candidate for governor of the new state. The idea had been offered by the editor of California's San Diego *Union*, but Greer was quick to disavow any interest in the job. Greer's lack of political interest may have been due to his failing health. In January 1907, the businessman spent a few days seriously ill in a Los Angeles hospital. Later that year he recovered and was listed as a developer of the San Antonio Hot Spring, a health resort about 17 miles north of Jamez Springs. Greer was also a promoter of the need for a paved highway between Santa Fe and Albuquerque.[14]

The Greers had sold their home in Deming in 1905. The *Headlight* had advertised the Zinc Street residence as a "bargain" and said, "This property will be sold cheap for cash." In 1907, the *Albuquerque City Directory* listed Greer's residence as the Commercial Club and "mining" as his business. Greer had only a limited need for a New Mexico residence because he was spending most of his days in southern California and it was there that he died, at 38, in late September 1910.[15]

Council Bill 26

Thursday, January 26, 1905, was the eighth day of the legislative session and on that morning the council held only a short meeting. A bill requiring traveling meat peddlers to carry the animal's hides with them and a bill prohibiting the use of unregistered brands were introduced. These two proposed laws were being requested by the Cattle Sanitary Board. Councilman Greer then introduced legislation labeled "Council Bill 26 — An Act to Organize and Equip a Company of Mounted Police for the Territory of New Mexico." The chamber's clerk was asked to read the entire bill to the lawmakers present. Nestor Montoya "moved that the rules be suspended and that Council Bill No. 26 be read the second time by title, ordered translated, printed and referred to an appropriate committee, which motion being duly seconded was put to a vote and carried." The *Council Journal* reports that Council President John S. Clark then referred the Mounted Police Bill to the council's Committee on Finance.[16]

The council finance committee was chaired by William E. Martin. "Billie" Martin was a bookkeeper from Socorro, "a very warm personal friend" of Governor Otero and a member the Republican Party's Central Committee. He was also a highly respected Spanish interpreter who was serving his third term in the upper chamber. Otero said his friend "had one serious fault: if he took one drink of strong liquor he had to take more, and when under the influence of too much liquor, he was rather dangerous." [17] In fact, Martin was convicted of killing a man in Socorro County and was sentenced to seven years in the territorial penitentiary. He entered the stronghold as Prisoner 131 on April 27, 1886. Less than a year later, on February 28, 1887, Martin was given three days in the "dark cell" for fighting with Prisoner 94. On October 24, 1887, Martin was again in trouble. This time he was given three days in the "dark cell"; each day he spent one and a half hours "with the bit," seven hours "with the buck" and was handcuffed in a standing position for 14 hours, and the day's final one and a half hours Martin could use for "personal needs." Following his three days in solitary confinement Martin was shackled for an additional 22 days. This punishment was for assaulting a night guard and using abusive language. During the rest of his confinement Martin was a model prisoner, so Governor Edmund G. Ross commuted his sentence "for good behavior" on March 18, 1889.[18]

The other four finance committee members were Jacobo Chaves, Charles Miller, David C. Winters, and Malaquias Martinez. Jacobo Chaves was a Los Lunas bookkeeper who was serving his first term on the territorial council. He represented Valencia County and the newly formed Torrance County. Charles Miller also had a lot of wide open range land in his district of Dona Ana, Grant, Luna and Otero counties. He was a first term councilman from Anthony, where his family ran a store, did some farming and raised a few head of cattle. David Winters was also a first term member of the assembly. He owned a drug store in Las Vegas and represented San Miguel and Quay counties. He was the only member of the council finance committee to vote against the mounted police legislation as it was finally drafted. Malaquias Martinez was a fourth term councilman representing the Third District composed of Taos, Rio Arriba, and San Juan counties. He had also served a term in the House and was a farmer-stockraiser from Taos County. The debate on a mounted police force was not new to him because Councilman Martinez had been a freshmen member of the upper house in 1899 when that body had discussed the Richardson Mounted Police Bill. It was Martinez who had made the motion to table action on the bill and caused the legislation to be returned to committee.[19]

Six years had made a vast difference in the prevailing sentiment among lawmakers. In 1905, a cross-section of commercial concerns endorsed the territorial police idea and the plan was even viewed by most legislators as a bipartisan effort. The Martin committee devoted many productive hours to refining the provisions of the Mounted Police Bill. No notes from these committee work sessions survive, but it is reasonable to assume that some discussion was held concerning the effectiveness of the mounted constabularies then at work in Texas, Arizona and northern Mexico.

In his 1905 report to the secretary of the interior, the governor of Arizona Territory commented on the formation of the New Mexico Territorial Mounted Police. The Arizona chief executive said, "Noting the good results accomplished by our rangers, the Territory of New Mexico this year established a similar organization—a company of 'mounted police'—and harmonious action on the part of the two forces will increase the efficiency of the Arizona Rangers. One of the strong arguments advanced for the creation of a force of 'mounted police' in New Mexico was found in the fact that many dangerous criminals were known to be hiding in that Territory, having been frightened out of Arizona by the activity of the [Arizona] rangers. It is obvious that if our ranger force should be discontinued this Territory would soon be an asylum for criminals that had been driven out of New Mexico."[20]

The council's Committee on Finance made its recommendation report to the upper chamber with a few amendments to Greer's draft proposal. The committee recommended the addition of a lieutenant to the officers' ranks and they also upgraded the recommended salary scale from the 1899 level to better reflect the higher 1905 cost of living. The number of privates was reduced from ten to eight to cover the additional cost of the lieutenant's post. The Martin Committee provided for a Mounted Police Fund to be supported by a special territorial tax and they also recommended a few minor changes in the authorized method of operation to be used by these new mounted rangers.[21]

On February 9, the council voted 9 to 3 to pass Amended Council Bill 26 that the finance committee recommended.[22] The three negative votes were cast by an odd trio. Winters did not like any type of legislation that would put an additional tax upon business interests, thus his "no" vote. The second no vote came from a Roswell Democrat named Charles Ballard who was a sometimes peace officer, cattle raiser and cattle brand inspector. Maybe he felt the new rangers would somehow cost him some fees, so his was a vote to protect his personal interests. Thomas B. Catron, now known as "Old Man of the Council" and still at odds with the governor over control of Republican Party politics, voted no for pure spite. If Governor Otero was supportive of an issue, then Councilman Catron was sure to be against the same measure.

Later that Thursday afternoon the clerk of the House received the Mounted Police Bill with notification that the council had passed it. On Friday, February 10, the House of Representatives suspended their debate rules and took up discussion

The Legislative Council Vote on the Greer Mounted Police Bill

The roll call vote took place on Thursday morning, February 09, 1905

Name of the Councilman	*Vote*
* W.E. Martin of Socorro, committee chairman	Y
* Jacobo Chaves of Los Lunas	Y
* Charles E. Miller of Anthony	Y
* Malaquias Martinez of Taos	Y
* David C. Winters of Las Vegas	N
* The Council Finance Committee	
John S. Clark of Las Vegas, council president	Y
Alexander Reed of Tierra Amarilla	Y
David J. Leachy of Raton	Y
Thomas B. Catron of Santa Fe	N
William H. Greer of Albuquerque	Y
Nestor Montoya of Albuquerque	Y
Charles L. Ballard of Roswell	N
The Official Vote Total	09–03

The House of Representatives Votes on the Greer Mounted Police Bill

All three roll call votes took place on Friday, February 10, 1905

Name of the House Member	*Vote #1*	*Vote #2*	*Vote #3*
Seferino Crollott of Albuquerque	Y	Y	Y
Maximinto Duran of Los Pinos	Y	Y	Y
John W. Hannigan of Deming	Y	Y	Y
H.H. Howard of San Marcial	Y	Y	Y
Jose Amado Lucero of Espanoia	Y	N and Y	Y
Florencico Luna of Las Cruces	Y	Y	Y
B.G. Lynch of Las Vegas	Y	Y	Y
Colin Neblett of Silver City	Y	Y	Y
Granville Pendleton of Aztec	Y	Y	Y
Cristoval Sanchez of Ocate	Y	Y	Y
Cornello M. Sandoval of Sandoval	Y	Y	Y
Matthias B. Stockton of Raton	Y	Y	Y
Pablo Vigil of Sapello	Y	Y	Y
F.L. Wright of Clayton	Y	Y	Y
Thomas N. Wilkerson of Albuquerque	Y	Y	Y
Carl A. Dalies of Belen The Speaker of the House	Y	Y	Y
Sylvestre Myrabal of San Rafael	N	Y	Y
Jesus G. Martinez of Taos	N	Y	Y
W.W. Williams of Hillsboro	N	N	Y
R.L. Baca of Santa Fe (a sheep raiser)	N	N	N
George F. Ellis of Portales (a school teacher)	N	N	N
M.C. DeLeon of Santa Rosa (a stockman)	N	N	N
Roman Sandoval of Cerrillos (a miner)	N	N	N
Nestor Griego of Sena (a stockman)	N	N	N
The Official Vote Totals	16–08	18–06	19–05

on Amended Council Bill 26. The House clerk twice read the title of the bill, then under continued suspension of the House rules the bill was read in full in preparation of the final vote. Amended Council Bill 26 passed the first vote 16 to 8, the second roll call tallied 18 to 6 and the final vote of passage had increased to 19 to 5 in favor of the new territorial rangers.[23] (See appendix for a copy of the bill.)

Governor Miguel A. Otero transformed the Mounted Police Bill into the Mounted Police Act with his signature on February 15, 1905.[24] New Mexico's northern neighbors were also interested in the new ranger force. The Denver *Republican* editorialized: "Cattle thieves and other outlaws have given much trouble in the southern part of the [New Mexico] territory and the new company will have its headquarters at Socorro. From that point it will scour the country in search of thieves. A force of this kind is well adapted to service in a sparsely populated country like the southwest."[25]

5

John Ferguson Fullerton: The Journey Begins

"Captain Fullerton looks the right man in the right place ... and it is expected, will prove a first class commandant of the [ranger] force."
Santa Fe *New Mexican*
01 April 1905

The Fullerton family lineage has its foundation with a small group of Phoenician mariners, who in the dim past became shipwrecked along the coast of present day Norway. These men intermarried with the natives and created a family that joined with the warriors who helped William the Conqueror and were part of the invasion of the islands that are now the British Isles. A family of brothers called the Fullartons eventually moved to the northlands in present day Scotland and befriended Robert the Bruce and helped him to become king. The brothers settled in Ayrshire and some of their descendants migrated to the new world in time to become part of the development of the United States of America. Today, the family crest of the Scots-Irish Fullerton clan contains the head of a camel surmounted upon the central part of the shield as a reminder of the family's ancient heritage.

The Fullertons were early settlers of the American countryside, as each generation seemed to move farther west just ahead of civilization. Thomas Fullerton was born in September 1753 in the British Crown Colony of Pennsylvania. When Tom was 23 years old, selected delegates to a citizen's convention declared that William Penn's colony was an independent state and was no longer subject to the direction of the British king or the British Parliament. Young Tom Fullerton joined with his neighbors and friends and became a private in a company of the new state's militia, the Pennsylvania Line. He served with honor over the next few years, as his state joined with other former colonies in a civil war for independence from England.

In the fall of 1779, Tom Fullerton took a leave of absence from his military service, and on August 22 he married his 18-year-old sweetheart. Tom and Hannah lived the life of a farm family after the war ended. They raised three sons, Bailey, William and James, and a daughter named Mary. The young family first lived on a farm in York County about 100 miles west of Philadelphia. Later, Tom moved his brood to Lycoming County about 120 miles north of York. The clan finally settled in Crawford County about 200 miles farther west near the divide with the Ohio country in the Northwest Territory. Tom Fullerton died just before Christmas in 1834 during his 81st year and Hannah joined him 15 years later.[1]

James M. Fullerton had been born in 1792. His wife, Ann Clark, was also a Keystone state native and they raised their family on a farm near New Castle. James and Ann's son, James S., was born on the bitter cold evening of February 13, 1830. Two decades later this winter baby met auburn haired Amanda J. Ferguson at Mt. Jackson in Lawrence County. She had been born in May 1834. On Thursday May 19, 1853, James S. Fullerton married his young sweetheart in a ceremony conducted by Rev. Dr. Aljorman S. McMarters. Their union lasted for 44 years until James died of old age at their San Diego, California, home in November 1907. Amanda joined him four years later.

James and Amanda had one daughter who was born to them early in 1854. She was christened Nannie Amanda, known as Amanda within the family, but called Nan by her friends. Nan grew up to marry J.C. Kutzner, manager of Albuquerque's electric trolley car company, and settled in the Duke City. This business was owned by William H. Greer and his business partner, D.K.B. Sellers. The former newspaperman would serve as Albuquerque's mayor from 1914 to 1916. Ten days before James and Amanda's third wedding anniversary, May 9, 1856, she gave birth to the couple's first son, who was christened John Ferguson.[2]

The War Between the States

This is not the forum to present a detailed discussion of the War Between the States, but a brief background would help explain the motivation for James Fullerton's march off to war. The November 1860 selection of Abraham Lincoln as president-elect of the United States was the match that lit the fuse of the sectional discord bomb that exploded with South Carolina's move to leave the Union in December and set their own course. Within six weeks, six more Southern states—Mississippi, Alabama, Georgia, Florida, Louisiana and Texas—had voted to terminate their participation in the federal government and joined the states' rights movement. On February 8, 1861, these same now independent Southern states voted to create a provisional government for a new national compact or confederation. A month later, the new provisional congress authorized Provisional President Jefferson Davis to form a central military authority "to repel invasion, maintain the rightful possessions of the Confederate States, and to secure public tranquility and independence against threatened assault" by the United States. President Davis asked his seven state governors to provide the infant central authority with a 100,000 man defense force.

On April 15, a month after taking office, President Lincoln asked the governors of the loyal states to supplement the federal military with 75,000 volunteers for a 90 day enlistment. Lincoln had used a law that President Washington had signed 70 years before giving the chief executive authority to request state militias to assist the federal government in the suppression of an armed insurrection. Pennsylvania's governor issued a call for troops and James Fullerton, with his brother Walter and other neighbors, answered the call on April 26. They enlisted as privates in Battery B of the First Pennsylvania Light Artillery. Following their basic training in June, the volunteer artillerymen selected their officers by naming Henry Danforth as captain, and as a sign of his leadership abilities, Fullerton was chosen as one of the two lieutenants. James even looked like a leader in his blue uniform with its red trimming. He stood six feet tall and his blue eyes looked even brighter against his black hair and light complexion.[3] John Fullerton was not quite five years old when his father marched off to war. He couldn't understand why his father was gone so long and why he had to work so long in the fields.

Two days after Lincoln called for volunteers to force the seven Southern states back into the Union, the Commonwealth of Virginia led the second wave of states to break ties with the Washington government. Arkansas, Tennessee, and North Carolina had left the Union before the Confederate government was relocated to Richmond in June. Missouri and Kentucky became the final two states to openly join the fight for Southern independence and earn a star on the Rebel national flag.

The Union volunteer enlistments were due to expire when the federal troops guarding Washington finally moved en masse on the Southern defense lines in northern Virginia. The two forces clashed at Bull Run Creek near Manassas and after a full day of fighting the Union army was in disorganized retreat toward Washington. Lincoln fired his generals and commissioned new ones, extended the volunteer enlistments and demanded a plan to end the armed rebellion. The new Union commanding general reorganized his demoralized troops into the new 100,000 man Army of the Potomac and developed a daring strategy to capture Richmond in the spring. George B. McClellan landed a formidable fighting force at Fort Monroe and slowly moved them up the Virginia Peninsula toward Richmond. McClellan's plan was to advance his forces toward the Confederate capital, with his flanks protected by Union gunboats on the James and York rivers, and to engage the enemy head on. This design also protected McClellan's extended supply line and scurried his lines of communication with Washington.

When the first federal troops landed on the Virginia Peninsula they made it very clear that they had no desire to change the established relationship between the races. These Yankee soldiers rampaged through slave settlements looting homes, killing livestock and raping the Black women. The freed slaves were forced into hard labor building camps for the army and in return they received some food and clothing. Less than three weeks after the Army of the Potomac landed at Fort Monroe, a race riot broke out and ended with over a hundred Black casualties. The military liberators had proved more oppressive toward the local slave population than the *status quo* Southern society had been.

Most of the Union army newspapers published on the peninsula carried ads about runaway slaves and printed reward notices. Some regiments, like the 99th New York, became runaway slave catchers and earned a $20 to $50 bounty per slave they returned to their masters. The official newspaper of the Fifth Pennsylvania declared that only "white folks" deserved "freedom" and pointedly stated "we do not wish it even insinuated that we have any sympathy with abolitionism." This newspaper statement was published during the same time frame that President Lincoln was working on the wording of his Emancipation Proclamation to free all slaves held in territory controlled by Union military forces. It should be noted that the almost casual cruelty that Union troops showed toward "contrabands" was still being investigated two years after the Peninsula Campaign was history.[4] It is unknown how the men of Battery B of the First Pennsylvania Light Artillery felt about slavery or freedom for the "contrabands."

The war effort in the Western Theater was going against the Confederate cause in the early part of 1862, but the strongest federal army in the Eastern Theater was still encamped on the peninsula and showed no signs of moving until President Lincoln ordered McClellan to attack the Rebels in force and take Richmond. The Army of the Potomac slowly moved up the land mass toward Yorktown and on May 3 the Southern defenders gave up the city and retreated toward their capital. Next, the Confederate troops lost Norfolk and their naval base at Hampton Roads and the fearsome CSA *Virginia* ironclad warship. The Union army's march-walk toward Richmond was in full operation and it seemed like the war was almost won, until a fateful bullet caused President Jefferson Davis to seek a new Confederate commander for the army defending Richmond. He called upon his military adviser, Robert E. Lee, to take field command and halt the Union army's advance.

Lee quickly took command in the field and changed the Confederate battle plan from a defense posture to that of an assault force. During seven days in late June, Lee's refocused army fought hard at Mechanicsville, Gaines' Mill, Savages Station, Frayser's Farm, Glendale, Malvern Hill and numerous other smaller skirmishes. The Army of the Potomac was roundly beaten and would have been destroyed had the federal artillery not held the high ground as the sun set on that last battle. The men of Battery B of the First Pennsylvania Artillery were among the hardest fighters and thirty-two years after that campaign a newspaper story said that young Lieutenant Fullerton had "distinguished himself by his coolness and bravery in many battles fought by that battery."[5] What remained of the 90,000 man Union army that had advanced in such triumph was now compelled to retreat to Harrison's Landing. Here, McClellan assumed a defensive position and his badly shattered army was out of action as an offensive fighting unit.[6]

The morale in the Army of the Potomac was gloomy and the weather was just as disagreeable. Steady rains now caused gloomy days, sodden fields and swampy camp life. In July and August, the weather and camp conditions caused Fullerton to become very ill with diarrhea, malarial fever and rheumatism. James' condition was so grave that he was unable to fight at the Second Battle of Manassas and at one point during these dark days the 32 year old officer was placed on the death watch list. Even his brother feared for his survival.[7]

In late August, Lee's 40,000 man Army of Northern Virginia defeated the federals at the second battle to be fought along Bull Run Creek, so Lee decided to take advantage of this opportunity and invade Maryland. He caused panic in Washington until a new 75,000 man army led by McClellan was able to stop Lee's advance at Antietam Creek near Sharpsburg. The Union victory caused 26,000 casualties and death lists filled both nations' newspapers. James Fullerton was one of the lucky ones who lived, but his health was broken to the extent that he was proclaimed unfit for continued active service. The Pennsylvanians were camped at Brooks Station, Virginia, on October 31, 1862, when James was given medical leave and ordered home.[8]

During his first few weeks home, James had difficulty keeping food in his system. Walter Fullerton would later recall his brother's physical condition: "The summer of '63 he was not able to work hardly any at home. After leaving the Service, I worked with him some days and [his] doing anything at all [was difficult]; his bowels where running at the time often 6 to 8 times a night." Slowly, under the watchful eye of Amanda and Dr. Patterson, a family friend, James made a recovery, but he remained "very poorly for a year or two." Fullerton never returned to active duty, but was granted an honorable discharge on February 4, 1863. The war had ended for him, but six months later his native Pennsylvania would run red with blood as General Lee once again took the fighting onto northern territory.[9]

The Fullerton Family in Northeastern Missouri

Fullerton's ill health motivated him to leave the damp Pennsylvania winters and relocate his family, in 1864, to Scotland County in northeastern Missouri. The county's northern neighbor is the state of Iowa and the area is located one county west of the Mississippi River. One person, in 1887, described the area's soil as "deep and dark, and rich in producing qualities." The land was a farmer's dream. "It is composed of a mixture of humus, clay and sand in such proportions as to make it very productive."[10] It was here that James Fullerton decided his health and his destiny were joined.

There is some evidence to support the idea that James may have moved to northeastern Missouri upon the recommendation of a distant relative who lived in the general area of Scotland County. During this time, a hat maker named Rice F. McFaden lived in Knox County, Missouri, a neighbor to Scotland County. Rice's grandfather, a Pennsylvanian, had been killed fighting with the Continental Army during the Revolutionary War. The grandfather's death left his son, John McFaden, an orphan, so John was raised by his mother's brother, William Fullerton of Lancaster County, Pennsylvania. As a young man, John left Pennsylvania, settled in the Commonwealth of Kentucky and married. Later, John settled his family on the Missouri frontier and it was here that Rice McFaden was born.[11]

Scotland County residents held strong Union sympathies during the War Between the States. In 1860, residents of Memphis staged an old fashioned Fourth of July barbecue, in a grove west of the county seat, that was "attended by a large concourse of people." The *National Democrat* reported the happy occasion by saying, "Two beeves, twenty-five sheep, several hogs, a large number of chickens, and bread and pies and cakes" were consumed at the country's birthday party.[12] It would seem that nothing has changed over the centuries, because people still like to eat, be with their family and friends and have fun on national holidays.

Not all Missouri citizens were as pro–Union as those who lived in Scotland County. In late October 1861, pro-Southern Missourians held a convention at Neosho and voted their state out of the federal union. They organized a provisional government and sent delegates to Richmond to seek admission into the newly formed Southern confederacy. The Confederate Congress granted Missouri's request on November 26 and added a twelfth star to their national flag. The Commonwealth of Kentucky became the thirteenth star in December, making Missouri and Kentucky the only two states with dual governments. The Confederate States of America was established by sectional political action in 1861 and was militarily extricated in 1865; the Confederate State of Missouri was already a historical footnote by the time James Fullerton settled his family in the "Show Me State."[13]

A few months after the national tragedy had ended, James helped to reorganize the local farmers' chamber of commerce and it was at that meeting that he was elected one of the directors for the new Northeast Missouri Agricultural and Mechanical Association. This should be viewed as a high honor for a man only one year after his arrival in the area.[14] In 1869, Memphis businessmen advertised their establishments in a county directory and this little publication listed Fullerton as conducting a "wagon manufactory" business. The community had four churches, five doctors and at least six attorneys. One of the doctors was D.B. Fowler, who kept a watchful eye upon James Fullerton's health.[15]

The Fullerton family was very active in the local Presbyterian Church led by Rev. M.G. Gorrin. Young John and his sister were regular attendees at the youth group meetings and the Wednesday night prayer service. The Fullerton family even gave an annual tithe for the right to have their own family pew on Sunday morning. The Presbyterian fellowship had been established in 1845 and the members built their first building in 1854.[16] In 1861, the country's Presbyterian churches split along sectional lines, but the Memphis congregation chose to stay within the southern assembly in spite of the community's pro–Union sympathy.[17] Over twenty-five member families pledged funds to construct a new two-story brick church in 1872, so the congregation sold their wooden structure to the local Baptist believers. The brick church burned in 1895 and the present day First Presbyterian Church was erected on the same site.[18]

In the summer of 1870, a federal census taker visited the Fullerton home in Memphis. James was listed as the 40 year old head of the household and his occupation was "wagon Manufacture." Amanda was "Keeping house" and teenagers John and Nannie were attending school. James had real estate valued at $3,000 and personal property valued at $2,500, so this would seem to place the wagon manufacturer and his family in the upper economic layer of Memphis society. The other fathers in the Fullertons' neighborhood were two wagon makers, a carpenter, an insurance agent, an attorney-at-law and two grocers. The combination must have been an interesting social mixture for the children and their parents. It also makes for interesting speculation to consider whether the two wagon makers and the carpenter neighbors may have worked for the Fullerton wagon company.[19]

In the fall of 1870, James Fullerton was called to civic duty; he ran for public office and was elected treasurer of Scotland County. He landed in the middle of a heated debate over the use of public funds to support the construction of a railroad line across the county. According to Missouri law, Fullerton signed the public bonds issued by the commissioner's court to support the Missouri, Iowa and Nebraska Railway. James completed his two year term and did not seek reelection, but the legal battle over the railroad bond issue carried on for years after the Fullertons had left Scotland County.[20]

St. Louis, in 1870, was one the country's largest cities and with over 100,000 people it was bigger than Baltimore and Boston. Hundreds of steamboats annually docked at the Gateway City and discharged thousands of passengers and 500,000 tons of goods for the western trade. These deeds were possible because three decades earlier a young Army engineer named Robert E. Lee had designed and constructed a dyke and revetment program to keep the main Mississippi River channel running by St. Louis and not creating a new channel through southern Illinois. The governor of Illinois was so upset with Lee that he issued an arrest warrant for him, charging the future Confederate general with "obstructing a navigable river."[21]

On June 30, 1870, a massive crowd gathered at St. Mary's Market in New Orleans and cheered as the *Natchez* and the *Robert E. Lee* set off on a 1,200 mile race north to St. Louis. The Great Steamboat Race lasted three days, eighteen hours and thirteen minutes. The Fullerton family was among the thousands who, at 11:33 on Independence Day morning, greeted the victorious paddlewheeler who broke the *Natchez*'s speed record by five hours. This race was the kickoff event for the ever popular annual Veiled Prophet Parade and festivities. This must have been an exciting family time, with no foreshadowing of future events.

We don't know when Amanda told her husband she was pregnant, but they were blessed with their third and last child in January 1871. The baby boy was named William Sharpe, but the family would always call him Will. The age difference between Nannie and John and their brother would always be a chasm between the siblings; they were never really close. This void may have added to Will's unstable sense of personal identity and his seeming isolation within the family.[22]

In September 1873, the nation's economic structure was shaken with the failure of the country's largest financial institution on top of the unstable insurance industry that was still depressed in the wake the losses caused by the Great Chicago Fire and a rash of other lesser blazes across the Midwest in 1871. The crash of the Vienna stock market earlier that year had caused European financial markets to tighten credit and demand that loans be repaid in gold. This monetary collapse caused a panic that deepened into a depression. It held sway over America until federal lawmakers enacted the Redemption of Specie Act that strengthened public confidence in the nation's paper money system. Over three million people would become unemployed and business failures would total over 500 million dollars during the five year depression; the nation's worst economic downturn up to that time.

A Memphis business directory from 1875 listed three companies under "wagon factory" category. Fullerton may have anticipated the rise of this new competition or the future depressed farm economy, or he may have wished for a less confrontational political climate, but for whatever reason he had moved his expanded family to St. Louis before the Panic of 1873 hit the West. The timing seemed to be right, because John and Nannie had completed their schooling and jobs were easier to find in a larger metropolitan area. James modified his design and established a carriage building factory along the banks of the Mississippi, and this crossroads of America was the family home for the next decade.[23] From the Fullertons' shop a person could see the giant steel railroad bridge across the Mississippi River between St. Louis and the Illinois shore. The revolutionary structure had been designed and constructed by an engineer named James B. Eads. The bridge still stands as a testament to the determination of mankind.

The carriage business grew and John helped his father with the sales department. The Fullerton family seemed to have adapted to their new life and their new Presbyterian Church home. The pastor family had come from Louisiana and John took a special interest in the dark eyed daughter named Susan Grayson Baker. She had been born in Tensa Parish near the village of St. Joseph, a settlement almost halfway between Vicksburg and Natchez, on January 15, 1864. Susan was the youngest child in a large family and grew up closest to her older sister Halle and her brother Frank. The Bakers had been among the thousands of displaced people who had lost their homes during the Yankee army's campaign to capture all of the river towns, so the Rev. Baker moved his family away from the war-torn South and found a new congregation in St. Louis. Susan was eight years John's junior, but the two young people fell in love and were joined as husband and wife. Their first son, named Frank after Susan's brother, died as an infant and it was during this family sadness that John and Susan decided to join the senior Fullertons in their expedition to settle a homestead in New Mexico Territory.[24]

Much of the family wealth had been lost when the carriage factory burned in the Winter of 1882, so still in semi-ill health, the senior Fullerton decided not to rebuild the facility. Fate has a strange way of adding irony to life. One of the blacksmiths that Fullerton contracted for labor in the carriage factory was a Prussian immigrant named Henry Hagerman. It would seem that at some point the two men had a disagreement and Fullerton no longer used the service of the blacksmith. Three decades later, John would have his own employment disagreement with a man named Hagerman, only this time it was a Fullerton who was dismissed.

The AJF Ranch

In May 1862, President Lincoln signed the National Homestead Act that gave a 21-year-old male citizen the opportunity to claim 160 acres of public domain lands. The qualifications for the free land were simple. The homesteader had to live on the land and make improvements to the property over a five year period to earn clear title. James decided to take advantage of the Homestead Act and searched for a climate with less humidity and dampness than the Mississippi River Valley. Somehow James saw a booklet published by the immigration bureau for New Mexico Territory and read about the clear air and beautiful mountain range lands of Socorro County.[25]

Fullerton took the gamble and in January 1883, he moved his family west. As it turned out for him, James made an excellent choice. In April 1900, the Socorro *Chieftain* reported, on page one, verifying effects of the New Mexico climate, "Several years ago he came from St. Louis weighing scarcely a hundred pounds. He has since then just about doubled his weight and is as fine a specimen of physical manhood as one would wish to look upon."[26]

James and John established a double homestead ranch in far western Socorro County on the south edge of the San Augustin Plains. There the normal precipitation of 15 to 20 inches per year makes this area good grazing lands. The Plains is a huge, stark inland basin from a pre-historical age, once home to Anastazis and Athabascans and other ancient peoples, where steep, round-top, rocky hills contrast with the flatness of the Plains. On the southeast side of the old sea is the Bat Cave, where archeologists have discovered ageless signs of agriculture in North America. The area is about seven thousand feet above sea level, where the air is dry and thin. The Continental Divide, the spine of the Rocky Mountains, was the western boundary. To the north is the area called the Playa because of the dryness of the topsoil.[27]

Susan Baker Fullerton was photographed in St. Louis about the time that young John Fullerton began to court his future bride. This was his favorite picture of her and he kept a framed copy on his desk (Irene Fullerton's photograph album).

The Fullertons' homestead was located about 61 miles southwest of Magdalena between the Mangas Mountains and the Continental Divide. Present day Fullerton Canyon is located southwest of the old ranch headquarters compound. The nearest community was the present day ghost town of Patterson, so the new settlers quickly felt the need to stock a trading post of their own at their ranch headquarters. Area livestock raisers, regional newspapers and mapmakers soon referred to the settlement as Fullerton, but the once lively hamlet is today only a fading memory of a past era.[28]

The Thirty-third Territorial Legislative Assembly, held in 1899, enacted a brand law that required all active cattle, horse and mule brands to be re-recorded with the Cattle Sanitary Board by July 1, 1900. The board published a pocket-sized book containing all these official brands. The AJF brand, for Amanda and James, was registered to the J.S. Fullerton and Son Cattle Company, while John's son Elmer used the JEF brand. When Will Fullerton was older he also joined the ranching business and recorded the 7+X brand for his personal use.[29]

Weather is the eternal nemesis of the farmer and the rancher. The winter of 1886–1887 was an extremely devastating time for ranchers all along the Rocky Mountains from Canada to Mexico and the Fullerton Ranch was no exception. The only thing many ranchers could salvage from the mass deaths was the hides from the decimated herd. Once more James Fullerton had suffered a huge financial loss and once again he resorted to the skill of wagon repair. Gold had been discovered in the Black Range Mountains of Socorro and Sierra counties, bloom mining communities had sprung up almost over night and chief among these was Chloride.

In Search of Gold

Wagon repair proved to be steady business and James Fullerton was slowly able to rebuild his fortune. The future looked bright until he was stricken with a severe case of rheumatism that kept him bedridden for almost a month. Two new friends, Benjamin McClure and Henry Myers, helped the family keep James' spirits high with almost daily visits. When he was able to get up and about, James decided that the cool, high mountain air was not the best climate for him, so the senior Fullertons returned to the warmer climate of the homestead with young Will.[30] James quickly regained his health at the ranch and he was able to play host to his brother William and his family in mid–October 1888. Will was also able to meet his namesake uncle and his cousin. Seven years later, James made a trip east to attend a reunion of Union veterans of the Grand Army of the Republic, and his own Battery B, held at Buffalo, New York. On his way home he stopped to visit with relatives at Mount Jackson, Pennsylvania.[31]

In June 1890, the Congress authorized a special pension for disabled Civil War veterans and James made an application based upon his constant state of ill health. One family member testified that James "has never recovered from his Army sickness," but the Pension Bureau took no action on the request. In 1897, Congress expanded the scope of the 1890 veterans' disability act and this time James was granted a small stipend. At the time of his death, James was seeking an increased allotment; it was granted to his widow.[32]

John and Susan had remained in Chloride, because John, like many young men of that era and locale, was working a mining claim in hopes of making the big strike. He was doing so when he and Susan received a special bundle of joy. Susan gave birth to her second son in December 1888, and the couple named him John Elmer. This mining adventure was short lived, however, and by the spring of 1889 John, Susan and the baby were comfortably settled on the family ranch.[33]

Past Indian troubles now seemed a distant memory and the rise of stock prices was a welcome new year greeting to the ranchers of the San Augustin Plains. However, an Apache raiding party did make one visit to the Fullerton Ranch. All the men were on the range and only Susan and John Elmer were at home. Susan had seen the Indians coming and hid herself and the baby in the barn behind a headboard for a bed and some wagon wheels. The raiders, from the now abandoned Warm Springs Apache Reservation, only stole some food and quickly rode away. Following this incident, John taught Susan how to use a rifle and she became an acceptable markswoman.[34]

Raymond Parish Fullerton, John and Susan's third son, was born in July 1892 and life was wonderful for John Fullerton until tragedy struck. Four days after Christmas 1893, Susan Fullerton died and less than two weeks later the year and a half old Raymond joined his mother as a victim of a fever epidemic. In his grief, John Fullerton somehow felt that God had betrayed him and stolen his joy and happiness, so he ceased active church attendance after he buried his loved ones. Family members have said that his pain and loss was so great that it never left John and that he may never have made peace with God. [35]

John Elmer also suffered from the fever, but following a long fight with the Angel of Death the boy grew stronger. This surviving son became very dear to his father and in his preschool years "his bright little son" accompanied John on many business trips to Socorro and Albuquerque. Just before the dawn of the twentieth century, Grandfather Fullerton bought "the Andrews property" in the southern section of the old Spanish community of Socorro and the house on California Street soon became a haven for their son John and his little boy.[36] A couple of years later, James added a windmill to his home water well and the *Chieftain* said, "He doubtless intends to be independent of the river's flow." Socorro is located along the west bank of the Rio Grande.[37]

When the senior Fullertons moved from their rural ranch to the city comforts of the county seat they left their cattle and sheep operation to their two sons. John let Elmer live with his grandparents so he could attend school at Socorro and these became lonely months for him on the San Augustin Plains.[38] Elmer attended the high school section of the New Mexico School of Mines. When John first visited the campus of present day New Mexico Tech, he was surprised "at the facilities for work in the Socorro institution" and he became a strong supporter of this facility of higher education.[39]

Will Fullerton was referred to as being a "dyer" person by members of the Fullerton clan, who said he always seemed to project a "strictly business" image.[40] Even so, Will may not have always been "dyer" as a young man. In 1905, Will was reported in the Duke City "greeting his numerous friends" and he, like his older brother, seemed to also enjoy festive dances as noted by the Socorro *Chieftain* in December 1901. When he was 27 years old, Will was helping a neighbor rancher repair a well pump, located down inside the well shaft, when the rancher "was overcome by foul air and fell" to his death in the well before Will could save him. At this late date it is uncertain what effect, if any, this tragic incident may have had upon Will's future state of mind.[41]

In March 1901, Will added 150 head of cattle to his personal ranch operation and by the end of the year he added more cattle and over a thousand head of sheep. The Fullerton brothers' joint sheep enterprise became so successful that in 1904 Will, who was the managing partner, increased the herd size by an additional 4,000 animals.[42] In the autumn of 1902, Will Fullerton wrote a friend, "I have for sale 107 hd of lambs turned out of The Patterson [area] herd this year." He said these lambs were better than the ones that he had sold the year before for $4.25 per head. "The Patterson sheep are said to be the finest in the Territory." Will bragged that his kind of cross breed sheep averaged "7¾ lbs per head twelve months clip." He concluded his sales offer by saying, "They are Thoroughbred."[43] The sale was done.

Cattle and sheep were not the only interest of John Fullerton. He also had an orchard at his ranch and once John's brother-in-law, J.C. Kutzner, visited the orchard and took some of the fruit back home to Albuquerque. An *Evening Citizen* reporter commented about the orchard, saying that Kutzner had "brought back with him a twig from a prune tree, literally loaded with ripe prunes, and it can be seen at the *Citizen* office." The news report further explained that Fullerton's orchard contained "at least 150 prune trees burdened with fruit."[44] The Fullerton Ranch also had a quality cantaloupe patch and the editor of the *Chieftain* claimed these melons were "as fine a specimen of cantaloupe as ever tickled the palate of an epicure."[45]

John began to shed his grief and take an interest in life outside of his ranch by attending social affairs in Patterson, Datil, Magdalena and Socorro. The *Chieftain* took note of the fact. "Mr. Fullerton seems to have some sort of an instinct that tells him when there is a dance in Socorro." One of his favorite activities was attending functions held by the Socorro Social Club. This group hosted parties and dances that sometimes continued into the pre-dawn hours. Once the *Chieftain* commented, "The ballroom was crowded with dancers. Everybody who could dance danced as though he thoroughly enjoyed it and the rest seemed to want mightily to learn." Two weeks later, Fullerton was back in Socorro but a local newspaper said his "instinct must have been at fault" because there was no dance that weekend. In fact, John had come to town to see his son and to attend to some ranch business. [46]

On August 6, 1903, John Fullerton gave up his reign as Socorro County's Most Eligible Widower. He married Katharine Lay Sleight and became stepfather to her daughter, Beatrice.[47]

Public Service

John developed an interest in civic affairs after he had the opportunity to serve on a district court jury in the summer of 1901. One of the peace officers who attended this session of the court was Deputy United States Marshal Fred Fornoff, but it is not known if the two men became acquainted at this time.[48] One thing is certain, from that point forward, their lives would cross paths many times.

Fullerton also took an active role in the local cattlemen's organization and was selected to represent Socorro County at a statehood convention held at Albuquerque in October 1901.[49] The Albuquerque convention heard both Arizona Governor N.O. Murphy and New Mexico Governor Miguel A. Otero speak in favor of the statehood movement. Otero told the statehood delegates that the assessed value of New Mexico Territory was less than 40 million dollars, yet in fact the real value was nearly 120 million dollars. "You must see to it that the proper men are elected to assess the property and equalize its value, so that we may appear to the world what we are in fact, as to our wealth and ability to pay our obligations," Otero told the delegates. True assessed property value and a properly collected tax was a key to future New Mexico statehood, prophesied the governor.[50] John Fullerton quickly understood the wisdom of the governor's comments and embraced Otero's ideas as his own.

The statehood movement failed in 1901, but Fullerton did not forget Governor Otero's fiscal plan. When the leadership of the Socorro County Republican Party asked John to run for the county assessor's post, he accepted the invitation. John Fullerton, now a candidate for public office, sold his brother a third interest in 600 head of cattle and 36 "saddle and work horses" for $500. John used the money to help finance his campaign.[51] Fullerton won the party nomination and the general election in November 1904.

John F. Fullerton, a successful stockman, now became a public servant and moved from his ranch into Socorro to take up his new county office. John took his oath of office on Thursday, December 29, 1904, after his friends H.T. Mayberry and August Kiehne posted a thousand dollars each towards Fullerton's office bond. Brother Will posted the additional $2,000 needed to guarantee John's performance of his official duty.[52]

When John and Katharine moved into Socorro he had a telephone line installed to his ranch headquarters so that he could keep in touch with his foreman. Pedro Perea was John's man at the AJF Ranch and was in charge of the day to day care of the cattle operation while Will handled the sheep and horse herd operations.[53] John assumed the assessor's office on New Year's Day 1905, but he occupied the office for only 77 days. He resigned his county office on Saturday, March 18, and he was replaced by local political favorite son Abdenago "A.B." Baca of San Marcial. The former Socorro town marshal, deputy sheriff–jailer and small time rancher was the brother of Socorro County District Attorney Elfego Baca.[54]

Governor Otero appointed John F. Fullerton as the first captain of the New Mexico Mounted Police on March 18, 1905, and Fullerton took his territorial oath of office the same day he was appointed. A reporter for the Santa Fe *New Mexican* recorded his impressions of the rangers' new leader when he described John Fullerton as "about five feet, ten inches in height, a rather heavy set man, well proportioned, with clean cut features, bright observing dark eyes,[55] black hair, strong thin determined lips, a firm mouth and rather bullet shaped head...." The capital city reporter claimed that Fullerton's head shape indicated John possessed "perseverance and energy." This positive assessment of John F. Fullerton was not shared by everyone who knew him during his lifetime, but as a whole the reporter's judgment does seem to have been an accurate one.[56]

Governor Miguel A. Otero had high respect for the territorial rangers and their new captain. On one occasion he wrote a friend, "I believe the law creating the Mounted Police force was a good one and will become more valuable to the territory each year. We have been very fortunate in the selection of officers and men and I have no doubt that in the near future we shall be entirely rid of an element that has been a disgrace to our territory."[57]

6

The Men of Fullerton's Rangers

> "And the men who trailed the desert
> Foot by foot and piece by piece
> Were the hard and dogged members
> of New Mexico's Mounted Police."
>
> Fred Lambert
The last living Territorial Mounted Policeman
1948 Poem

The annals of the American southwest can lay claim to the adventures of no other company of territorial peace officers more misunderstood, and underrated, than the men of Fullerton's Rangers. This first company of New Mexico Territorial Mounted Police was composed of fearless men who became a legend as they blazed a new trail of law enforcement with perseverance and tenacity of purpose.

Fullerton's Rangers were not larger-than-life heroes. They were just ordinary family men doing a job and as a group they had little in common. The officers hailed from Pennsylvania, California and Alabama. Three rangers came from Texas, while the others where from Missouri, Wisconsin, Minnesota, Kansas, Illinois, California and the Sunshine Territory. These first mounted police were rugged men who were cattlemen, schoolteachers, professional lawmen, salesmen, stock inspectors, newspaper editors and politicians. These men were Republicans and Democrats. They were Presbyterian, Methodist, Southern Baptist, Roman Catholic and non-believers.

Most of these range riders were crack shots and would shoot to kill if forced to take lethal action. They were flesh and blood men who lived an exciting, dangerous adventure, yet none of them felt, at the time, they were doing anything heroic and certainly they held no dreams about making law enforcement history or becoming folk heroes in another generation.

Many of Fullerton's Rangers were hard drinkers and frequent users of tobacco. They could hold their own in a hard-fought fist fight or a heated cussing match. Most of the rangers were family men who cried when they lost a child or a beloved pet. They understood that their ranger duties demanded that they spend many days away from their families on lonesome patrols and a few of them suffered the bane of lawmen of all ages—a divorce from an estranged wife. None of the rangers became wealthy while working for the territory, but a few of them were able to make a successful financial leap after they left the mounted police.

Captain John Fullerton enjoyed jelly donuts and loved cherry pie. Lieutenant

Cipriano Baca could eat a bowl of beans, and drank a pot of hot coffee with each meal. Sergeant Bob Lewis and Fate Avant were both steak and potatoes men, but "Stuttering Bob's" real love was watermelon. Rafael Gomez could cook up a tasty and highly seasoned manudo, while Julius Meyer loved a big plate of hot German sausage topped with sauerkraut. George Elkins smoked cigars, Bob Putman smoked Chesterfields and Dick Huber smoked his strong smelling tobacco in a large German bowl pipe. Will Dudley read Shakespeare, quoted the Bible and wore shoes, not boots, when he was out on scout duty. John Brophy wore wire rim eyeglasses.[1] They were a mixed lot with a common desire for justice and a steady paycheck.

Cipriano Baca

"[Lieutenant Cipriano] Baca is said to be a fearless and capable officer, speaks both languages fluently and has a natural instinct to hunt criminals."
— The Tucumcari *News*
23 June 1906

Cipriano Baca rests between two strangers in an unmarked grave in Albuquerque's Sunset Memorial Park. Baca was just four days short of his seventy-eighth birthday when he died after having been a New Mexico peace officer for 52 years.[2] Cipriana Baca Randolph told the author that her father, called Sipriano on the old family baptismal record, had been born on September 26, 1859, in Martinez, California.[3]

Baca's youthful marriage ended with the tragic death of his wife and daughter in a boating accident. Later in Arizona Territory, Baca worked on a farm-ranch and lost a second wife due to divorce before he settled in Deming, New Mexico Territory. In Grant County, he was an undercover range detective while openly working as a railroad meat contractor, and may have helped Wyatt Earp with his clandestine return to Arizona in the summer of 1882.[4]

Cipriano Baca accepted an offer, in March 1891, to wear a deputy's star for Grant County Sheriff James A. Lockhart. His first arrest was enacted like a classic B-grade western movie when he brought William "Bronco Bill" Walters out of Old Mexico.[5] A few years later, Baca moved to the boom mining camp of Mogollon and continued his peace officer career as a Socorro County deputy sheriff.[6] Baca won election, in November 1896, as the Socorro County tax assessor and quickly took charge of his new duties by adding many new names to the county tax rolls.[7] Baca not only ran the assessor's office, but he continued to serve as a deputy sheriff and special deputy U.S. marshal, invest in mining development, and court a young woman named Mary Berry.[8]

Third time was a charm for Baca when he and Miss Berry were married, on Lincoln's birthday 1898, in the small mountain mining village of Kelly. Cipriano and Mary's 15-year union produced 11 children, but only five of them lived long enough to reach adulthood.[9]

On January first 1899, Baca relinquished his desk as county assessor to become a full-time deputy federal marshal,[10] but within months he had resigned to become the yard master at the territorial prison in Santa Fe. Two years later Baca was Grant County's chief deputy sheriff and was stationed at Silver City.

In 1901 the territory's Legislative Assembly created a new county from the eastern part of Grant County[11] and Baca was appointed its first sheriff. "Even Governor Otero's enemies must admit that, in appointing [Cipriano Baca the sheriff] of Luna County, he made an excellent and discriminating choice."[12] In November 1902, Cipriano Baca lost his bid, by 58 votes, to serve a full two year term as Luna County sheriff. The Deming *Herald* complimented Baca for having been "a safe, conservative and business-like officer" and editorialized, "His has not been a flashy or brilliant reign perhaps, but it has been what is better — modest, safe and substantial."[13]

Once again Cipriano Baca became employed by Uncle Sam and there are numerous accounts about his service as a federal peace officer. Good judgment, stern determination, a quick smile, and a sense of justice by law were qualities that made Cipriano Baca a respected officer and this was a rare quality on the New Mexico frontier of the Twentieth Century.[14]

In April 1905, Cipriano Baca became lieutenant of Fullerton's Rangers and once again located his family in Socorro. Baca set an excellent record as a territorial policeman until he resigned his ranger commission in January 1907. The news of Baca's resignation surprised and stunned people across the territory. The Albuquerque *Morning Journal* said Baca "has done yeoman service during his incumbence [*sic*] in rounding up rustlers and other criminals and preserving order in his district."[15] The Territorial Mounted Police never again had a Spanish surnamed officer.

The 47-year-old ex-territorial lawman finally accepted a detective job with the El Paso and Southwestern Railroad Company, but by the fall he had became the marshal of the coal mining town of Dawson. However, within a few months Baca had became disenchanted with Dawson and returned to his former job as a special agent for the El Paso and Southwestern Railroad.[16]

In September 1910, Cipriano Baca's world changed again. Mogollon was a tinderbox divided over the death of a saloon owner killed by mounted police officers in a shootout. Socorro County Sheriff G.E. Sanchez needed a good deputy in the mining camp to settle the tempers and restore order.[17] Baca and his growing family spent nearly three years in Mogollon and during this time Mary Baca and her newborn son died. The joyful light in Baca's life went out and a year later he was forced to make his toughest decision. A popular church hymn of the day reflected the mood of Baca's troubled mind. One verse says, "In the midst of faults and failures, Stand by me; When I've done the best I can, and my friends misunderstand; Thou who knowest all about me, Stand by me."[18]

Cipriana Baca Randolph remembered, "Mogollon as a very tough town and a hard place to raise a family. Father tried to make it a safe place for us, but he had a tough job. Father had to make a difficult decision because he felt he could no longer care for us children and perform the demands of his jobs."[19] Louise Nazareth Baca recalled that her husband, Florentino, "never would talk about his father due to a grudge he held against him for putting him [a ten year old] in an orphanage. I never knew Cipriano but he must have had what he, at least, considered a legitimate reason."[20] Baca gave his three daughters to his in-laws to raise and he placed his two sons in an Albuquerque orphanage.

A few years of Baca's life after he left Mogollon are unclear. In 1918, the New Mexico Mounted Police were reactivated for scout duty along the Mexican border and Captain Herb McGrath selected his former boss to be one of his full time rangers.[21] Captain McGrath's company of Mounted Police served until the last day of December 1918. The world was once again at peace and 60-year-old Cipriano Baca was employed as a mounted inspector for the state's Cattle Sanitary Board. In the late 1920s, Cipriano Baca was serving warrants as a Bernalillo County deputy sheriff, but his advancing age and ill health finally caused him to give up his deputy star and become a night watchman.[22]

Finally, he could work no longer due to his failing health, and in September 1936 Cipriano Baca underwent an operation on his lower colon. "I really don't know who is paying for this treatment," Baca wrote Cipriana. Cipriano Baca may have felt his hours were numbered because he did not end this letter in his usual manner. This time Baca wrote his daughter, "Good Bye Father." A week later, Cipriano Baca died from colon cancer.[23]

In the fall of 1936, the nation's newspapers were full of stories about a new band of federal crime fighters called G-Men. The cowboy and the western outlaw was the backbone of the Saturday motion picture serials. Few New Mexicans remembered the deeds of their own territorial rangers and even fewer could recall the soft-spoken Spanish peace officer who had once been a living legend. Cipriano Baca had simply outlived his era.

Robert W. Lewis

"Sergeant Lewis rarely fails to get the man he goes after."
— The Socorro *Chieftain*
18 May 1907

Robert W Lewis

Robert W. Lewis was a man of action and for over a quarter of a century few possies rode in Socorro County, New Mexico, that did not have him as a member. He was an excellent tracker, a crack shot and a man who would stand his ground against the odds. Lewis carried his Colt .45 in a shoulder holster under his left arm and was quick to use it when the need presented itself. He was a competent lawman with a propensity to play practical jokes.[24]

The War Between the States had ended and the Reconstruction Era was under way in the Deep South when, on Wednesday, March 10, 1866, Carlyne Lewis gave her husband, Ben, a son they named Robert. Following three years of difficult economic times in Leboron, Alabama, the Ben Lewis family moved to the cattle country of Comanche County, Texas. Sixteen years later tall and handsome Bob Lewis saddled his horse and headed for New Mexico Territory.[25] He said years later, "I wanted to grow up with the land."[26]

Bob Lewis did grow up and became a big man, standing six foot, two inches tall and weighing in at well over 200 pounds. The young cowboy developed a taste for fine whiskey and a good cigar and never out grew either of these vices. Bob had a speech impediment that sometimes caused him to stutter when he got excited, so he was given the nickname "Stuttering Bob" by his friends, who used the name in a friendly manner because no one dared to make fun of him. Lewis was a cheerful, happy-go-lucky man, with a strong left hook and a swift gunhand, who could turn serious at the wink of an eye.[27] Lewis was always a true son of the South and often showed that allegiance by eating large quantities of watermelon; saying once, "It's always been my favorite."[28]

Lewis first rode into far western Socorro County, present day Catron County, in 1885 and started working on the Bar N Ranch. Lewis grew to love the high range country and in spite of his brushes with the law, he proved to be a hard working cowboy and a good manager of men and animals.[29]

On October 10, 1896, Bob Lewis married Flora Higgins. She was one of seven daughters and five sons of Socorro County rancher Pat Higgins. Bob and Flora Lewis were a team who enjoyed the life on the open range and their union produced seven children with the oldest, Patrick, born in 1897. The couple had four other children, sons W.T., Ben, Robert, Jr., and a daughter named Velma, who grew to adulthood. Two other daughters, Carrie and Una, died as young children and are buried in the Lewis family plot in Socorro.[30]

Leandro Baca, the Democratic candidate, was elected sheriff of Socorro County, in November 1902, and asked Bob to become a deputy sheriff and jailer. Lewis accepted the offer and quickly gained a reputation as a man-hunter.[31] It was this reputation that earned "Stuttering Bob" Lewis the honor, at 39, to be selected as the sergeant of Fullerton's Rangers.

Following three years of service as mounted police sergeant and a year as the rangers' second-in-command, Bob Lewis resigned from the range riders, effective March 31, 1909, to take a better paying and less stressful job in the cattle business. Lewis became the range foreman for the Adams Cattle Company's Vermejo Park operation in Colfax County.[32]

By June 1910, "Stuttering Bob" was once again settled in his believed Socorro County as a deputy sheriff at Magdalena. The territory's largest cattle and sheep shipping center held his interest for a year before Lewis hung up his shoulder holster and turned in his badge to become a hotel proprietor. Lewis bought Socorro's historic Plaza Hotel and re-christened the place the Park House Hotel.[33] Bob's rheumatism continued to give him trouble and the hotel life was not Bob's calling, so late in 1912 he was back on the range once again as a cow foreman in Colfax County.

Mogollon experienced a new gold discovery in 1913, and Lewis was part of the boom by swinging a hammer as a carpenter in the new building craze. The boom did not last and Bob returned to Socorro as a range inspector for the state Cattle Sanitary Board.[34] Bob Lewis was a Socorro County peace officer, often a deputy sheriff or the chief deputy, from 1916 until his retirement in 1938. Lewis is best remembered, however, as the tough, yet loveable, town marshal at Magdalena. The town council gave Bob a gold-plated marshal's badge that is still a family treasure.[35]

Lewis, like many New Mexicans, had searched for the Lost Adams Gold Diggings. "I first met Adams in Reserve [Upper Frisco Plaza] in 1889, while working as a cowboy near there on the Bar N ranch," he recalled. Over two decades later Lewis was still searching for the diggings. "It was in 1918 that I finally located the skeletons Adams had described. In fact, I found everything but the gold."[36]

A major fire went out of Bob Lewis when his wife of 39 years died in 1935, but the old peace officer was able to find some solace in his grandchildren. In old age Bob had his memories. "The times were tough in the old days and we had a few shootings, but they didn't happen as often or in such large proportions as we see in the usual western movie" of the 1920s through the 1940s.

"People didn't try to beat their debts in the old days. A stranger could always walk into a Magdalena store and get anything he wanted on credit, with no questions asked. The western cowboy was usually always good to his word."[37]

Retirement came hard for a man like Lewis. His adventuresome life included having been shot in the leg and having two of his coats shot with bullet holes.[38] He was easily called back to the active life, in 1939, to run the new Civilian Conservation Camp at Sandia Park near Albuquerque. Lewis still enjoyed the rugged outdoor life, but he soon found that age was beginning to demand that he slow down, so at 73 his lifelong fight with rheumatism finally called a halt to his over-active life. Bob's hearing and eyesight also became concerns for his family.[39]

Robert W. "Stuttering Bob" Lewis returned to his maker on Friday, August 18, 1950. That evening a cerebral hemorrhage took his life. He was buried alongside Flora and their children in the family plot in the Socorro Cemetery, following a Masonic Lodge service. The mortal remains of Bob Lewis now rest beneath an unmarked grave.[40]

George M. Elkins

"George Elkins, the well known range rider...."
The Silver City *Independent*
11 July 1905

George Elkins,

George M. Elkins was born in Waldrip, Texas in 1878. The village's remains are in the northwest corner of McCulloch County. Two decades later George was the tall and lean foreman for the Al Watkins spread in a remote section of New Mexico Territory. A short time later Elkins found his true home at the Hatchet Ranch in the rugged mountains of the boot-heel. George liked being called a "cowman" and he became a star among the best of his breed.[41]

Elkins enjoyed the taste of a mild cigar and the range life pumped through his veins. Many people called the cowboy fearless. George knew cattle, hard men and a tough and untamed section of the Land of Enchantment.[42] At 27 years of age he wore badge number one of Fullerton's Rangers and he had the personal endorsement of the rangers' founding father, Col. William H. Greer.

Following his 91 days of service to New Mexico Territory, George Elkins went to work on the vast Diamond A Cattle Company ranch. A few years later, he rode the range lands around Best near Mescalero. Elkins wrote, in 1909, that the Best range country had "water all over it in fact the best watered range I ever saw."[43]

In 1913, George Elkins was back at the Hatchet Ranch and this time he was the general foreman. Today, Elkins is remembered on the Hatchet Ranch by having an impound lake named in his honor, located between the main ranch house and the Big Hatchet Mountains.[44] Following the Villa Raid on Columbus, New Mexico, in 1916, George did some scout duty for General John J. Pershing's forces in Old Mexico. For their protection, George Elkins housed his family near the U.S. Army camp near the international gate at Palomas, Mexico, just south of Columbus.[45]

After a short stint as a state cattle brand inspector, Elkins became an independent cattle trader in Old Mexico and was there when he was murdered in the early 1930s. M.T. Everhart, whose family has owned the Hatchet Ranch for over a century, told the author that Elkins was assassinated near his ranch. The murder "was generally attributed to hirelings of Jim Regan who was also given discredit for the Kingsbury [a prominent border rancher] killing." No one seemed to know why Regan may have wanted Elkins dead, but Mr. Everhart just assumed that "there were sound economic reasons." The rancher also said, "Regan was a bad man, but not bloodthirsty." Regan himself was later killed by another man he had once tried to ambush.[46] Was this border justice?

Chandler Elkins said that his father, a good family man, was more at home around a cow camp than in a ranch building. George Elkins was "a fine horseman and a good judge of livestock."[47] Maybe he was the only true range rider in Fullerton's Rangers.

Julius Meyer

"By reason of his vast knowledge of the country, his coolness when in the work and his splendid character throughout the [mounted police] appointment is more than fitting."

— El Paso *Times*
28 March 1905

The author had the opportunity to visit and correspond with three of Julius Meyer's wonderful grandchildren. Meyer had three wives and over a dozen children.[48] Julius' last name was often misspelled Meyers or Myers in the newspapers and in official records. He was born near Paris, Missouri, on July 18, 1866.[49]

Meyer's first wife died, leaving him three small children to raise on a homestead near Clairmore, Oklahoma. It would seem that Julius Meyer may have left his children with his sister when he moved to New Mexico. A Meyer family member told the author that Julius' sister ran a "house of ill repute."

Julius Meyer, who spoke excellent Spanish, next married Librada "Libby"

Sanchez of Albuquerque. The couple was married nearly a quarter of a century and they had ten children. Libby, born in 1879, died at the couples' home in Willard on the day before her birthday in 1914. Libby was the wife Julius was "searching for" after she had left Estancia and moved to the Duke City, while he was on an extended mounted police scout in 1905.[50]

The new county of Torrance was formed in central New Mexico in 1903 and Julius Meyer gave up his many odd jobs to become a deputy sheriff. Meyer rode with the territorial rangers for four years before he was elected sheriff of Torrance County in November 1908. Early in his law enforcement career Meyer made friends with a deputy federal marshal named Fred Fornoff.

During his years as sheriff, Meyer and Captain Fornoff became long term partners in a cattle ranch operation and a salt mining business in Torrance County.[51] Earl Scott, cashier at the Estancia Savings Bank, was the third partner in the salt business and was always keeping a watchful eye on Meyer's handling of the business. Scott once wrote Fornoff, "This is no reflection on Julius as he is simply careless."[52] Meyer was still working the salt licks as late as 1918.

When Julius Meyer left the Torrance County sheriff's office, a few years after statehood, he opened a garage and service station in Willard and became an auto mechanic and let his son Charlie operate the family ranch and farm. Julius also served as a Torrance County commissioner.

In 1915, the 49-year-old Julius Meyer married for the last time. His bride was 27-year-old Geneva Epler[53] and together they had two sons and a daughter. An advanced case of consumption caused Julius Meyer to seek a dryer climate than the mountainous plains of central New Mexico, so in the late 1930s he and Geneva moved to southern California. Julius Meyer died in the Golden State and is buried in Santa Anna.[54]

John James Brophy

"We are pleased to state that Mr. J.J. Brophy has received his appointment to the Territorial Ranger force. If the same standard of excellence prevails throughout the force New Mexico may well be proud of her Rangers."
The Clayton *Enterprise*
24 March 1905

John James Brophy was the only one of the original Fullerton's Rangers to be assigned to duty in northern New Mexico. John had been a brand inspector at Clayton, but was a Union County deputy sheriff at the time of his appointment to the mounted police. Union County citizens had sent Governor Otero "a strong petition" asking that Brophy be appointed one of the new rangers.[55]

The Oconto, Wisconsin, native, born October 24, 1863, was an experienced stockman. While working as a cowboy he had single-handedly recovered some stolen horses while working on a ranch in the Texas Panhandle. Later these same rustlers, out of jail on bond, tried to murder John while he attended a dance in Liberty, New Mexico, but he survived the two bullet wounds.[56]

John was an early day Tucumcari businessman before he relocated to the newly formed Union County. Brophy and Quay County Sheriff Alex Street, a future mounted policeman, remained good friends and over the years spent time in each other's homes. The two men often worked together on possies and civic events.[57] Many a would-be lawbreaker was fooled by Brophy's appearance as a glasses-wearing dandy.[58] John was in fact a hard working, no nonsense peace officer who, at 42, was the oldest member of Fullerton's Rangers.[59]

John completed his one year appointment as a territorial ranger, then he resigned to become the night marshal at Clayton. One of the jobs that the new town council asked Brophy to do was to locate a dumping ground for dead animals and to serve as the town's pound master. The marshal was also required to collect the $25 a month license fee from the local brothel owners and the $5 a month fee from each of the girls.[60]

In the summer of 1906, Marshal John Brophy prevented the lynching of a man he had arrested for murder and this action earned him high praise from the territorial governor and his fellow lawmen. By the end of 1906 John Brophy was working as an inspector for the Sheep Sanitary Board and some time later he again became a Union County deputy sheriff. In 1915 Brophy was working a ranch in the Oklahoma panhandle county of Cimarron.[61]

The untimely death of Brophy's eldest son was a tragedy that clouded John's last days. The Brophys had lost two children as infants, so Frank held a special place in his dad's life. Frank George Brophy had been a pleasant and helpful boy, while his younger brother was reported to have been as fiery tempered as his red hair would have indicated. Young John seems to have been a source of worry to his parents because he was always in trouble.

On a spring day in 1915, the two Brophy boys went duck hunting near Black Mesa outside Kenton, Oklahoma, and only young John Duran Brophy returned alive. The boy claimed his brother Frank had accidentally shot himself while crawling through a barbed wire fence, but many Union County residents had trouble accepting young Brophy's tale. One historian noted, "There were rumors and speculation, but such accidents happened just the way [young] John said this did."[62]

John Brophy died of ptomaine poisoning on June 5, 1916, and was buried next to his son Frank. The grave is unmarked. Rosaria Duran Brophy died of cancer in April 1925 and was buried in an unmarked grave beside her husband in Clayton's Kilburn Cemetery.[63]

William E. Dudley

"Among the force no one is more efficient or better qualified than Ranger Dudley."

The Alamogordo *News*
17 November 1906

William E. Dudley was a native of Tyler, Texas, and was called Will by family and friends. He was born on February 17, 1869, and 23 years later was a homesteader on Yellow House Creek in Crosby County, Texas. Here, Will married Mary Josephine Burleson in July 1896 and they moved to a Parker County, Texas, farm. A short time later both were teaching in the public school system in Brownsville, Texas.[64] However, a few years later the lure of a larger paycheck and a desire to run his own school brought Will and Josie to New Mexico Territory.

In the fall of 1902, the Dudleys were teaching at the public school at Nogal in Lincoln County, New Mexico. Two years later the teacher team and their young children made Alamogordo home. By now Will had become a recognized orator and was also fluent in Spanish.[65] Professor Dudley was a life member of the fraternal order called the Knights of Pythias and always tried to live up to the organization's motto of "Be Generous, Brave, and True." The very popular Dudley was elected as the grand vice chancellor of the New Mexico Grand Lodge in the fall of 1905.[66]

Will Dudley served five and a half years with the Territorial Mounted Police. His last year was as the company's sergeant before resigning, in September 1910, to become marshal at White Oaks. Later, Will served 37 months as the deputy sheriff and marshal at the Dawson coal camp. It was during these years that he became an excessive drinker and developed a pot belly.[67] He seemed to have trouble dealing with the death of his only son and his role as a mine company enforcer.[68]

In 1915, Will Dudley undertook the job of a mine guard in southeastern Arizona and one source claims that Dudley was really an undercover federal agent for the Justice Department. It would seem that during these pre–World War I years that Dudley may have sustained a head injury during an assassination attempt.[69]

Will's health was never the same following his stay in Arizona and he suffered extended periods of delusion. One of Dudley's grandsons has said that Will just packed up his bag one day, told his family good-bye and disappeared. Extensive research has located Will for a few of the years following his family desertion. During these mystery years Will Dudley is known to have posed as a wealthy Texas rancher, passed worthless checks to government officials, worked in a small Texas granary, raised money for the American Red Cross and in 1918 was appointed as the pastor of the First Baptist Church in Herington, Kansas.[70]

Will and Josie separated during this period, but they never were divorced. Court records show that Will Dudley had married a woman in Wichita, Kansas, and then left her there when he moved to Herington. He was arrested and charged with "wife desertion" in a Kansas state district court, but before his trial date Will had skipped his bond.[71] Will Dudley's remaining years and his final resting place are clouded in mystery.[72]

Josie Dudley returned to Alamogordo and became a beloved schoolteacher and church volunteer. She was 101 years old when she died in 1978, and she rests today in that city's Monte Vista Cemetery next to her only son. An Alamogordo public school was named in her honor.[73]

Octaviano Perea

"Mr. Perea appears to be a man well chosen for his work, that of a mounted police or range rider."

Durango (Colo.) *Evening Herald*
01 September 1905

Octaviano Perea was the only native-born New Mexican on Fullerton's original ranger force. He was born the son of Demetrio and Crucita M. Perea, at Torreon in Valencia County, in March 1868. Perea married in the spring of 1891 and settled his small family at Fort Stanton[74] where he was a Spanish teacher, translator, court interpreter, notary public and a legislative session interpreter.[75] He was once called "one of the bright active and intelligent citizens of Lincoln county."[76] Perea loved to play cards and race horses.[77]

Octaviano moved to Lincoln to become chief deputy sheriff and jailor for his father.[78] Two years later the new sheriff retained Perea's services. A news account stated, "While being a careful and strict official he is kind and just to the prisoners in his charge."[79] In 1904, Perea moved his family to Otero County and started a Spanish language newspaper in Alamogordo.[80] Following his year with Fullerton's Rangers, Perea worked for some time in Old Mexico and he finally resettled in Lincoln and became "one of the old timers and best known Lincoln county citizens." [81]

Herbert James McGrath

Herb McGrath was "one of the best known and most resourceful peace officers in the southwest."

The Silver City *Enterprise*
06 October 1933

Herbert James McGrath was a true gentleman and businessman. Herb was a veteran deputy sheriff and constable at Lordsburg.[82] McGrath had not sought his appointment to the mounted police and in fact he was somewhat reluctant to accept the post. The native Californian and college (New Mexico State University) football quarterback had recently earned a reputation as a "two gun peace officer" because he shot to kill. On the weekend Governor Otero announced McGrath's ranger appointment the young lawman had shotguned two bandits in a face-to-face shootout.[83]

McGrath served only nine months with Fullerton's Rangers before he resigned. Herb entered the local political wars and in November 1908 he won election as Grant County's sheriff. McGrath held this post for almost a decade before he resigned to become captain of the reorganized mounted police in the summer of 1918.[84] When the war time rangers were disbanded, Herb McGrath married his secretary, retired to his vast FM Bar cattle ranch west of Silver City and continued his civic duty by serving as a member of Cattle Sanitary Board.[85]

Herb McGrath died in October 1933 and sleeps forever with his first wife and their families in a large plot of the once opulent Concordia Cemetery in El Paso.[86] Herb was only 58 when he died. He was survived by his second wife, a son and his two nieces he had raised.

Charles Richard Huber

"Mr. Huber has done some very clever work on this [horse stealing] case...."
Albuquerque *Morning Journal*
22 August 1905

C R Huber

Minnesota born Charles Richard Huber was a colorful character who wore his Colt .45 affixed to his cartridge belt on a swivel pin and was an expert at shooting from the hip.[87] To some people, Huber, a son of a German immigrant, was a windbag because in his later years Dick was known to spin some wild and exciting tales of an adventurous youth.[88] One of Dick's longtime acquaintances described him as a loveable old rogue.

Huber had a few encounters with the law before he crossed over to become a law enforcer as a Santa Fe County deputy sheriff and deputy game warden. The smiling, six-horse hitch stage-coach-driver-turned-peace-officer did not always abide by the letter of the law even after he had sworn an oath to enforce that law.[89] His conduct caused his removal from office as one of Fullerton's Rangers. He was reemployed by a new captain, but was fired again. After he was asked to leave the mounted police a second time, Huber served as a marshal in Santa Fe, and again as a Santa Fe County deputy sheriff. Drink became his chief enemy and finally Dick was encouraged to work for himself, so he formed his own moving and transfer business. He ran this business until his marriage fell apart and at the time of his death he worked as a janitor and was living at the Santa Fe Elks Club. He is buried in an unmarked grave, under a driveway, in a Catholic cemetery in Santa Fe.[90]

Jessie LaFettie Avant

"Avent [sic] is one of the fearless and daring officers who has rid his locality of some very undesirable characters."

The Tucumcari News and Tucumcari Times
20 April 1907

L.iFt.Avent

Fate Avant and Cipriano Baca were the only two left-handers in Fullerton's Rangers. Jessie LaFettie Avant first saw the light of day on the family ranch near San Antonio, Texas, on November 11, 1856. He was the youngest of 12 children and learned early how to farm and ranch.

Avant married Ella Simons in January 1881 at Chadbourne, Texas, and they settled on a ranch near Cotulla. A long, difficult South Texas drought caused Avant to seek a new future in New Mexico as a sewing machine salesman. Fate became a successful salesman and earned enough to move his large family to Roswell before finally settling on a ranch near Capitan. Here he became a beef contractor for the government and also sold timber to the mine owners at Colora. In 1905, Fate Avant, at 48, was a successful businessman and a leader in the Baptist church.[91]

The 53 year old Avant retired from the ranger service in December 1909.[92] Six years later, he sold his Lincoln County holdings and relocated to a ranch in Sierra County. After five years of fruitless labor in an unbreakable drought, Avant was broke and separated from his wife.[93]

Once more the six foot, two inch Fate Avant accepted an appointment to ride with the mounted police. It was 1920 and the state rangers were now commanded by A.A. Sena. Fate served the year and was reappointed under Captain Lorenzo Delgado. Fate and his son Howard were the only father and son team to serve as rangers in the New Mexico Mounted Police. They were together just over a month before the rangers were permanently abolished in February 1921. Avant was the only ranger to have been present at both the mounted police's birth and at their funeral. He served under four of the mounted police's five captains.[94]

After leaving the mounted police, Fate Avant spent the next two decades earning a living doing a variety of odd jobs in central New Mexico. In the hot summer of 1940, the 84-year-old former rancher-ranger became very ill and he knew he might die, so he asked to be taken to a hospital in El Paso. Fate Avant's last wish was to die in, and to be buried in, the Lone Star State. On Saturday, July 13, 1940, Fate Avant found his final peace. He is buried in El Paso's Evergreen Cemetery near the grave of the deposed Mexican President Victoriano Huerta.[95]

Robert G. Putman

"Mounted Policeman [Bob] Putman after a month's chase, including his following old trails over dangerous mountain passes and lying for hours in wait for the desperadoes arrested ... the head of a gang of outlaws, whose depredations have lost the ranchman thousands of dollars."

The Santa Fe *New Mexican*
02 May 1906

Robert G. Putman (signature)

Robert G. Putman was born in Kansas on July 3, 1869, and during his youth migrated to New Mexico Territory. Few details of his movements before the turn of the century are known.

In 1901, Bob Putman married a woman 14 years his junior and settled near the hot springs at Los Palomias in Sierra County. The couple had a son they named Rhody. Putman had a small ranch and worked part time as a cowhand for bigger ranch operations. In the spring of 1905, the Putman family lived near the mining community of Fairview.[96]

Bob's first ranger assignment was on a mountain scout with Sergeant Lewis.[97] Six weeks later Putman had his family settled in a rented house in Socorro near the area were Fullerton and Lewis lived.[98] When the officers were away from the rangers' headquarters Putman was in charge and on other occasions Bob was named to lead ranger patrols in place of Baca or Lewis.[99]

Captain Fred Fornoff kept Putman on the force, but reassigned him from Socorro to Silver City. In early October 1907, Bob left the ranger service to become chief deputy sheriff of Grant County. Bob Putman had left the mounted police on a high note by completing a murder investigation, arresting his suspect and for good measure also arresting a horse thief suspect.[100]

Following Sheriff Charles Nelson's re-election loss to Herb McGrath in November 1908, Bob Putman became a constable at the Carthage coal camp in Socorro County, but a short time later he left the camp to become an inspector for the Cattle Sanitary Board. A lucrative salary offer in 1910 brought Bob Putman to the high mountain mining town of Mogollon as a special officer.[101] In this Socorro County gold camp Putman joined forces with Mounted Policeman John Beal in a shootout that made them both living legends. Their fearless stand against organized outlawry in the camp earned them an honored place in mounted police lore.[102]

In 1916, Putman was the Sierra County deputy sheriff who policed the construction camp at the Elephant Butte Dam project. One night in a barroom fight Bob had his throat cut, but he was still able to arrest his men and take them to the lockup before he passed out from loss of blood. The legendary Bob Putman now became the lawman you could not kill.[103] Before World War I, Bob served as the day desk officer on the Deming Police Department.

Putman spent the last seven months of 1918 with Herb McGrath's Mounted Police company and following this service as a state ranger Bob became a state cattle inspector at Hachita. He, like many lawmen before him and after him, became a divorced man.

In old age, Bob Putman settled in Deming. He spent his last six weeks in the Deming Hospital where he died, on October 9, 1947, of an obstruction of the bile ducts. A small cement slab marks Robert G. Putman's grave in the Deming Cemetery.[104]

E. Rhea Stewart

> E.R. Stewart is a man "of nerve and experience in frontier police duty, and doubtless will be of valuable assistance to the Mounted Police."
> The Las Vegas *Weekly Optic & Stock Grower*
> 23 December 1905

E. Rhea Stewart served New Mexico Territory as a policeman for less than six months. He was born in Illinois during the summer of 1873 and as an adult made his home at Aztec in San Juan County. He knew the range life and was a veteran cowman and stock inspector when he replaced Herb McGrath as one of Fullerton's Rangers in December 1905.[105]

During the summer of 1905, Lt. Baca and his ranger squad had worked undercover in San Juan County to break up a stock thief ring. The 32-year-old Stewart had helped in this effort and Baca may have recommended the former livestock inspector to Captain Fullerton.[106] Stewart was the only member of Fullerton's Rangers to be stationed in the northwestern corner of the territory.

Rhea was re-commissioned a mounted police in April 1906, but six weeks later Captain Fred Fornoff asked him to leave the ranger service. Stewart resigned, via a letter postmarked from El Paso, Texas, and disappeared from New Mexico history. Official mounted police records suggest that Rhea Stewart did little or nothing to earn his $75 a month as a territorial policeman.[107]

Rafael Gomez

> "The efficiency of the New Mexico Mounted Police was proved again yesterday when Rafael Gomez captured...."
> The Albuquerque *Morning Journal*
> 31 August 1911

Rafael Gomez was born in Socorro County, New Mexico, in February 1866. He attended public school and learned to read and write English. By the turn of the century, Gomez was married and owned his own home and a farm in Santa Fe County.[108]

In December 1905, the 39 year old Gomez replaced Dick Huber and became the last man to be appointed to Fullerton's Rangers. Rafael was re-appointed in 1906 and served under Captain Fred Fornoff until April 1907. Beginning in January 1909, Gomez once again wore the territorial ranger star and this time he remained on the force until he resigned to become a city marshal in Santa Fe in the summer of 1912. A year later, Gomez returned to the state rangers and was with Captain Fornoff when the State Mounted Police was unofficially disbanded in December 1913 due to lack of funding.[109] Gomez compiled one of the best arrest records of the territorial rangers.

During the years before World War I, Gomez operated a small horse ranch. When a full time salaried company of mounted police was resurrected during the summer of 1918, Rafael Gomez was selected to serve as one of Captain Herb McGrath's rangers. His arrest record for these seven months is impressive and it shows once again that Gomez was an outstanding peace officer. Following his mounted police service Gomez returned to his Valencia County home and it was here that he died, in 1924, at the age of 58 years.[110]

Appointed but Did Not Serve

Two other men had been given the opportunity to serve as privates in the first company of New Mexico Territorial Mounted Police. They had ranked high enough on the selection committee's short list to earn a recommendation for appointment. Both of these men were appointed to office, but both finally chose not to accept Governor Otero's offer to serve with Fullerton's Rangers. They are the only men to ever turn down an appointment as a private in the New Mexico Territorial Mounted Police.

Francisco Apodaca

In 1937, the Sierra County courthouse was relocated from Hillsboro to Hot Springs, present day Truth or Consequences, and many of the county's historical files were destroyed so that the county would not have to pay to have them moved. This lack of contemporary information has hampered historical study of the county and its citizens. Francisco Apodaca lived at Cuchillo Negro, wide open range country, a few miles north and west of Hot Springs.

Census data seems to indicate that Apodaca was a farmer and a *nuevomexicano* who must have earned high respect among his fellow ranchers for his knowledge of the outdoor life, thus his nomination to become a ranger. One possible reason Apodaca declined his appointment to the mounted police may have been his age. In April 1905, Francisco Apodaca would have been nearly 50 years old and this was not the ideal age to spend long days in the saddle or even longer nights sleeping on the ground in a cold camp. Such was the demanding life expected of a range rider.[111]

William M. Taylor

Even though his mounted police appointment notice listed his address as Deming, William M. Taylor's mail was better delivered to Feywood Station, some 24 miles northwest of the Luna County seat, along the Santa Fe Railroad tracks. Bill Taylor's family had owned a ranch in that valley for decades.[112] In 1901, Governor Miguel Otero had named Taylor one of Luna County's first county commissioners. Like Cipriano Baca, Taylor had lost an election bid to the post to a heavily Democratic victory in November 1902. However, unlike Baca, Governor Otero was able to reappoint Taylor to his former post because one of the elected commissioners resigned in March 1903.[113]

At first, Taylor did not accept his mounted police appointment, but a short time later he changed his mind and asked Governor Otero to restore the appointment. The governor told Taylor that he no longer had a vacancy on the force.[114] Had Taylor been patient he might have received his wish, because George Elkins, in June 1905, became the first active duty ranger to voluntarily resign his commission. By this time, William Taylor had left New Mexico Territory and he had settled his family on a border ranch near Douglas in southeastern Arizona Territory.[115]

7

"The Governor Shall ... Organize a Corps of Mounted Police"

> "The Mounted Police force is made up of experienced men, all dead shots, who can be relied on to capture or kill [the outlaws they seek]."
>
> *Otero County Advertiser*
> 22 April 1905

In mid–March 1905, Governor Otero received a letter from the general superintendent of a large land holding company that was headquartered in southern California. The man's company also held mining claims in western Socorro County. "I wish to thank you kindly for your prompt action in signing the Mounted Police Bill." H.A. Jastro went on to write, "I assure you that the people of the territory are greatly indebted to you for the benefits the territory will derive from the passage of this bill. From my own knowledge, in some parts of the territory, no legitimate business can be carried on at this present time, and will not be until a number of those outlaws, who are infesting that portion of the [western mountain] country are routed out."[1]

Under the provisions of the Mounted Police Act, the territorial governor had 60 days to appoint the leadership and the field rangers for the new force of territorial police. Within days of the law's passage, the governor's office was flooded with over 200 letters, petitions or formal applications for the range rider jobs. Otero decided not to review all the applications himself so he formed a screening committee to locate the best candidates. Holm Bursum and Solomon Luna were asked, by Otero, to perform this thankless task and to make the formal recommendations. Otero, except for two personal requests for special consideration, gave Bursum and Luna full authority to recommend a slate of candidates. One ranger request concerned Octaviano Perea and the other was for Deputy United States Marshal Cipriano Baca. Some of the candidates had nominated themselves, while others were proposed by friends or employers without the knowledge of the prospect. It would appear that even the screening duo may have added a few candidates to the application pool.[2]

Holm Bursum was a stockman, a former sheriff of Socorro County and a former member of the Territorial Council, who was presently serving as the superintendent of the territorial penitentiary. He was also the chairman of the Republican Party's Territorial Central Committee. The future United States senator accepted the selection assignment with his usual zest for a new challenge.

The 1905 Mounted Police Selection Committee: Soloman Luna (left) of Los Lunas, N.M., and Holms O. Bursum of Socorro, N.M. Governor Otero named these two ranchers and political leaders as the selection committee to review the 200 applications and make final recommendations of appointments to the mounted police (NMMP/AC).

Solomon Luna, head of Albuquerque's Bank of Commerce, was a wealthy, soft-spoken sheepman and former sheriff from Valencia County, where he was the county's patron and a territorial *jefe politico* lovingly nicknamed "King Saul" by his many friends. Luna was highly respected for his extraordinary political ability and for his service as the treasurer of the Republican Party's Territorial Central Committee. One night in late August 1912, Luna went to the privy at his home. He suffered a stroke or heart attack and died after falling in a sheep dip tank.[3]

John Fullerton was in Santa Fe on "official business" during late February 1905.[4] It is uncertain as to the nature of his business, but this was about the time that John's old friends Luna and Bursum were starting to discuss recommendations for the mounted police. No evidence exists to suggest that Fullerton actually ever met with his friends during his stay in the capital. However, the idea that John might have discussed an appointment with one or both of the "selection committee" does make for some interesting speculation.

The governor was repaying a political debt he owed Octaviano Perea for the votes he had delivered, in Otero County, during the November general election. Perea was presently serving as one of the Spanish interpreters for the House of Representatives and was busy every day,[5] but two days before Governor Otero signed the Mounted Police Bill into law he found time to make a social call upon the chief executive. Otero's day journal records nothing concerning the nature of their conversation, but some believe it might have addressed Perea's pending mounted police appointment.⁶ This selection is a good example of how the political reward system was used during this era.⁷ Political reward appointments were prohibited, under the regulations established for the re-organization of the Mounted Police force in 1918.⁸

The Cipriano Baca appointment was no political payoff. Baca was the most effective Hispanic lawman of his era. The *New Mexican* reported Baca's visit to Santa Fe "on official business" and almost as an afterthought the reporter wrote, "He incidentally visited the legislature this morning."⁹ The governor and Baca held a frank "personal-social" meeting later that same morning, concerning the mounted police and Otero's wish to offer the captaincy of the rangers to Baca. However, both men had agreed that an Anglo, with stockmen's support, would receive wider acceptance for the new force. Baca had agreed to accept, if offered, the second-in-command.¹⁰ A short time after that meeting someone, most likely his friend Holm Bursum, told Baca that his territorial appointment was set, because Cipriano dated his two week resignation notice to U.S. Marshal Creighton M. Foraker on March 14. A few days later, Deputy U.S. Marshal Cipriano Baca was in Socorro County serving jury summons for the next session of federal court when the general public learned of his mounted police appointment.¹¹

The real discussion concerning who would make an effective officer may have been over the position of sergeant. No records of these talks survive, but surely someone brought up the fact that the top two officer candidates were Republicans. So to avoid the charge of partisanship with the mounted police appointments, the sergeant had be a Democrat from the Southern part of the territory and the top contender was Robert W. "Stuttering Bob" Lewis, the former chief deputy sheriff of Socorro County. An unpublicized morning "personal-social" get acquainted visit was arranged between Lewis and the governor for 10:30 on Tuesday, March 7. During this encounter the statuesque Bob Lewis impressed Otero enough for him to offer Bob the post of ranger sergeant.¹²

Hard money was in short supply in New Mexico and the Alamogordo public school had closed its doors due to a lack of funds. This was the reason that private schoolteacher-principal William E. Dudley¹³ lobbied diligently for a slot with the rangers with numerous letters from Otero County businessmen and a lengthy petition of support.¹⁴ One letter even recommended Dudley for the post of ranger lieutenant.¹⁵ Twice during the 1905 legislative session Will Dudley had been invited, by lawmakers, to address a joint session. Will was a gifted orator, in both English and Spanish, and was considered an "expert in handling the native population."¹⁶

John J. Brophy, a Union County deputy sheriff, had conferred with Governor Otero on the morning that he made his mounted police appointments, but no record of the meeting's purpose was recorded in the chief executive's official logbook. The meeting may have been a last minute lobbing effort by Brophy to win a ranger's post, or the governor may have felt a need to size up John in person, or it might have just been a simple social visit. The timing, however, does give one cause to question the visit's purpose because Brophy had actively pursued a position with the territorial police by sending a letter to Otero requesting an "appointment as range rider." John Brophy was known as a businessman, cowman, and a good vote getter, but he was not known as a tough guy even though he was a respected lawman at Clayton.¹⁷

Herb McGrath, a Democrat, also had high-placed political connections. Twice during the legislative session he and John McCabe, the Republican precinct chairman from Lordsburg, traveled to Santa Fe to lobby the lawmakers to create a new county out of the southern section of Grant County. The men wanted to call the new county Pyramid and set the seat of government at Lordsburg. The effort was felt to be ambitious at that time, but the idea was sound and a decade later Hidalgo County was born.[18]

On the deadline day, Friday, March 17, Holm Bursum and Solomon Luna presented the governor with a letter containing their recommendations.[19] The list contained both Democrats and Republicans and the governor agreed to the duo's proposals. To a degree the new ranger company was non-political or at best bipartisan in configuration. By prior agreement, Bursum and Luna recommended Fullerton be named captain, Baca to be lieutenant and Lewis to be the company's sergeant. Eight additional men were suggested to be the privates or rangers of the Territorial Mounted Police.[20]

Governor Otero accepted the recommendations and asked to visit with Fullerton, so a quick message was sent to John requesting a meeting with the governor at 11:30 A.M. on Saturday. Otero and Fullerton had a short discussion concerning John's appointment as captain and the formation of the new mounted police company. Fullerton accepted the governor's formal offer to head the new rangers and a second meeting was planned for Monday afternoon.[21] Following their first meeting Fullerton tendered the governor a one sentence resignation as assessor of Socorro County and Holm Bursum presented Otero the name of a suggested replacement, which the governor accepted, and A.B. Baca was named to replace Fullerton.[22] Governor Otero's secretary, Miss Clara Olsen, released the names of the Mounted Police appointees shortly after Fullerton was administered the territorial oath of office by Secretary of the Territory J. Wallace Raynolds. During the next few days some of New Mexico's weekly newspapers published the names of the men who would form the new ranger company. However, these appointments were second tier news to the story that President Roosevelt attended the wedding of his niece Anna Eleanor Roosevelt to Franklin Delano Roosevelt and that the President had authorized, by executive order, a pension for Civil War veterans over 62 years old.

John Ferguson Fullerton. This photograph was taken in Socorro, N.M., in the late 1890s (Irene Fullerton's photograph album).

Was John Fullerton the best candidate to lead the mounted police? Probably not, because he had no background in law enforcement, but his two officers were seasoned lawmen and half of the privates were veterans of law enforcement. John was an organizer and his men were the field agents. John was a successful cattleman and was popular among the stockmen of the southern region. He was a Republican, supported Otero's economic development plan and he had won a very impressive election victory. He could be very personable and charming, an asset he used well as an insurance salesman in later years. Fullerton may not have been the best candidate, but he was acceptable.

Otero and Fullerton met as planned on Monday and it would seem that the two men discussed all facets of the organization steps. Otero may have felt like he was reliving the long days he had spent in 1898 organizing New Mexico's Rough Rider troops. These cavalry units served in the volunteer army that fought in Cuba during the Spanish-American War.[23] It is the author's conjecture, based upon circumstantial evidence, that Otero viewed the territorial police, very much as Richardson had in the original Mounted Police Bill of 1899, as a para-military unit. The governor was also completing final plans for his own extended working vacation trip to

John Fullerton's mounted police commission (courtesy of Susan Leverett).

the west coast, but he wanted to spend the needed time in conference with Fullerton to finalize the rangers' muster. The two conferred again on Tuesday and Wednesday.²⁴

When John Fullerton left Santa Fe he carried with him a certified copy of the Mounted Police Act, a list of his men and a fancy, large, wall size commission signed by the governor and countersigned by the secretary of the territory.²⁵ Fullerton was now faced with a special opportunity to formulate an organization plan during the two weeks before the formal muster ceremony. His only guide was the legislative act of creation and the best wishes of the governor, "Reposing, Special Trust and Confidence in the Prudence, Integrity and Ability."²⁶

Fullerton was in Socorro for the weekend and so where Cipriano Baca and Bob Lewis. How much contact, if any, the two men had with their new captain during the last few days of March is unknown and how much input, if any, they had on Captain Fullerton's command decisions is unclear at this late date. No tangible records remain to help document the thinking that must have influenced John Fullerton's actions. However, strong circumstantial evidence does exist and deductive reasoning can also help resolve some of the mystery.

Patrol Squads

One of Captain Fullerton's first moves, in accordance with Section 10 of the 1905 Mounted Police Act, was to separate his command into two squads under the direct command of one of his officers. This type of structure was being employed by Captain Tom Rynning of the Arizona Rangers.²⁷ One can only speculate on why Captain Fullerton composed his squad as he did. The patrol squad commanded by Lieutenant Baca consisted of George Elkins, Julius Meyer, John Brophy and Will Dudley,²⁸ while Sergeant Lewis was assigned William Taylor, Herb McGrath, Francisco Apodaca and Octaviano Perea.²⁹ Fullerton's design gave both squads rangers from the northern and southern sections of the territory. Fullerton may have felt this arrangement would give each command the ability to function across the territory, but when put into operation during the first few months, this system seemed to produce an overlap of effort. One squad would be covering the same ground right behind the other squad.

Hindsight would suggest that Captain Fullerton should have formed a northern and southern detachment or an eastern and western detachment structure. These squads could have had primary responsibility for their section and support function for the other detachment. This would have eliminated the endless overlap of patrol areas and the embarrassing lack of communication between the rangers living in the same general area, but serving in different scout squads.

The Company Muster

It was 5:51 when the sun broke over the mountains at Santa Fe on Saturday morning April 1, 1905; it was April Fool's Day. Looking back, with over a century of perspective, the choice of this date was almost a forecast of the future of Fullerton's

7—"The Governor Shall ... Organize a Corps of Mounted Police"

Rangers. Brophy, Dudley, McGrath, Perea, Meyer and Elkins were the six privates that joined Fullerton, Baca and Lewis in the governor's paneled office at 3:00 that afternoon. Taylor and Apodaca had not yet accepted their ranger appointments. Governor Otero and his family were en route to California for a month long business and vacation trip,[30] so Acting-Governor J. Wallace Raynolds presided at the half hour muster ceremony for the new ranger force.

John Fullerton had signed the standard territorial oath form on March 18. Cipriano Baca, Bob Lewis and each of the ranger privates were issued a crossed over National Guard Oath of Office form with its long worded promise that the signer would serve the territory "honestly and faithfully." The oath closed with the admonition of "So help me God." Beginning in 1906, the standard territorial oath form was used by all of the mounted police.

Cipriana Baca Randolph recalled, "Captain Fullerton quoted his men two verses from the Book of Proverbs. One was about riding the path of justice [08:20] and the other one was something about defending the rights of the poor [31:09]. It seems funny now, but I remember the rangers' motto best. It was the same as the Canadian Mounties. Maintain the Right. Father would sometimes quote one of those Bible verses or the motto, especially the motto, when we kids needed some attention paid to our backsides. Captain Fullerton must have been a closet romantic."[31]

The "Certificate of Mustering Officer" document, used by Fullerton, was a converted New Mexico National Guard form. He crossed out the military term and wrote "Mounted Police." This roll was required under Section Two of the Mounted Police Act.[32] When Fred Fornoff assumed command of the rangers in April 1906, he also held

Cover sheet of mustering certificate for mounted police Company One. The New Mexico Mounted Police was such a new concept that the legal forms needed to organize the company had not been designed at the time of their enrollment so Captain Fullerton used National Guard muster forms (New Mexico State Records Center and Archives).

an oath-taking ceremony, but he didn't, for whatever reason, fill out a muster roll as required by the mounted police law.[33]

Captain Fullerton informed his men that they would be governed by the rules and regulations of the U.S. Army "as far as the same may be applicable" because Section 9 of the Mounted Police Act prescribed that the territorial police would function under these guidelines. Fred Fornoff, however, choose to abandon this para-military style when he assumed control of the range riders and instead reorganized the new rangers into the district system used successfully by New Mexico's deputy U.S. marshals. No one at the time seemed to have questioned the legality of his action.

A local newspaper heralded the muster: "There was noticeable about the streets of Santa Fe today several strangers who attracted a good deal of attention by their manly and independent bearing, and by their general appearance which indicated that they were men of strong character and nerve and of the true western stripe — men who were used to outdoor life, could ride and manage a bucking bronco, as well as a gentle gelding and handle a Winchester or a Colt's six-shooter with the greatest of ease and accuracy should occasion require."

The Santa Fe *New Mexican* printed that run-on sentence as the lead to a page one feature on the muster of the mounted police. The capital city paper headlined the report, "Are Sworn Into Office." Further into the account the mounted police were described as "men in the prime of life, strong of feature and build, active and energetic selected for their peculiar fitness and experience which will be required of them and which will be not only not easy and light but on the contrary will be arduous, dangerous, and strenuous."

The *New Mexican* inserted an editorial comment, near the end of the news report, which predicted the rangers "will prove, within a year, a great factor for the preservation of the peace and the protection of the lives and property of the people in the isolated and stock-growing sections of the Territory."[34] This prediction proved to be both right and wrong.

Mounted Police Headquarters

Captain Fullerton had, as directed by the law, selected "as his base the most unprotected and exposed settlement of the territory" as his headquarters by locating the ranger office in Socorro. With this act the mounted police became the only territorial agency not to be headquartered in Santa Fe.[35]

In many ways the New Mexico Territorial Mounted Police was like a modern state police force. Captain Fullerton tried to outfit his men with the latest state-of-the-art police equipment and over the years Captain Fornoff continued the update procedure. Captain Fullerton provided the Socorro office with a set of research books containing registered livestock brands and he began a central criminal history file. He must have been concerned about the health and comfort of those who visited the mounted police headquarters because the office contained three cuspidors.[36]

John Fullerton established his office in the Chambon Building on Court Street. The room was rented to the territory for $9.00 per month by Henry Chambon.[37]

7—"The Governor Shall ... Organize a Corps of Mounted Police"   75

The Chambon Building at Socorro contained an office that served as the mounted police headquarters during John Fullerton's years as ranger captain. This photograph was taken in 1968 during a remodeling phase.

Elfego Baca, Socorro County's member on the Republican Party's Territorial Central Committee and the newly appointed district attorney, vacated his former law office for the mounted police's use, but he left his furnishings. On March 28, 1905, Captain Fullerton issued Mounted Police Voucher Number 2 in the name of "E. Baca." This territorial warrant was written for $51 and was to cover the sale price of Elfego Baca's used office furniture. Fullerton purchased Baca's desk and chair for $25, a $12 carpet, an old heating stove for $1.50, a wall lamp for $1.00, two wood chairs and a typewriter table for $3.00, two rocking chairs for $6.50 and a blank file box for two dollars.

A year later when Captain Fullerton closed the Mounted Police's Socorro headquarters he bought some of these same office items from the territory.[38] Captain Fred

Fornoff accepted Fullerton's offer to buy the desk and chair for $15, the carpet for $3.00, the old $1.50 stove for $5 and the $1 coal-oil lamp for twenty-five cents. The best bargains were the chairs, two rockers and two straight back wooden, originally purchased for about $8. They were sold to Fullerton for just $3. The cuspidors went to the Santa Fe office.

Captain Fullerton asked C.E. Ross, the territory's assistant traveling auditor, to provide the ranger office an account ledger. Fullerton completed his initial purchases by acquiring a typewriter and when the Socorro office was closed the typewriter was sent to Santa Fe in the care of Mounted Policeman Bob Putman. Putman also took with him the "maps and all papers in [the] office including [field report] blanks."[39] The maps that Bob Putman took to Santa Fe were the linen paper postal route charts sold by the U.S. Post Office Department. On June 3, 1905, Fullerton had purchased maps of Colorado, Utah, Arizona, Texas and three of the Sunshine Territory at a cost of $6.40. Each postal map sold for 80 cents, except for the double sized Lone Star State chart, which was $1.60.[40] These maps not only contained the postal route and a notation of the frequency of mail delivery along that system, they also located the mining districts, rivers and creeks, forest reserve boundaries, county lines and railroad routes. Baca and Lewis each had one of the New Mexico maps for use on patrols or scouts and the other maps were kept for use at headquarters.[41]

Following the conclusion of the 1905 legislative session the secretary of the territory compiled the 134 new laws and the joint resolutions and memorials into book form.[42] The published edition of the compiled code has an extensive index to assist the researcher in locating the information they seek. Each law is listed as a separate chapter and is numbered in the order that Governor Otero approved the legislation. Chapter Nine deals with the mounted police and the index for this chapter contains 17 subsections; each deals with a separate function such as "Tax Levy," "Supervision," or "Salary of Officers." The first 16 subsections deal with their stated topic, but the last is misleading. The subsection called "Uniform" actually deals with the mounted police badge and contains nothing about the ranger's dress. The person who did the indexing may have become confused with some wording in the text; it says, "a badge, uniform in size and shape" when identifying the emblem of office. The subsection should have been called "Badge" and this change was made in later years as the territorial law books were updated and republished in new editions.

One of the items John Fullerton discussed with his rangers was the company's uniform. The new police force was authorized to wear a gray suit modeled after the Northwest Mounted Police, except the New Mexico police would be issued a cowboy style hat instead of the Canadian pill-box hat.[43] The 1905 law, unlike the Mounted Police Bill of 1899, did not require that a uniform be worn by the territorial police and it is uncertain who designed or even authorized the gray uniform that was worn by Fullerton's Rangers. Governor Miguel A. Otero was an exponent of a show of state authority and a good example of Otero's showmanship was the governor's own personal staff, called the Otero Guards, who were brilliantly uniformed and omnipresent. Since 1894, Otero had been a member of the colorfully uniformed fraternal organization called the Knights of Pythis.

The governor, the ranger's commander-in-chief, may have been responsible for the semi-military favor of the police uniform by ordering Captain Fullerton to have his command dress in some type of identifiable clothes. The Fullerton uniform was seldom worn after Governor Otero left office and was totally discontinued after Fred Fornoff took charge. Another official mounted police uniform was not adopted until 1918 and then that suit was worn for the next two and a half years.

One question that begs for an answer is, why a gray uniform? Both the Otero and Fullerton families were strong union supporters during the War Between the States. Cipriana Baca Randolph recalled that her father once had a book, which Captain Fullerton had given him to read, about the Civil War exploits of John Mosby and his partisan rangers.[44] The book presented the cavalier "Gray Ghost of the Confederacy" and his men as dashing heroes in their colorful *gray* uniforms. In 1905, the romantic Mosby legend was still alive as shown by an old man's boyhood impression of having seen the rangers in action. He wrote that Mosby's Rangers "had for us all the glamour of Robin Hood and his merry men, all the courage and bravery of the ancient crusaders, pirates and the stealth of Indians."[45] Could the answer be that simple?

Nathan Salomon, owner of "The Only Up To Date Dry Goods Store In Santa Fe," was awarded the contract to provide the uniforms in mid–April. The store's stationery said, "Specialty in Ladies and Men's Taylor Made Suits." The Las Vegas *Daily Optic*, one of the territory's top three newspapers, reported the contract award on April 17 and then added, "The new uniforms are of gray cloth and tailor made. They have already been received, together with the hats and other accessories."[46] The news that the rangers already had their uniforms must have been a real surprise to the rangers, and to Nathan Salomon. This is the type of contemporary misinformation that makes recording a factual history of the mounted police so difficult.

A week after the *Optic* announcement Captain Fullerton sent each ranger a letter saying, "I enclose a blank for a suit measure. Try and get some man that will understand this and give you a good measurement and be particular in giving your description and shape of neck and shoulders."[47] When the uniforms arrived, Fullerton inspected each for quality and craftsmanship and rejected the whole shipment. "They did not look good to me and I hardly think they would hold their color," wrote Captain Fullerton in a letter to Private Will Dudley. "I hardly think the shirts were all wool. I examined the workmanship on them thoroughly."[48] Mr. Salomon next sent a first class outfit. The all-wool shirts cost $2.50 each. The gray uniform coat came with turned down collars, matching gray pants and a gray wool vest. The headgear was a top grade gray felt westerner style hat. Fullerton authorized payment of $354.35 for the 11 uniforms.[49]

In June, Captain Fullerton sent a territorial warrant to the M.C. Lilly Company of Dayton, Ohio. The $7.68 government draft was in full payment for eleven sets of hand embroidered, gilded, half-inch "NMMP" letters to be sewn on each collar of the mounted police's uniforms.[50]

Section 1 of the Mounted Police Act of 1905 contains the statement, "The pay herein provided shall be full compensation in lieu of all other pay and compensation, including clothing and all other expenses for officers and men." Captain Fullerton must have interpreted this proviso to mean that each of his rangers was responsible for the expense of his own police uniform. This belief is borne out by

Mounted Policeman Will Dudley in uniform, mounted on his horse Keno (courtesy of Frank Shofner).

the fact that the captain charged George Elkins $35 for "one suit of clothes" when he resigned from the police.[51] There is, however, no record to indicate that Fullerton charged Herb McGrath or Dick Huber for their uniforms when these men resigned in December 1905. It is most likely that McGrath and Huber, and the rest of the rangers, may have already paid for their uniforms via some type of deduction from their paycheck. It is interesting that Captain Fullerton claimed the "cost of uniforms, firearms" as two of the new territorial police's organizational expenses and these costs are listed in the first annual Mounted Police Department report made by Fullerton to the governor in August 1905. John made no mention of the possible reimbursement of this expense by his rangers themselves, nor is there a record of this money being logged in the police accounts.[52]

A comparison of prices in large contemporary mail order catalogues against Captain Fullerton's reported cost for the ranger uniform is enlightening. A quality "cowboy style" hat and the all-wool gray shirt prices were in line with Fullerton's cost. The catalogue retail price and storekeeper Salomon's tailor-made price are not even close for the rest of the uniform parts. The roughly $29.21 paid for each of the wool suits ordered by Fullerton appears to be an excessively high price. Mail order all-wool suits ranged from $4 to $12, with a vest for $1 to $3. Even adjusting for a special tailored outfit, the nearly double cost is hard to explain. A true evaluation of the worth of the Fullerton Rangers' uniform, however, cannot be ascertained due to the lack of sales records or an original uniform for a hands-on inspection.[53]

Mounted Police Badge

Section 15 of the Mounted Police Act of 1905 prescribed that the territory should issue a badge to be worn by the mounted police. Captain Fullerton presented Cipriano Baca a shield identifying him as the ranger's lieutenant and "Stuttering Bob" Lewis was given the sergeant's shield. Each private was issued a plated shield with the wording "New Mexico Mounted Police 1905" inscribed on the face with the ranger's number stamped above the wording. These badges might have been produced by a national or regional police supply company,[54] but it is more likely the Fullerton Ranger badge was crafted by a silversmith or jeweler in Socorro for about $2 a piece.[55]

George Elkins was issued shield number one and Julius Meyer was ranger number two. John Brophy wore shield number three and Will Dudley carried badge number four. Badges number five and six were issued to Herb McGrath and Octaviano Perea. Captain Fullerton retained badge number seven to give to the recently appointed Fate Avant and badge number eight was held in reserve pending the decision of William Taylor to accept his appointment.

When Fred Fornoff took command, he felt the need to have a new badge to identify the new ranger force, so he had a different style badge crafted for his men. The new emblem was a handmade, five pointed, ball capped, sterling silver star that featured a raised galloping horseman attached in the center. The crafted horseman was semi-circled with the legend "New Mexico Mounted Police" engraved on the face.[56]

Fullerton's Rangers received some additional police authority in May 1905 when they were each sent a deputy commission issued by Territorial Fish and Game Warden Page Otero.[57] This new badge gave the rangers a chance to make a little extra money because a deputy game warden was paid on a fee basis. A ranger who made an arrest for violation of the territorial fish and game laws while acting under his deputy game warden powers could earn the arrest fee. Some legal concerns were raised about this arrangement of overlapping police power, but the territorial attorney general finally settled the questions when he issued his views on May 19. The opinion upheld the legality of the dual appointment, but also held it was not necessary because the mounted police already held authority to enforce all federal, territorial and local laws.[58]

John Fullerton explained to the new recruits that Section 3 of the Mounted Police Act authorized the territory to provide "the most effective and approved breech-loading rifles" for the rangers. The same section also said that each man was "to be furnished with the arms to be used by him at the price the same shall cost the territory, which sum shall be retained out of the first money due him." Section 4 said that each ranger would have a "six-shooting pistol (Army size) and all necessary accoutrements."[59]

Fullerton, a sportsman, had chosen the Model 1895 Winchester lever-action, .30-caliber Army, with a five round box magazine. The rifle's prospectus said that the "moving parts are few and strong," and that the weapon was designed to fire only the soft nose or steel jacketed smokeless powder cartridge. The barrel was round, nickel steel, 28 inches long, and could be fitted with Lyman sights for more accurate

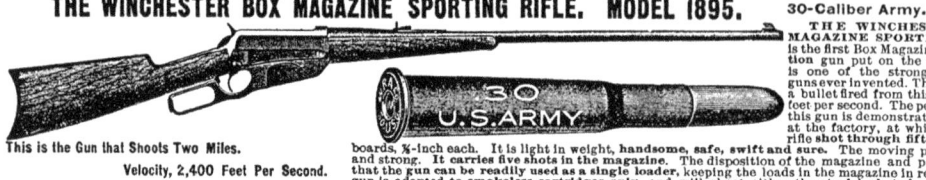

Winchester model 1895 rifle (Sears Roebuck and Co. Catalogue #111, 1902).

shooting. The rifle fired a 220 grain lead bullet propelled by 37 grains of smokeless powder. This was the same standard longarm then being used by the Arizona Rangers and many members of the reorganized ranger force of Texas.

Winchester advertising proclaimed that their 1895 model rifle was the first box magazine rifle on the market and that it was "one of the strongest shooting guns ever invented. The velocity of a bullet fired from this rifle is 2,400 feet per second." The manufacturer claimed that factory tests showed that a steel jacketed bullet fired from the 1895 Winchester could penetrate 48 pine boards, each ⅞ of an inch thick, and could shoot two miles. An effective and accurate range was about 1,500 to 2,000 yards, because it is difficult to see most game at 500 yards, and a man becomes almost invisible at 1,000 to 1,500 yards. Ammunition manufacturers suggested the soft nose cartridge — "The soft point gives the best satisfaction for large game shooting" — because it expands upon hitting a target and produces a shock upon impact. Steel jacketed bullets may go right thorough a target "as they do not tear or shatter the bones of a man when hit, but disable him, unless he is struck in a vital place."

In mid–April 1905, Captain John Fullerton shipped each mounted police a new 1895 model Winchester. He also sent them 140 rounds for the rifle and 50 rounds of .45 pistol cartridges. The Whitney Company, of Albuquerque, supplied the rangers with both soft nose lead and steel jacket cartridges for their rifles.[60] In April 1906, there

Colt single action army .45 (Sears Roebuck and Co. Catalogue #111, 1902).

were still nine boxes of .30–40 ammunition and three boxes of .45 Colt cartridges remaining in the mounted police inventory. In a companywide letter Fullerton wrote his police, "The rifle scabbards and belts that were ordered were not satisfactory and I returned them. I will have some made to order later on."[61] The author has not located any record to suggest that this special order was ever placed. Perhaps Fullerton found more pressing matters to deal with.

When Fred Fornoff took charge of the mounted police he conveniently forgot about the standard issue territorial rifles and the required regulation handguns. There is no evidence that he even supplied his men with legislatively mandated ammunition. Fornoff gave no public reason for his violation of territorial law and no formal request was made to have the law amended. In fact, Captain Fornoff seldom wore his pearl-handled Colt .41 unless he was on a case, but he favored the Winchester .44–40 Model 1873 for outdoor use. In later territorial years, both Rangers John Beal and J.B. "Slim" Rusk each carried an automatic pistol, while Ranger Fred Lambert favored a Colt .32–20 or sometimes he used a Colt .38–40 and a Winchester .25–35. Sergeant John W. Collier was known for his love of the Occidental double barrel shotgun and Ranger Jim McHughes, a National Guard award winning marksman, favored the German made Mossier pistol.[62] Some of these rangers may not have known they were "law breakers," but their captain knew of these violations of the police empowerment act and still he condoned the non-enforcement. This is just one more example, in a long line, of abuse or neglect of responsibility by a charismatic leader.

The large mail order companies of the era offered the Winchester 1895 model rifle for around $18 each. When shipping costs were added to the retail price, the cost was about $20 per rifle, what Captain Fullerton charged each of his mounted police. Rifle cartridges were $4.37 per 100 or about five cents apiece with freight costs added. A 100 round case of .30 cartridges weighed about seven and a half pounds.[63]

Once, Ranger Will Dudley had to tie his prisoner's hands and feet to the man's saddle before he could take him to the nearest jail, because Will had no handcuffs.[64] Fullerton tried to provide his men with the best

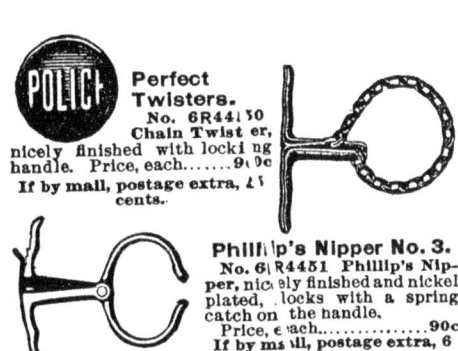

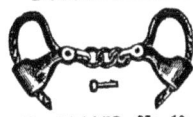

Twister and nipper and handcuffs (Sears Roebuck and Co. Catalogue #111, 1902).

handcuffs and transport come-alongs, commonly called twisters or nippers, he could locate, but sometimes John was faced with unavoidable problems. The modern expression for this is "They're on back order." It took nearly three months of paperwork for the mounted police to finally receive their handcuff order.

Captain Fullerton had properly placed his handcuff order and had issued the required voucher. The supplier had accepted the order and sent the territorial auditor a request for payment. The auditor took weeks to issue a territorial warrant. The supplier's bank then requested payment of the warrant. Following yet another delay, the supplier was finally paid and the long awaited order was shipped. In the meantime some of the mounted police had bought their own handcuffs and come-alongs or used the ones they already owned. Lt. Cipriano Baca's April 3, 1906, inventory of the mounted police office at Socorro included "three pair of chain handcuffs."[65]

Horse and Camp Gear

Section 4 of the Mounted Police Act of 1905 stated that each ranger was "required to furnish himself with a suitable horse ... and camp equipage." If a mounted policeman was "deficient" in any of these things then the territory would buy them for the ranger "and charge the cost of the same to the person for whom the same shall be provided." This section also stated that the territory would pay for any ranger's horse that was "killed in action."[66] It was expensive to be one of Fullerton's Rangers. A new uniform cost $35 and a new Winchester rifle was $20. These expenses were charged against a ranger's first paycheck and a territorial policeman's salary was only $75 per month. John Fullerton tried hard to keep some field expenses to a minimum. He even provided his men the use of his own personal camp equipment. John once wrote one ranger to come to headquarters, "I will supply you [with pack equipment]." He worked out an arrangement with the railroads to ship the saddles, camp outfits, rifles and ammo free of freight charges. Once, Fullerton even wrote Santa Fe County Sheriff Charles C. Closson, "Dear Charley," and asked the sheriff if he would please pick up Ranger Dick Huber's "roll of bedding" from the Santa Fe railroad depot "so as to avoid storage charges."[67]

In the Greer Mounted Police Bill, before it was amended in committee, the territory was authorized to furnish the officers and the privates "with provisions, ammunition, and forage for horses when necessary and when on duty."[68] The removal of this expense provision from the final draft of Council Bill 26 would prove to be a serious flaw in the Mounted Police Act of 1905. New Mexico Territory did provide Fullerton's Rangers with ammunition. However, the issue of horse care and the expense of room and board for the rangers while on patrol soon became a real concern. One territorial newspaper was quick to point out the nature of the expense account problem.

The *Western Liberal* reported, "If in the field two horses would be necessary, and a horse cannot be kept on grain, as such would have to be kept, for less than fifteen dollars per month each. Then add to this the personal expenses of the men, and there would be very little of the $75 [monthly salary] left."[69] The same paper addressed yet another problem. "If the law requires them to take the field, and put in their entire time at the work most of them will resign. If the men are to be used as emergency men, called out only when there is a necessity for them, most if not all of them can serve, and do good work when sent out."[70]

Captain John Fullerton once remarked, "The Mounted Police are not short on healthful exercise though they may be [short] on salary."[71] Fullerton was unable to deal effectively with the amount of personal expense required of his men to perform their public duty as a mounted police while he led the force, so he continued to lobby for a salary increase for the men after he left office.[72] Fullerton was, however, able to curb some of his men's complaints about spending weeks at a time away from home and family, by not sending them on so many extended scouts or patrols. The travel expense problem was an issue that continued to plague the mounted police far beyond the Fullerton era.

In 1907, the members of the Territorial Legislative Assembly authorized an additional $25 per month salary increase for the eight rangers, but not the three officers, "in lieu of expenses and railroad fare." Two years later, the New Mexico lawmakers provided, in the Mounted Police Reorganization Act of 1909, that the territory should pay the reduced force, four rangers and two officers, for "their actual and necessary expenses" while on duty.[73]

Preparation for Scout Duty

To conduct a successful extended scout, a ranger needed to do some planning to ensure the comfort of himself, his horse and his pack animal. Most of the new rangers were experienced outdoorsmen and knew the best use of their camp outfit. In 1967, the author and Fred Lambert, the last living member of the territorial police, discussed what he did to prepare for scout duty. One of the first chores Lambert would undertake was to study a map of the area he expected to cover so that he was familiar with the topography, settlement locations, telegraph and long distance telephone connections, railroad lines, ranch boundaries and local water sources. He next estimated the distances to be traveled and the amount of time this might take barring no major mishaps. Lambert would then double his estimate and then he would use this measurement to determine the quantity of supplies he needed for the trip.

Fred Lambert always believed that he would catch his man, so he planned for the extra supplies needed for his prisoner. If he felt that a re-supply stop along his projected travel route was possible, then Lambert would plan to utilize the establishment as a checkpoint for communications with mounted police headquarters. Fewer supplies for the ranger's pack animal to carry meant more time the animals could be used before they needed to be rested or replaced. Animal feed was the largest single supply item needed for an extended scout. The success of a mission often hung upon the health of the ranger's horse and pack animal, so the mount received priority care so he could stay strong and healthy. To help his working horses remain dependable, a range rider often provided his mount and pack horse with grain or oats to supplement grazing. Most times, the mount and pack animal were cared for before the ranger started to make his evening camp or even started to prepare his own meal.

In 1905, the 59th Congress tried unsuccessfully to establish regulations concerning the operation of motor vehicles and that same year a man in St. Louis reported to police that someone had stolen his new automobile. Just two years before, in 1903, two men and a dog made the first 6,000 mile transcontinental automobile trip. Time does not stand still. During the mounted police's last seven years, gasoline replaced oats and grain as the commodity needed to keep the ranger's "steed" mobile. The first ranger to use a gas powered "motor pony" to patrol the state was Fred Lambert during the four years (1914–1917), he was the state's only regular mounted policeman. At first, Lambert didn't like giving up his pinto horse to ride a new Indian motorcycle, but he soon came to really enjoy the speed and freedom of the two-wheeler.

In 1918, the automobile replaced the motorcycle when the new mounted police captain, Herb McGrath, chose to drive a Ford Model T flivver that the state bought for $521. Six months later a new captain sold the Ford for $150 because the auto was "pretty well worn and while it was not run so long it had hard usage and in rough country." In the spring of 1919, Captain A.A. Sena purchased a Dodge touring car for $1,264.65 for his office use and two years later, when the mounted police was disbanded, the vehicle was transferred to the inventory of state adjutant general's office.[74]

How open a ranger could be about his presence in an area would be determined by the nature of the ranger's mission. When possible many ranchers were willing to help the rangers by providing fresh mounts and food supplies. Sometimes the rangers were able to spend the night as a guest at a ranch bunkhouse or at a line camp and in the morning they and their animals might even get a free breakfast. The rangers were very thankful for these small acts of kindness.

On a typical scout Fred Lambert would pack a flour sack he called a "greasy bag" that contained a five pound slab of smoked beef and some bacon. A tin of Arbuckale coffee and a tin of Luzianne tea with a small brew pot, a small iron Dutch oven, a pound of potatoes, a small sack of yellow onions, some well packed eggs, two loaves of German rye bread and three or four cans of Campbell's Condensed Tomato Soup made up the food store for one of Lambert's short trips.

Fred Lambert's warbag, which is used as a pillow at night, contained two suits of underwear, a spare shirt and trousers, two bandanas, a couple of pairs of socks, leather gloves, and an extra pair of boots. He also had a sack coat and in cool weather he packed a cardigan sweater and a muskrat cap. His normal dress might include a vest, neckerchief, riding spurs, pocket knife, Stetson hat and leather shirt cuffs. Fred's personal hygiene kit contained the new Gillette safety razor.[75] His pack animal also carried a rain slicker, two full water canteens, a folding water bag, a rope coil, a half side of a military camp tent, a camp lantern, a flashlight, a camp ax and folding bow saw, cook gear and his own self-designed, oversized sleeping bag. Fred was a man who enjoyed a restful night's sleep, so his bag was made of a folded waterproof tarp with ring holes down one side and the bottom so he could use a leather strip to sew up the side to keep it closed. Inside the tarp he used two soogans, light cotton quilts, and depending upon the weather one or two Navajo blankets.[76]

For many years, Lambert's mother received a case of pine tar soap from her relatives who lived in the Commonwealth of Kentucky. The brown colored, tar smelling soap would lather with white foam and Fred's mother used this soap as a hair sham-

Mounted Policeman Fred Lambert on scout duty in the fall of 1911 as he returned from a hunt for rustlers. Note the extra large bed roll tied behind Lambert's saddle and the lumberjack style cap he is wearing to keep his ears warm (courtesy of the Fred Lambert Collection).

poo, even though it was called a toilet soap. Many people also used this soap as a natural insect repellent and this tar soap made many mountain scouts with Lambert.[77]

Living away from home was expensive. When camping out, even in the summertime, the trip required portable food supplies for both man and horses. The outdoor menu was not always first class due to the time it took for the camp chores or the Dutch oven cooking. Good drinking water for horse and man was always a problem, especially during the dry season or during a drought. Laundry needs and personal hygiene were other challenges of an extended patrol. A few examples should illustrate the expense of trail camping in 1905. The mounted police could buy a pound of coffee for about seven cents, a dozen eggs for 14 cents, a pound of sugar for four cents, a pound of butter for 24 cents and a pound slab of beef for about seven cents. These five items would have cost the ranger about 56 cents with no sales tax. If this cost is adjusted for inflation to the 2000 rate, the 1905 costs of 56 cents would be $10.97 compared to the 2000 cost-of-living price of $12.11, plus state and local sales tax, for the same set of supplies.[78] A mounted policeman, in 1905, was paid $60 a month or about $20 per month more than the average range hand. The ranger had to pay all his patrol expenses from his salary while a range hand received free horse care, plus room and board from his employer. The question might well be asked, who had the better deal?

Railroad Transportation

Bad weather in the spring of 1905 caused bad road conditions across the territory. Muddy and pothole infested roads made horseback or wagon travel difficult. The main roads were hard enough to navigate, but off-the-beaten-path trails made travel a true adventure. Distance was measured in days instead of miles.[79] During the Thirty-third Legislative Assembly lawmakers enacted a law to deal with smoother travel across the territory. The law established the El Camino Real, the territory's first hard surface road improvement project, which was designed to connect Colorado with Texas via Raton, Las Vegas, Mora, Santa Fe, Albuquerque, Socorro, Las Cruces and on to Anthony. Today, this basic route is Interstate 25.

Under these circumstances, rail travel was the only truly dependable and swift means of conveyance over long distance, but this travel method was only effective in areas crossed by the bands of steel, and it also carried with it a certain amount of expense. By today's financial standards a 1905 arduous train trip could be financed by the cost of a day's supply of bubble gum.

Management of the major railroads doing business in New Mexico Territory had supported the effort to enact a ranger law during the Thirty-sixth Legislative Assembly. So, upon formation of the mounted police, Captain Fullerton felt he could make a request for complimentary passes for the territorial police. A few local railroad branch lines quickly responded with annual tickets for free transportation the length of their service line. These annual passes were issued to the rangers stationed in the railroad's geographic area.

John Fullerton was frustrated and he vented his disappointment to Governor Otero: "I beg to inform you that the organization of the police force has been very much retarded on account of the force not receiving transportation over the AT&SF also the Santa Fe Pacific."[80] These two railroads controlled the major north-south and east-west access across the territory.

Fullerton's frustration level had reached its peak when he wrote, "If they [the large railroad companies] ever expect us to respond to their calls [for help] they should grant what little we ask." The mounted police captain concluded, "I am inclined to think that these R.Ry. officials do not realize what valuable service the Mounted Police could give them."[81] It would seem that Captain Fullerton made a valid point, but in fairness to the railroad company moguls, they may not have truly understood the nature of these new territorial police.

The state or territorial police concept was a new idea. In the west only the Texas Rangers had been in service for any length of time, having been reorganized in 1874 following the Civil War's Reconstruction Era; Arizona's ranger force was only four years old in 1905. In the eastern states, Massachusetts and Connecticut each had organized small state detective forces, Pennsylvania was in the process of forming a statewide police force and on the west coast California had only recently created a central Bureau of Criminal Identification. It would be three more years before Nevada would organize their state police force and another decade would pass after that before other states followed these early state police examples.[82]

Governor Miguel A. Otero finally composed a personal request to each corporate general manager of the main railroads operating in New Mexico Territory. He asked them to issue free annual passes for the mounted police to ride their trains within the territory. This was a big request and some of the railroad company executives may have felt the governor's appeal was excessive or maybe some new kind of "shankdown" scheme.

It took months before any of the railroads acted upon Governor Otero's request. This may have been a delaying tactic because most astute politicians of the day understood that Theodore Roosevelt had won election to the presidency in his own right and had just started his new administration in March. They knew that Roosevelt would quickly make new appointments to top federal government posts like territorial governors. The president had said that he would reward his fellow Rough Riders and Otero was not a veteran of Roosevelt's former cavalry corps. So the question was, how long would Miguel Otero remain governor of New Mexico?

On the other hand, spite could have been the real reason. In 1903, powerful business interests headed by the territory's railroad and mining companies were successful in getting a protectionist bill passed by both houses of the 35th Territorial Legislative Assembly, only to have it vetoed by Governor Otero. He felt that the Hawkins Bill was a violation of an individual's constitutional right to seek damages for injury caused by negligence on the part of business management, but the bill became law when the lawmakers passed the measure over Otero's veto. In 1905, Otero added his support to a bill designed to repeal the Hawkins Act, but the legislation

These are examples of the different railroad passes issued to the mounted police during Fullerton's tenure as captain. The railroad watch was used to keep Julius Meyer on time.

was killed before it could reach Otero's desk. The management of the railroads and the mining companies were not pleased with the governor's active support of the general public against corporate interests. Another effort to abolish the Hawkins Act was defeated in 1907 and again in 1909, but the Congress finally listened to New Mexico citizens and nullified the law in May 1909.[83]

Finally in midsummer, the Atchison, Topeka and Santa Fe Railroad gave up the wait and agreed to Governor Otero's request. They became the first major rail system to issue all the mounted police a courtesy pass for themselves and their pack equipment. Otero's father had been a founding officer of the AT&SF Railroad and was active in the company's New Mexico business until his death in 1882. In 1899, during the building of the new territorial capital complex, Governor Otero had managed to negotiate some reduced freight rates for the large stone building blocks and other construction supplies shipped from Illinois and Indiana via the railroads.[84]

Fullerton could not win. When the long awaited notice arrived it came via a collect telegram. Miss Olsen sent the following message on July10, "Have annual passes for you all over Santa Fe. Shall I mail them or will you be up." Fullerton's reply was short. "Mail them to me here." Otero received Fullerton's message at 7:32 on July 11 and later that morning wrote the captain, "I am just in receipt of your telegram and take great pleasure in forwarding your passes." The governor continued, "I have no doubt but what the action of the Santa Fe Road in granting passes will bring passes from other roads." Otero ended by suggesting that "should you desire to settle up this pass question it might be well when you have your Santa Fe pass to come up here and dictate letters [to Miss Olsen] for the others [railroad systems]."[85] Fullerton followed up on the governor's offer.

A short time later Captain Fullerton tried to get the Santa Fe system to reimburse him for tickets he had purchased before the railroad issued him a free pass. The giant railroad company's general manager said no to this fine example of the "Yankee two-step" and he might even have entertained a second thought concerning the free passes he had recently issued.[86]

There were some bright spots in the battle for the free railroad passes. One of New Mexico's regional railroads supported the mounted police with more than free rail transportation. A first-class stamp in 1905 cost two cents, but when adjusted to 2000 standards that same stamp would cost forty cents. So it was very helpful when the Santa Fe Central Railway provided the mounted police with two books of "postal stamps" to help with the rangers' start up expenses.[87]

Captain Fullerton's hard fought effort to gain the rail transportation for the rapid mobility of the police was scuttled when the Congress enacted the Hepburn Act in 1906. This federal law prohibited railroads operating within the western territories from providing complimentary transportation to government employees. The measure was designed to curb the railroad's practice of "rewarding" lawmakers and executives with "trip benefits" for their legislative and administrative support or from providing judges "holidays" for rendering the right judicial ruling.

It was a cruel twist of fate that one of the charges leveled against Fullerton's Rangers was that they worked to closely with the railroads. The White Oaks *Outlook* stated this view by saying, "Now let these uniformed and ornamented gentlemen get out into the mountains, and into the secret rendezvous of the badmen — and it is well known that there are such — and not confine themselves strictly to the towns along the lines of railroads as detectives for the railroad companies."[88]

The controversy over funding for the mounted police's railroad transportation did not end with the removal of Captain Fullerton. The transportation expense was used by anti-ranger factions as a key issue in both the 1907 and the 1909 Territorial Legislative Assembly debates over the level of funding for the mounted police operation. The transportation issue proponents finally won the debate, as the issue was a major factor in the company's disbandment in 1913.

Communications

The vastness of New Mexico Territory compounded the mounted police's need for quick communications. Many farm villages and logging and mining camps were miles from a long distance telephone line or even a telegraph wire. The mail was dependable in most rural areas, but not all settlements had a post office. The stage coach was still the best way to reach non-railroad areas. Some of these local passenger lines were equipped with motor cars, but most still depended upon the horse team. In many areas the local newspaper was published only weekly and in the remote back country even this news source was hard to find. When Socorro was the headquarters for the mounted police, the town did not have electricity. The ranger office was lighted by the coal-oil lamp and was heated by a coal and wood burning stove. Fullerton rented a telephone from the Colorado Telephone Company for the mounted police, at $2.50 per month, and he later connected the office with the long distance line to Las Vegas, Santa Fe and Albuquerque. He was also able to reach other smaller communities connected to the main long distance line.[89]

Fullerton designed mounted police stationery because much of the ranger service's communications was conducted via the U.S. mail. The letterhead was a mark of authority that was understood by all who received the correspondence. Fullerton's first stationery, printed in Socorro, contained a masthead that listed the breakdown of the two ranger squads and was printed before Francisco Apodaca and William Taylor refused their commissions. It also continued a second mistake by misspelling last names of two of the rangers. Julius Meyer was given the "s" that belonged at the end of Elkins' name. The mistake was most likely taken from Governor Otero's appointment order because Miss Olsen had taken the name spellings from the Bursum-Luna recommendation letter. These errors are easy to explain, because at this point in the organization Fullerton may not have known any of his new rangers personally. When the original supply of paper was depleted, Fullerton simply discontinued the listing of the privates and only used the names and rank of the officers. The three line heading said simply "Headquarters," "New Mexico Mounted Police," and "Socorro, New Mexico."[90]

When Fred Fornoff illegally moved the ranger headquarters to the capitol building he kept Fullerton's basic letterhead design, but added a fancy logo in the upper left corner. The emblem depicted a scene of miners and cowboys at work with an idealized version of the territorial seal in the center. On April 6, 1906, Fornoff ordered

HEADQUARTERS
New Mexico Mounted Police.
JOHN F. FULLERTON, CAPTAIN.

CIPRIANO BACA, LIEUTENANT

PRIVATES: GEORGE ELKIN
JULIUS MEYERS
J. J. BROPHY
WM. E. DUDLEY

R. W. LEWIS, SERGEANT.

PRIVATES: WILLIAM TAYLOR.
HERBERT McGRATH
FRANCISCO APODACA.
OCTOVIANO PEREA.

SOCORRO, NEW MEXICO.

HEADQUARTERS
New Mexico Mounted Police,
JOHN F. FULLERTON, CAPTAIN.

CIPRIANO BACA, LIEUTENANT.

R. W. LEWIS, SERGEANT

SOCORRO, NEW MEXICO.

Two examples of the official stationery used by Captain Fullerton's company of the New Mexico Mounted Police. The first example contains the listing of patrol assignments and the misspelled names of two rangers. The second example was generic (New Mexico State Records Center and Archives).

the new letterhead printed by the territory's public printer. Six days later the captain received 1,000 copies of the new design with his name on it. Fornoff next ordered 500 "6½ envelopes" from the same printer and eight days later, April 20, the envelopes were delivered to the new mounted police office in the capitol. The cost was $4.50 for the letterhead and $2.50 for the envelopes. The concept was short lived and Captain Fornoff soon returned to the simpler 1905 design.[91] In 1909, the mounted police's post office address, Box 451, was added to the upper right corner and Fred Fornoff's name moved to the top left corner. No other personnel were listed on the letterhead.

Field Reports and General Orders

In late June 1905, Lieutenant Baca left Socorro "on a scouting trip with no definite clue of any particular mater." He spent 12 days in the saddle and finally had to rest "on account of our horse being rode down."[92] If the horses were "rode down" what was Baca's physical condition? Sometimes the mounted police found that when their patrol time was extended they ran short of money to buy supplies. Other times they could not find supplies even when they had the needed money. That was another reason some of Fullerton's Rangers found the long patrol scouts so lonesome and so very frustrating.

Ranger Julius Meyer once wrote to headquarters, "I am out here [in remote

Guadalupe County] a long way from anywhere, get no news."[93] On another occasion Meyer returned home following a scout of several months to find that his wife and children had packed up and left the area. When Julius finally located his bride in Albuquerque, Libbie Meyer told her husband she had found the 100 person outpost settlement of Estancia just too small, too isolated and too lonely. Estancia was so small in 1905 it could not even qualify for a territorial saloon license.[94]

Captain Fullerton felt he would have a total lack of knowledge concerning the movements or actions of his rangers without some type of weekly contact. So among the first letters Fullerton sent was to Arizona Ranger Captain Tom Rynning. John asked for help from the veteran ranger chief concerning his mode of communications. On April 17, Rynning mailed Fullerton copies of his weekly report form and his general orders of operation. In his reply Fullerton said, "They are just what I want and will be much help to me getting every thing established." John extended Rynning a pledge to "co-operate with you and render you any assistance possible." Fullerton had also contacted Captain William J. McDonald, at his headquarters in Madisonville, and asked for copies of the report forms and general orders in use by the Ranger Force of Texas. The legendary Texas lawman also supplied the requested samples and offered the assistance of his rangers if the need ever presented itself.[95]

Fullerton introduced the new field form in his "General Order #1, Making and Rendering Weekly Reports" issued on May 4, 1905. He asked two basic questions. What was the policeman's weekly patrol action and did he make any arrests during the report week? The weekly report form measured the standard 8½ by 11 inches and was printed on off-white paper. The heading said, "Capt. John F. Fullerton, New Mexico Mounted Police, Socorro, New Mexico." The report began, "Sir, I submit herewith report of operations for the week ending _____ 1905." Two-thirds of the way down the page was the single word "Arrests," then at the bottom was the page ending "very respectfully, _____, New Mexico Mounted Police." The back of the form was designed so that the report could be folded in thirds and filed. The printed heading on the back's center said, "New Mexico Mounted Police, Report of _____, Week ending _____ 1905."[96]

Some of the territorial police viewed this mandatory weekly report as a sign of mistrust by Captain Fullerton and to some others it was viewed as an invasion of their independent nature; or worse, the plan was seen as long distance spying into their private affairs. Most thought the weekly report was needless paperwork and few of the police provided Captain Fullerton with more than the basic outline requested. A good example of this simple style is a report filed by George Elkins. "[May] 26 from Deming to Victoria, 27 from Victoria to Hachita, 28 from Hachita to Deer Creek, 29 from Deer Creek to Hachita, 30 from Hachita to Columbus, 31 on duty in Columbus, June 1st returned to Hachita, 2–3 on duty in Hachita."[97]

Captain Fornoff discontinued the use of the weekly report in April 1906 and it was over a year before he developed a new arrest report system. Only a few of the Fullerton era field reports survive and most of these are from a select group of the faithful and active rangers who reported weekly in compliance with Captain Fullerton's general order.

It is uncertain how many general orders were issued by Captain Fullerton. The content of general order number two is unknown, but order number three, dated June first, said, "Effective during the month of June, 1905 ten days of absence is granted private Julius Meyer." Ranger Julius Meyer had requested the leave time to tend to some personal business and it would be a safe bet that the time was granted without pay. However, the financial records needed to prove or disprove this point of view are no longer available. Captain Fullerton sent Meyer his May paycheck at the same time he sent him the general order.[98]

Modus Operandi

The adventures of Sherlock Holmes, "the world's first consulting detective," were — and still are — very popular on both sides of the ocean. This Victorian era English pulp hero often set forth revolutionary investigation principals that are now commonly used by real investigators; "There is no branch of detective science which is so important and so much neglected as the art of tracing footsteps." The New Mexico Territorial Mounted Police were not as good as Holmes with "footstep" tracking, but they were good at locating missing livestock trails. The mounted police, like most 1905 law enforcement agencies in the United States, were mainly dependent upon good guesswork, sheer luck, eyewitnesses, paid informants and criminal confessions to make a criminal case hold up in court.

The concept of police science was in an infant stage when Fullerton's Rangers was created. The Italian crime researcher Cesare Lonbroso had developed, in 1895, a method of monitoring a person's heartbeat to detect truthful or false statements made by that person. Yet a decade after police had first used the device in Europe, few American lawmen had even heard about the lie detector instrument and there were none to be found in New Mexico. The anthropometry system of suspect identification, by body part measurements, was in use by 1882 and blood types were well established by 1902. Few of New Mexico's frontier doctors, however, were experts in blood typing, so in most cases this detective tool was unavailable to the mounted police.

In July 1901, London police began to fingerprint all persons that they arrested. However, the world's first in-depth fingerprint program had been established in 1892. New York City police started a limited scale program in 1902. The prevailing identification system of the day was the Bertillon system that involved measuring a suspect's fingers, feet and skull with a set of calipers. Even in this new age of DNA analysis, the fingerprint is still the backbone of police crime solving. The new science of fingerprint identification was gaining acceptance by 1905 and dusting kits were even sold in national mail order catalogs. St. Louis was the host city that summer for many law enforcement delegates who attended the first international conference on fingerprint identification and criminal justice. The big drawback to local police using this technology was the lack of a central criminal fingerprint file and in the United States a national fingerprint file was three decades in the future.[99] Fullerton's Rangers depended mostly upon physical descriptions and photographs to establish identification of suspects. The author has found no records to support the idea that fingerprint detection was used by any of Fullerton's men.

The science of nose printing cattle for identification purposes was just in the trial stages during the reign of Fullerton's Rangers. Today cattle can be nose printed just like people can be fingerprinted for security measures and identification. It almost seems funny to think about the rangers riding up to a herd of cattle and checking nose prints from their wanted poster book.

Command Structure and Public Relations

John Fullerton seems to have tried hard to conduct the mounted police in strict accord with mandates set forth in the authorization legislation; however, his pleasant, sociable personality must have made it very hard for John to be formal and command a stiff military tone of operation. He may have tried to pattern his new formal style of conduct after his commander because Territorial Governor Miguel A. Otero was renowned as a stickler for proper protocol, pomp and ceremony. Fullerton often followed the governor's protocol and addressed Otero "Hon. Governor, Commander in Chief, N.M.M.P." and in his letters to his rangers John would address them as "Dear Sir" or "Dear Private."

Governor Otero and John Fullerton held their first official meeting on March 18, 1905. The governor's *Executive Ticker* lists John as "Mr. Fullerton" for this meeting, but subsequent log entries refer to him as "Capt. Fullerton." During the ten months that Otero and Fullerton worked together, all of John's visits to see the governor were recorded as "official." Not one social visit was exchanged. Meanwhile, during this same time frame Cipriano Baca and Octaviano Perea felt free to have "personal-social" visits with the chief executive of the territory.[100]

Captain Fullerton tried to stay abreast of the political climate in the capital by reading the Santa Fe *New Mexican,* while also reading the Albuquerque *Morning Journal,* the Denver *Republican* and the El Paso *Times* for regional information. These papers told him what had happened or what might be planned, but could not tell him what was taking place that day. Fullerton quickly learned firsthand that political power comes from proximity to center of authority and that he was isolated in the backwoods of Socorro. This distance factor would prove to have long range consequences for Fullerton and the rangers. This same factor was at play in Arizona and would, in 1909, end in the abolishment of their ranger service.[101]

It is noteworthy that Captain Fullerton often referred to "the boys" when he talked about his territorial rangers being furnished lodging, fresh mounts and information, but he never said "we" when discussing the actions of the mounted police. Fred Fornoff also used the term "the boys" when referring to the mounted police, but he often used "we" in his remarks concerning their actions.

Another problem John Fullerton had was his formal public presence and his business-only relationship with some of the territorial press corps. This attitude may have projected an erroneous image of John Fullerton to the general public and this same Fullerton image may have carried over to the mounted police themselves. Dick Huber was openly hostile toward his captain. Other rangers, like Julius Meyer, seem to have held little respect for his leadership. Fullerton's strongest supporter among the rangers was Will Dudley and this may account for the fact that he was the only

Fullerton man to be given a probationary reappointment under Captain Fornoff in April 1906.

Leadership

The early history of the Texas Rangers is centered on the actions of the captains who led the frontier companies. These men rode against roaming bands of Indians and outlaws. The individual exploits of Arizona Ranger Captains Burton Mossman, Tom Rynning and Harry Wheeler are law enforcement legends. These captains were field officers who led by example and shared the cold camps, long, hard trails and danger with their rangers. New Mexico Mounted Police Captain John Fullerton was also a rugged outdoorsman. He was a hands-on rancher and a crack shot game hunter. John and his son Elmer enjoyed camping and fishing and the high mountain country during any season. Captain Fullerton loved the open range life, but he also enjoyed the elegant comforts of city dwelling.[102]

John Fullerton traveled widely during the year he led the territorial police. He is known to have made overnight trips to Santa Fe, El Paso, Albuquerque, Las Vegas, and Alamogordo on official business. Each of these communities was accessible by railroad and required no camp gear, pack horse or overland journey. This method of travel also meant that Fullerton could reach an area quickly when his presence was most needed and take the field on a rented horse. It would be fair to say that Fullerton may have seen himself as a hell-fire Mosby style leader, but was in reality more of an organizer and cheerleader. John was efficient at the needed paperwork, but he lacked the public relations skills to develop a popular following among the territory's populace. He also lacked the day-to-day personal contacts to assist him in building a political support system or a large cadre of press contacts needed for his success in the world of territorial politics. Fate did not provide him with the opportunity to face battle with a rustler gang or to apprehend a famous fugitive; in fact no official records remain to suggest that Captain John F. Fullerton ever personally made an arrest while he was the head of the territorial police. Does this mean that he was not an effective ranger leader? Does this suggest that he lacked courage in the face of danger? No. It simply means that John Fullerton was not in the right place at the right time to face that type of challenge.

Fullerton personally investigated a Socorro County connection to some horse stealing in the eastern part of the territory on the vast Bell Ranch. The captain wrote the ranch general manager an update on his findings. "I also have located in this county two parties that hold two Bell horses that were stolen from your ranch. I don't expect to make any arrests for several weeks as I wish to get more evidence of who are the parties that cut [the] fence this last time. I have not and don't intend to give up this fence cutting affair." Fullerton closed by adding, "Will see you personally just as soon as possible and talk the matter over with me."[103] Fullerton and O'Donnel met a short time later at an Albuquerque social club and over drinks they discussed the last fence cutting affair and the recent cattle and horse stealing. An action plan was formulated to capture the rustlers.

In mid–December 1905, John Fullerton told a reporter, "I have been making a personal inspection and find that game is being killed in large quantities regardless of the laws." Fullerton was investigating complaints that Indians in western Socorro County were illegally killing deer and antelope off their reservation. This out-of-season hunting was against both federal and territorial laws. "I am now undertaking the difficult task of arresting all Indians breaking the law," stated Fullerton.[104]

From the outset the specter of the new police force clashing with local law enforcement officers over "turf" was raised by New Mexico's media. In late April 1905, a ranger force detachment took control of Hampstead, a Texas border town, to stop a riot local officers could not contain. A few days earlier, a squad of Arizona Rangers had raided a gambling den, also in a Mexican border town, and had arrested a local deputy sheriff for condoning the illegal gaming activity.[105]

The Albuquerque *Morning Journal* asserted, "The [Arizona] rangers were created for the purpose of clearing the territory of cattle thieves, murderers and desperadoes and not for the purpose of performing the ordinary police duty in cities and towns."[106] A week earlier the Lordsburg paper had made a similar comment. "It is to be hoped that the New Mexico rangers will be able to get along with the local police officers better than do the Arizona rangers. There seems to be a constant quarrel between the rangers and the sheriff's office in both Cochise and Graham counties, and neither set of officers can do their best work while this continues."[107]

The first mounted police company suffered growing pains and John Fullerton was in a constant state of migraine headaches. Relations with many local law enforcement officers was less then top rate and some county lawmen gave only arm's length cooperation to the mounted range riders. Some sheriffs were active detractors. Only a few sheriffs were openly glad to accept the free help that the mounted police offered them and their deputies toward the protection of the livestock interests in their counties.[108]

Four of the 25 county sheriffs in office in 1905 would later become territorial rangers. These men were Alex Street, Quay County; Cicero Stewart, Eddy County; Boone Vaughn, San Juan County; and Leandro Baca of Socorro County. Cipriano Baca, Luna County, and Fred Higgins, Chaves County, had each completed their term as a county sheriff before their mounted police appointment. Herb McGrath was a ranger before he was elected Grant County sheriff and became the third mounted police captain after he left the sheriff's office, while Leandro Baca served as Socorro County sheriff before he became a ranger and after his ranger service he was appointed the first sheriff of the newly created Catron County.

The United States marshal and his deputies were authorized to enforce only federal laws and the county sheriff and his deputies had no jurisdiction outside their own county. A precinct constable was the police arm of a justice of the peace court and the local marshal's power reached no further than his community's boundaries. The deputy game wardens[109] and the cattle and sheep inspectors worked in districts and had limited authority outside their own assigned area and what enforcement power they did have was limited to game and livestock laws. The mounted police shield gave the rangers legal arrest power to enforce any law, at any time and in any place within New Mexico Territory. The mounted police were New Mexico Territory's chief law enforcement officers and their supreme jurisdiction was the root of jealousy among other peace officers.

An additional area of contention centered on money. Local and county lawmen were paid on a fee system and the rangers drew a salary that was not based upon court fees, capture bounties, rewards, or transportation allowances. What the mounted police lacked in support from local and county officers, the territory's livestock owners compensated for in double. These men knew firsthand the service provided by Fullerton's Rangers.

"Our men report that they have been greatly aided secretly and openly by ranchmen and stockgrowers all over the territory, who are mighty glad to see the law enforced," Fullerton told reporters. "Often the boys are furnished lodging, fresh mounts, and what is more important, they are given information which leads to the arrest of cattle rustlers."[110]

The men who composed Fullerton's Rangers were selected to achieve political balance first, and secondly because of their police experience. The men were provided no formal training for their new task; they had no classes in law enforcement techniques or legal procedures. They were expected to use their common sense, and good judgment, and have a lot of good luck.

A century later, the cadets at the New Mexico State Police Academy are chosen by competitive merit without regard to political connections. They spend four months in dawn to dusk military style training, learning all aspects of modern law enforcement. After graduation, new officers will spend two years as probationary troopers before they are granted an unsupervised patrol assignment. A century has made a world of difference in police operations.

Fullerton's Rangers Appointment Date and Oath of Office Date

Commissioned by Governor Miguel A. Otero   Appointment   Oath

	Appointment	Oath
Captain: John F. Fullerton, Socorro	March 18	March 18
Lieutenant: Cipriano Baca, Albuquerque	March 18	April 01
Sergeant: Robert W. Lewis, Frisco	March 18	April 01
Private: 1 George M. Elkins, Hachita	March 18	April 01
2 Julius Meyer, Estancia	March 18	April 01
3 John J. Brophy, Clayton	March 18	April 01
4 William E. Dudley, Alamogordo	March 18	April 01
5 Octaviano Perea, Alamogordo	March 18	April 01
6 Herbert J. McGrath, Lordsburg	March 18	April 01
7 Francisco Apodaca, Cuchillo Negro	March 18 *	
8 William M. Taylor, Deming	March 18 *	

Commissioned by Acting-Governor J.W. Raynolds
Francisco Apodaca resigned his appointment on 31 March 1905.
Private: 7 L.F. Avant, Capitan   March 31   May 02

William M. Taylor resigned his appointment on 07 April 1905.
Private: 8 Charles R. "Dick" Huber, Santa Fe   April 07   April 07

Commissioned by Governor Miguel A. Otero
George M. Elkins resigned effective 30 June 1905.
Private: 1 Robert G. Putman, Fairview   June 30   July 08

Herbert J. McGrath resigned effective 05 December 1905.
Private: 6 E.R. Stewart, Aztec   Dec. 14   Dec. 14

Dick Huber suspended on 17 November; resigned effective 01 December 1905.
Private: 8 Rafael Gomez, Santa Fe   Dec. 14   Dec. 4

Octaviano Perea resigned effective 31 December 1905.
Private: 5 Left vacant for new governor's appointment.

John J. Brophy resigned effective 01 April 1906.
Private: 3 Replacement was named with 1906 annual appointments.

This data is compiled from the appointment and the resignation notices in *Executive Record Book #6* and the Mounted Police Oaths of Office. Secretary of the Territory Records, NMSRCA.

The Twenty-five County Sheriffs of New Mexico Territory during the tenure of Fullerton's Rangers 1905–1906

(These men were all voted into office in the general election of November 1904)

County /County Seat	Sheriff	Party
Bernalillo/Albuquerque	Tom S. Hubbell*/ Perfecto Armijo	R
Chaves/Roswell	K.S. Woodruff	D
Colfax/Raton	S. Marion Littrell*	R
Dona Ana/Las Cruces	Jose R. Lucero*	R
Eddy/Carlsbad	Miles Cicero Stewart*+	D
Grant/Silver City	Charles A. Farnesworth	R
Guadalupe/Santa Rosa	Felipe Sanchez y Baca	D
Lincoln/Lincoln	John W. "Jake" Owen	D
Luna/Deming	Dwight B. Stephens	R
Mora/Mora	J. Demetrio Medina	R
McKinley/Gallup	J. Harry Coddington	R
Otero/Alamogordo	A.B. Phillips	R
Quay/Tucumcari	James Alexander Street*+	D
Rio Arriba/Tierra Amarilla	B.C. Hernandez	R
Roosevelt/Portales	Joseph Lang	D
Sandoval/Sandoval	Emiliano Sandoval	R
San Juan/Aztec	Boone C. Vaughn+	D
San Miguel/Las Vegas	Cleofes Romero*	R
Santa Fe/Santa Fe	Antonio J. Ortez	D
Sierra/Hillsboro	William C. Kendall	D
Socorro/Socorro	Leandro Baca*+	D
Taos/Taos	Silviano Lucero	D
Torrance/Progresso	Manuel C. Sanchez y Valdez	R
Union/Clayton	Tranquilino Garcia	R
Valencia/Los Lunas	Carlos Baca*	R

*Denotes the eight incumbent sheriffs who were reelected to office
+Denotes the four sheriffs who later served as mounted policemen

This list was compiled from the voter records of the Secretary of the Territory.

8

"The Mounted Police ... Shall Have Full Power to Make Arrests"

> "In my opinion the moral effect of this Mounted Police force would be to stop these criminal depredations, break up the organized bands of bank robbers and stock thieves and lessen the amount of all classes of crime within our boundaries."
>
> Col. William H. Greer
> The Santa Fe *New Mexican*
> 26 January 1905

Documenting the movements and actions of Fullerton's Rangers is a difficult task. This fact is illustrated by the simple attempt to identify the first mounted police patrol. It is not certain who led this outing, where the patrol went or even which rangers composed the squad. What was the mission? Was it a success or a failure? The confusion rests with the lack of official records detailing this action and the conflicting information printed in the contemporary newspapers.

The confusion begins with an account in the El Paso *Times*. "The members of the New Mexico mounted police company recently mustered into service at Santa Fe will meet in Socorro today [April 17, 1905] to receive their first assignments to duty by Captain Fullerton." The *Times* concluded by saying, "The men have been given two weeks in which to close up their personal affairs and get in shape to give their whole time to the service."[1] The Las Cruces *Citizen* told its readers, "Immediately after the mustering in [ceremony] Capt. Fullerton will bring his force to Socorro and at once proceed to put his men into condition for active operations." Meanwhile, the El Paso *Evening News* added to the confusion by saying the "territorial mounted police were mustered in at Santa Fe and have gone to headquarters at Socorro."[2]

The El Paso *Times* report, concerning the mounted police's taking leave time before they began their official duties, is also called into question by an Albuquerque *Evening Citizen* account of Sergeant Bob Lewis leading a ranger squad into Lincoln County "with sealed instructions from Captain John Fullerton" to search for a band of cattle thieves during this time frame.[3] At the same time, the Socorro *Chieftain* reported that the mounted police would "assemble at headquarters in this city on the 15th instant for assignment to duty."[4] Another El Paso *Times* account states, "There has been no indication as to where the first work of the mounted police will be done, but it is considered probable that they will take the first turn in the saddle in southwestern Grant county." The *Times* story explained this reasoning by saying that the Bootheel section was a place "where conditions have been unpleasant for some time owing to the influx of desperadoes driven in from Sonora, Ariz. [*sic*] and Texas by the rangers of those states."[5]

A further complication as to what happened first is told in the Albuquerque *Morning Journal*. Their muster ceremony story reports that Captain Fullerton, Lieutenant Baca and four of the rangers had been in Albuquerque the night before headed for Socorro. "It is understood that the larger division of the company will proceed at once to southwest Grant county. Two members were sent east over the Santa Fe Central [Railroad] last night."[6] The two men headed home via the Santa Fe Central train would most likely have been John Brophy and Julius Meyer. Julius Meyer simply rode the Central south a few miles and got off the train in Estancia. Brophy, from Clayton, could reach home by way of Dalhart, Texas. John needed to take the Central south to Torrance than catch the El Paso, Rock Island to Santa Rosa. Here he caught the Chicago, Rock Island Railroad east to Dalhart, where he would have transferred to the west bound Fort Worth and Denver City train that would have delivered him to Clayton. The Santa Fe Central had its maintenance shops and their engine terminal located at Estancia.

Fullerton, Baca and maybe Lewis used the Santa Fe Railroad, via Albuquerque, to reach Socorro. The other four rangers also used the Santa Fe main line to go south but they traveled on through Socorro south to Rincon. Here Herb McGrath took the western branch to Deming to catch the Southern Pacific westbound to Lordsburg. George Elkins, Will Dudley and Octaviano Perea stayed on the Santa Fe until they reached El Paso. Elkins could have caught the "Drummer's Special" for the El Paso and Southwestern westbound train, leaving El Paso at 7 p.m., and traveling along the Mexican border until he reached his home at Hachita Junction. In the Pass City, Dudley and Perea would have made connections with the El Paso and Northeastern Railroad to go north again to reach their own homes in Alamogordo, however, the daily 7:30 train was delayed that weekend because snow closed the tracks through the Gallinas Cut until early evening on Sunday.[7]

Sergeant Lewis was not mentioned in the Albuquerque *Morning Journal* story and his location at that time is unknown. He may have remained in Santa Fe for some reason or he may have even joined Brophy and Meyer at Estancia and led them in the sweep into the central part of the territory that was reported by the Albuquerque *Evening Citizen*.[8] There are reasons to believe that was not the case. It is most likely that Lewis was in Albuquerque and that his presence was just overlooked by the reporter who saw the rangers gathered at the train depot.

It is doubtful that Fullerton's Rangers did any mass patrol into Grant County in April 1905. Six feet of snow covered the western mountains and 15 more inches fell on Silver City the first weekend in April. The Silver City *Independent* reported that McGrath spent Sunday, April 2, and an additional "few days" in town. He was doing some official business at the Grant County sheriff's office, but the weather may have also kept him at the county seat.[9] The Silver City paper added that Deputy Sheriff Herb McGrath "has not yet decided whether or not he will accept the position as ranger." Herb and Sheriff Charles Farnesworth may have discussed McGrath's remaining as a deputy while jointly serving as a ranger; dual appointments were quite common during that era. Some arrangement was agreed upon because McGrath preformed both jobs until December 1905.[10]

The Socorro *Chieftain* was still leading the cheers for the mounted police: "It is safe to predict that the wisdom of the legislative assembly in providing for this force will be amply vindicated shortly after the force begins active operations." The paper then said, "Lawless characters will be suppressed or driven from the territory, crime will be diminished in number, the heavy expense heretofore borne for the trial of criminal cases will be reduced. New Mexico's reputation for law and order will be enhanced, and the business and social life of the territory will feel a new impulse." The report ended by saying, "These results are greatly to be desired and the territorial police force will therefore enter upon active service backed by the hearty approval and best wishes of all good citizens."[11]

The Santa Fe *New Mexican* must have worked under the assumption that Captain Fullerton had called the rangers to Socorro to give them their marching orders. "The Mounted Police of the Territory which was assigned to duty Saturday [April 15] will immediately proceed to take steps looking to the driving out of the numerous 'badmen' who have infested this Territory." The short report concluded on a very optimistic note. "When the New Mexico force begins to drive them from the north it is expected that a number of important arrests will be made as there will be the Mexican Rurales on the south and the Arizona Rangers on the west to hem in the outlaws and effect their capture."[12]

At least one of the new rangers took the initiative and made patrol visits on his own. "W. E. Dudly [*sic*], formerly a Nogal pedagogue [schoolmaster] and later engaged in the same occupation at Alamogordo, made White Oaks a running visit a few days ago. Mr. Dudley

John F. and Susan Fullerton in Socorro, N.M., in the fall of 1892. Susan is holding Raymond Parish Fullerton and the boy sitting on John's lap is John Elmer Fullerton (Irene Fullerton's photograph album).

was appointed a territorial ranger by the governor and has entered upon his duties." *The Outlook* account concluded, with what proved to be a false prophecy, by saying that the mounted police's "operation will probably be confined to the territory west of the Rio Grande, where its services are needed worse than in this section." The week before, the newspaper had announced that "Communications addressed to Capt. John F. Fullerton at that office [the Socorro headquarters] will receive prompt attention."[13] It is possible that a few more of Fullerton's Rangers might have made some "show of force" before the muster call at Socorro, but the matter is unclear at this late date. If Sergeant Lewis did not lead the first patrol into Lincoln County, then that honor of first patrol command devolves to Lieutenant Baca.

Mounted police documents record that Cipriano Baca did, in fact, lead his squad out of Socorro headed northwest into the mountain country following the muster call held at ranger headquarters. They were followed a day later by Sergeant Bob Lewis and his two-man patrol unit, who struck out for the east central range country. The Deming *Graphic* was right when it said, "Capt. John Fullerton's mounted police are now mustered in and the New Mexico cattle thieves will soon hear something drop."

The Hicks Brothers

Meanwhile, B.F. Knight, a rancher from Ancho in Lincoln County, had informed mounted police headquarters about a missing sorrel and burro. Fullerton notified his men to be on the alert for the animals and the suspected thieves, the Hicks brothers. "Private Avent [*sic*] came in through San Antonio; he did not see or hear of them [Hicks brothers] coming that way, though they may have crossed the river ahead of him," Captain Fullerton wrote to Will Dudley. "I notified Serg. Lewis about them. He is out west of Magdalena and will probably see them if they pass that way. I also notified Privates Huber and Meyer thinking they might go by way of Belen then to Estancia, as I understand they once lived their [*sic*]."[14]

Fullerton's Rangers was finally a full company when Ranger Fate Avant took his oath of office on May 2. The ranger and his 11 year old son had traveled over land to Socorro from the Capitan country. The father-son trip took about two weeks due to bad mountain roads, lack of roads across the lava flow in the Valley of Fire and the vast Jornada del Muerto wasteland.[15]

Avant and his son spent a day in Socorro, enjoying the big city sights, before they began their return trip. The father and son again crossed the Rio Grande near San Antonio and headed east toward the mountains. A few hours into the trip Avant came across a couple of rough riders headed for Arizona. Fate Avant's case report said, "I found 2 Hicks...." He was quick to show his steel; the men were surprised when a territorial ranger questioned them on suspicion of being horse thieves. Avant continued his report by saying, "[I] inspected their stock which concisted [*sic*] of 8 head of horses. And [a] mare in harness and loose animal[s] in various brands." The new ranger was looking for the missing mare and burro from the B. F. Knight ranch.[16] Captain Fullerton had briefed Avant about the reported stock lose and the possible suspects. None of the missing Knight stock was found with the two men, so

Avant simply reported his search to headquarters then continued his homeward journey.

A couple of days later, Captain Fullerton, acting on Avant's recommendation, wrote Mr. Knight, "You had [should] probably make [local] inquires about your stock as it may not have been stolen."[17] Quick and decisive action was to be the hallmark of Fate Avant's ranger service and his weekly field reports show that he was on patrol almost every day upon his return home.

The Fountain and Chaves Murder Cases

Shortly after the mounted police's formation Captain Fullerton compiled much of the information that had been gathered during the numerous local investigations into the murders of two prominent New Mexico politicians. It would appear, however, that Fullerton's Rangers had little or no success with either of these cases, if in fact they even undertook an active investigation of the homicides.

One of these unsolved murder mysteries concerned Albert J. Fountain and his young son. The former New York native was well traveled and had practiced law in San Francisco before accompanying the California Column to New Mexico, during the War Between the States, to help defend the southwest against a Rebel invasion from Texas. After the war, Fountain stayed in the new territory and fought against Victorio, Geronimo and the other Apache chiefs before becoming a leader in the fight against the outlaw bands that rode across the southern part of the territory. Fountain was married and had 12 children.

Few records remain to help establish the depth of the mounted police's investigation into the 1896 murder of Col. Albert J. Fountain, a vigorous prosecuting attorney who disliked horse and cattle thieves, and his young son.[18] However, in a 1949 newspaper interview, "Stuttering Bob" Lewis claimed that Tom "Black Jack" Ketchum had killed both Fountain and the boy. Lewis said Tom's brother Sam had told him all the details of the murders after his brother's hanging at Clayton in 1901.[19] It is very likely that when Fred Fornoff succeeded Fullerton as mounted police captain that he and Baca both took a special interest in using the territory's resources to solve the Fountain case. The large posted reward was still active. Former Dona Ana County Sheriff Pat Garrett devoted the last years of his life to the Fountain investigation and this chase was a cause of his own death. Captain Fornoff investigated Pat Garrett's 1908 murder and included his findings in a confidential communiqué, *The Fornoff Report*,[20] to the governor and the attorney general. The identity of the cold-blooded murderer of Albert J. Fountain and his young son in the Chalk Hills remains an unsolved mystery.

Fullerton's Rangers also developed a case file on the 1904 political assassination of the territory's superintendent of schools.[21] Col. J. Francisco Chaves had been born in New Mexico under Mexican rule, but he was educated in St. Louis and attended medical school in New York. Chaves fought with the New Mexico Volunteer Infantry during the War Between the States and after the war he entered the territory's political wars and served as the territorial delegate to Congress. He also served 14 terms in the Territorial Council and was president of the 1889 Constitutional Convention. Chaves owned a 10,000 acre sheep ranch in Valencia County.

Lieutenant Cipriano Baca may have still been investigating the Chaves murder when he unexpectedly resigned from the rangers in January 1907.[22] Baca claimed to have "entirely reliable" knowledge concerning the killers' identity and claimed that the men could be "captured in short notice." Within days of his resignation, Cipriano Baca had tried to telephone Captain Fornoff with his new discovery but found that the captain was out of town, so he wrote to Governor Hagerman about his information.[23] A month later, in February 1907, the mounted police arrested a suspect in the Chaves case. However, the case never came to trial and the $2,500 reward was never paid. The whole Chaves affair was a volatile political hot potato that had divided the territory along racial, religious and political party lines. Hagerman soon left office and his successor, recently returned from overseas duty, seemed to have had no interest in the case. Was it a case of let sleeping dogs lie? The Chaves murder remains officially unsolved.

"The Bootheel"

George M. Elkins had a deep love for the hard, free life, the spirit of independence on the open range. He holds a special place in the annals of the New Mexico Territorial Mounted Police. Elkins was ready to accept his ranger appointment because to him it was the best part of two worlds, because he could work outdoors in the livestock business and earn twice as much as a regular cowhand. The rangers had been told that their duty was to apprehend "any outlaws, law breakers, marauding Indians or bands of hostile Indians or for the purpose of carrying out any measure that may contribute to the better security of the frontier...." All the rangers were exempt from military or jury service and had "full power to make [an] arrest of criminals in any part of the territory...."[24] Most of Fullerton's Rangers were very aware that they had taken on a big responsibility, yet they were as "tickled over their jobs as a boy with an all day sucker."[25]

In mid–April 1905, George Elkins left his home near Hachita Junction and bought a ticket on the spur line train to Deming. Here he spent the day checking on the brands in the cattle shipping pens and the feed lots. An area paper, reporting on the trip, called Elkins "the well known ranger." A few days later, Elkins sent Captain Fullerton a report of his uneventful trip[26] and Fullerton replied, "I shipped your rifle to you on the 14th together with one hundred rounds of thirty-forty cartridges. Also fifty rounds of forty-five Colts." The captain felt that Elkins would soon need this ammunition shipment because of his imminent encounter with the border outlaws in the Bootheel. Fullerton concluded his letter by saying, "There is nothing new as to [free railroad] transportation" for the rangers.[27]

The Silver City *Independent* next printed a single line report on the Grant County ranger, saying, "Hachita Ranger Geo. Elkins left Friday [April 21] for a trip along the frontier."[28] The *Otero County Advertiser*, meanwhile, was telling its readers that the mounted police were planning a major in force move into the Grant County Bootheel and intoned, "Several of the most desperate men of the southwest are known to be hiding in that section."[29] This outlaw stronghold was believed by many territorial lawmen to be located in the foreboding Animas Mountains.

A few weeks before these events, the other Alamogordo newspaper had published an interview with Councilman William H. Greer. This long report concerned the need for the mounted police troop to clean up the Bootheel section.

> It is all a mistake, the supposition that the ranger company will benefit only the cattle interest of New Mexico. People who are informed of the geography of New Mexico know that on the southwestern corner of Grant County there is a little neck of land which runs down into the state of Chihuahua. I say a little neck of land, and it is, in comparison to the rest of New Mexico. In reality, this neck is eighty miles or more from east to west and nearly as wide from north to south. On either side of the mountains which run through this neck of land are rich pastures. In it is Guadalupe canon [canyon], one of the richest mining districts in New Mexico, for the continuance of this range in southern Arizona and Sonora carries the great cooper fields of Bisbee and Cananea. Yet in Guadalupe canon there has been almost no development of mining property. The reason is simple enough, for you can not find a prospector in all New Mexico who will go down there to drive a pick. It is almost impossible to get men to tend cattle in the valleys on either side of the range. They are afraid to go; but it would be foolhardy for any man to risk his life and property in that section under present conditions.
>
> The mountains [of southwestern New Mexico] are literally full of the worst class of desperados in the country, men who have found that there is no other section of the West so safe. In that neck of land there are gathered now a few of the most notorious outlaws of the time.[30]

George Elkins is standing on the front porch of the Hatchet Ranch headquarters building near Hachita, N.M., circa 1914 (courtesy of Chandler Elkins).

Captain Fullerton took Greer's comments to heart and meant to uphold his prediction concerning the effectiveness of the rangers. Greer had said, "I venture the assertion that a ranger force of twelve men of the right sort, sent into that country, would clean it out in a very few months. In my opinion the development which would follow a reign of law in Guadalupe canon would in a year or two meet the expense of the ranger force needed in increases of assessed valuation [and collected taxes]."[31] Col. Greer's prediction was correct. Within a few years, wagon loads of turquoise, gold, silver and tin were extracted from the Little Hatchet

Mountains and mineral wealth joined livestock shipping as the lifeblood for the two railroads serving the Hachita area.

For a second time, a mass invasion of the Bootheel by Fullerton's Rangers failed to materialize. This time it was due to bad weather. The southern mountain regions had experienced heavy rain daily for over six weeks and the drenching downpour had made overland travel almost impossible. One Albuquerque newspaper was prompted to comment: "New Mexico ranchmen say that seaweed is likely to be the pest of the range this year."[32]

In the early spring of 1905, much of the Sunshine Territory was still blanketed in white and a final cold snap almost wiped out the Mesilla Valley fruit crop. The bad farming weather soon caused many central New Mexico small homesteaders to seek backbreaking work in the rock quarries near Watrous. The need for hard cash drove other settlers to seek day work as harvest pickers in the southern Colorado beet fields, while still others became livestock thieves.

Early in May, George Elkins began a new series of scouts in the "high lonesome" along the mountain divide. In his first report that month Elkins told Captain Fullerton, "I have been down on the line until a few days ago. I went to Lordsburg the 6th." Elkins continued, "There has been 5 head of horses stolen near Deming branded 5 ... tryed [sic] to catch there [sic] trail but could not. There is nothing going on here now." George then noted that the cattle shipping season would start in a few days and he was optimistic that this action might cause the would-be thieves to show their colors. The ranger ended his report by saying, "I received my gun [Model 1895 Winchester .30–40 lever action rifle] and am well pleased with it."[33]

Elkins' optimistic bubble was busted, but not by rustlers. "Lack of cars at Deming is working great inconvenience to cattle shippers. Droves of cattle are being herded in the vicinity waiting on the railroad." Local cowhands kept close watch on the herds and long ropers had no chance to swing a loop. Ranchers had another problem to confront. The larger horse herds running wild on the open range had developed an infestation of mange that was spreading across the southwestern part of the territory. The Cattle Sanitary Board quickly set up dipping pens in hopes of quelling the plague before it became an epidemic in the territory.

Meanwhile, in the northeastern section of New Mexico, a series of violent early summer hail storms had not only damaged buildings, but had killed livestock. Hail had destroyed numerous adobe buildings in Colfax County and broke most of the windows in Raton. The prairies of San Miguel and Colfax counties were dotted with carcasses of dead cattle. The Cattle Sanitary Board later estimated that over 10,000 cow hides from these nature-killed animals reached the hide market. At least some ranchers were able to recover part of their loss through these hide sales. If dead cattle were not a big enough problem, the Dry Cimarron River, filled with runoff from Johnson Mesa, became a river and raced across northern Union County, washing out bridges as it overran its banks on its journey east toward the Arkansas River.[34]

In mid–May, George Elkins again sent a field report to headquarters. The young ranger told Captain Fullerton, "I will write you a few lines as I start to the Animas vally this evening to look after some horses that has diapeared and will be gone for 8 to 10 days." Elkins also reported that the five horses he had been seeking for a few weeks "have shoed up all right they had just driffed off."³⁵ "Well there is nothing going on down here now everything is so very quite." On his next trip, George located some stray horses. "There were no one with them when I found them."³⁶

The Hatchet Mountains and other southern New Mexico mountain ranges were once home to hundreds of desert bighorn sheep. But over time, the once free-roaming animals that were so familiar to Elkins became an endangered species by the 1990s due to mountain lions, disease and hunters.³⁷ In Spanish the word *animas* means departed souls and this is just how Elkins found the Bootheel. It was the "high lonesome" for a ranger who was supposed to be stationed in the heart of "outlaw country" and was unable to locate any sign of illegal activities.

During the legislative debate over the demand for the rangers, the chief reason cited was the need to rid the southern mountains of vicious outlaw gangs, and the reasoning continued, "This is not the only section of New Mexico which needs attention and with which the [local] peace officers are unable to cope."³⁸ Rangers in other sections of the territory were making real progress. Fullerton wrote Elkins, "I just returned [to Socorro] from a trip to Lincoln and Otero Counties. There has been something doing in the Capitan Mts. and hope to have that country cleaned up before long."³⁹

It seems that George Elkins could not do anything that pleased Captain Fullerton. His only arrest was for forgery and the accomplishment was dutifully reported on the ranger field report. A reprimand was received by return mail. "Particular care must be exercised in listing the arrest." The ranger chief wanted to know the name of the person arrested and the disposition of the case. George's reply to the request is missing from the records of Fullerton's Rangers and local contemporary records do not contain any information about this case.⁴⁰ The loss of a head of cattle was serious business, but the act of passing funny money was almost commonplace in the western territories and states due to the large amount of counterfeit banknotes in circulation. This is one reason why most westerners preferred to deal with gold or silver coins.

In spite of George Elkins' reports to the contrary, Lieutenant Cipriano Baca, his squad commander and former Luna County sheriff, held firm to the belief that there must be some kind of trouble in the "outlaw country." Fullerton agreed and he wrote Elkins that Baca "thinks there is quite a goodeal [*sic*] of work down on the line."⁴¹ Unsaid, but understood, was the question, why haven't you shown some results? Captain Fullerton keep up the drum beat by telling Elkins that he was "very anxious to make a trip down in your country and will do so as soon as I can get transportation over the AT&SF." In that letter the captain softened his tone, "Use your own judgment about the work that is necessary until I can come down." John Fullerton signed off by saying he was still having trouble finding the right kind of uniform for the rangers.⁴²

It is a good guess that George Elkins was not overly concerned about not having a mounted police uniform. The uniform was to be worn at official musters and special company functions and no one was going to see him wear it in his patrol area were the range camps were days apart by horseback ride. A century later, an even more sparsely populated Bootheel country is still mostly accessible only by unpaved roads and horseback trails. Present day drug runners, illegal worker smugglers and other border outlaws still use the area's vast ruggedness to hide their activities.[43]

The discouraged George Elkins continued to try and locate some trouble. In late May, Elkins rode out of Hachita with a pack team for a scout through the Valley of the Playas and did not even find a horse track.[44] In early June, he rode east toward Deming and still found no trouble, so a week later George crossed the mountains and rode through the Guadalupe Canyon area along the Arizona line. He told Captain Fullerton, "(I) do not find anything of interest down there. I see a few stray horse tracks but they are old."[45]

The frustrations proved too much for George Elkins, so he chose to leave the rangers. Elkins' resignation also put an end to the paper crusade to rid the Bootheel section of outlaw gangs. In July 1905, Bob Putman was appointed to replace Elkins and Captain Fullerton ordered him to Socorro "just as soon as you can possibly get here.... I have some very important work on hand."[46]

In a strange twist of events, mounted police arrest records show that shortly after Elkins left the ranger service McGrath reported making an arrest in Elkins' hometown. McGrath had taken the Arizona and New Mexico Railroad's morning coach down to Hachita, known locally as the Lordsburg-Hachita Line, and later that day McGrath took his prisoner back to the Lordsburg jail aboard the afternoon passenger coach. McGrath had not acted as a territorial ranger, but as a deputy sheriff when he arrested a man for shooting up the village of Hachita. Once again McGrath had charged taxpayers twice for the same service by claiming an arrest fee and a prisoner transport fee, while also seeking credit for being an effective salaried territorial ranger.[47]

Harris L. "Lod" Littleton, the 39 year old Texas cowboy who "treed" Hachita, was given a one year sentence in the territorial prison for "unlawfully carrying [a] deadly weapon" by District Court Judge Frank W. Parker. He was released a month early due to "good time" conduct.[48]

Looking back, it would seem that the Bootheel outlaw menace of the spring of 1905 was much more psychological than real. This may have been due to the territory-wide publicity campaign concerning an impending ranger strike force moving into the Bootheel. The image of a massive, well armed and determined mounted police incursion may have had the desired effect of driving the gangs from the Bootheel, thus making the need for the raid unnecessary. W.H. Greer had the right idea when he said, "The moral effect of the word 'ranger' is great. Outlaws do not care to meet a well armed body of that kind."[49] Greer's idea is supported by the fact that neither Fullerton's Rangers, nor their many successors, ever undertook a mass raid into the Bootheel.

The Spring Patrols

In late April 1905, Rangers Meyer and Huber rode into Socorro and reported to headquarters to confer with Captain Fullerton. The two rangers spent a few days "acquainting themselves with affairs at headquarters and preparing themselves otherwise for active duty" by helping Bob Lewis search the local watermelon patches.

The Socorro press gave the reason: "Sergeant Lewis is from Alabama and they say he has a hankering for melon."⁵⁰ Following these field training days, the two rangers felt they were ready for action, so with the captain's blessing they headed east in search of trouble. The two men escaped Socorro in such a hurry that Julius Meyer left a pair of his boots at the hotel, so Captain Fullerton sent them, via railroad express, to the ranger's home in Estancia.⁵¹

The day before Huber and Meyer left Socorro, Captain Fullerton warned Private Perea that the two men would "start in the direction of your county [early] tomorrow [morning]."⁵² Fullerton's letter gave Perea no direct orders concerning his part in the men's proposed actions while in Otero County, so Perea did nothing about the information. He just continued to edit his newspaper and await orders. A few days after Fullerton wrote Perea he sent a letter to Will Dudley. "I am glad you are in the mountains [around Nogal] getting what information you can. Everything here has been going very slow.... On last Tuesday the 25th I started Private[s] Huber and Meyer to Alamogordo. I instructed them to report to you, thinking that perhaps that you might have something on hand."⁵³

Julius Meyer, photographed at Estancia, N.M., while he was the sheriff of Torrance County, circa 1910 (courtesy of Mrs. I. B. Singer).

In early May 1905, Rangers Dick Huber, Julius Meyer and Will Dudley joined forces to make a detailed investigation through the White Mountain and the Capitan Mountain regions. It had rained almost daily for nine months prior to this mountain scout and the area had received well over 16 inches of rain. The Rio Grande flooded the ancient Spanish riverbank settlements of San Marcial and Tome along with farmlands near Las Cruces, while the average daily temperature was four degrees below normal. Perea was still sitting at home while the ranger trio traveled over 350 miles on horseback. They summed up their extended patrol with a simple report to Captain Fullerton: "From information gathered [we] believe [the] district is quite [sic]."⁵⁴

It had turned into an very extended scout for Will Dudley, Dick Huber and Julius Meyer and the ranger trio had began to run low on food supplies, so they decided to close their mission and return to their homes for some much needed rest. Dudley turned south and headed for Alamogordo while Meyer and Huber, with their pack horses, struck out north into unknown range country.

The word "smog" was coined in 1905 by a newspaper reporter to describe the condition of the air over some of America's largest cities. Smog would seem to be a difficult concept for Meyer and Huber to have understood as they rode the vast plains of central New Mexico for a few days before they finally reached the Torrance County seat. In their report the two rangers told Captain Fullerton, "We ought to have written you sooner but could not figure out where we could be." The next day they left the village of Progresso and continued north only to stumble across a stock shooter who was randomly killing horses and mules for the sport of it. The man invited the two trail riders to join him in the fun before, to his misfortune, he discovered their profession. Justice was served because these two weary rangers had spent a couple of extra days and nights on the open plains in southern Torrance County.[55]

Back at headquarters, Captain Fullerton tried to keep up on the paper work. "I am very sorry to hear of your ware-house being burned," wrote Fullerton. The barn was located on the vast Block Ranch and H.A. Scott, the ranch manager, had notified the rangers about the crime. "You no doubt have some idea how it occurred. Will be glad to hear from you at any time how things are going on in that country [around Richardson]."[56] The ranger chief made no offer to assist local lawmen with the investigation.

Meanwhile, Sergeant Lewis was on a solo patrol in the western part of Socorro County. He spent Friday, May 5, at Captain Fullerton's ranch before he took up the trail of a horse thief. That same weekend Herb McGrath arrested four men for "aiding & abeting [sic] unlawful Chinamen to enter & pass through the United States." The suspects, C.A. Wise, A.N. Howel, W.B. Aken and J. Goddard, were lodged in the Deming jail in lieu of a $1,000 bond.[57]

A week later, Ranger McGrath wrote Captain Fullerton how he had been able to track down a suspected cattle thief through the butcher who had bought the stolen stock. However, McGrath said he was unable to make an arrest because the steer's rightful owner would not make the needed complaint against the rustler suspect.[58] A hundred years later, the word "intimidate" still means to frighten someone or to make them afraid of some kind of reprisal. Nothing seems to have changed. McGrath's pocketbook was luckier a few days later. This time Herb locked up a man who was wanted in Old Mexico for stealing six mules. This time no reluctant witness was necessary to prove the suspect's guilt, because Miguel Fierra still had four of the stolen mules in his custody when Herb arrested him near Lordsburg.[59]

Herb McGrath, acting as a Grant County deputy sheriff, earned a prisoner transport fee when he traveled to Tombstone, Arizona, in June to take custody of two Grant County horse thieves being held in the Cochise County jail. Sheriff Stewart Hunt had used some country psychology on his prisoners when he told the men that he would have to transfer them to Phoenix, a more secure long term jail, if they chose to await an extradition hearing on their case. The men knew that the Phoenix jail, in midsummer, was hotter than an oven, so they were quick to select the offer of the cooler New Mexico mountains and voluntarily asked Sheriff Hunt to send them to back to Silver City for a summer vacation sojourn in the county jail.[60] It would be interesting to know if, while he was in Tombstone, McGrath had expressed his support for some local girls who wanted to form a basketball team.[61] Herb had been an outstanding college athlete and seemed to approve of female sports, because he supported his nieces' athletic endeavors.

Travelers along the railway headed west from Lordsburg had the joy of seeing vast patches of wild wheat growing along the right of way. The crop probably came from seeds that had fallen from supplies shipped aboard the passing freight trains. On the high plains near Silver City, McGrath and his prisoners could have seen some wild peas growing along the roadway. Both of these sights were by-products of the abundant spring rains. In other parts of the territory, the rains were causing train delays due to overflowing arroyos and rivers.[62]

In late June, Captain Fullerton wrote a Faywood area rancher that he would send him some help. "I have detailed Private Herbert McGrath of Lordsburg to take this work for you." Fullerton continued, "I am anxious to stop the [cattle] killing and stealing." A few weeks later, Fullerton asked McGrath for a progress report. "Please let me hear from you about the work at Faywood. I have not heard from you for some time." The details concerning this case are missing from the mounted police records, but it would seem that McGrath did little about the matter. Herb told Captain Fullerton that "it has always happened for me to be out some where & could not make the [weekly] reports as I should."[63] McGrath had told a tall tale, because he spent most of early July in Lordsburg supervising a street cleanup project. "Mr. McGrath has been invited to repeat the operation often." He did. Three weeks later the Lordsburg paper again reported on the street cleaning saying, "They have improved much in appearance." The next week it rained every day in southern Grant County.[64]

When Bob Putman was named to the rangers, Captain Fullerton had sent orders to report to Socorro ready for actions. "You need an extra good horse also a pack horse if you can bring one with you. Pack saddle and what ever you need for a trip through the mountains. It is not necessary for me to mention what will be needed as you know as much about that as I do. We have adopted the .45 colts revolver, I suppose you have a good one. I have a .30–40 rifle here for you."[65] A week later, Bob took his oath of office and was ready to take the field in search of outlaws. However, the plans for the big Bootheel raid had gone bust, so Bob found he spent his time acting as a clerk at the mounted police headquarters. He also took a few days and moved his family to Socorro.

The Lincoln County Roundup

Will Dudley spent many late spring nights on lonely mountain scouts where he discovered numerous simple signs that when added together meant big trouble.[66] Dudley wrote Fullerton, "There has been something doing in the Capitan Mountains, and I hope we have the country cleaned up before long."[67] Rangers Avant and Dudley were spreading their wings and testing the scope of their mounted police authority. Captain Fullerton understood this desire for action and wrote Avant concerning the process. "When you need advice on any case the prosecuting attorneys of each and every county in the territory are supposed and duty bound to furnish the mounted police with all the required [legal advice needed] free of charge." Fullerton concluded by saying that if "such information should be refused by any prosecuting atorney please report him to me."⁶⁸

On Monday, May 8, 1905, Will Dudley and Octaviano Perea joined Fate Avant in Capitan. Dudley and Perea had used their railroad passes and taken the El Paso and Northeastern Railroad up from Alamogordo to Carrizozo, then changed trains to ride on into Capitan. Details of this conference are unknown, but about a week later Avant bought a new $2 pair of shoes on credit in anticipation of some extended travel. A few days later, Will Dudley was back in Capitan and this time Captain Fullerton was Dudley's traveling companion.⁶⁹ The *Otero County Advertiser* commented on Fullerton's visit to Otero and Lincoln Counties. "The captain became acquainted with many of our citizens and expressed himself as well pleased with his first visit to Alamogordo."⁷⁰ The three rangers conceived the first of a series of plans that were designed to break the back of the livestock thieves in Lincoln County. Captain Fullerton gave Dudley and Avant his approval of the new Lincoln County cleanup plan and it was decided that Dudley would make a big show of his coming and going in the area, while Avant would fade into the landscape. Mounted Policemen Dudley and Avant quickly developed a close working relationship that would soon cause trouble for long ropers in the area. The Capitan *News* dutifully reported many of Dudley's "regular visits to Capitan."⁷¹ When the would-be-raiders saw Dudley leave the area, the rangers thought the badmen would make their move. Avant would keep his eyes and ears open for the suspected action and then he would send for Dudley to come help him with the outlaw roundup.⁷²

Ranger Perea was not in Alamogordo when Captain Fullerton visited in the Otero County seat. He was still in Lincoln County and later he would write Fullerton, "I waited there [at Coalora] for Private Dudley, 3 days and he never showed up and I came on down to Alamo[gordo]."⁷³ The mounted police records are not clear as to why Perea thought that Dudley would meet him in the tiny remote mining camp on the same day that he was scheduled to be in conference with Captain Fullerton and Fate Avant in Capitan. Even if Dudley and Perea had arranged a meeting and Will later found that he could not keep that appointment, he could have easily gotten a message to Perea. Just as interesting is why Perea, if Dudley knew he was just a few miles away, was not summoned to join the Capitan conference. The mining company office at Coalora had a telephone line that was connected to Capitan, but Will Dudley made no telephone call to Coalora.

The mounted police's first *nuevomexicano* ranger seems to have once again operated in a vacuum while dancing to his own tune. Coalora was located a mile northwest of Capitan in the Salado Flat area. This is the area were Fate Avant had his ranch and there is no indication that Perea even once tried to contact Avant while he was in the area. Avant and Perea were both assigned to Sergeant Lewis' patrol squad. It would seem that Perea had spent four or five days riding around the Ruidoso and Capitan country visiting family and friends. It would seem that the Lincoln County rustler element did not consider Perea's mounted police connection as any real concern because he had caused them no trouble. If the local rustlers had feared Perea as an active lawman, then his presence could have accidentally upset the Fullerton-Avant-Dudley long-roper roundup plan.

This group photograph was taken in front of the public school at Lincoln, N.M., circa 1890s. Octaviano Perea was one of the teachers (courtesy of the Lincoln County Historical Society).

Captain Fullerton, and maybe even Ranger Will Dudley, had many reservations concerning Octaviano Perea. The ranger chief expressed the idea that Perea "seems to be rather extravagant ... [and] he does not seem to take hold of this [police] work." Fullerton's comment is interesting in light of Perea's experience as a Lincoln County deputy sheriff and jailor. Perea may have had an extravagant nature, because he had borrowed money from Captain Fullerton as an advance on his salary. He had also borrowed money from Will Fullerton and Col. W. H. Greer. John promised Greer that he would put a stop to Perea's credit.[74] Captain Fullerton warned Lieutenant Baca about Perea's problems with overspending. Once on an extended scout Baca was forced to loan Perea an advance on his police salary. Fullerton wrote Baca, "You had better keep a strict account of all the expenses and settle up the first or as soon as the money [the monthly paycheck] is received."[75]

In the summer of 1902, the Nogal *Republican* had supported Perea's ill-fated bid to become Lincoln County sheriff. The newspaper had said, "He has served several terms as chief deputy sheriff and made a most excellent officer. He is well qualified, obliging and broadminded, brave and courteous."[76] It is very likely that Octaviano Perea was the victim of the Hispanic culture that caused him to show differed respect toward Captain Fullerton and may have caused Perea to appear timid. Perea may also have shown the *la familia* attitude of helpfulness toward those *nuevomexicano* who found themselves in trouble and thus he may have seemed to be overly friendly toward some of the suspected outlaw element. He was a man caught in the middle of two worlds. When Perea's father was nearing the end of his tenure as Lincoln County sheriff, the Santa Fe *New Mexican* praised his work: "Cattle stealing, once a common crime, has been suppressed. Law and order prevail."[77] The rustlers had returned to Lincoln County and Perea's son wanted to restore the family's tarnished reputation, but he was unsure how to accomplish that mission.

When Fullerton left Alamogordo that May afternoon, he gave Dudley some straightforward instructions to impart to Octaviano Perea. Perea finally returned to Alamogordo on Saturday and the two rangers held a private conference on Monday that must have been a very pointed conversation. "I told Private Perea what you said and what his duties were in a good kind manner," Dudley wrote Captain Fullerton. "I could not have felt so kindly disposed Saturday evening [after he learned about Perea's Lincoln County visit]. I could remember 'Caution after reflection' and the 'Pardon was granted'."[78]

Dudley had to deal with a critical family problem before he could devote his full energy to the planned rustler roundup. His youngest daughter had been badly injured in an accident when an iron bed frame had collapsed on the child. The couple finally decided that Josie Dudley and her mother would take the baby to Fort Worth for special medical treatment. Dudley's wife and their two daughters then spent the remainder of the summer at Grandmother Burleson's ranch in Crosby County, Texas. Even after a couple of operations, Lois Ann Dudley Shofner was unable to walk, even with her special built shoes, without a limp as a result of that childhood accident.[79]

Even during his troubles with his fellow ranger and his own personal concerns, Dudley kept his vigil for a fugitive wanted by the Arizona Rangers. The official records are unclear concerning the nature of this case; however, it would seem that the former schoolteacher turned lawman was finally able to arrest his prey and return the wanted man to Arizona.[80] Meanwhile, Perea wrote Captain Fullerton that he had joined Dudley "as requested" on a scout into the White Mountains, then up the Hondo Valley and across the Capitan Mountains. Perea did not include Fate Avant in his report for some unknown reason. The trio was unable to make any arrests, but they did investigate a "calf case on the Bonito River but there was not enough evidence to do anything about it." Perea puffed himself up a bit and added, "I think crime is stopping a good deal in that county since we've been riding that country." The territorial policeman concluded by saying, "I am here at Alamogordo awaiting further orders." Fate Avant's report of the scout said simply, "I was assisted in making the search by Wm. E. Dudley and Perea, privates of our company."[81]

A relative of Avant's would later recall this tale:

> Did you ever hear tell of the cabbage snake? You known the boys ... the rangers ... would spend sometime weeks on the trail chasing after some rustlers. On one of those trips Grandpa Fate had a newspaper with a story about a new kind of snake that had been discovered in the South. It seems that this new snake was almost colorless so you couldn't see him. He was very fast and deadly poisonous, but the best part was that he ate cabbage plants. Can you see a snake eating a cabbage plant? Well, Grandpa Fate told them about that snake one night during one of them trail camps. There was a Mexican ranger [Perea] with them and he really got spooked. Didn't like

no snake, no how and an invisible one really spooked him. That Mexican rigged up some kind of hammock between two trees and spent the night half awake. Next morning, Grandpa Fate told him that those snakes could climb trees. He never rode with them again and resigned from the rangers sometime after that camp out.[82]

The myth of the cabbage snake started in Kentucky and spread across the southeast during 1905 and caused an economic disaster on the farms as cabbage crops were unpicked and left to rot in the fields by frightened laborers. The cabbage snake is now a part of southern folklore, but it seems that a century ago the myth was a real event in the life of a New Mexico mounted policeman.

Captain Fullerton kept in mind Perea's friendship with the governor, but he had reached the end of his tolerance. So, he summoned Perea to Socorro. The town's weekly newspaper reported on the visit and one of the *Chieftain*'s editorial comments said Perea was "a good political manager, as is indicated by the fact that although his county is a close one he carried it [among the Spanish voters] for the Republican ticket last November." Interestingly, nothing pro or con was said concerning the quality of Octaviano Perea's outdoor, ranching or law enforcement skills.[83] Perea was reassigned to Lieutenant Baca's squad and was ordered to the far northwestern part of the territory.

Horse Racing

Mounted Policeman Octaviano Perea was well known around Lincoln County for his love of fast horses. It was said he would race his favorite mare on any occasion that involved a reasonable bet or sometimes he would race just for the fun of it. One such occasion was reported by the Capitan *Progress*: "A horse race was pulled off at Lincoln last Monday between the well known Brady mare and the equally well known horse owned by O. Perea which attracted a great many people to that town on that date. The race was won by the Perea horse which crossed the line several feet ahead of the mare."[84] There was no mention of the amount of money that changed hands that afternoon in Lincoln.

Perea was not the only ranger that enjoyed a good horse race or a game of chance. Rafael Gomez, the second *nuevomexicano* ranger, was also an expert horseman and poker player. While on scout duty in the summer of 1906, Gomez found an occasion to take part in a horse race with C. E. "XIT Buck" MacConnell, the old range cowhand turned writer, who was working for the Turkey Track Bars Ranch, near Coyote, that summer. One day Buck and his range boss, Bob Kelly, rode into the settlement and here the two men met Gomez. "This fellow was one of the prettiest sights I ever saw on a horse," remembered Buck. "Pearl handled six gun, silver conchos lining his Texas flap chaps, silver ornamented spurs, bridle and saddle. Wore an expensive Stetson at a rakish angle." Nearly seven decades later the outcome of the race was still clear to MacConnell: "I didn't win." The race had not been Buck's idea but he did have a good horse. "I was riding a blue roan which the boss thought was very fast." The bets were made and the two horsemen lined up at the mark. The signal shot was fired. "At the crack of the pistol shot to start the race people popped out of the adobe houses lining the dusty street. The blue roan [horse] broke in two [bucking] and headed for the country while trying his best to unload me."[85]

The Back Trails

While Baca's squad was hard at work in the northwest country, Dick Huber was working close to home. He had not yet been issued any railroad passes so he had to travel on horseback and was "riged [sic] out with a pack [horse]." Huber wrote ranger headquarters that "some bad carecters have been seen lately [in Santa Fe County]." Dick's character assessment proved to be correct because a short time later he was notified that a man had shot and wounded a woman at Galisteo. Ranger Huber took up the hunt and tracked Miguel Fernandez to Pinos Wells, where he arrested him. The man was charged with attempted murder and Huber turned him over to the deputy sheriff at Cerrillos.[86]

Julius Meyer was on patrol in Guadalupe County when he found a Texas horse thief ready to start a new business in the Santa Rosa district. Meyer decided not to sponsor him for a chamber of commerce ribbon cutting but instead sent him back to Crockett County in chains. It would have been interesting to have read the story about this horse thief's "triumphal return" to his hometown, but unfortunately the early files of the Ozona *Kicker* were lost in a fire and no copics have been located.

In mid–May, two men escaped from the El Camino Real road building crew near Las Vegas, so Meyer kept a close watch on the canyon trails heading south toward the San Miguel County line. Meyer told the "vacationing" prisoners that he hated to cut their spring break short, but they were needed back at hard labor so they could earn their room and board from the territory.[87]

Lost Chaves Cattle

In late May, Captain Fullerton received word that a band of long ropers were at work on the central plains. "There seems to be a bad lot of men in that vicinity," Fullerton wrote the territorial game warden. "I am going to stop that stealing business."[88] Rangers Julius Meyer and Dick Huber along with rancher James W. "Jimmie" Chaves, a son of the late Col. J. Francisco Chaves, undertook a search for the missing cattle heard. The men started their horseback trip from Estancia with a ride along the eastern slope of the Manzano Mountains. En route the trio passed the ancient apple orchards that gave their name to the nearby mountains, and headed south over pastoral lands that were once an inland lake toward the red-bluff and pinon pine country around Mountainair.

The Mountainair settlement was only a few years old and contained the only deep well water supply for miles in all directions. The water holes dug south of the village were all alkaline. Even the railroad engineers found that they needed to fill their locomotives at Willard before they came west over the pass to Belen. The Mountainair region was excellent for raising pinto beans and was soon called the Pinto Bean Capital of the World. The ranger posse watered their animals at Pop Shaffer's blacksmith shop and visited with the locals about range conditions in the pass region.

Meyer, Huber and Chaves then rode on southwest through Abo Pass before doubling back to the Torrance County plains on the old Indian trail now used by ranchers to move their herds through the mountains.

Estancia was another new settlement made possible by the court order that declared the ownership of the Baca and Sandoval land grants void. The valley was quickly opened to claims by homesteaders and "the resting place" became a trading center for farmers. A post office opened in late 1903 and the Estancia *News* started publication the next year. Forty men and two women attended Rev. A. P. Morrison's first service in the community church and 60 children attended the first day at the community school. Meyer, Huber and Chaves spent a day in Estancia while their horses were re-shod. The next day found the posse camped in the high mountains on the road to Albuquerque. Here they finally picked up the trail of some cattle and the next day the herd and four Mexicans were located south of the Duke City. The men were promptly arrested and charged as rustlers, because the 33 head of livestock they had in their herd wore the Chaves Ranch brand.[89]

Jimmie Chaves gave an interview to the Albuquerque *Evening Citizen* concerning the chase. Fullerton wrote Meyer that he felt that this kind of publicity could "spoil all the work you have done" by letting the outlaws understand the rangers' methods. He told Meyer to "be very careful in the future in regard to our work and not let the reporters know anything of our movements."[90] Chaves wanted to be a mounted police and when the opportunity arrived he was highly recommended by both Meyer and Huber, but for some reason, maybe this faux pas, Chaves never received a mounted police appointment.[91]

A few days after the newspaper interview Meyer and Huber were back in the Manzano Mountains. On the third day into the scout the rangers spilt up and Huber headed back east toward the open plains along the Lincoln County line. Finally, Dick turned north and after a six day ride reached his home in Santa Fe. The next week, Huber was once more searching for missing Chaves Ranch cattle as he rode over western Santa Fe County and finally south again into Torrance County. He spent the weekend resting in a soft bed at Julius Meyer's ranch near Willard.[92]

Meanwhile, Meyer continued his scout through the Manzano Mountains and his forth night in the high country was no fun. The Rio Grande Valley north and south of Albuquerque and west to Gallup received a three hour downpour and then a slow rain settled in for the rest of the night. Meyer wrote Captain Fullerton; "Rode in Mts. Slept out in Mts rained all night." A light rain continued all weekend, but Meyer finally reached Albuquerque and the home of his wife's family. The next morning Meyer took the train down the Rio Grande to Socorro and had a talk with Captain Fullerton concerning the hunt for the lost Chaves ranch herd.[93]

Ranger Meyer may have left his hard ridden horses at his in-laws because his field report says he returned to Albuquerque "by rail" and the next day went on to Estancia "by Rail." Meyer may have shared a coach ride with Captain Fullerton on Wednesday, June 14. The ranger chief was headed to Santa Fe to attend an evening soiree at the Palace of the Governors on the old city square. This by-invitation-only event was to honor Governor Otero's eight years as the territorial executive. Unfortunately, however, John Fullerton missed the most prestigious "smoker" of the political season due to "his train not making connections" at Albuquerque.⁹⁴ Captain Fullerton reached the capital early Thursday morning and conducted his "official business" before returning to Socorro.

Julius Meyer soon returned to the central mountain region and spent a few days riding the Old Mission Trail hunting for some missing horses in the grazing lands adjacent to the small land grant communities along the route. On Saturday, June 17, he was at Ranger Perea's birthplace, a small farming community 14 miles west of Estancia, and his field report contains an unexplained comment under this date: "Got horse out of pond at Torreon." A side note says, "costs $7²⁵/₁₀₀." Meyer gave no further information concerning this adventure or the $7.25 expense. Julius Meyer may have simply misspelled the word "pound." The horse in question may have been being held in Torreon at some sort of local animal impound and the $7.25 was the fine or board cost for the horse's care. It is unclear why Meyer took custody of this horse or what he did with the animal after he retrieved it, but it is clear that he was at home with his family on Sunday.⁹⁵

The extended hunt for the Chaves ranch cattle came to a sudden end the next week. With good luck, Ranger Dick Huber located the cattle trail south of Willard and followed the signs south into Lincoln County and then west toward the Socorro County line. The whole area had been pounded by heavy rain that made roads into lanes of mud and fields into marshland. Travel was measured by yards, not miles. The mountain snow was still melting and the normally dry arroyos were abundant with water.⁹⁶ In the area called Sierra Oscura the ranger and the cattle's legal owner located the missing herd. Huber notified headquarters about the find and in his report said, "The cattle showed that they had been hard driven." The rustlers were now on the run, because they felt the hot breath of the mounted police on their necks. Sergeant Lewis and Ranger Putman had set out from Socorro to stop the rustlers from reaching Arizona, while Herb McGrath was sent to search along the Mexico border. The rangers were too late, however, to stop the rustler gang's disbandment. Their leader made his escape, via the railroad, to El Paso and he was able to cross the Rio Grande into Old Mexico.⁹⁷

Dudley's June Scout

Livestock conditions throughout New Mexico continued to improve during June. The sheep shearing season was almost complete and the wool

William E. Dudley, photographed in Alamogordo circa 1905 (courtesy of Frank Shofner).

growers were headed for a record setting season. Lambing season was also coming to a close and new births had reached a record high. The sheep and cattle growers were in a very happy mood and would remain so as long as the mounted police protected the range form unwanted visitors and the grass continued to grow.[98]

Will Dudley told a reporter from the Las Vegas *Daily Optic* that he never saw "finer ranges and fatter stock than may be seen now in Lincoln county. There are fewer cattle and horses to be seen than in years previous, but the improved condition of the ranges and the excellent condition of stock of all kinds is reassuring to the stockman." Dudley didn't tell the newsman that these same conditions were also a disadvantage to stockmen because the loss of even a few of his herd to the elements, wild beasts or human thieves could cause financial damage to the rancher. Lincoln County sheep, Dudley also reported, were "shearing 8½ lbs. per head, and the flocks are in excellent condition."[99] It would seem that Lincoln County had more outlaw prospects than the Bootheel.

In June, weather was still playing havoc with the mounted police's scout duty in Lincoln County. The rains made the area seem like the tropics without the mosquito netting. The Salado, Bonito and Ruidoso rivers were at flood tide and were "doing great damage to ranches along their courses."[100] Will Dudley was finally able to make a lone scout through the Sacramento Mountains and found sign of illegal activity. A few weeks later he joined Fate Avant for a ride across Lincoln County. Their hard work finally produced a suspect and the two rangers were ready to make the arrest. A few days after the arrest, Dudley reported to Captain Fullerton that the livestock owner "would not file [a] complaint and we had a circle. He must have been fixed for he reported to us after we caught his man he would not prosecute."[101]

Comida para Dos — A Meal for Two

For many people, the "sport" of dog fighting and cockfighting are cruel and inhumane events indulged in by the low class of society. Today dog fighting is a felony in 46 states and a misdemeanor in the other four, while cockfighting is illegal in all states, except in Louisiana and nine counties in New Mexico. The cockfight is staged in a pit and is a fight-to-the-death match between similarly sized roosters. These fighters usually wear gaffs or small knives tied to their legs and they try to cut their opponent to death. Cockfighting and dog fighting have been called the worst kind of cruelty to animals, because they're done for excitement and gambling. Cockfighting has even been labeled a "sport of honor" because "being game" is more important than winning the fight, thus the name gamecock fighting. To the fighting bird trainers and dog trainers, these bloody "honor sports," and their fight winnings, are their way of life. In most states the animal and bird fighting laws are rarely enforced and if they are enforced judges rarely give heavy fines or jail sentences to the purveyors.

Late one afternoon, Avant and Dudley heard the noise of a cockfight coming from inside an old dilapidated barn near a small Mexican settlement. The onlookers, including women and children, gave only slight notice as the rangers rode up to the scene because almost everyone had a bet on the outcome of the bloody match that ended with both roosters dying in a bloody pool. Avant decided to change his trail menu that night, so he bought the mangled body of the biggest rooster from the former owner. The two territorial policemen then made a camp near the barn and Avant set about cleaning his chicken for supper. Dudley disapproved of cockfighting, but he didn't disapprove of eating some of Avant's spit-cooked chicken.[102]

A disheartened Will Dudley left Avant the next morning and made a swing northeast toward Tucumcari. In Quay County, he located a stolen horse, but he could not locate a horse thief suspect. The long days in the saddle and the cold camps had begun to take their toll on the former schoolteacher, so Will loaded his horses and pack gear on the Rock Island Railroad and headed for a soft bed in his Alamogordo home. While the train halted at the water stop in Jarilla, Dudley discovered a man called Hudson that he suspected was a fugitive, so he arrested him on suspicion. Will was correct in his judgment of the man and he was later able to identify him as W. L. Smith. The man was in the mining camp hiding from a warrant issued in the state of Kansas charging him with rape. Smith was soon returned to the Prairie State to face a judge and jury.[103]

Broken Glasses

Veteran county lawman John Brophy had been assigned to Baca's squad, but he seems to have been another ranger who misunderstood the nature of the new mounted police and distance precluded the lieutenant from giving active leadership to Brophy. Distance also kept him from joining the Four Corners scout. Captain Fullerton wanted his men in the field actively seeking out livestock thieves and he also wanted to know what his men were doing with their time. In short, he wanted a full-time commitment. Captain Fullerton wrote Ranger Brophy in early July 1905. "Please let me know how you are getting along and if there is any thing doing [in your area]. It has been sometime since I heard from you."[104] It took John Brophy a few more weeks to catch the ranger spirit, but when he did John proved to be an effective territorial peace officer.

John Brophy visited Tucumcari to attend the summer session of the district court and to visit with his good friend Quay County Sheriff Alex Street. Brophy may have eaten something that disagreed with him while visiting in the town formerly known as Six-Shooter Siding, because he spent a few days in early July bedridden, suffering from some kind of trouble with his bowels or liver.[105] Maybe he had time to reflect upon the economic future of a new business that rented a "gasoline launch" for fishing or pleasure trips on Springer Lake or the new breed of enterprising Indians that were now personally selling their crafts in front of the Santa Fe depot at Albuquerque. The old ways were changing, but was it progress?

A short time later, John felt well enough to return to his mounted police duties, so he rode up to Folsom and arrested Ike Bass upon a true bill issued by the Union County grand jury. John didn't want to take Bass to jail, so he tried to help his prisoner secure the money needed to post a court appearance bond for the cattle stealing charge. Bass and Brophy visited the suspect's friends and family to seek their support for his bond, but Bass had no luck in raising any of the needed bond money.

Finally, Ike became so frustrated that he vented his anger upon Brophy. Bass hit John in the face and broke his glasses, which caused Brophy several ugly face wounds. John was quick to subdue his prisoner and just as quickly took him to the county jail at Clayton with an additional charge of assault upon a peace officer.[106]

The Shootout at Capitan

Livestock crimes were not the only cases investigated by Fullerton's Rangers, as shown by one of Fate Avant's duty reports. In July, Avant took into custody Robert Russie and charged him with "house breaking" at Capitan. The young man was escorted to the county seat at Lincoln to await his preliminary hearing before the local justice of the peace.[107] Sometime during the evening of the same day that Avant took Russie to the Lincoln County jail an accused arsonist escaped from that same jail. The man was Robert Rusher and on Wednesday morning Deputy Sheriff Phil Blanchard was in Capitan looking for the escapee. The Capitan *News* remarked that Rusher had "left jail, without hobbles, or bell, and without any instructions to the sheriff about forwarding his mail."[108] Five years earlier, the Santa Fe *New Mexican* had called the Lincoln County jail "a good one, better than found in most of the counties of the Territory."[109] What had happened in those intervening years? Had the jail building not been maintained for security or had the current jail guards just become lackadaisical in their duty?

L. F. Avant in a picture taken from his wedding photograph, made in San Antonio, Texas, circa 1881 (courtesy of Jettie Avant Sullenger).

Avant's field report for the first week in August was upbeat. "I saw one of the parties yesterday that we were expecting to catch ... says he has quit [stealing cattle], he is scared [I'll catch him]. I believe his intention is to leave the country. We can not arrest him on any charge yet as we have no evidence against him." Fate also said the cattle stealing had stopped and that the "noted thieves" were packing up and heading for new vistas. "One went about 2 weeks ago and 2 more of them are going today from Capitan." The ranger's final comment was "sent me cartridges to Capitan."[110] Ranger Avant's next report seemed to reflect a frustration with his "Operation at Capitan." Fate told Captain Fullerton about his fruitless all-night stakeout at the Welch & Titsworth Store. Avant also explained his pre-dawn patrol's trying to trap some of the remaining local stock thieves. Neither of these efforts had yet produced results.[111]

For four days during this stakeout period, E.B. Welch, George Titsworth's partner from El Paso, and his friend T.H. Rogers were visiting the Capitan area. The countryside was a beehive of excitement because the Baptists' annual camp meeting revival was in full swing a few miles south of Capitan along the Rio Bonito at the village of Angus.[112]

George Titsworth was one of Capitan's community leaders and he was a visionary businessman. He lived in a large, two-story house a block west of his store. His store was a single level building with a high pitched roof running down the center length and he had bicycles hanging from these center rafters. Each week he offered his patrons a chance to win a prize from the store. Each dollar of purchase earned a chance on the weekly prize. This contest boosted store sales and kept return business. Titsworth was also very liberal with his store credit, but he was not beyond seizing property if the high interest credit payments were not kept current. He eventually foreclosed on many of the old Spanish homesteads in the area. One present day Capitan resident remembers, when she was a young girl, how her relatives lost their heritage to the mercantile company. "Mr. Titsworth was such a churchman, but he was not a nice man to our family. I'm sure the meek and lowly Jesus would not have approved of him."[113]

Three days after Avant mailed his weekly report to Socorro, he got more excitement than he ever dreamed about experiencing. August 22, 1905, began as a normal Tuesday in the high mountain country around Coalora. Fate Avant was at home resting from his past week spent in the saddle when his son Bundy rushed into the house to tell him that he had found a VV branded cow tied up in the Avants' north pasture. The ranger suspected that his slippery cattle rustler neighbors were planning their latest move, so he was going to be there to catch them in the act.

About sundown, three men riding in a hack drove up to the staked out cow. One man got out of the wagon and hit the cow in the head to kill it. All three then joined in the skinning process, while Avant watched the butchers from his hiding place. Soon, a fourth man rode up to join the group. Avant decided it was time to make the arrest. Captain Fullerton described the gang's arrest to the governor, in a very concise report, "These [men] were caught red-handed and in the act of killing beef. A running fight ensued there being five [four] of the thieves—upward of twenty-five shots being fired."[114]

The Capitan *News* reported the incident with a little more excitement. "He [Avant] jumped up from his hiding place, threw down on them and ordered them to hoist their hands." One man quickly complied, but the other three "responded with rifles, after taking refuge in the weeds and underbrush. However, the policeman worked his 30–30 in such a scientific manner that, if they didn't, 'like the Arab', fold their tents, they 'silently stole away.' This was a pretty risky affair for the policeman, yet Avent's [sic] muzzle is just the color to indicate that when once started he was enlisted for the war."[115] Bundy Avant was with his father that day and told of the adventure over 70 years later. "Father raised up from our hiding place and told the [four] men to put their hands up, that they were under arrest. The bullets went to flying but as we had the protection of the canyon bank, the men soon saw it was the better [part] of valor to surrender."[116]

Fate Avant was able to arrest Abran Miller and Severo Perez and he charged both men with cattle stealing, in a preliminary hearing, before Justice J. A. Haley. He placed the two men in jail upon their failure to post a $50 bond each. Avant turned over to the court the hack and team, a rifle and a bottle of whiskey. The Angus VV Ranch kept the dead cow and the hide.[117] The Santa Fe *New Mexican* bragged, "Private Lafayette Avent [sic] of the mounted police, stationed in Lincoln County, is evidently the right man in the right place at the right time. There will be less cattle stealing in Lincoln county if Private Avent's [sic] station is not changed."[118]

Two days after the canyon shootout Avant received a message from one of Capitan's 'lewd females' claiming that one of her "johns" was planning to rob the Welch & Titsworth General Store that evening. Avant passed the word to George Titsworth and the two men hid in the store after closing to await the arrival of the thief. This was the second time the two men had spent pre-dawn hours at the large merchandise store in anticipation of a robbery.

Avant had described that first stakeout to Captain Fullerton in his August 9 report to mounted police headquarters. "I had information that a certain party who was in jail at Lincoln [about 10 miles southeast of Capitan] and was allowed the liberty of a cook intended to breakaway from jail and come to Capitan and break into this store. This prisoner did get away from [the] Lincoln jail and was away one day and was captured by a ranchman and taken back to jail that evening."[119] Thus Avant spent a long night and no attempt had been made to rob the store.

The Alamogordo *News* narrated the story of Avant's second watchful night at the Capitan store. The paper told how Fate Avant and George Titsworth "secreted themselves in the store to await the burglar. In due time the thief entered [via a side window] and was ordered to hold up his hands but instead of obeying the officer's command he proceeded to empty a six shooter, shooting at random in the dark room and without touching either the Ranger or Mr. Tittsworth [sic]." The newspaper said Avant, hiding in the dark, had an advantage over the burglar because the would-be bad-man stood under the dome of a skylight.[120] "Buckshot, as well as pistol balls were soon flying thick and fast," reported the Capitan *News*. "Ten buckshot took effect on [Robert] Rusher's body, and he fell near the front of the store, and his body was found face downward, a 32-calibre pistol grasped in his right hand, all six of the chambers empty."[121]

The Las Vegas *Daily Optic*'s "special correspondent" datelined its account August 25, via Santa Fe, and wrote that Rusher had fired at Avant after being ordered to surrender. "This was answered by a load of buckshot, from a gun in the hands of the officer, which put and end to the earthly career of another desperate criminal." The *Optic* account added the fact that Rusher's pistol was a "double action gun" and that he continued to fire it after being hit by Avant's buckshot. The report concluded by saying that Avant had "demonstrated the cool judgment and undoubted valor so essential in an officer. Lincoln county may well feel proud of such an officer." The subheading for the story said, "One Criminal Dead and Several Missing as Result of Efforts of Young Man to Enforce Laws Against Cattle Stealing."[122] Avant must have felt flattered to be called a "young man" because he was three months short of his fiftieth birthday.

Avant had remembered the words of Captain Fullerton when he had told his men that some of the outlaws that they would face "are well equipped with arms and ammunition and will fight if they have half a chance so do not risk one movement" but shoot to kill. Attorney General George W. Prichard, in Opinion 252, had also ruled that the mounted police "may use sufficient force, in making arrests, where resisted, to effect his purpose."[123] When the coroner's jury examined the body, the next morning, they found five finger rings and four pocket knives, with the Welch and Titsworth's mark, in Rusher's pocket. The inquest found that Rusher death "was justifiable homicide, and that the deceased met his death while resisting lawful arrest."[124]

The Capitan *News*, "A Journal Devoted to the Interest of Lincoln County," concluded its front page report on the Rusher killing and the official inquest by saying, "The county has been rid of a desperate, dangerous character, and the parties responsible for his taking off, and the manner surrounding the homicide deserve and receive the heartiest commendation of the citizens of the county."[125] Robert Rusher was unceremoniously buried, at county expense, in an unmarked grave in the Capitan Cemetery.[126]

Unfortunately for the history of Fullerton's Rangers any mounted police report that Avant may have filed concerning the Rusher shooting affair is not now a part of the official records. Historians have no firsthand account of Avant's feelings concerning the shooting incident. It would seem, from their inquest testimony, that George Titsworth joined Avant in returning Rusher's fire. However, the contemporary press makes it clear which man fired the fatal shotgun.

A Santa Fe *New Mexican* editorial seems to have caught the general feeling of citizens in the territory's rural areas. "It cannot be denied that the New Mexico Mounted Police are having a wholesome influence in repressing lawlessness in sections where police protection has been out of the question." The final comment concluded that the ranger service was of great value "in making known the fact that the days of desperadoism in New Mexico are of the past."[127]

Just to keep Avant's heroic actions in the proper focus, it should be noted that on the same day that the Capitan *News* lauded Avant's police actions they also published the county's delinquent tax list. It seems that Avant owed Lincoln County $51.68 for the value of his personal property, plus $2.58 in late penalty and thirty-five cents for court costs. Avant, like most people, did not like to pay taxes. He was human after all.[128]

Within a few months Fate Avant had gone from a small rancher to a territorial ranger to a man-killer. There was no training course to prepare Avant for that transformation. The author has found no evidence to indicate that Avant ever publicly bragged about having killing Robert Rusher. It is doubtful that anyone in 1905 had any concept of what the medical profession today calls posttraumatic stress syndrome. Available evidence doesn't indicate that Avant ever suffered any lasting trauma from his two shootouts with men bent upon doing him severe bodily injury. Ranger Fate Avant's blazing gun had set the tone for the reputation of the infant New Mexico Mounted Police. People came to believe that the mounted police, like their Canadian namesake, would stand their ground and defend the law, if needed, with their life. L.F. Avant's action had set the pattern that the mounted police would give no quarter. He had been in two life and death shootouts in one week and this was a record that no other ranger would have the opportunity to equal. Captain Fullerton told the press that during their first five months of operation the rangers had made nearly 50 arrests, but that only Avant had "been called upon to spill blood in fulfilling their duties as guardians of the peace."[129]

The ranger from the Capitan country would spend nearly four more years with the mounted police. Territorial ranger records and contemporary newspaper accounts contain tales of Avant's many fearless arrests as he brought in wanted men accused of cattle, goat, sheep and horse theft, murder and arson. Fate Avant even made arrests for drunk and disorderly conduct and assault cases. However, at no other time would he ever again reach the zenith he had reached during that week in the late summer of 1905.

The Early Fall Patrols

Major diseases infected wide areas of the Sunshine Territory in the fall of 1905. The older section of Alamogordo and parts of Old Albuquerque reported cases of typhoid fever. The Alamo City had one death, while the Duke City recorded 15 cases of the fever; the water supply was the main suspect in both towns. Smallpox raised its head in Silver City, but was quickly contained. Both Isleta Pueblo and San Marcial, located along the Rio Grande above and below Socorro, suffered from an outbreak of screw worm. Gallup had a measles scare, and to the community's relief, the outbreak proved to be less dangerous than the local health officials had at first expected.[130]

Lieutenant Baca was unable to take the field for a few days in late May due to sickness in his family. On the other side of the territory sickness hit another ranger. Will Dudley felt he was only suffering from some type of fatigue, but discovered he was wrong when he landed in bed with the fever that hit many people in Otero County. Dudley became very ill and longed for Josie and the girls to come home. He had a slow, up and down recovery and was in a weakened condition for several weeks. Captain Fullerton wrote Fate Avant concerning Dudley's illness. "He will not be able to do much riding for a few days. There seems to be considerable work around in that country and I think it best for you to work together." Fullerton continued, "I will leave it to your own judgment as to the plans you may follow. I know that you will do the best you can."[131]

When Dudley was finally able to think about returning to work he discovered that he had lost his ranger's shield, so he had to have an Alamogordo jeweler make him a new badge. This new emblem of his legal authority, made with a special clasp, cost Will Dudley five dollars.[132] Will was not the only ranger to have the misfortune to lose a valuable tool of the police business. Lieutenant Baca lost his railroad passes. The next day a good citizen of Socorro found them and returned the lost cards to Baca. "A few little dodgers printed at the *Chieftain* office brought the passes to light in less than twenty-four hours," bragged the local press.[133]

A much improved Will Dudley was happy to once again take up the scout when he received a message from Avant asking him to come up to Capitan. Will shipped his saddle and camp pack on the train with him to Capitan, and then used some of Avant's horses for the patrol. The two rangers sent Captain Fullerton a joint message saying they were taking the field against the local long ropers. Dudley told Captain Fullerton that Avant still did not have any railroad passes "so I go out on the road and he writes me to come there [to the Capitan area]."[134] A happy ranger captain sent a quick reply. "Glad to hear from you both. Am also glad to hear that Private Dudly [sic] is better and able for duty again."[135]

A mounted police scout patrol often spent many nights around a campfire. Here the men discussed politics, sports and current events. Local newspapers contained accounts of the men who found a one pound diamond in South Africa, the Japanese naval victory over the Russians, the tornado that killed 87 people in Snyder, Oklahoma, and the 50 women who were burned to death in a shoe factory in Brockton, Massachusetts. The highlight discussion to have witnessed was most assuredly the debate over the Congressional proposal to build a federally funded settlement for the nation's lepers in New Mexico.[136]

During some of those lonely nights the rangers would entertain each other with readings, games, stories or skits. On one of their scouting trips together Dudley taught Avant a little ditty that was popular during that era.

> I come before you
> > to stand behind you,
> To tell you without doubt
> > something I know nothing about,
> One dark night
> > when the moon was bright,
> Two dead boys who were brothers
> > drew their swords and shot the other,
> A deaf and dumb policeman heard the noise
> > and came and shot the two dead boys.

It is easy to envision Dudley acting out this tale in the glow of a dying campfire. Avant seemed to like the ditty, because he passed Dudley's rhyme along to his family and they have passed the simple tale along to new generations.[137]

Within days, Avant and Dudley had scored. Will Dudley's field report covering this roundup reads, "I have made one arrest and one assist...."[138] A rough translation of this message would mean that each ranger claimed credit for an arrest. Once again Dudley asked Captain Fullerton for a war council. He wanted the meeting "so we can have a talk about our work in these parts."[139] Fullerton suggested the men meet in Santa Fe for the "war council" so that Governor Otero could be informed of the plan. Sergeant Lewis was placed in command of the strike force composed of Mounted Policemen Avant, Dudley and Brophy.

Almost before the rangers could take the field the Albuquerque *Evening Citizen* reported on the territorial lawmen's planned mission. The paper said that Sergeant Lewis left Socorro "with sealed instructions from Captain Fullerton" and headed his squad east toward Lincoln County. "Lincoln County is supposed to be the rendezvous of a band of cattle thieves and this pilgrimage may have more than passing significance with this fact."[140] The *Citizen*'s report proved to be correct and a week later the mounted police raid was over and the arrested suspects went to jail to await the action of a grand jury. Brophy and Avant returned to their homes while Dudley boarded the train to Socorro, via El Paso, with Sergeant Bob Lewis. After spending a couple of days at ranger headquarters, Dudley took the morning train south to El Paso and then later that afternoon he took the coach up to Alamogordo.[141]

The Hunt for the Magnum Brothers

The Socorro *Chieftain* had once said, "Sergeant Bob [Lewis] has had a great deal of experience in dealing with fugitives from justice and it is a sorry day for such characters when he strikes their trail."[142] Once the success of Fullerton's Rangers became common conversation among ranchers and businesses, the requests for their services became overwhelming. "I haven't enough men for the amount of work, am having calls most every day," Fullerton wrote to W. C. Barnes, secretary for the cattle sanitary board. "Men are all busy and doing well." Fullerton then thanked Barnes for some information. "I have known of the [cattle] stealing in the vicinity of Gallup and the lumber camps for some time and think that with your assistance, in time, we can put these cattle thieves out of business."[143]

In another letter to Barnes, Fullerton promised to help ranchers in McKinley County "providing the stockmen will furnish them [the rangers] with extra good horses, as it is too far to ride and would take to [*sic*] much valuable time." The McKinley County ranchers agreed to furnish the mounted police horses, so Fullerton assured Barnes that if he "can possibly get away, [I] will go up with them."[144]

Lieutenant Baca had been prepared to lead his squad into the Bootheel until two unexpected occurrences changed the master plan. First, Baca's wife became ill and he was needed at home. Secondly, real rustlers became very active in the northwestern part of the territory. Finally, Baca and Rangers Meyer and Perea were able to begin their extended patrol after the fast moving rustlers. The three men were prepared for a long trail and Captain Fullerton sent extra supplies to his men. He ordered an Albuquerque mercantile store to "ship by [railroad] express 100 rounds of 30–40 soft nose cartridges, 100 rounds of 30–40 steel jackets, also two boxes of Colts .45 to Cipriano Baca [at] Ft. Wingate N. M." The captain knew his rangers would need all their cash for personal supplies so he added, "Please prepay the express and send [the] bill to me." Fullerton issued Voucher #38 for $18 payable to the Whitney Company to cover the cost of the ammunition he had sent to Grant County.[145]

Baca seemed to always have a book with him and on this trip he had Owen Wister's novel *The Virginian*. You can almost envision Baca reading the book to Meyer and Perea and the trio discussing the tale over a beer and some tamales. For weeks, Meyer would end his conversations with, "Smile when you call me that." Perea tried to teach the squad how to sing "In the Shade of the Old Apple Tree" like a barber shop trio, but Baca couldn't stay in tune. While they were on this long stakeout duty Meyer taught Perea the fine art of shooting marbles and finally won back his poker losses.[146]

A Mounted Police mountain scout. This photograph was in the mounted police collection assembled by Fred Lambert. The ranger leading the pack horses is believed to be Octaviano Perea, who was on a long scout with Julius Meyer and Lieutenant Baca. Baca had taken a Kodak camera with him on this scout (courtesy of the Fred Lambert Collection).

For a time the rangers had traveled north toward the Mormon community of Farmington along the old trade road that became U.S. 666 in the 1940s. The two-lane rural highway was nicknamed the "Highway to Hell" or "Satan's Highway" due to the reference in the Book of Revelation to the number name of the beast of the world's Last Days. After a decade of protest by the spiritually centered Navajos, the road designation was changed to U.S. 491 in the summer of 2003.[147] The Navajo Indian Reservation stretches for miles along the New Mexico–Arizona boundary running south from the Four Corners region down toward Gallup. Baca discovered the now famous Navajo rugs and blankets on this trip and bought one of these intricately designed rugs for Mary and a large blanket for himself. These were made by hand on the looms at Teec Nos Pos.

During their three months in northwestern New Mexico, Baca's squad was able to see some of the area's natural wonders and ancient settlement ruins. San Juan County is a contrast between the Nacimiento Badlands with it grotesquely shaped terrain of mesas, cliffs, canyons and the plateaus, low hills and open range country along the San Juan, Animas and La Plata rivers. Angel Peak is the sentinel for the Wastelands formed millions of years ago by a long ago vanished inland sea. The ancient Anasazi Indian ruins at Aztec, Chaco Canyon and Salmon provided excellent hiding sites for rustled cattle. San Juan County was also a vast agricultural oasis with large, fragrant orchards and abundant crops. The area was the backdrop for numerous conflicts between cattlemen and homesteaders. Today the region has a

The mounted police bring a prisoner to justice. This photograph was in the collection assembled by Fred Lambert. This group picture is believed to be Lieutenant Baca (riding beside the prisoner) with Rangers Perea and Meyer as they bring in one of the Magnum brothers. Note that the prisoner has on handcuffs (courtesy of the Fred Lambert Collection).

renewed life endowed with oil, natural gas and coal reserves large enough to supply the nation's needs for generations.

"Lieutenant Cipriano Baca of the New Mexico Mounted Police earns his salary," a newspaper proclaimed in a dispatch detailing Baca's actions. It said the rangers "had trailed the Magnum brothers, with 100 head of stolen stock, from Ramah [in southern McKinley County] to Bloomfield [in northern San Juan County] and had corralled the stock and captured the Magnums. If the report is correct, this is a very important capture, as the Magnums are known as desperate cattle rustlers." The report proved to be accurate and the Silver City *Independent* called the Magnums "a terror to the neighborhood in which they operated and have for some time past been running off stock and terrorizing ranchers." During this sojourn in San Juan County, Baca worked with two future mounted police; Sheriff Boone Vaughn and Territorial Cattle Inspector Rhea Stewart.[148]

Baca, Perea and Meyer had been on the scout for three months trailing these outlaw brothers. "Captain Fullerton is to be congratulated upon having in his service such men as Baca [and his squad]," commented the *San Juan Index*.[149] Rangers Julius Meyer and Octaviano Perea were not listed in many of the newspaper stories concerning the Magnum brothers' arrests, nor were they mentioned in most of the official reports. These two mounted police, however, did quality undercover work and were an important part of the successful San Juan County operation.

It would seem that Captain Fullerton's strategy of reassigning Perea worked because two months after he was sent on scout duty to the Four Corners area, a Durango, Colorado, newspaper headlined a short story, "Mounted Policeman Perea Makes Arrest." The report concluded that "Mr. Perea appears to be a man well chosen for his work, that of a mounted police or range rider." The *San Juan Index* agreed with the Colorado paper that Perea was a fine officer and wished him well. "May the good work go right on."[150]

During the extended absence of his three rangers, Captain Fullerton kept a watchful eye on the families of Baca, Meyer and Perea. Fullerton gave Mrs. Perea $25 to help her and her children with family needs, while he also deposited $55 at Price Brothers Store in Socorro so that Mary Baca could feed her family. He once wrote Libby Meyer just to reassure her that Julius was "all O.K." The captain would forward personal mail to the wives that he had received from his men and he often enclosed family letters along with his official communiqués to Lieutenant Baca.[151]

John Fullerton was not physically on location in the San Juan Basin with his rangers, but he was with them in spirit and supported them with supplies and encouragement. Fullerton and the Magnum brothers never met, but the shadow of these rustlers' misdeeds was to cast its evil over the destiny of the mounted police and the integrity of their captain.

The Claude Doane Dragnet

Claude Doane and his pal Jose Baca were the most wanted men in New Mexico during the summer of 1905. The former convicts were being hunted for horse and cattle stealing, plus the murder of a McKinley County schoolteacher. Day after day the dragnet got tighter around the fugitives, as most of the lawmen in central New Mexico actively joined the hunt for the elusive duo and the chance to collect the handsome reward.

The Las Vegas *Daily Optic* headline said, "Horse Thieves Make A Raid," and told how the Doane gang had stolen some horses from a ranch near Albuquerque. Sheriff Hubbell and a deputy had trailed the gang to an isolated location, but found the encampment well fortified; they got back in their buggy and returned to the Duke City empty handed. "A posse was at once organized, headed by Captain H.S. [sic] Fullerton of the New Mexico mounted police and it has gone after the rustlers." The report also said, "The horse thieves are all heavily armed and are expected to put up a hard fight when over taken." Fullerton told his men "do not give him [Doane] any chance what ever as I have orders from our chief [the governor] to kill him on sight," so it was fortunate for both Doane and Jose Baca that the territorial police were not located in the right area to get them.[152]

In early July, Doane and Baca were finally cornered and captured by veteran manhunters Fred Fornoff and Ben Williams—using a tip provided to them from a mounted police informant—at a ranch house on the river at the mouth of the Rio Grande Canyon near Embudo. The outlaws were trying to exchange their tired mounts for fresh horses when they were captured. The bounty hunters took their prisoners to Santa Fe, collected the reward money, and made no acknowledgement of the assistance provided by the rangers. "The good work of Ben Williams and Fred Fornoff in landing the outlaws, Doane and Baca, is worthy of very favorable commendation," a newspaper account read. Fornoff and Williams basked in the public praise, while the mounted police continued the dull job of collecting the vital physical evidence that would be needed to build a strong court case against the two fugitives.[153]

Ranger Dick Huber had spent over a week in Bernalillo County rounding up stolen horses that Doane's rustler gang had driven into that county for resale to the local ranchers. Most of these animals were ultimately returned to their rightful owners. "Mr. Huber has done some very clever work on this case and the conviction of Doane will be in a great measure due to his hard work," said the Albuquerque *Morning Journal*.[154] Claude Doane was a veteran of the territorial prison, having served two years at Santa Fe for cattle theft and another four years, with a $500 fine, for horse theft. Huber's "hard work" paid dividends during the November 1905 murder trial when Doane pleaded guilty and received a 90 year prison sentence that was later commuted by the governor to 25 years.[155]

Meanwhile...

Western Socorro County, present day Catron County, was an area of high sagebrush grazing land and rugged mountain canyons. In the Mogollon Mountain range, ponderosa pine, pinon and juniper trees cover the slopes. Miners gave life to towns like Mogollon, Alma and Clear Creek. Ranch trading posts like Quemado, Patterson and Datil were located along the Magdalena Cattle Drive Trail that originated in Arizona. The route was nicknamed the "Beefsteak Trail" or the "Hoof Highway" and operated from the early 1880s well into the 1950s. During the peak year of 1919 nearly 22,000 cattle and 150,000 sheep were driven over the trail that today is roughly U.S. 60 from Quemado to Magdalena.

In the early fall of 1905, Sergeant Lewis took a trip to his old homestead and visited the "locals" at the bar in Frisco, near present day Reserve. Here he learned that the stills were operating in Moonshine Canyon. The whiskey makers were area farmers who found it easier — and more profitable — to convert their grain into liquor then to freight it to market. Bob made a raid on the stills, but did not find anyone working that day, so he headed up to the Beefsteak Trail where he found the tracks of some wandering cattle. A week into his patrol, Lewis met Ranger Bob Putman on his maiden scout tracking a suspected horse thief.

The two rangers teamed up and a few days later they found Putman's suspect and arrested him. The 27-year-old Jose Lozano, a married cowhand with two small sons, was taken to Socorro for a preliminary hearing.[156] His plea, at his trial before District Judge Frank W. Parker, was not guilty, but the jury did not agree with him and he was sentenced to one year in the territorial prison. Lozano had a "scar from bite of dog on inside left thigh." He was released 36 days early, on November 16, 1906, due to "good time."[157]

Public Duty

In his autobiography George Curry, territorial governor from August 8, 1907, to February 28, 1910, wrote a concise account of the political turmoil among the leadership of New Mexico's Republican Party in 1905. He clearly defined the factions and their power struggle. "In the feud between Otero and [Frank] Hubbell, the Governor won the first battle."

Frank A. Hubbell was a wealthy Bernalillo County sheep owner, the political boss of the county, and was a member, and some times chairman, of the Republican Territorial Central Committee. He was a friend of Otero's bitter antagonist Thomas Benton Catron. Curry wrote: "His brother Tom Hubbell, a big jovial man and a tower of strength in the Hubbell county machine, had been sheriff for a number of terms. He was charged with padding fees and expenses of feeding prisoners in the county jail. Frank Hubbell, then county assessor, was charged with favoritism to Albuquerque merchants in 'fixing' their assessments in return for political support. The Hubbell machine had elected Eslavio Vigil, boss of the suburban precinct of Barelas, as county school superintendent. Vigil, while an honest man and a good citizen, was wholly unqualified for the job. Even his knowledge of the English language was quite limited." The Albuquerque *Morning Journal*, the territory's largest newspaper, called the group "The Hubbell Gang."[158]

The long hearing concerning charges of malfeasance in office by three of Bernalillo County's top elected officials finally came to a close on August 31. The three men appealed to Governor Otero the hearing officers' recommendation that they each be dismissed from office. The governor reviewed all the testimony and the evidence and upheld the results of the misconduct review commission. He ordered that the three public employees be removed from their offices and that the hearing testimony be turned over to the grand jury for any criminal charges. In accordance with the duty of his office, Otero appointed a new county treasurer, a new county school superintendent and a new sheriff for Bernalillo County. This executive action was challenged by the three ousted "public servants" in a legal action before the territorial courts. The court ruled that the governor's action was legal and proper and ordered the men to give up their courthouse keys and leave their former duties to their successors.[159]

In Arizona and Texas the rangers had been used by the governor to enforce unpopular court orders issued against workers in labor conflicts and poll tax enforcement in elections. These actions had not made the rangers very popular among the "common man" or native populations, so some of the territorial police where concerned that Otero might call upon them to go to the Duke City to help place Perfecto Armijo in charge of the sheriff's office. These men believed that Armijo was a good choice to be the county's chief lawman, he had served as sheriff of Bernalillo County from 1878 to 1884, but they were apprehensive about the rangers becoming involved in what some felt was a local political matter that was best handled by local people.

Fullerton kept Baca updated concerning Tom Hubbell's refusal to vacate the Bernalillo County sheriff's office to his appointed successor. "I understand that the

County Commissioners will not pay any of the jail expense from the time Profecto [sic] Armijo was sworn in [as the new sheriff]." In a half joking comment Fullerton added, "Tom Hubbell will have quite a bill to pay in keeping up the jail."[160] The captain assessed the situation and told his men, "I don't expect we will have a call [from the governor] to settle matters there."[161] Fullerton's prediction proved to be right. Tom Hubbell finally accepted the fate of his removal from his post and vacated the sheriff's courthouse office and the jail. A Bernalillo County grand jury ultimately indicted the three former county officials for a number of crimes; however, none of these men were ever tried in a court of law for any of their alleged crimes. The Hubbells did lose their bid to be reelected to public office.

Four factors controlled the very nature of Miguel Otero; friendship, politics, ego and public accountability. Each of these four factors held equal importance to the governor. This time public accountability overruled friendship; Tom Hubbell had been a member of the governor's fishing party just three weeks before the governor removed him and his brother from office. The Hubbell family never forgave Otero for what they considered to be a personal insult and used their wealth and influence to help deny Otero another term as governor.

During these three months of uncertainty Captain Fullerton had been in and out of Bernalillo County almost weekly assisting area lawmen and keeping current on the local political climate. During his many overnight stops in Albuquerque, Captain Fullerton took the opportunity to visit with his sister and her family and his son Elmer. Also during this time, John was able to complete some personal business with the sale of a moving transfer business that he owned in the Duke City. This divestiture enabled him to repay some outstanding debts and provide himself with a better financial outlook for the near future.[162] Fullerton had an overdue bank note and an overdrawn checking account at his Albuquerque bank during the fall of 1905. John was also late with a monthly payment to his friend Holm Bursum, the prison warden, who was selling him a horse.[163]

Kidnap Rumors

Socorro's massive Windsor Hotel caught fire in mid-July, and the whole business section of the county seat was in danger of being consumed in the inferno. Fullerton had joined the town's fire brigade and helped to save the business district, including the mounted police office in the Chambon Building, from destruction. In a happier business matter, the Arizona–New Mexico Internal Revenue District reported that the two territories had a record $80,343.00 tax revenue year and this helped the government coffers.

The same ex-convict informant that had told Fullerton where to locate Doane and Baca also warned him about a plot by Doane confederates to kidnap Governor Otero's son. The plan was for Doane to organize a gang of ex-convicts to capture young Miguel and to hold him captive in the wilds of the Carrizozo Malpais (badlands) lava flows of western Lincoln County, present day Valley of Fires State Park, until the governor paid a large ransom and did some other things that Doane would also demand. Otero was told of the kidnap plan and he took precautions, including telling the press about the plot, to protect his son until the gang was captured.[164] The kidnap threat subsided after Doane's arrest, so the governor and his friends H.O. Bursum, territorial prison warden, and Bernalillo County Sheriff Tom Hubbell planned a fishing trip at the Otero ranch.[165]

Captain Fullerton spent Tuesday and Wednesday, August 8 and 9, in Santa Fe. Each afternoon he had a meeting with Governor Otero. The two men discussed the Claude Doane and Jose Baca cases, the plot to kidnap the governor's son, the hunt for the Magnum brothers, and the livestock theft investigation in the central part of the territory, as well as other mounted police business. On Thursday afternoon Otero and his outing party took the train for Las Vegas. Otero claimed that later that night Judge Henry Waldon called at his residence and the old family friend told the governor that his son was in real danger. The judge said that he had just returned from Glorieta and conveyed a tale told him by a woman who worked at the Red Cliff House, a lodge on the Pecos River, about raiding bandits searching for the governor or his son. Governor Otero became very concerned about these new rumors that an outlaw gang was going to kidnap his son.[166] Young Miguel, his Uncle Page,[167] who was the territorial game warden, and Page, Jr., had spent a few days fishing on the Upper Pecos River and staying at the Red Cliff House lodge. The governor had picked up Miguel, Jr., during a stop at Glorieta that afternoon, and the boy had accompanied his father to Las Vegas.

Following his uncle's death in 1933, Miguel wrote his Aunt Lottie, "I recall the old days here [in Santa Fe] and the many good times I had with Uncle Page, especially on the famous fishing trip to the red house on the Pecos which we took years ago at a time when Page Jr. and I were both little kids. Page Jr. probably remembers the episode where we killed the chickens and received some heavy discipline at the hands of Uncle Page."[168] This is one of those letters where historians wish that the writer would have included a bit more information. What about the chickens? It would seem that a young boy's fishing trip still held strong memories even three decades after the events.

To really understand the governor's innermost fear concerning his son, a person must first understand the personal side of the governor. "Gillie" Otero always felt he had married above his social status in 1888 when he wed Caroline Virginia Emmett, the daughter of a Minnesota state supreme court justice. The couple had three children; two boys and a girl. The oldest boy, Miguel III, died young and in January 1901 the Oteros lost their seven month old daughter, Elizabeth. The governor had trouble dealing with his grief and privately began to abuse alcohol, so that after three years of marital discord the Oteros separated early in 1904. Otero wrote a massive three volume autobiography, but only wrote a few lines about his first wife and nothing about their daughter. Governor Otero had named his second son Miguel A. Otero IV and after his split from Mrs. Otero the governor became very protective of the boy. The Oteros divorced in October 1909.

Governor Otero notified Fullerton about the threatened kidnapping and the captain rushed to Las Vegas with some of the rangers. Friday afternoon the governor told a Las Vegas reporter, "Captain Fullerton, of the mounted police, has assumed charge of the hunt for these men. He has in his posse Lewis, McGrath, Brophy, and other picked men. The Upper Pecos region will be thoroughly scoured and the men will be captured if possible." Thirty-five years after the Pecos River adventure, Governor Otero altered the facts and wrote, "I soon had reached several of the mounted police and appointed Charles Closson [a one time peace officer and at the time of the incident a livery stable owner in Santa Fe] in command, I sent them immediately on horseback to find Miguel and bring him home." Young Miguel was already with his father in Las Vegas.

Sergeant Lewis and Rangers Putman, Dudley, McGrath and Huber gathered at Glorieta for a tactical assessment with Captain Fullerton and they developed a search plan. Fullerton went down river to meet the governor's party at the Ribera train station a few miles north of San Miguel on the Pecos River. Fullerton then accompanied Otero, his son and Superintendent Bursum back to Santa Fe, while the other territorial lawmen rode all day and through a stormy night searching for the mysterious would-be kidnappers. It is interesting that contemporary newspapers make no mention concerning the whereabouts of Sheriff Hubbell during the excitement. At noon on Saturday, Fullerton met with the governor and updated him on the field investigation led by Sergeant Lewis. Years later Otero wrote, "The group of bandits must have heard the posse pass the house in which they were sleeping or protecting themselves from the rain, for they disappeared from sight."[169]

It would seem that Governor Otero's usually dependable memory failed him concerning this misadventure if an Albuquerque newspaper presented an accurate account. This editorial is a fine example of Victorian Era prose: "A great cock and bull story went out over the territory about a week ago, and was telegraphed to all parts of the country, to the effect that a desperate band of fierce and bearded land pirates, armed to the teeth, were scouring the Pecos woods with the diabolical intention of kidnapping our governor or, worse yet, of shooting him full of holes. Indeed the reports did not make quite clear just what it was they wanted to do with him or to him, but it was something too awfully awful to be talked about except in whispers."

According to this report some young men from Santa Fe, "inoffensive as little kittens," were camped near the lodge that housed the Otero family. One morning one of the "native boys" became ill after eating breakfast and wanted some "liquor for his stomach ache," so some of the group went to the lodge looking for Page Otero and the "medicine" for their sick friend. It should be noted here that Page Otero held the reputation of a man who enjoyed his "spirits" and thus the boy's belief that he might have some with him at the lodge.[170]

The part about armed men seeking one of the Otero family was true. The young campers were armed with their hunting weapons during the hikes to and from their camp. The rest of the story seems to have developed a life of its own. An Albuquerque newspaper account stated, "The mounted police, as well as the governor's own guard [led by Charles Closson], were sent for to scour the country for the 'kidnappers.' But, as you know, they failed to find them. The boys taken for kidnappers did not hear of their being the cause for the commotion until the country was full of mounted police and detectives and they availed themselves of their first opportunity to explain to some of the officers the circumstances resulting in the search for bandits. Since their return to Santa Fe some of the boys have gone to the governor and explained things." The editorial claimed "there was nothing, absolutely nothing, in that reported attempt to kidnap our little governor, and he and his comrades knew it, and that is why they say no more about it." [171]

A few days after the "rescue" assignment, Captain Fullerton gave the governor a final report on the rangers' investigation during an afternoon briefing session. Later that day, Fullerton told a Santa Fe reporter that his men had informed him "that there was no foundation for the stories which circulated" concerning a kidnap attempt on the governor's son in the Pecos River Forest Reserve.[172]

Otero always publicly stated that he believed his son had been in real danger during August 1905. Time has a way of confusing dates in a person's mind. Miguel Otero, in his autobiography, claimed the kidnap incident took place on August 17, but Dick Huber's field report clearly shows that the mounted police rode on the night of 11–12 August "from Santa Fe to Glorieta and return."[173] Otero may have been the most hands-on commander-in-chief concerning the operation of the mounted police during the territorial era, yet the "kidnapping incident" is his only reference to the police in his lengthy account of his nine year leadership of New Mexico's executive branch.

The Territorial Fairs

Handbills and newspaper advertisements proclaimed the twice-a-day exhibition between a horse and Whirlwind, "the wonderful trotting ostrich" from Hot Springs, Arkansas, as the highlight of the 25th annual territorial fair to be held at Albuquerque. Thomas Cockbarn's "big bird" was clocked at two and a half minutes over a two and half mile course and was a real challenge to any horse. The promotion also highlighted a baseball tournament, the stock show and the produce and crop exhibitions. Horse racing, bronco busting, Indian dancers and army cavalry drills were other fair attractions. The territorial fair committee had purchased 10,000 yards of green, cream and cardinal bunting to decorate the city for a festive atmosphere.[174]

The Grand Street Parade had become the fair's kickoff and it normally drew a large crowd of visitors to Albuquerque. Word quickly spread that the new mounted police would ride in the opening event and special trains brought the throng of visitors to the city. The rangers rode at the head of the fair's grand march and were seen, and judged, by the largest audience to that date ever gathered in the Duke City. Overnight the 1905 parade became a historical event: it was the first of only two times that the complete company of Fullerton's Rangers publicly appeared together.

It had taken a personal request from Councilman W.H. Greer, and a pledge from D.K.B. Sellers, secretary of the fair committee, to pay the rangers' travel expenses and to provide them with horses for the parade, before Governor Otero would ask Fullerton to muster the territorial police in Albuquerque.[175] The captain agreed with the governor's request, saying that the experience would be a nice "change for all the boys." John sent a company-wide order for all the rangers to gather in Socorro on September 19 so they could travel as a group to Albuquerque. Dick Huber was the odd man out and chose not to go to Socorro as ordered, but arrived in Albuquerque a day after the other rangers. He had spent the extra day searching for some missing sheep.[176]

The Albuquerque *Evening Citizen* told readers that the appearance of Fullerton's Rangers would "afford fair visitors an opportunity of judging for themselves whether this branch of the law is formidable or not." The paper concluded that the "verdict will most likely be in the affirmative."[177] Ranger John Brophy appeared at the parade still showing the results of the face wounds he suffered while he was subduing a prisoner. In addition to the mounted police, another highlight of the fair was a demonstration of a wireless telegraph system. A wireless message was sent between Albuquerque and Trinidad, Colorado, with no signal interference from the mountains in between.

The territorial fair committee had agreed to pay for the mounted police's hotel bill, but this promise quickly became a hot political issue. So many false claims were filed with the fair committee by hotel owners that Captain Fullerton was finally forced to intervene and help decide the true accounts that where due payment. The final bill for housing the rangers was $100.60 and if all these fake claims had been paid, it might have bankrupted the fair committee. No criminal charges were filed against the hotelkeepers for their "mistaken claims."[178]

In Albuquerque, the municipal court levied a $10 monthly fee on each prostitute who worked in the city's Red Light District. This "fine" helped to fund the city government, but even a good thing could be too much. It took 50 "special officers" plus the whole regular Duke City police force to remove the extra "ladies of the night" from the city following the close of the fair.[179]

Fullerton was not always conducting official police business. While in Albuquerque, John had a meeting with W.H. Greer and later that afternoon he wrote a personal letter to a man at Jamez. Greer had told Fullerton that he had borrowed some money from this Jamez man and had used his pistol as collateral. Now the man was refusing to return the weapon. Fullerton told the man to return the handgun to Greer, accept the payment and not to cause any more trouble. "If it is not at his office by that date [August 29], I will take the matter up with you and it will cost you considerable time, trouble and expense."[180] The pistol was returned before the requested time. This incident would not be the last time that a mounted police officer became an "enforcer" to help out a friend in need.

The next week the mounted lawmen were mustered for the Northern New Mexico Territorial Fair.[181] Representatives from the New Mexico Driving Park and Fair Association asked the governor and his new ranger force to appear in Otero's hometown. Fullerton and Otero discussed the regional fair during their visit on Saturday afternoon, September 2. The two men worked out the details for the Las Vegas muster, the projected budget request was conveyed to the fair committee and the arrangements were finalized for the mounted police to ride in the parade.[182] The northern fair followed the Albuquerque show, so the rangers first appeared in the Duke City even though the Las Vegas committee had been the first to arrange for the rangers' appearance.

The Santa Fe Baptist Association, the officers of the National Guard, the Grand Lodge of the Odd Fellows and the Grand Lodge of the Knights of Pythias were all meeting in Las Vegas during the fair dates. It was going to be a big party in the Meadows City. Will Dudley was a local celebrity and the popular ranger was elected the grand vice chancellor at the Knights of Pythias convention.[183] Other rangers pointed out among the crowd were the fast shooting Herb McGrath and Fate Avant.

The first day of the fair was clouded by a downpour and the Grand Floral and Industrial Parade was postponed a day, but the new parade day dawned as a wonderful, clear fall day. Governor Otero, with other territorial and local dignitaries, led the march followed by a large display of business floats with pretty girls waving to the assembled crowd. Finally, the third division came into view led by Troop A of the National Guard. The soldiers were followed by the local undertaker driving his new ambulance. "He was followed by the entire mounted police, who were liberally cheered," the local newspaper reported.[184] Fullerton's Rangers wore their new gray uniforms and full "battle gear" as they rode in the two fair parades. Captain Fullerton had bought each ranger a new gray hat for the occasion because some of the men had already "seasoned" their original issue hat.[185] The horsemen were led by Captain Fullerton with Lieutenant Baca and Sergeant Lewis leading their squads. One ranger carried a 45 stared national flag, while Dick Huber carried the Mounted Police flag.[186]

These two fair parades were the only times that the complete corps of Fullerton's Rangers was ever assembled at the same place at the same time. It would have been enlightening to have been a mouse in the corner silently observing as these eleven rangers took the measure of each other.

This silk 45 star United States flag (1890–1908) was carried by the mounted police during their company muster at the territorial fair at Albuquerque and the regional fair at Las Vegas, fall 1905.

The fairs had been a fun time for the rangers. Some of the men, like Sergeant Bob Lewis, brought their families with them to the festivities.[187] Ever so quickly the fun faded and duty called.

The New el Gorras Blancos

Some of the rangers, including Captain Fullerton, had already left Las Vegas before an urgent set of telegrams passed between the Meadows City and the City of Holy Faith. A fence cutting gang had struck in Guadalupe County and a brutal murder had been committed at Monero in Rio Arriba County. The governor's office had been requested, by local county officials, to send the mounted police to aide in both of the investigations.[188] Ranger Dick Huber was dispatched to Rio Arriba County to help Sheriff Benigo Cardenas Hernandez, while four of Fullerton's Rangers were headed south for the Bell Ranch.[189]

In June, the decomposed body of a man was found along the Canadian River near Tucumcari. The body had a bashed in head and was still unidentified at the time the fence cutters struck the ranch. Was this man a victim of the White Caps? What if anything had he seen that caused someone to kill him?[190] The Deming *Graphic* had added to the discussion in mid–August: "It is reported that a gang of lawbreakers, of from one-half to a dozen men, are at work in Central New Mexico stealing cattle and sheep and being ready for any devilish work that way turn up. The mounted police should go after this gang. That is the kind of work for which the police was organized. The *Graphic* would like to hear of good results in that line and will give due credit if they are obtained."[191]

In northern New Mexico, small ranchers, mostly of Spanish-Mexican heritage, were angry because the large ranchers, mostly Anglos, were fencing in land that they felt should remain open range for everyone's use. The Anglos claimed that they had rightly homesteaded the land and it was their property, while the Hispanics held that the land was a community range under terms of Spanish or Mexican land grants issued before New Mexico became part of the United States. To fight for their cause, these Hispanic ranchers became white hooded raiders and held midnight "devil's wire parties" as they cut down the hated fences.[192] "*Tierra o Muerte*— Land or Death" was the battle cry of open rebellion by *nuevomexicanos* in northern New Mexico in 1967. The armed conflict was finally quelled by the state police and the national guard. Nearly four decades later, the fight continues in state and federal courts and in the media. The fight this time is not against large, private land owners, but against the regulations of the large landowning United States Forest Service and its legion of faceless government bureaucrats.[193]

In September 1904, the *Gorras Blancos* (White Caps) again raided across San Miguel County, but this time it was different, because this time the mounted police took the field. Julius Meyer, Fate Avant, John Brophy and Will Dudley made a wide sweep through San Miguel and Guadalupe counties and the four man ranger patrol quickly located ten suspected *Gorras Blancos* and arrested them for illegal fence cutting. The men were taken to Las Vegas and lodged in the San Miguel County jail. The *Santa Fe New Mexican* proclaimed, "Every settler in those sections will breathe easier, and will bless the Thirty-sixth Legislature for enacting the Mounted Police law."[194]

In anticipation of possible trouble on the eastern ranges, Captain Fullerton sent Rangers Avant and Dudley a notice that he had employed an informant to assist them. "I will give him [William Pierce] a note to you so that you will know and understand the situation in which he is working under as he will have to be with these parties [cattle rustlers] in order to find out just what they are doing and he promises to keep you posted."[195]

William Pierce had been a former prison friend of Claude Doane. "I had a talk with him while in Albuquerque," Fullerton wrote to two of his men, "and Doan [sic] was caught through him getting the information for us." Bounty hunters Fornoff and Williams had caught Doane using the Pierce information and then they claimed the reward that Fullerton had promised to get for Pierce for his information.[196] It is uncertain how much help Pierce was to the mounted police in Lincoln County, but the records do contain a clear picture of another informant. Jose Sosteno Baca was an undercover spy within the Guadalupe County fence cutter ring. Governor Hagerman had given Fullerton strict orders, "I want everything to be done that possibly can be done properly by the territorial and county authorities, to put an end to this fence cutting. Nothing should be resorted to, however, which will in anyway open the mounted police, or any other territorial officials, to any criticism." Lieutenant Baca soon discovered that Jose Baca was really a double agent and told Captain Fullerton that "he was all wrong." Jose Baca had once presented himself as a mounted police and had used his "authority" to intimidate the people around the ranching community of Anton Chico. In short order, a real ranger arrested the fake ranger and sent him to jail.[197]

The Alamogordo *News* told its readers that "Ranger W.E. Dudley came in Friday morning from the northern part of the Territory where he has been on ranger duty for some time." While at home Will learned of his youngest sister's death. He was, however, unable to attend her East Texas funeral because he was called back to duty. "Ranger Dudley was up the road Wednesday night on official business and was caught in a snow storm."[198] Will Dudley was still not fully recovered from his summer bout with the fever, so this early winter weather did not help his recovery.

A new campaign by the fence cutters began in late September and the manager of the vast Bell Ranch wired Governor Otero about the depredations. "Eight miles of my pasture fence near *Bado* [*de*] *Jaun Pais* cut and destroyed. I anticipate further destruction. Please assist with Mounted Police."[199] An Albuquerque paper said, "Dudley left home ... expecting to be away four days. The job took him and his comrades six weeks, but it was successful. Fence cutting [is] a serious offense."[200] Even the best outdoorsman would have had trouble expanding the supplies for a four day trip into a 44 day expedition without having a re-supply point.

Will Dudley told an El Paso reporter that "the white caps in bands as large as twenty five are terrorizing that section, going about at night on their horses and themselves wrapped in sheets, cutting fences and posting notices that anybody undoing their work will be killed."[201] Dudley had told the truth, but his forthrightness was not appreciated by Captain Fullerton.

"I am very much surprised to think that you would give to the newspapers an article for publication of our work when it is not more than half finished," Fullerton wrote Dudley. "I wish you would be more careful hereafter and if there is anything published before the work is finished I want it understood that such publication should come through the office." Fullerton added a second thought. "We have obtained quite a little information about these fence cutters since this piece has been published about the White Caps of New Mexico. I don't object and rather think it is a benefit to us to have our work published when it is finished, but not before."[202] Dudley's reaction to Captain Fullerton's confusing message has not survived, but it was just this type of misdirection that caused some rangers to misunderstand their captain's wishes.

The mounted police kept after the *Gorras Blancos*. Putman and Meyer accompanied Sergeant Bob Lewis on an extended scout through Quay County. They covered the lands drained by the Conchas and Canadian rivers as the trio continued to search for additional clues as to the identity of the new fence cutters. Bob Putman was able to demonstrate his fishing skills and treat his companions to a supper of trout as they camped near the adobe ruins of Fort Bascom. While they were at this camp Bob Lewis was adding a log to the campfire when a hot spark injured his eye. "Hope your eye is better and [the injury] will not prove serious," wrote Fullerton to his sergeant.[203] Bob's eye needed to be covered with a patch for a few days, but Lewis did recover his sight. The Lewis patrol was not as lucky, because it ended with little new information for the rangers.

The *Gorras Blancos* hit-and-run raids continued off and on over the next nine years. Finally in 1914, Mounted Policeman Fred Lambert was able to locate the White Cap's secret meeting place and in a daring undercover mission discovered their plans. Lambert gathered enough evidence against the chief leaders of the night riders to finally break the back of the fence cutting gang's effort to disrupt the cattle industry in central New Mexico.[204]

Death on the "Upper River" and the Motor Stagecoach

Monero, named after the Italian word for money, was first settled in 1884 by a group of Italian coal miners seeking the "good life" in America. The dream lasted a few generations, but today the site is mostly home to ghosts. The settlement was built near the mine on the edge of the Apache Reservation and among the Hispanic farmers of the *Rio Arriba*, the Upper River Country. It was not racial tensions, labor unrest or social conflicts that brought bloody death to Monero. It was hard liquor and hard words. In 1905, most of New Mexico's 2,354 coal miners lived in company owned houses, shopped at the company store, labored long days and drank stiff whiskey to forget the unfulfilled dreams of their youth.

It had been almost a decade since the soil of the Upper River Country had been stained with blood and even Sheriff Hernandez[205] was unsure of how to handle the investigation of a murder in the fall of 1905. He asked the mounted police for help and Captain Fullerton assigned Ranger Dick Huber to the case. The manhunt consumed over two weeks of Huber's time as he ranged over the rugged Continental

Divide and the forest region along the Colorado border around Dulce. He even took the train up to Cumbres Pass to question railroad construction repair workers. No one had seen the phantom suspect. In anticipation that the murderer might try to escape to the south, Captain Fullerton ordered Herb McGrath to search the mountain mining camps in Socorro and Sierra counties. "Not a trace of the wanted man could be found," reported McGrath's hometown paper, "and the rangers finally concluded he had skipped the country."[206] When Ranger Huber finished his search in Rio Arriba County he took the narrow gage railroad down the Rio Grande and headed for home.

Some peace officers spend their total career and never have to deal with a murder investigation, but Dick Huber was not one of these officers. The sight of violent death affects individuals differently and it is hard to evaluate the effect this case may have had upon Huber. One thing is sure, he did not stay home very long. Dick may have needed a new challenge or just a solemn country ride, so he made a swing south through the Estancia Valley and was able to locate a suspected horse thief hiding out on an abandoned homestead. He also took in tow a man he charged with assault with intent to kill. Both of these men were bound over to the Torrance County grand jury for indictment.[207]

It may have been on this trip that Huber encountered the motor stagecoach on its run from Roswell across the rugged plains to the railroad junction at Torrance. The passenger and freight line service had started in May 1905, over a homemade road, with a large red and brass trimmed six-passenger Winton Model C. The auto made the one-way overland journey in nine hours, stayed over night in Torrance and returned to Roswell the next day. A one-way ticket cost $10.[208]

Governor Hagerman commented on the new motor stagecoach in his 1906 report to the secretary of the interior. "A very successful automobile line has been established between Roswell, in Chaves County, and Torrance, on the line of the El Paso and Northeastern, putting the constantly growing sections of the Pecos Valley in much closer communication than ever before with the rest of the Territory."[209]

Huber, a horse stagecoach driver in his youth, knew that the motor stagecoach route was in service, so when he heard it approaching and saw it in the distance he became interested in a close-up look at the operation. Dick ground hitched his pack horse. He then rode alongside the coach for a few miles and talked to the passengers until his horse could no longer keep up the pace. For a magic moment the past and the future had shared life's stage together.

Day by Day

Following the Las Vegas fair, Lieutenant Baca and Rangers McGrath and Putman took the railroad south to Socorro. En route they prevented a holdup of the Santa Fe train just south of Belen. The three uniformed and well armed territorial police "frightened the would-be robbers, who escaped in the darkness."[210] This incident causes one to wonder if the holdup men had seen the rangers in Albuquerque or Las Vegas and knew that these gray-suited men were territorial lawmen.

In early September, the Capitan *News* was discussing a rash of horse stealing.

"Horse thieves are said to infest the Ruidoso country, and three small bunches are reported to have been driven off recently." The newspaper also reported that Will Dudley was once again making visits to Capitan.[211] The print voice of the territorial capital crowed, "It cannot be denied that the New Mexico Mounted Police are having a wholesome influence in repressing lawlessness in sections where police protection has been out of the question."[212]

Estancia become a major player in the stock business during the 1905 fall shipping season when over 3,000 head of sheep were sent from the new rail center. Territorial commerce took another step forward when the St. Louis, Rocky Mountain & Pacific Railroad began laying tracks out of Raton toward Cimarron and Clayton. This new rail system further opened the range country and connected the area's mining camps to regional and national markets.[213]

New Mexico has many breathtaking scenic vistas and most of these physical wonders are enjoyable all year. In late September or early October, Mother Nature adds an extra visual wonder to the landscape when she majestically changes the colors in the high mountain Aspen country. This flamboyant act can sometimes take place overnight; sometimes it lasts for two weeks. This is truly God's Country. The green Aspen forest changes to chartreuses, to a pale yellow, to a liquid gold; sometimes the delicate leaves turn orange and even pink. Today many mountain resort communities stage golf tournaments, old timer picnics, antique car rallies, dances, arts and craft shows and horse races to attract tourists to the glorious Aspencades.

In the fall of 1905, the mounted police seemed to be everywhere at once and they were making their presence felt among the criminal element. No matter how successful Fullerton's Rangers had become, some taxpayers still thought that the range riders were an unnecessary expense to the territory's land owners. Captain Fullerton tried to counter the rangers' detractors when he said, "The duties of a Mounted Police are hard, and only men of staying qualities can withstand the hardship imposed on them, as they are required at times to ride practically all night, sleep in the open whenever necessary and always to keep their life in their hands."[214] Fullerton's words had little or no effect upon the naysayers. In another case where a rancher demanded quick action from the mounted police, Captain Fullerton answered the complaint by saying, "*You must* remember this is a large Territory to work with so few men [for patrol duty]. I can assure you *we are* [now] and will [continue to] give good service to the people in the Territory."[215] There is no public record concerning the rancher's reaction to Captain Fullerton's reply; however in his annual department report, in an awkwardly worded phrase, John made a prophetic statement, "The men now mustered in are hardened to their work. They can be looked forward to make the name of a Territorial Mounted Police a terror in any bad man's country."[216]

Even an accomplished manhunter like "Stuttering Bob" Lewis could make a mistake. In September 1905, Sergeant Lewis arrested a suspect he believed to be wanted for larceny in Colorado. The suspect was a very close resemblance to the wanted man. However, Bob finally released the man, because he was unable to satisfy himself beyond a reasonable doubt that this was the wanted man.[217] Lewis was tough, but fair. He could also have fun with a prisoner. A week before Christmas 1905, Lewis delivered a reluctant charge to El Paso because Texas authorities wanted the man on a bond jumping charge. The prisoner had boasted to his cell mate how he would fool Sergeant Lewis when they reached the Texas line, but it was the escapee who was surprised when Bob did not stutter a bit as he shoved the man over the territorial-state line. A Texas officer gladly helped the man to his feet and just as happily escorted him off to jail for a nice Christmas celebration.[218]

It would seem that as the days ticked off to close his nine years as governor, Miguel Otero became less and less the "man of the people" he had been over the years. Mrs. Clara A.B. Corbin of La Gran Quivera had almost become a pen-pal as she wrote to the governor on a wide range of subjects, always imparting her wisdom concerning how he could rid the territory of the "evil forces" at work in her area. She always had the inside "secret" information he needed to prosecute these persons, and she would only give it to him if he would come to see her. "The duties of my office are such that it is impossible for me to take these matters up personally," wrote Otero in late October 1905. Astounding as it may seem, Otero was never able to visit her area in almost a decade of public service. Otero told Mrs. Corbin, in his last letter, that the mounted police might be able to give her aid, but he cautioned her that "unless positive information can be given regarding criminals, it is useless to put them to [the] expense in visiting sections [of the territory] merely on suspicion of people." The chief executive passed the baton when he suggested that "it might be well for you to correspond with the Captain."[219] The remaining official records do not show that Mrs. Corbin ever communicated with Captain Fullerton.

Shortly after assuming the governor's office Herbert Hagerman received a letter telling him of "evil forces" at work near La Gran Quivera. Evil is worldwide and has many faces. In November 1905, a man living in Detroit, Michigan, erected a monument to satan at the corner of Stinton and McGraw avenues. This remembrance of the Bible's Prince of Darkness had little impact upon daily life in New Mexico Territory, but the incident does point up the fact that twisted minds lived among "civilized people" as well as people living in the developing frontier territory of the southwestern United States.[220]

Winter Illness

If it was not fence cutters it was cattle or horse thieves. Ranger Fate Avant had been away at the two fairs and a quick swing across the plains before returning to Capitan. He had not been home long before he had the opportunity to arrest Arch Parker, a suspected long roper, who was stupid enough to try working his magic not far from Avant's own Lincoln County ranch.[221] Parker, a Texas fugitive, won an "all expense paid vacation" in the Lincoln County jail. It would seem that some people never get the word that a policeman lives on the block.

Fate Avant was, by nature, a robust individual, but in the fall of 1905 the long weeks of horseback scout duty had begun to wear on his system. In mid–October, the local newspaper told its readers that Avant had returned home "from a month's trip to various sections of the territory." A few weeks later it was reported that Avant was "suffering from an attack of rheumatism."[222] The old cowman was forced to his bed for nearly two weeks and Captain Fullerton wrote Fate Avant, "I am sorry to hear of your sickness; hope you will be able to work soon, although I don't want to send you any orders until you are able for duty. Let me hear from you as often as possible."²²³ At least one other ranger, Bob Lewis, could identify with Avant's plight, because he too suffered from this ailment and was occasionally confined to bed.

The mounted police captain needed Fate Avant healthy again because cattle rustlers were active near Encino. Fullerton wrote one of the victims, "We are very busy at present and can hardly keep up with the work. However, we will do all we can to find your cattle that are missing." Fullerton told the rancher he would soon send Ranger Avant to investigate. "He is sick at present and is not able to work, will know in a few days how he is."²²⁴

The Apache Kid and Football

The Denver *Republican* published a special dispatch from their Santa Fe correspondent, "at the headquarters of the New Mexico rangers," describing how Apache Indians had raided a ranch in southwestern Socorro County and were "committing depredations" in the area. "Considerable stock has been taken from settlers, who have organized a posse and are now pursuing the Indians. The later are believed to be under the leadership of the Apache Kid. Arrangements are being made to send out rangers after the marauders." The Indians had attacked the Kiehne Ranch, located along the Negrito near Frisco, and killed two horses with arrows and drove off two mules. A five man posse, including Bob Lewis' father-in-law, tracked the raiders into the Elk Mountains where the mules and camp equipment were found abandoned. Camp signs indicated that there were only two persons on the raid.²²⁵

Fate Avant's rheumatism keep him from joining Lieutenant Baca on a mountain scout, so Herb McGrath joined Baca and Julius Meyer on a hunt through the Mogollon Mountains for the legendary Indian outlaw Zenogalache, Crazy One, commonly called the Apache Kid. Up until 1894 the Arizona Legislature had offered a $5,000 bounty for the Indian. The mounted police took up the hunt and spent days searching for the renegade and his woman, but Baca's patrol was unable to locate any sign of the elusive Indian and his companion. Meanwhile, Sergeant Lewis was tracking some suspected cattle thieves in western Socorro County when he made a disturbing discovery. According to a news account, "He found tracks which induced him to believe that the 'Kid' and his squaw are still hiding in the Mogollon mountains and it is but a question of time that they will find themselves in a white man's calaboose." ²²⁶

It is claimed that a few weeks later, six stockmen found the Indian camped in the San Mateo Mountain range and today a gravesite for the Apache Kid is located on the north slope of the 10,000-foot Apache Peak in the Apache Kid Wilderness area in the San Mateo Mountains.²²⁷ The legend of the Apache Kid still lives. He is the only hostile Indian ever to have successfully defied the army in the field, and baffled law enforcement officers and scrofulous bounty hunters in two territories.

In the fall of 1905, President Theodore Roosevelt threatened to ban intercollegiate football in the United States due to the massive number of injuries and some deaths among players. A new set of game rules and some degree of protection for the players was established by a select committee of college representatives and presented to the president for his review. He agreed to the improvements and the gridiron competitions continued. It would be interesting to know if Baca, McGrath and Meyer discussed the college football controversy around a campfire during their search for the Apache Kid. Herb McGrath had firsthand knowledge of the problems, because as a freshman at New Mexico Agriculture and Mechanical College (New Mexico State University) he had been injured in the big game against their rival, "The University," in a game that was played in Albuquerque before a raucous crowd of University of New Mexico fans. McGrath was the freshman quarterback for the "the boys" from Las Cruces in the hard fought loss. Doctors benched Herb's football career, so he took up the sport of tennis and won two major tournaments during his only season on the court.[228]

Trouble with Indian Hunters

The Mounted Police Act required the rangers to deal with "marauding Indians or bands of hostile Indians." Using colorful turn of the century language, the Socorro *Chieftain* told the story: "The noble redmen of New Mexico are showing a reckless if not a contemptuous disregard of the game laws of the territory and also the laws regulating their absence from their reservations."[229] In early November, Captain Fullerton wrote the territorial game and fish warden concerning the wayward Indian hunters. "Lieut. Baca and Meyers [sic] will leave Rahma [Ramah] the first of the week, and go Southwest from there into the Datil country and will investigate those Indian affairs, and will arrest any and all [Indians] that [they] find out hunting and confiscate their belongings."[230]

Page Otero was excited about the proposed help from the mounted police. "I am heartily glad that some action will be taken at once to stop the depredations of these raiding devils. I have repeatedly notified the Indian Agents, but with, apparently, no results." The territorial game warden suggested a plan to Fullerton, "The only remedy which I can now see, is to arrest, prosecute, and give them the extent of the law." In concluding Otero said, "I earnestly hope that Cipriano [Baca] and Meyers [sic] will accomplish something, and should be glad to hear of it when they do."[231]

A few days later Page Otero wrote to the superintendent of the Navajo Indian Agency at Fort Defiance, Arizona. "I am receiving letters from the settlers there [western Socorro County] complaining of these Indian Depredations. In many instances when game was scarce they have killed cattle & sheep. I have notified the New Mexico Mounted Rangers and a party of them left for the area the first of this week." Otero also said he was concerned that if the killing did not stop "there will be serious trouble." He concluded, "My instructions to the Rangers are to arrest, prosecute and confiscate all carcasses."[232]

Baca and Meyer were in San Juan County finishing up some court business connected with their recent outlaw roundup. When they completed their court business they planned to pick up their horses and pack gear at Bluewater, located in western Valencia County in the shadow of majestic Mount Taylor, and head south into western Socorro County. The two men left Farmington via the Denver & Rio Grande Railroad, went north into Colorado, then south along the Rio Grande into Santa Fe. The rangers left San Juan County just before a smallpox outbreak ravaged through the D&RG crew based in that area. In the City of Holy Faith the two rangers switched to the main Santa Fe line and traveled to Albuquerque, then west toward Bluewater. This long roundabout rail trip saved the two lawmen many days in the saddle.

A few days later, Captain Fullerton wrote a Socorro County rancher concerning the Indian hunters and the mounted police's investigation. "They [Baca and Meyer] went by way of Albuquerque and from there to Bluewater were they had left their horses. From there they went to the Datil [Mountains]. I instructed them to arrest everyone they could find and bring them in. We will see what the law will do for them."[233]

Most Native Americans were treaty wards of the federal government. In the fall of 1905 some Pueblo Indians were hunting out of season on national forest lands, yet federal officers were reluctant to help with the search for the culprits. In fact, the U.S. marshal for New Mexico Territory had expressed the sentiment that it was "high time that the Territorial officials of Arizona and New Mexico devoted some of their energies in this behalf."[234] To one of his Socorro County ranch neighbors Fullerton wrote, "The government does not seem to care to take hold of the matter and we want to do all we can to stop the Indians from killing this game. I should have sent more men had I had them." The ranger captain then brought the Patterson area rancher up to date on the search. "I sent two men about 10 days ago, Lieutenant Baca and Meyers [sic]. No doubt they will arrest all that they find and bring them in; that was the instructions I gave them. I am looking for them anytime."[235]

There is an old maxim that not every problem that a person faces can be changed, but that nothing can be changed until the problem is faced. Page Otero faced his Indians' illegally hunting out of season problem when he wrote Captain Fullerton that he had two reasons why he didn't personally go after the Indian violators. He said his deputies were paid on commission and that they would only receive money if they made an arrest and won the prosecution. "Were I to go out I would soon be without anyone to help me." Otero's second reason also dealt with money — his. "I carry [life] insurance and have been warned on three different occasions when I went after Indians, not to do so again or

Page B. Otero, territorial game and fish warden (New Mexico Department of Game and Fish).

my policy would be cancelled." Otero continued by telling Fullerton he would appoint every rancher in the southern part of the territory as a deputy game warden if they would go after the rebellious Indians. "I think if the settlers would kill off a few of them it might be the means of attracting a little attention from the Department [of Indian Affairs] at Washington & bring about the desired result. I heartily wish this would be done."[236]

The tenor of Page Otero's message is disturbing to many individuals in this era, because killing people to attract "a little attention" has the ring of a racist with a barbaric nature. Even so, as difficult as it may seem, we today should not transpose our society's human life values and our social judgments upon the people who lived in 1905 New Mexico Territory. Both Page Otero and John Fullerton had each experienced close encounters, less than 20 years before, with "hostile Indians" during the bloody Apache Wars and they still held vivid memories of the events, because the ghosts of our youth never leave us. It would appear from the tone of this letter—"I heartily wish this would be done"—that deep within the soul of Page Otero a hatred of Indians still ran untamed.

Fortunately for the wandering Indians and the Anglo-Spanish settlers in western New Mexico, Captain Fullerton put duty above whatever personal feelings he may have harbored toward the Apaches and their Pueblo brothers. Fullerton took no action toward helping Otero make deputies of Socorro County ranchers so they could legally hunt Indians and kill them on sight. He did not want another Indian war just to get "the desired results" of the Indians observing the game laws. It was not a simple matter of right or wrong, but new laws vs. old ways and Fullerton felt the incident could be settled without the loss of human life.

A.J. Abbott, a former territorial judge who was then special counsel for the Pueblo Indians, presented the Indians' side of the hunting controversy in a report to Governor Hagerman.

> The Pueblo Indians are not criminally inclined. During the last four years not a single arrest has been made among them for any of the lower and especially disgusting crimes, such as rape and incest. In this regard they are an example for both the Caucasian and the African.
> The Pueblo have been accustomed for centuries to take an annual hunt for meat in winter time. This has been a communal event for centuries with these people. The round-up hunt in November, after the crops were matured and gathered and the winter fuel provided, has gone into history as a fixit custom among them; and they have been accustomed to regard the elk, the deer, the mountain sheep, and the wild turkey, as well as the game fish of the mountain streams, as the peculiar provisions of nature for their benefit. Territorial game laws have restricted them in this regard until no citizen of the Territory can kill more than one deer in a year, and that must be a deer with horns. The open season for deer hunting in this Territory (when there has been an open season) has been the months of November and December, until the year 1905. The Indians had come to know that all the privileges allowed them for deer hunting were to be enjoyed during these months.[237]

The 1905 Legislative Assembly changed the hunting season from November and December and established it as September 15 to October 31. Prior to 1905 the statutes required that the Indians be notified of the hunting dates, but no one notified the Indians of the 1905 change. So in November and December the Indians went hunting as usual, with the resulting clash of culture and language.

The national forest concept, and all its federal regulations, was also new to the territory. The Gila River National Forest Reserve, established in 1899, was only the second reserve in New Mexico; the first area was formed along the Pecos River in Santa Fe County in 1892 and a third reserve was created in the mountains of Lincoln County in 1902. A second problem that the rangers faced was the language barrier, because neither English nor Spanish was their primary means of communication and not all Pueblo Indians speak the same language. The three major hunting bands represented on this trip each spoke a different dialect. In San Felipe Pueblo the Keresan language is spoken. In Jemez Pueblo the residents converse in Towa, while on the 210,000 area Isleta Reservation the cousin Tiwa language is spoken.

Discretion is the better part of valor and Cipriano Baca understood that principle. He and Julius Meyer conducted an investigation and discovered that 150 Indians from San Felipe, Jemez and Isleta Pueblos were illegally hunting deer in Socorro County out of season and without a permit. The two rangers ordered the Indian hunters "back to their respective reservations and that nearly all of them have complied with the order."[238]

Captain Fullerton commented on the troubles to the press by saying, "The lieutenant did not make any arrests, as he states that they [the Indians] were in an ugly frame of mind and that he would have had to kill some of them to accomplish an arrest." Cipriano Baca may have had flashback memories of a similar incident he had with a drunken, angry mob of Indians. The year before Baca had been at a Taos Pueblo dance, as a deputy U.S. marshal, with federal warrants to arrest some of the Indians. He was almost killed during this encounter and it is only reasonable to assume that Baca did not want a repeat of that near death experience.[239]

Lieutenant Baca and Territorial Fish and Game Warden Page Otero had corresponded about a similar incident in October. Then no action was taken because the federal Indian officers would do nothing to assist the mounted police. This time the rangers went to the Pueblos and with the help of the local Indian police officers they found the homes of the Indian suspects and had them arrested by local deputy game wardens. About 30 Pueblos were charged with killing game out of season and bound over to the district courts because the alleged hunting incidents had occurred off the Pueblo lands.[240] None of the arrests for the Indian hunters are recorded in the mounted police field reports or in their official arrest records.

According to fish and game warden records, "Ignorance of the law not being a defense, and it being true that deer had been killed by some of them out of season, fifteen pleas of guilty were entered and one conviction was procured on the evidence. As to the others, the prosecutions were dismissed. The sentences which the court must necessarily pronounce under law were suspended, and the Indians were allowed to go, under promise of future good behavior and with the warning from the court that further violations would set the law in operation as to the suspended sentences, as well as to provide prosecutions and incur heavier penalties."

Deputy U.S. Marshal Fred Fornoff always seemed to be in the middle of something that Fullerton's Rangers were investigating. Page Otero had been trying for months to get the Indian superintendent or the federal prosecutor to help him restrain the Indians from over-hunting on federal forest reserves. Finally, Otero turned to the mounted police for action. The rangers were quick to respond and headlines across the territory heralded their actions. In the wake of this favorable press attention, the slow-to-move federal officers were forced into action to save face, so they staged a raid on the 400-year-old Jemez Pueblo. "Three Indians were arrested by Fred Fornoff, as I understand, for violation of game laws," wrote Page Otero to Captain Fullerton. "I do not understand by which authority Mr. Fornoff acts, or whether it is part of his duty. Anyhow the offense was committed in Socorro Co. & the Indians should be tried there. Will you look into this?"[241] Once again Fullerton and the mounted police were asked to clean up behind Fornoff. However, John and Page were both out of office before the Indians' trial date, so neither man played an active role in the prosecution of the cases. Fornoff was then captain of the mounted police.

Trouble Along the New Railroad

The management of the major railroads that operated in New Mexico, as well as the locally owned smaller companies, had supported the effort to create the mounted police. An interlocking railroad system was the cornerstone to the development of the Sunshine Territory and it was also important to the function of mounted police. A direct east-west rail system would provide the rangers with a means for a quicker response time into troubled areas and the so-called "Belen Cutoff" became this much needed connecting rail route.

The work on the Belen Cutoff had first started in 1903, but the "Rich Man's Panic" of that year hurt investment efforts and halted further construction until August 1905. The railroad company was laying track from the New Mexico–Texas line, at Texico, west across the plains to Abo Pass and then on west to the Rio Grande. Near the little river town of Belen the new Santa Fe rail line would connect with the main north-south rail line. For the first time passengers and shippers from El Paso and Denver would have a direct road into the heart of Texas and the South. Over 500 men were working on the massive construction project in May 1905 and an additional 200 men soon joined that work force. A few months into the construction schedule, a Santa Fe Railroad executive wrote Captain Fullerton detailing the actions of a band of thugs operating along the construction line. Fullerton told the official, "I have been planning for two or three weeks to send three men over to [the] Torrance [community] and the Belen cut off." Fullerton next promised he would station some rangers in the triangle area so that they could patrol the Torrance, Guadalupe and Lincoln County country. He further said, "I have also had other reports from there say that there was considerable trouble, no doubt there is a hard lot of men in and around Texico."[242]

It is uncertain whether it was the presence of a ranger patrol or the advent of bitter winter weather that ended the 1905 railroad troubles. The truth is, the troubles continued to plague local lawmen off and on over the next few years, until the mounted police made mass cleanups of the gambler dens and red light areas scattered along the length of the new rail line. On one day in July 1910, Sgt. John Collier single-handedly apprehended 21 persons. This feat took place at Vaughn, a railroad junction in Guadalupe County, and was for enforcement of the territory's Sunday saloon closing law. Collier's roundup stands as the all time arrest record for a territorial policeman.[243]

Routine Duty Continued

The last part of 1905 found Will Dudley on an extended scout along the New Mexico–Texas border. Finally he turned west toward the mountains, then headed for Santa Fe. In the capital city, Dudley visited a penitentiary inmate "securing a little information" for his range theft investigation. Back in Alamogordo, Will Dudley arrested a man named Vancouver Williams for theft of some wholesale goods, but the arrest was not as easy as it may appear from the newspaper accounts. Will attempted to take the man into custody in a simple arrest, but he made a run for freedom. Following a mad dash through a couple of downtown Alamogordo stores the would-be robber was finally cornered and jailed. Dudley recovered a large stash of stolen hardware equipment in the man's home, and the *Otero County Advertiser* proclaimed, "What is thought to be quite an important arrest was made Thursday."[244]

Mounted police patrols had become almost routine duty for most of the rangers. Sergeant Bob Lewis discovered Albert Mongdon, a Texas fugitive, hiding out at the Engle mining camp. The would-be miner was wanted for forgery. Ranger Bob Putman went on escort duty to La Junta, Colorado, to return an escaped penitentiary inmate to Santa Fe. James Sanders had been serving a one year sentence for an Albuquerque burglary when he escaped.[245] John Brophy also made a trip to the north. He took the train up to Trinidad seeking a fugitive. John found the man he wanted at the Tabasco Coal Camp and arrested him on a murder warrant from Union County. Pedro Baldanero had beat up a Folsom man so badly that the man died from the assault. The fugitive was lodged in jail at Clayton just in time for the big New Year's Eve party.[246]

Winter's bitter cold caused New Mexicans to seek shelter and even the would-be outlaws wanted to stay near the comfort of a fire. An out of control fire, fanned by strong winds, proved to be devastating to Clayton. Buildings in the downtown business section had to be torn down to stop the raging inferno. Across the territory, at 1:34 p.m. on January 25, 1906, an earthquake hit the McKinley County seat. The minute long quake was severe enough that it caused the large pendulum clock at Gallup's railroad depot to be frozen in time.[247]

Some of Fullerton's Rangers were always on the move. The Clayton *Enterprise* told its readers, "The territorial rangers are rounding up a gang of cattle and horse thieves in Union and Quay Counties. Seven men have been arrested and 150 stolen sheep and a number of horses and cattle have been recovered. This breaks up one of the most thoroughly organized gangs of desperados in northeastern New Mexico."[248] John Brophy had done his homework and when the time was right he asked Captain Fullerton for help to make the arrests.

A local rancher had high praise for this winter rustler roundup. He wrote Captain

Fullerton, "I have the pleasure to report that the recent operations of your men in the Salado Pastura district resulted in the capture of nearly all known law breakers of the locality. [You have my hearty] appreciation for [the] good work of the Mounted Police under your command."[249] The *Salado Pastura* spread over a vast area of northeastern New Mexico. *Salado* means salty and *pastura* refers to an area used for grazing. The Charles Ilfeld Company, of Las Vegas, ran a trading post along the Southern Pacific Railroad southwest of Santa Rosa and called the settlement Pastura.

In early January an El Paso newspaper reported that "W.E. Dudley of Chihuahua is in El Paso on one of his periodical visits" and a couple of days later reported that he had stayed at the Sheldon Hotel, but "has returned to Chihuahua." Dudley and M.D. Gaylord, from Nogal, had made the trip to check with the El Paso and Juarez police about Mexican bandits operating in the Capitan-Alamogordo area. Dudley had developed the "Chihuahua" identifier as a means of keeping a low cover. The trip proved to have limited immediate success, but a month later Dudley, the Alamogordo town marshal, and the area constable discovered a plot to rob a large retail store in the town's main business section. A loose gang of Mexican thugs were suspected of robbing local stores and then setting a fire in the business to cover their crime. The Alamo City had suffered a number of small fires during the winter of 1905–06, so Dudley was now conducting an investigation into the possibility of a conspiracy to commit a crime.[250]

Bob Lewis and the Long Hunt

Late in December 1905, Sergeant Bob Lewis packed his camp outfit and kissed his wife Flora good-bye. He took up the trail of the murderer Howard Chenoworth, who on Christmas Day evening had escaped from the Grant County jail at Silver City.[251] It is possible that Chenoworth was not trying to gain his freedom, but just wanted to escape the whooping cough epidemic that was descending upon Silver City, so with that idea in mind Sheriff Charles Farnesworth only posted a $600 reward for Chenoworth's recapture.

Howard Chenoworth, a local area cowboy, had been arrested at Silver City by Grant County Deputy Sheriff John Collier on August 27, 1904, for shooting ex-city marshal Perfecto Rodreguez through the heart and mortally wounding City Marshal W. H. Kilburn. The two men had tried to break up a fight between Chenoworth and two other cowboys. Chenoworth wounded one cowhand before he shot the lawmen. When Deputy Sheriff Collier arrived on the scene he ordered Howard Chenoworth to drop his pistol, so when he refused Collier emptied a load of birdshot into Chenoworth's face. The man's head wounds were painful, but not fatal. Chenoworth escaped the Grant County jail following his double murder conviction and a sentence of 50 years in the territorial penitentiary.

Sergeant Bob Lewis had learned that Chenoworth was trying to make a run for Old Mexico, while the Grant County lawmen were huddled in Silver City. The area was in the depths of the coldest season the community had experienced in seven years; the temperature hung at zero for days. Undeterred by the weather, Lewis took up the fugitive's trail and headed south into the Bootheel and on into the mountains of Old Mexico. It is interesting to note that the finance conscious Grant County Deputy Sheriff Herb McGrath, stationed at Lordsburg, made no effort to apprehend Chenoworth and collect the reward. Could weather have been a factor in this lack of action?

Near the international border Lewis located four Texas Rangers who were in pursuit of cattle rustlers. Jurisdictional legalities did not seem to matter as the five rangers rode south together in a quest for wanted men. West Texas was awash with renegades during the winter of 1905 and one rancher posted a $500 reward for "evidence to convict" cattle thieves who raided his ranch. He also offered an additional $50 for each year the thief spent in the penitentiary. These long ropers were so active along the border and along the plains east of El Paso that Ranger Company C was ordered to relocate their base camp from Colorado City southwest to Alpine in the crest of the Big Bend Country. Captain John H. Rodgers assigned four of his rangers on detached duty with orders to scout along the Rio Grande and to cooperate with Captain Ponce de Leon and his "Mexican rangers" who were riding along the south side of the big river.[252]

Meanwhile, the Texas adjutant general responded to requests from county law enforcement officers in the western mountain region and dispatched some rangers from Company B to this area of large ranches, thousands of cattle and a small human population. Captain Bill McDonald's rangers were headquartered at Alice. The adjutant general had arranged for the Texas Pacific Railroad to transport these lawmen and their equipment from Alice to their detached duty assignment at Sierra Blanca. The Company B rangers were given orders to scout the vast range lands west of Sierra Blanca toward El Paso and on along the Rio Grande hunting for cattle rustlers who were raiding the isolated ranches. This ranger squad was led by J.D. Dunaway and was composed of M.G. Delling, H.B. Smith and W.A. Millican. These south Texas lawmen may have been the rangers that rode across northern Mexico with Sergeant Bob Lewis.

Texas Ranger captains were required to file two different monthly service reports and a monthly payroll voucher. One report, the Duty Report, contained quartermaster information concerning state owned equipment, the health status of the men and officers, and an overview of any arrests made that month. The second report, the Scout Report, was a detailed day-by-day account of patrols and the activities of each ranger in the command. Today these two monthly reports are part of the Texas Ranger history files housed in the Texas State Archives in Austin.

Fate sometimes has a way of derailing the recording of history and this seems to be the situation with this case. The files for Company B, for 1905 and 1906, are complete. However, the Company C records are missing all the Scout Reports for 1906. The Company C Duty Report for January 1906 contains some information that might relate to the long hunt. Under "remarks" is found this note: "Private Millican sick & went to [word unclear] on Jany 24th." Under the section dealing with arrests is a long run-on sentence containing a number of different unrelated topics. One of these topics reads, "assisted Private Dunaway in securing evidence in horse stealing case & scouted in Durango [words unclear] & watched for cattle thieves who had been killing [words unclear] cattle." Dunaway and Millican were two of the rangers sent on detached duty to West Texas in late 1905, but it is still difficult to determine if these men where the Texas Rangers who rode with Bob Lewis.[253] Finally, the rangers from the Lone Star State gave up the hunt and started the long ride home. Back in El Paso, they sent a telegram to Captain Fullerton stating that Sergeant Lewis would keep up the pursuit until all hope of finding his 20 year old fugitive was lost.[254]

Sergeant Bob Lewis had been on the hunt for 36 days when, as a resolution in his hometown newspaper stated, "the fell destroyer entered his home, and gathered to his icy bosom his little daughter...."[255] It was the afternoon of January 31, 1906. Una Jane Lewis, four and a half years old, was playing in a large vacant lot west of the family house on the western edge of Socorro. Neighborhood children had built a bonfire to help keep warm while they were playing their games. Somehow Una's dress caught fire and the little child was severely burned before the fire could be extinguished. The youngster was deeply and badly burned in two places on her abdomen and hips.

Dr. C.F. Blackington was summoned to the Lewis home to treat the little sufferer. Una was in great pain, but Blackington felt that the little girl would be up and about in a few days. A few days later, however, territorial newspapers were reporting that young Miss Lewis might die because of the wound's complications. Una

Sergeant Robert W. Lewis. This photograph was taken at Magdalena, N.M., about the time Lewis served as the town marshal, circa 1935 (courtesy of Howard Bryan).

was in constant pain and her little body would not react to the medication, so she became weaker by the hour.[256] During these tragic hours, Flora Lewis asked Captain Fullerton to locate her husband and inform him of Una's condition, so the ranger chief sent twelve telegrams to the major points he felt that Lewis might cross during his manhunt.[257]

It was St. Valentine's Day and Socorro was not yet alive with mid-week commerce. Una Lewis had awakened and "with her own baby lips and voice constantly bade her mother not to weep, that she, Una, would not die and leave her." The girl was dead by nine o'clock that morning and her father was still in Old Mexico.

The Socorro *Chieftain* carried an account of the Una Lewis funeral on the front page. "In a little white casket, laden with delicate flowers, no more pure in their innocence than the jewel it held, little Una was laid to rest in a grave prepared for her little body in consecrated ground." The Fullertons and others of the "mounted police family" were present at the memorial service. Resolutions of sympathy and condolence were issued by church and civic groups. The *Chieftain* voiced the community's feelings by saying, "An extremely sad feature of the case is that the father, who is on Mounted Police duty in Mexico, could not be reached in time to attend the funeral...."[258]

Captain Fullerton had recently talked about the rangers with a reporter and was quoted as saying, "Since the force was mustered in last April, not a man has been killed, although several of them have been under fire."[259] Fullerton had not been discussing his missing sergeant, but Flora Lewis read the remark and began to feel that her husband would become the first territorial police killed in the line of duty. Fear is a four letter word for deep dread. A feeling of loss overtook Flora Lewis. She was 29 years old and had lost her young daughter, had three other small children to look after, and was terrified that she might have also lost her husband. Now even Flora's friends and relatives became concerned about the safety of Sergeant Bob Lewis, but they were really much more concerned about Flora's state of mental health.

On Tuesday morning, February 20, 1906, Fullerton returned to Socorro from a trip to El Paso. When he reached his office he found a delegation of Lewis family friends awaiting him. They had a petition asking that Captain Fullerton order some of the rangers to go in search of Sergeant Lewis. Bob's friends also pledged funds to support such a search. "I told them," Fullerton remembered, "that I had no fears for Sergeant Lewis' safety, and that if he did not report in a short time I would search for him myself."[260]

The next day a telegram from Mexico was received at mounted police headquarters. Sergeant Lewis reported that he was in Montezuma in the State of Sonora. Lewis had not been able to locate Howard Chenoworth, but he had found Claude Barbee, an escaped murderer from Socorro County. Lewis said he needed a legal request for the Mexican police to arrest Barbee. Captain Fullerton was very relieved and he must have run to the telegraph office to send a couple of messages. First thing Fullerton did was to wire Lewis about his daughter's death and requested that he remain in Sonora a short time longer.

A second telegram went to the governor's office. "Please request [the] governor of Sonora Mexico to order [the] perfecto at Sahauriha to arrest and hold Claude Barbee."[261]

Captain John F. Fullerton's message to the governor offered no word about Bob Lewis' safety or why Fullerton wanted Barbee arrested. Captain Fullerton just assumed that the new governor would understand the message in the same way that Governor Otero had always understood.

Captain Fullerton next called at the home of Sergeant Lewis and told Flora he had received a telegram from her husband and that he was doing fine. The Socorro *Chieftain* reported the news with a classic understatement when it said, "This telegram was a source of great relief to the Sergeant's friends in Socorro."[262]

Thursday morning, John Fullerton caught the northbound train for Albuquerque. He was headed for Santa Fe to see the governor. In the Duke City a reporter questioned him about rumors that Sergeant Lewis was dead, so he told the Albuquerque reporter that Sergeant Lewis was very much alive and had reported to headquarters on Wednesday. Thursday evening, the Santa Fe *New Mexican* headlined a page one story "Officer Killed? Sergeant Lewis in Pursuit of Jail Breaker, Has Been Missing Two Months." The opening sentence stated flatly, "Sergeant R.W. Lewis, of the New Mexico Mounted Police, has in all probability been murdered by cattle rustlers."[263]

On Friday morning Captain Fullerton reached Santa Fe to discover that the capital city was alive with rumors about the murder of Bob Lewis. That evening the *New Mexican* printed Captain Fullerton's reply to the murder rumors on page one. "I am at a loss to know where this rumor originated. It was reported that Lewis had not been heard from for two months which was quite true, but should not have caused fears for his safety as the mission upon which he was sent would necessarily keep him away from railroad or telegraph communication. I was not worried about the safety of the officer as I felt confident he could take care of himself."[264]

Captain Fullerton went on to explain that he and Lewis had made plans for the trip, but the captain was uncertain how close the ranger sergeant was able to follow the trip plan. Fullerton told the press he expected a full report, via the mail, upon his return to Socorro.[265] He also took the opportunity to detail some recent successes of the other rangers. Fullerton showed the reporter a telegram he had received that morning from Lieutenant Baca saying he was at Santa Rosa with four stolen horses and the horse thief under arrest. John Fullerton finished his interview by saying he was sending some of his mounted police on a scout into Grant and Luna counties.[266]

These closing remarks were in reply to recent press criticism over the resignations of Herb McGrath and George Elkins. The two rangers had worked the southern border area, but their replacements were now stationed in the northern part of the territory. Some southern ranchers considered these new appointments a violation of the gentlemen's agreement that had been reached by lawmakers during the debate over the creation of the mounted police. The understanding had been that a ranger would be stationed in the territory's southwestern section because of the outlaw strongholds in that region's mountains.[267]

Herbert J. Hagerman, the new governor, was unaware that Captain Fullerton was on his way to the capitol building when he sent the ranger chief a telegram. The message was in reply to Fullerton's request for a requisition to extradite Claude Barbee from Sonora. "Governor has no power to make such [an arrest] request [of the

Mexican governor] until [a] warrant and requisition [are] issued in New Mexico."[268] Fullerton met with no success during his unscheduled meeting with Governor Hagerman because the governor just restated the message of his morning telegram and said he would not issue a request for an international arrest until a proper New Mexico warrant had been issued for the crime. Fullerton had wasted his time and had needlessly tested the support of his new commander-in-chief.[269] Fullerton telegraphed Sergeant Lewis that he needed to stay in Sonora for a few more days until the proper paper work could be completed and sent to him.[270]

Captain Fullerton and Sheriff Leandro Baca appeared before a Socorro County judge early Monday morning to swear out an arrest warrant for Claude Barbee. He was charged as an escaped prisoner convicted of murder in Socorro County, New Mexico. Fullerton mailed the arrest warrant and other supporting court documents dealing with Barbee's conviction to Governor Hagerman and on Thursday Captain Fullerton personally picked up the signed requisition papers from the governor's office.[271] It would be interesting to know if Fullerton felt a sense of impending doom on that visit because evidence indicates that Hagerman had already begun thinking about replacing him as field chief of the range riders. The undercurrent between the governor and the captain was not yet public knowledge, and may not have been known by Fullerton, so the ranger captain was still able to continue his duties as if nothing was amiss between the two men.

Many newspapers printed Captain Fullerton's praise for the actions of the territorial police following one of his infrequent news conferences. On this occasion he told the press that the rangers "have been greatly aided secretly and openly by ranchmen and stockgrowers all over the territory, who are mighty glad to see the law enforced. Often the boys are furnished lodging, fresh mounts, and what is more important, they are given information which leads to the arrest of cattle rustlers." John Fullerton concluded his remarks by saying that most lawbreakers "surrender as soon as the [territorial] police find them, which speaks well for the men of the service."[272]

Any hint of political intrigue concerning the appointment of a new ranger captain was unimportant to Sergeant Robert W. Lewis. He was hundreds of miles from home and very ready to return to his family. The package of official papers, personal letters and Socorro newspapers finally arrived and the arrest was made by the Mexican authorities. Lewis wired Fullerton he had Barbee and would be home in a few days. Bob added a personal note and asked Fullerton to tell the *Chieftain* that reports of his death were "greatly exaggerated." The ranger sergeant read his own remarks later that week.[273]

"Stuttering Bob" Lewis had been gone from his family for 71 days and it must have seemed like a life time to Flora Higgins Lewis. She had lived through the nightmare of their daughter's death without the aid and comfort of her mate. In the cold, hard retelling of historical fact, the deep hurt of human misery is often glossed over. Robert W. Lewis never forgot that he was high in the mountains of the Republic of Mexico when his sweetheart needed him most. Duty, like fear, is a four letter word.

Baca's Lone Scout

Cipriano Baca had also left Socorro on December 30, 1905. Unlike Bob Lewis, Baca did not leave by horseback but took a train north. On the open plains a few miles west of Albuquerque the snow was so deep that trains had to worry about windblown drifts blocking the tracks and at Laguna Pueblo the snow was "so deep that it will hardly allow going out and the temperature is 15 degrees below zero." Weeks later the weather was still dangerously cold because the postal carrier between Magdalena and Burley had his horse freeze to death under him as he tried to deliver the mail.[274]

Lieutenant Baca spent New Year's Eve 1906 in Las Vegas and the next morning, with a rented pack team, he started cross country searching for some reported stock thieves. For the next 18 days he slowly made his way across San Miguel and Guadalupe counties, always one day ahead of bad weather. There was 15 inches of snow at Epris, in the area southwest of Vaughn, with "prospects of more" and the Pastura locality had over two and a half feet of snow on the ground as Baca continued searching for clues and hoping each day to connect with his missing ranger squad. While Baca was laboriously traveling the back trails of New Mexico Territory, Wall Street investors were blazing their own trail. On January 12, 1906, the Dow Jones Average closed above the 100 mark for the first time in the history of the New York Stock Exchange.[275]

Always on the lookout for misconduct, Baca found and arrested three men he charged with horse theft. It took him four more days before he could arrange a preliminary hearing for his prisoners. When Baca finally located a peace justice it took the judge two days to locate his law books and official trial forms, and two more days were needed before witnesses could reach the court for the hearing. By this time the three prisoners, tired of wearing handcuffs and unable to post a bond, had waived their hearing rights and had asked to be locked up in the nearest jail. Repair work at the Guadalupe County jail was still under way, but Sheriff Felipe Sanchez y Baca accepted the prisoners and housed them in the secure section. After a hot meal and some needed sleep Baca filed his case report.[276] The Santa Rosa *Sun* was the local newspaper and it almost certainly published an account of the Mounted Police's extended journey across the frozen snow covered rangeland of central New Mexico. Unfortunately for the historical record, no known issues of *The Sun* survive from the era of Fullerton's Rangers.

One newspaper reported that the region Baca was traveling through had two and a half feet of snow on the ground in the low country and over three feet in the mountains. "Stock and sheep are suffering greatly from lack of food," said the report, adding that some ranchers were "at present cutting down pine trees for the starving animals to feed on." Wild animals were also searching for food during this territory-wide storm. "The coyotes are still plentiful around Tres Piedras. They come right into town before dark and keep the dogs barking all night."[277]

In late January, Rangers Julius Meyer and Rafael Gomez were finally able to reach Santa Rosa. "On account of snow, bad weather and long distance they were delayed on [the] road from 26th December 1905 until January 22nd 1906"[278] These two bone-weary rangers had traveled on horseback for 28 days through two feet of snow on muddy roads and continued to endure daily foul weather to locate Lieutenant Baca.²⁷⁹

Ranching had been the main business in Guadalupe County since 1824 when Don Antonio Sandoval settled his wife on the vast Hacienda de Agua Negra (Dark Water Estate) Land Grant. By the 1870s this area, and much more, was controlled by Don Celso Baca, who had built the Territorial House as his headquarters and established a private chapel near the ranch house named in honor of Santa Rosa de Lima. The ranch settlement, later a railroad junction, adopted the name of the place of worship. By the time Lieutenant Baca brought his prisoners to Santa Rosa, the town's economy had added another industry. It was a railroad supply center and home to thousands of railroad construction workers, and as such had also developed a proliferation of saloons, dance halls, gambler dens and an assortment of general undesirables.

In February 1906, newspaper readers found some good news concerning the actions of Fullerton's Rangers. Many territorial papers proclaimed that the "Robber's Roost" had been cleaned out in Guadalupe County and that Lieutenant Baca and Rangers Meyer and Gomez had done the deed. The ranger raid had netted six horses and 148 head of sheep, plus three stock thieves that were turned over to the grand jury for action.²⁸⁰ Baca and his two man squad were next seen in northern New Mexico, where another gang of cattle rustlers were at work. John Brophy now joined the squad for this scout. The Tucumcari *News* took note of the area's trouble and told readers, "The New Mexico Mounted Police should run these desperados out of the country as soon as it is possible to do so, and we understand Cipriano Baca is doing it as fast as he possibly can. He with two or three other [territorial] police have been making it warm for this class of criminals in Union County lately"²⁸¹ The Clayton *Enterprise* put the cap on this adventure story. "Seven men have been arrested and 150 stolen sheep and a number of horses and cattle have

Lieutenant Cipriano Baca, photographed in Deming, N.M., about the time he served as the sheriff of Luna County, circa 1902 (courtesy of Cipriana Baca Randolph).

been recovered."²⁸² The men of Fullerton's Rangers had broken up another large, well organized gang of long riders and Fullerton told the Socorro *Chieftain* that Baca's squad "has the worst assignment of the whole force, but is doing effective work."²⁸³

Following two months of cold camps and back trails, lonely stakeouts and tough detective work, Baca dismissed his squad. Julius Meyer stayed out on the range. John Brophy returned to Clayton and sought a new job, while Baca and Putman headed home to Socorro. The *Chieftain* bragged that Cipriano Baca's ranger team was "a good example of the service which the Mounted Police force as a whole is rendering the territory."²⁸⁴ The final sweep had netted six rustler suspects and 40 head of stolen sheep and the same number of lost or missing horses.²⁸⁵

The Last Roundup

Captain John F. Fullerton gave orders that during the spring the rangers would ride non-stop scouts until the long riders were captured, killed or driven from the territory. Late in March, Will Dudley was searching for some men who had raided a number of boxcars of the Rock Island Railroad.²⁸⁶ Will lost the trail of the robbers but his close pursuit caused them to discard the stolen merchandise. A few days later Dudley picked up the trail again and this time he was able to capture three of the men who broke into the box cars. A three day and three night chase through the Gallinas Mountains ended when the men "although heavily armed were surprised by the ranger and captured single handed."²⁸⁷ Later, some railroad workmen were able to capture the other two boxcar robbers without a fight.

In mid–February, the local news column of the Socorro paper reported that Captain Fullerton had been to Santa Fe "on official business before Governor Hagerman."²⁸⁸ A few weeks later the content of that "official business" was printed as a rumor on the front page of *New Mexican* by saying that Hagerman was going to appoint a new mounted police captain.²⁸⁹ A few days later, the rumor was stated as fact. Fullerton's Rangers were to become a part of New Mexico's history and a new company of mounted police would be organized under a new captain.

It was quiet at headquarters that last week in March 1906. Captain Fullerton's movements are unclear, but Lieutenant Baca was in Globe, Arizona, questioning the wife and other relatives of a kidnapping suspect. The man was wanted for questioning concerning his part in a Grant County crime. Baca was unsuccessful, as the El Paso *Times* reported, "He has left Arizona without his man." With Baca back in the office Thursday morning, Bob Putman saddled up and rode over to the high mountain mining camp of Kelly searching for a man wanted by Quay County Sheriff Alex Street.

Kelly had been founded as a sawmill site and lead-zinc mining settlement in 1870. When Putman visited the community a couple thousand people made the town home and supported two churches, seven saloons, two dance halls and two hotels. A decade after Kelly's birth a new town called Magdalena was built at the base of the mountain as a railroad shipping point. The two towns became intense rivals over the next half century.

The next day Putman rode down the mountain to Magdalena then took the road following the railroad tracks back to Socorro. This was the easiest way to travel horseback between Magdalena and Socorro because Putman was riding down "The Elevator" that dropped or climbed, depending upon your destination, about 2,000 feet in about 16 miles. Bob spent Saturday at home with his family. In his final report to Captain Fullerton he said, "The chances are good he [the man Sheriff Street wanted] is laying around some of those thief lovers that live round Magdalena and [in] the Western portion of Socorro County."[290] It is uncertain if Fullerton ever read Putman's report, but one thing is certain and that is this hideout problem did not disappear. Bob Lewis, as marshal of Magdalena, was still combating this menace well into the 1930s.[291]

Governor Hagerman may not have meant to compliment the territorial police, but he summed up the positive service of Fullerton's Rangers when he wrote about the peaceful state of the territory during the summer of 1906. "The condition of the Territory from the standpoint of law and order has been satisfactory during the past year, the percentage of crime, taking the Territory as a whole, being considerably decreased." He further stated that the real problem was not with law enforcement, but with the territory's legal code. "Our criminal code is in many respects much more advantageous to the accused than it is to the prosecution, resulting often in greater difficulty to secure convictions than is warranted by the circumstances of the case. A revision of our criminal laws is very desirable, if not absolutely essential."[292]

Arrests Made by Fullerton's Rangers

APRIL 01, 1905-MARCH 31, 1906

Name	*Offense/Charge*	*Arrested By*
01 Sam Ballard	Larceny of stock	Dudley
02 C. A. Wise	Aiding & Abetting the	McGrath
03 A. N. Howel	unlawful entry of a	McGrath
04 W. B. Aken	Chinaman into	McGrath
05 J. Goddard	USA	McGrath
06 Robert Russie	House breaking, Lincoln Co.	Avant
07 Abran Miller	Cattle stealing, Lincoln Co.	Avant
08 Severo Perez	Cattle stealing, Lincoln Co.	Avant
09 Unknown	Cattle stealing, Lincoln Co.	Avant
10 Unknown	Kidnapping	Baca/Lewis
11 Unknown	Forgery	Elkins
12 Miguel Fernandez	Shooting at woman	Meyer/Huber
13 L. Shylisky	Insanity, Otero Co.	Dudley
14 Miguel Fierra	Mule stealing, Luna Co.	McGrath
15 Unknown	Texas fugitive	Dudley
16 Charles Garword	Horse stealing, Grant Co.	McGrath
17 Dean Lamb	Horse stealing, Grant Co.	McGrath
18 Fred B. Malone	Cattle stealing, Grant Co.	McGrath
19 Lod Littleton	Shooting up Hachita	McGrath
20 Francisco Aldazo	Attempted murder	McGrath
21 W. L. Smith/ Hudson	Rape, Texas fugitive	Dudley
22 Unknown	Cattle stealing, Chaves Co.	Dudley
23 Casamiro Chacon	Escaped convict	Huber
24 Jose Cano	Murder/horse stealing	Huber

Arrests Made by Fullerton's Rangers (continued)

25	Donaciano Quesnel	Order of the governor	Huber
26	Felipe Perea	Escaped convict	Huber
27	Robert Rusher	House burning, Lincoln Co.	Avant
28	Jose Lezano	Horse stealing, Socorro Co.	Lewis/Putman
29	— Magnum	Stock stealing, San Juan Co.	Baca/Meyer/Perea
30	Tom Magnum	Stock stealing, San Juan Co.	Baca/Meyer/Perea
31	Ike Bass	Assault on police, Union Co.	Brophy
32	Unknown	Cattle stealing, Lincoln Co.	Avant
33	Unknown	Cattle stealing, Lincoln Co.	Avant
34	Unknown	Cattle stealing, Lincoln Co.	Avant
35	Robert Rusher	Burglar killed at Capitan	Avant
36	Unknown	Cattle stealing, Lincoln Co.	Avant/Dudley
37	Unknown	Horse stealing, Rio Arriba Co.	Perea
38	Unknown	Horse stealing, Rio Arriba Co.	Perea
39	Unknown	False arrest, released	Lewis
40	Jacobo Flores	Escaped convict	Lewis
41	Robert Embree	Horse stealing, Mora Co.	Brophy (?)
42	Arch Parker	Horse stealing, Lincoln Co.	Avant
43	J. J. Jones	Larceny, Union Co.	Brophy
44	Micario Torres	Horse stealing, Torrance Co.	Huber
45	Lee Longino	Assault to kill, Torrance Co.	Huber
46	— Delgado	Fence cutter, San Miguel Co.	Brophy
47	Isadro Tafoya	Fence cutter, San Miguel Co.	Brophy
48	Unknown	Fence cutter, San Miguel Co.	Dudley/Avant/Meyer
49	Unknown	Fence cutter, San Miguel Co.	Dudley/Avant/Meyer
50	Unknown	Fence cutter, San Miguel Co.	Dudley/Avant/Meyer
51	Unknown	Fence cutter, San Miguel Co.	Dudley/Avant/Meyer
52	Unknown	Fence cutter, San Miguel Co.	Dudley/Avant/Meyer
53	Unknown	Fence cutter, San Miguel Co.	Dudley/Avant/Meyer
54	Unknown	Fence cutter, San Miguel Co.	Dudley/Avant/Meyer
55	Unknown	Fence cutter, San Miguel Co.	Dudley/Avant/Meyer
56	Albert Mongden	Texas bond jumper	Lewis
57	Vancouver Williams	Larceny, Otero Co.	Dudley
58	Pedro Baldanero	Murder	Brophy
59	James Sanders	Escaped prison trustee	Putman
60	Unknown	Horse stealing, Socorro Co.	Baca
61	Gregorio Romero	Horse stealing, Guadalupe Co.	Baca
62	Ciborio Lucero	Horse stealing, Guadalupe Co.	Baca
63	Eliseo Chaves	Horse stealing, Guadalupe Co.	Baca
64	Claude Barbee	Flight and murder, Socorro Co.	Lewis
65	Unknown	Horse stealing	Baca
66	Unknown	Horse stealing	Baca
67	Unknown	Horse stealing	Baca
68	Dwyer	Railroad car theft, Curry Co.	Dudley
69	— Valiercroux	Railroad car theft, Curry Co.	Dudley
70	— Fitzmoses	Railroad car theft, Curry Co.	Dudley
71	— Hauley	Railroad car theft, Curry Co.	Dudley
72	— Edwards	Railroad car theft, Curry Co.	Dudley

There is no official action report concerning the 72 known arrests made by the New Mexico Territorial Mounted Police under the command of Captain John F. Fullerton.

The author has compiled this arrest list from the information contained in Captain Fullerton's department report to Governor Otero, the mounted police's weekly field reports, Fullerton's official correspondence and contemporary newspaper accounts of the rangers' actions. However, name identification is a problem because the name of the arrested party, and sometimes even the mounted policeman's name, was not always listed in the official reports or the newspaper stories.

9

Fullerton's Personnel Problems

"It is not glory I work for."
Ranger McGrath to Captain Fullerton
5 December 1905

"The force as you well know consists of eleven men including officers and as there are twenty-five counties in the Territory it can readily be seen that it is impossible with the above limited force to police the entire Territory," wrote Captain Fred Fornoff in a report to Governor Hagerman. "I respectfully recommend that additional men be provided, and I also recommend that provisions be made for clerk hire at the headquarters of the organization. One additional sergeant should be provided for."[1] The captain was presenting his department's personnel recommendations to the 1907 Territorial Legislative Assembly. Fornoff was unsuccessful with all three of these requests, but he was able to acquire the cost of living adjustment he had requested for his eight rangers and a limited account to reimburse their travel expenses.

Fred Fornoff had been mounted police captain only a few months before he came to understand the handicaps under which his predecessor had operated. "By a study of the history of the Texas Rangers and the Arizona Rangers it will [be] seen that the New Mexico Mounted Police have met with the same difficulties for the first two years of its existence that the older organizations have met with." Fornoff praised the work of New Mexico's rangers, "The men have at all times been anxious to do the work allotted them and have undoubtedly been a great factor in preserving the peace and enforcing the laws of the Territory." In time, even Fornoff learned that not all of the men appointed to the mounted police were "anxious to do the work allotted them."[2]

New Mexico's range land was home to over a million and a half head of meat cattle, six million head of sheep, and more Angora goats than the territory had people. The livestock industry, conservatively estimated at over $50 million in value, was the leading source of income for New Mexico.[3] This was a major reason why the mounted police needed to be at full authorized strength. Fullerton and Acting Governor J.W. Raynolds quickly dealt with the need to bring the ranger company up to authorized strength. The problem of what to do about Francisco Apodaca proved easy to solve; he refused his ranger appointment, citing a business conflict.

The Capitan *News* had supported the formation of the mounted police, but was disappointed when none of the new force had come "from among its [Lincoln County] many capable citizens." However, the White Oaks *Outlook*, another Lincoln County paper, had claimed both Will Dudley and Octaviano Perea by crowing "that two Lincoln county citizens, who have but recently taken up their residence in the Otero county seat, were lucky enough to gather in the ripe persimmons [of a government appointment]." The *Outlook* concluded its story thus, "If our neighboring county has any more fruit of that kind to be gathered, they can always depend on Lincoln to help them out."[4] On April seventh the Capitan *News* was also able to proclaim a belated victory. The story was titled "Lincoln County Policeman" and said, "This, however, has been partially remedied by the resignation of Francisco Apodaca, of Sierra county, and the appointment in his stead, by Acting Governor Raynolds, of L.F. Avent [sic], of Coalora, this county. Mr. Avent [sic] is a good man, and will no doubt, fill the position satisfactorily, for all of which, evidently, we must thank the mission that called Governor Otero away, and left Secretary Raynolds in charge."[5]

But what should they do about William Taylor? Taylor was a personal friend of Governor Otero and neither Raynolds nor Fullerton wanted to move too hastily in the matter of a new appointment. William Taylor took nearly two weeks to decide he would not accept his mounted police commission. Another week ticked by before Acting Governor Raynolds notified Captain Fullerton he would name Santa Fe County Deputy Sheriff Richard Charles Huber to replace Taylor. Fullerton may have had some premonition of future difficulties, because he wired a word of caution to Raynolds. "Investigate Huber thoroughly if not satisfactory don't appoint him."[6] It is unknown how much investigation Raynolds made concerning Huber, but the deputy was offered the ranger appointment and he took his territorial oath on April 7.

Trouble in the Ranks

George M. Elkins became the first mounted policeman to resign his commission. By June 17, 1905, he had become very frustrated and discouraged, and he had finally experienced enough disappointment to offer in his field report to Captain Fullerton his resignation effective on August 1. A couple of days later the captain wrote Elkins, "I have some work planned out which will take two or three months. Now if you cannot be with us during this time mentioned please send your resignation by return mail so that I can appoint someone in your place."[7]

Captain Fullerton had given Elkins a second chance for some real police work, but he was not taking any chances. Fullerton needed a dependable ranger to help carry out his planned outlaw roundup in the northern mountains, so he wrote the first man on his stand-by recruit list. "As there will be a vacancy soon on the Mounted Police Force I wish to know if you are still wanting to accept a position as Private." Robert G. Putman's answer was a quick yes. Fullerton's reply to Putman was equally quick. "Hold yourself in readiness as you will hear from me in a few days."[8] Meanwhile, Captain Fullerton held out hope for Elkins and wrote Herb McGrath, "If you need any help wire Elkins." Earlier Fullerton had written Elkins to inquire, "Do you hear or see anything of Private McGrath?" Was this a question concerning McGrath's police work or was it just some encouragement for Elkins to contact McGrath to help him with anything he was currently investigating? Maybe it was just Fullerton's wishful hope that McGrath and Elkins could develop the same style of teamwork that Avant and Dudley had working in the eastern part of the territory.⁹

Governor Otero accepted Elkins' resignation, effective the last day of June, and on the same page of the *Executive Record Book* that Miss Olsen recorded the Elkins resignation she also recorded the appointment of Bob Putman to replace the tall cowman from Hachita.¹⁰ Captain Fullerton sent Elkins a short note in late June. "If you do send your resignation send your badge, [and also send] all your [railroad] transportation [passes]." George Elkins' 91 day career as one of Fullerton's Rangers was finished when he forwarded his badge, rifle and railroad passes along with his resignation to ranger headquarters.¹¹

Shortly after his resignation, Captain Fullerton sent his former ranger the gray suit that had been tailor made as Elkins' uniform. "It is a good suit and I think worth the money." It did not matter how George felt about the gray suit because the $35 cost was deducted from his last paycheck. Fullerton had allowed Elkins a $20 credit for the Winchester and sent him a $60 territorial warrant. Fullerton concluded his letter by saying, "Will be glad to hear from you at any time."¹² Records, however, suggest that the two men never corresponded after the resignation.

The infant mounted police was struck a painful personnel blow in December 1905 when three of Fullerton's eight rangers resigned their commissions. The first letter came from Herb McGrath. The next to quit was Dick Huber and he was followed by Octaviano Perea.

It is uncertain how long Perea had been planning his resignation before he acted, but it is known that he and Governor Otero held a 10:30 Saturday morning "personal-social" visit on November 18 and one can only speculate on the nature of the visit. The *New Mexican* reported that Perea stayed at the Claire Hotel and was in the capital city on "official business." Had Otero and Perea discussed his family situation? Did the two discuss the mounted police and had Perea sought another political appointment from his old mentor before he left office? The true nature of the discussion may never be known. However, it was a month later that Perea claimed that "domestic affairs render it impossible for me to remain ... there is [*sic*] many things I can do which are more profitable to me in a financial way. My wife is very sick and I shall have to take her to El Paso to have an operation perform [*sic*]."¹³ Fullerton expressed his best wishes for Mrs. Perea's recovery when he sent Octaviano his final paycheck.

Huber-Fullerton

The Huber-Fullerton confrontation was an issue of authority. Dick Huber had been on leave from active duty, having been placed on suspension by Captain Fullerton, under authority of Section 6 of the Mounted Police Act. Available records seem to support the allegation that Ranger Huber blatantly disregarded the regulations that the captain had set forth to govern the ranger's operation. "I wish you would keep me posted," Fullerton had once written Huber, "so that I will be able to reach you at anytime if necessary."¹⁴ In July 1905, Captain Fullerton wrote Huber, "I have not been able to keep up with you as you have been going around from one place to the other. You seem to have ignored my order [to report to headquarters]. I have over looked it so far thinking perhaps you had not received the order.... I will not allow this thing to occur again...."[15]

Dick Huber often acted independently and at his own direction, while shielding his conduct by hiding behind his friendship with Governor Miguel A. Otero. As commander-in-chief of the mounted police, Governor Otero would occasionally order the Santa Fe based ranger to undertake a special assignment. In 1885, Miguel A. Otero had been appointed chief deputy to United States Marshal Romulo Martinez and 12 years later he had been an active candidate for the post of United States marshal for New Mexico Territory when President William McKinley named him the territorial governor.[16] It would seem that Otero had a latent desire to be a lawman and this may help to explain why he was so involved with some of the mounted police's day-to-day operations.

In mid–July, Governor Otero covered for one of Dick Huber's acts of rebellion. "I sent for Huber and told him to get his horse and start out, so you will understand that if there was any break in your general arrangements that it was caused by my instructions."[17] In a few other incidences, Otero had neglected to notify Captain Fullerton that Huber had been assigned a special duty and was unavailable to do something Fullerton needed done. This accounted for some of the shaky relationship between Fullerton and Huber. "While I want Huber to do his duty the same as any other member of the force [at] the same time I feel that I have been responsible for his apparent dereliction of duty. I have had him doing some work on the case that I mentioned to you, and I do not want you to be too severe on him in reprimanding him."[18] It would seem that Huber was aware of Otero's communication to Fullerton, because he now showed an openly superior attitude toward his fellow mounted police and especially toward his captain.

Ranger Huber had been warned twice by Captain Fullerton to obey the mounted police regulations; even Lieutenant Baca had to reprimand Private Huber. During the time Baca was directing the mounted police office, while Fullerton was in Albuquerque dealing with the Bernalillo County courthouse mess, the lieutenant demanded that Huber keep headquarters informed of his location and his actions. He told Huber to make a weekly report—even if he did not have any official report form, "take a sheet of writing paper and make it out." Then Baca issued another directive. "On your return from the cattle stealing matter come to Socorro without fail."[19]

Cipriano Baca had felt that a face to face discussion was needed with this headstrong ranger. No record of this meeting remains, but it would seem from his future actions that the dressing down had little or no permanent effect upon Ranger Dick Huber because he remained a tough-nosed hardhead who felt his friendship with the governor combined with his arrest record gave him the edge on anyone who took issue with the way he did his job. Old timers remembered Huber as "an expert on the draw and on the fire ... there was no better man with a gun."[20] For some time Huber was able to walk the thin line between official police rules and his own course of action.

On September 22, 1905, Governor Otero left the territory on a month long vacation and business trip. Otero wrote that during his last year in office he "was somewhat run down in health and greatly in need of rest." He also claimed he wanted to take a trip to Europe with his son. So in early October, Otero visited Washington and had a short conference with President Roosevelt. Otero later claimed that he had told TR he did not wish to be reappointed for another four year term as New Mexico's governor and that the president had reluctantly agreed to his wish. He later admitted that he and Roosevelt had clashed several times and "in place of seeking a reappointment under him, I always considered myself lucky to be able to serve out my term." Otero added that he "had very little confidence in his [Roosevelt] statements or in his actions. He was too egotistical and overbearing. He ... would sacrifice anyone in his way, even though it be a friend." The two men had agreed that the White House would make the official announcement of a new governor's appointment on November 24. "I saw no reason to give publicity to my plans immediately. I certainly wanted to keep my enemies guessing as to what I would do." However, to Otero's open disdain the Associated Press released the leaked news three days early.[21]

By mid–November 1905, Governor Otero had removed himself from any direct involvement with the territorial police's operations. "I told him [a man who requested that the governor assign a mounted police to help him] that I had nothing to do with the distributing of the privates throughout the territory, and that the matter was entirely in your [Fullerton's] hands."[22]

On Friday, November 17, Ranger Dick Huber stepped off his tightrope and disobeyed a direct order from a squad leader. Huber had been instructed to operate under the guidance of Ranger Bob Putman during a robbery investigation. Huber left the crime scene and returned home in defiance of Putman's order to continue the search for crime scene evidence. Putman immediately notified Fullerton of Huber's actions. Huber had finally given his captain a *casus belli*, a reason to act, and Fullerton suspended his single-minded ranger from active duty.

Dick Huber again sought redress from Governor Otero. Captain Fullerton wrote to his commander concerning Huber's rebellion. "No doubt Huber has had an interview with you as I suspended him on the 17th inst. for leaving Willard against [Bob] Putman's orders. I must have discipline from this time on in order to accomplish anything. I rather think that I will have to suspend two more of the men very soon if they do not respect orders as they should."[23] Fullerton did not identify the other two rangers. Even in Texas and Arizona, discipline always seemed to have been a major problem among the 20th Century rangers.

In his own defense, Huber claimed that the holdup investigation was useless and a waste of his time. District Attorney Frank W. Clancy had wanted Huber to make an appearance in an Albuquerque court case, but Captain Fullerton had told Clancy, "I have ordered him out on some special work at Willard, they had a hold-up there night before last."[24] Dick Huber wanted to be in the limelight, wearing his mounted police uniform, during the court hearing and not on a cold, back-breaking chase that had no chance of catching the bandits who had robbed a railroad agent. The mounted police closed the Willard robbery investigation about a week after the holdup. Railroad officials and the rangers jointly agreed "that a further search would be of no avail."[25]

It would seem that Putman may have seen Captain Fullerton in Albuquerque and briefed him about the Willard investigation and Huber's actions. Fullerton was headed to Las Vegas on "a business trip" with his Uncle Milton Fullerton. John had been entertaining his uncle and a traveling companion at his Socorro County ranch and at his sister's home in Albuquerque. A newspaper recounted, "When asked what he thought of central New Mexico [the area were Fullerton had his ranch] the Pennsylvania Fullerton [Uncle Milton] said that he found it to be a big country with nobody at home."[26]

Captain Fullerton sent the governor a full account of the reason for Huber's suspension and then met with Otero on December 6 to discuss the whole affair. Governor Otero agreed with Captain Fullerton's position and upheld Dick Huber's suspension.[27] Fullerton now asked the governor for permission to deal with another thorny problem. He wished to issue a general order prohibiting "moonlighting" by his rangers because he felt that some of his men were not devoting enough time to their duties as territorial police. Governor Otero understood Fullerton's concern and authorized the captain to issue the general order.[28] Dick Huber, upon notification of the new general order, sent Captain Fullerton his resignation and the ranger chief accepted the voluntary removal of the troublesome private. Fullerton backdated acceptance of the resignation to the first of December because he had no desire to reward his suspended ranger with an additional week's unearned salary after all the trouble he had caused.[29]

General Orders

The New Mexico Mounted Police were not the only ranger service with personnel problems. In 1907, six years after the force was organized, Arizona Ranger Captain Harry C. Wheeler found it necessary to issue a set of seven general orders detailing what he would consider proper conduct for the rangers. On June 2, Wheeler wrote Arizona Governor J. H. Kibbey, "I do not wish to tramp upon the liberties of the men under me, nor take advantage of my position in any way, however, incidents that to my personal knowledge have occurred ... made necessary, the promulgation of the orders ... for the information and guidance of all Rangers personally and for the good of the service in general."

Wheeler, like Fullerton before him, was faced with a near mutiny. "They [the general orders] have not met cordial reception by some of the men, but I intent they be obeyed, even to the extent if necessary, of letting those go, who feel they are unable to abide by them."

Wheeler's general orders instructed the rangers not to "congregate in saloons, nor in any bawdy house, for the purpose of amusement, or out of idleness." The rangers were to honor their "financial obligations on time and according to promise" and they were also prohibited from entering Mexico "in any official capacity what so ever, armed or unarmed."

Orders number four and five demanded strict and impartial enforcement of the laws against gambling and women and children visiting a saloon. Number six said that all ranger prisoners were to be shown "the greatest humanity," but the ranger was not to "endanger his life by taking foolish chances with desperate criminals and if any one must be hurt, I do not want it to be the Ranger." The final general order stressed that "Obedience to orders must be observed." Wheeler said, "To obey is honorable. To disobey, dishonorable, in this organization."[30]

If Captain Fullerton had been delighted to accept Huber's resignation, he may have been more reluctant to accept the termination letter of the popular Herb McGrath. Fullerton should not have been surprised by McGrath's resignation, because Herb had made his position very clear nine months earlier. "If it is required to put in all his time [as a ranger] he cannot afford to accept the position. There is not enough money in it," reported McGrath's hometown paper in March 1905.[31]

McGrath expressed the truth when he wrote, "My constable & deputyship are worth more money [in collected fees] every month to me than the territory pays you as captain. It would be very foolish to give them up to work [solely] as a [mounted police] private." McGrath was also candid when he remarked, "A little glory is about all a man can possible [sic] have left at the end of the month [after paying his field expenses with his ranger's salary], it is not glory I work for." John Fullerton must have been moved when he read of McGrath's willingness to ride just as hard and just as far to assist his former captain as any of his present rangers. "I am at your command."[32]

Herbert J. McGrath, photographed at Silver City about the time he became mounted police captain in the summer of 1918 (courtesy of Tom McGrath).

Money was always an important concern to Herb McGrath. Even on his trip to Santa Fe for the mustering-in ceremony as a mounted police, Herb found a way to have Grant County taxpayers foot the bill for the trip and his expenses. Deputy Sheriff Herb McGrath accompanied Sheriff C. A. Farnesworth as a guard for some county prisoners being "routinely" transported to the territorial prison. Captain Fullerton understood the desire to collect reward money. As early as June, he had made an inquiry concerning "what reward is offered, if any." In October, he asked a New York City detective agency the same question. However, there is no evidence to suggest that Fullerton ever received any reward money for the efforts of his rangers.[33]

Herb McGrath had the best individual arrest record during the first few months of the new ranger services' history, yet none of these arrests had been accomplished while Herb was on ranger scout duty. All of Herb's reported mounted police arrests had been made in a town or village and he double reported most of his arrests. McGrath's arrests were, if possible, always made as a deputy sheriff so he could collect an arrest fee from Grant County. He then reported the same arrest on his weekly ranger field record. Contemporary newspapers seldom ever referred to Herb McGrath as a territorial ranger, but most often spoke of him as a constable or deputy sheriff.[34]

It is interesting to note that neither Fullerton nor Baca seem to have ever openly questioned the actions of Herb McGrath, whose hometown area of Lordsburg was just a few miles northwest of George Elkins' home at Hachita Junction. Yet no one, not even McGrath's squad leader, suggested that McGrath's service area was overrun by outlaw gangs or that he was not fulfilling his ranger duty. In an unusual arrangement of command, Captain Fullerton had placed George Elkins under Lieutenant Baca and Herb McGrath under Sergeant Lewis.

Stewart and Gomez

Governor Miguel Otero granted Captain Fullerton's request to appoint E. Rhea Stewart, of Aztec, and Rafael Gomez, of Santa Fe, to the mounted police. Fullerton had written the governor, "I have made a thorough examination as to the fitness" of Stewart and Gomez and find they are "in every way qualified to act in this capacity." Fullerton even noted that Stewart had "good references."[35] Stewart, a brand inspector for the Cattle Sanitary Board, had helped Baca and his squad break the Magnum gang's hold on northwestern New Mexico. It is possible that Lieutenant Baca had also recommended Gomez to Captain Fullerton, because Baca and Gomez knew each other from their days working at the territorial penitentiary. Baca oversaw the prison yard guards, while Gomez did special projects for the superintendent.[36]

Stewart and Gomez met Captain Fullerton at the capital on Thursday afternoon, December 14, and accepted their appointments. Both men were then sworn in to office and briefed on their duties.[37] It is interesting to note that there are no official records to indicate that Captain Fullerton ever discussed the need to order a mounted police uniform with either of these new rangers. In fact, the dress uniform is never mentioned again after it was ordered worn by the rangers during duty at the two territorial fairs.

One newspaper told its readers that both of the new rangers were "men of nerve and experience in frontier police duty, and doubtless they will be valuable assistance to the mounted police."[38] Stewart, however, did little more than check some local San Juan County butcher shops for misbranded cattle hides. Meanwhile, Rafael Gomez picked up the same scout area that Huber had traveled and he quickly made his presence known to the local ranchers. With the year 1905 nearing a close, Captain Fullerton was quoted as saying, "The territory is pretty free of crime at present. I have been doing a little work on misdemeanor cases but there has not been a crime of any prominence during the past few weeks."[39] This may have been one reason that the new governor felt no urgent need to replace Mounted Policeman Octaviano Perea.

The Stewart and Gomez appointments still left the company short one ranger, but Governor Otero chose to leave this open post to be filled by his successor. The new governor decided not to fill the three month vacancy left by Ranger Perea's departure.[40]

In late March 1906, Captain Fullerton received one final resignation. It was from John Brophy and he told Fullerton that he did not wish to be reappointed to another term as a mounted police, at $75 per month, when he could become the night marshal at Clayton and earn $125 per month.[41] Brophy had been doing double duty as a Union County deputy sheriff since November 1905 and interestingly Brophy never made one mounted police arrest in Union County. Fullerton must have had some sympathy for Brophy's desire to be home with his family and friends and the added desire to earn more income to support his growing family.

John Brophy continued to earn his territorial salary until his final day. John's last mounted police duty was a 220 mile trip down to Tucumcari and back to Clayton. This final week-long horseback scout followed his attendance at the district court session held in Clayton. Some of Fullerton's Rangers seem to have had a strong work ethic and John Brophy was one of them.

10

The New Mexico Mounted Police Fund

> "There shall be annually levied and collected in addition to all other taxes authorized by law, a tax of one-half mill on taxable property in this territory, to be placed in a fund by the Territorial Treasurer, to be known as the New Mexico Mounted Police Fund, and upon which fund all warrants and payments made under any of the provisions of this act, shall be drawn and made."
> Section Three — Mounted Police Fund
> **New Mexico Mounted Police Act of 1905**

In early August 1905, Captain Fullerton sat at his desk in headquarters trying to compose his response to a request from Governor Otero. Miss Olsen had sent Fullerton a letter explaining that the governor wanted to include information about the rangers in his annual report to the secretary of the interior. Clara Olsen said Otero wanted "a statement regarding the organization and operation of the Mounted Police since the passage of the law." The governor's private secretary then added, "Will you kindly prepare such an article and forward, if possible, sometime before the 15th of August?"[1]

Captain Fullerton began a review of the mounted police's weekly field reports, the purchase orders and the payroll vouchers. John must have also reread the legislative act of creation to help him outline the territorial police's duties. All of this data must have had a very sobering effect upon the Captain Fullerton. The territorial auditor had honored Captain Fullerton's request for salary warrants amounting to $3,708.13 for the mounted police. Fullerton had also requested payment of $1,026.30 in day to day field expenses for his men. During four months of operation the captain had also paid to outfit his rangers and equip the ranger headquarters at a cost of nearly $600.[2] John Fullerton was a successful businessman and he understood budgets and cash flow. He also understood the accounting term deficit financing.

Deficit Financing

Section 12 of the Mounted Police Act made it the duty of the territorial auditor to authorize the territorial treasurer to pay approved mounted police expenses at the end of each month. The accounts due were to be paid from the Mounted Police Fund that was to be established according to Section 13 of the same act. The territorial treasurer was authorized to annually levy and collect a one-half mill[3] tax on all property for the support of the ranger force. The section further stated that "said tax shall be levied and collected in the same manner, and at the same time and by the same officers as other territorial taxes."[4] The Arizona Rangers Fund was financed by "a tax of five cents on the hundred dollars of taxable property in this territory."[5]

The Mounted Police Act also ordered the treasurer to "pay the same [all mounted police bills] out of any funds, except the interest and sinking funds in the Territorial Treasury," until the new levy could be collected.[6] This last provision had been added to the original bill as a means to support the immediate formation and activation of the rangers. It was a necessary measure because the annual territorial tax levy was made based upon the fiscal budget starting each December 1. The first Mounted Police Fund levy would not be made until the fall of 1905.

William G. Sargent, the longest serving territorial/state auditor in the history of New Mexico. He was not a supporter of the mounted police, but was a distant relative of Cipriano Baca (courtesy of Cipriana Baca Randolph).

Fullerton saw his department's financial boat was in danger of sinking. Budget projections revealed that a fully staffed mounted police company would cost $11,900 in salaries for one year. Because of some vacancies during the first few months and the possible further lack of manpower, Fullerton knew he would not overspend this allocation. However, the operational expense for Fullerton's Rangers during the first four months had reached $1,026.30.[7] The captain could see no way that the range riders could function within the specification set down by Section 14 that "the total cost and expense of the organization, equipment and support of said company shall not exceed the sum of Thirteen Thousand Dollars for any one year."[8]

If Section 14 constituted the total mounted police appropriation then Captain Fullerton had less than $75 to operate the rangers over the next eight months. After careful reading of the Mounted Police Act, Fullerton found what he felt was an additional annual appropriation of $1,200 for the ranger's contingent expenses.[9] Fullerton quickly contacted the territorial auditor about the use of these newly discovered funds since the law stated that the auditor approved payment upon the captain's recommendation. Territorial Auditor William G. Sargent took the stance that the mounted police were only entitled to $13,000 a year and not a cent more. He told Fullerton he would not honor any request for money over the legislatively approved appropriation.[10]

Fullerton and Sargent had experienced an initial disagreement when the auditor approved the captain's first paycheck. Fullerton wrote Sargent, "My salary ... figure it is at the rate of $2,000 per annum divided by 365 days and that gives $5.48 per day." The captain returned the check and asked Sargent for a new one. Fullerton felt the territory had overpaid him by $1.25 for his first month's work.[11] A new check was issued.

John Fullerton would not accept the position advocated by the auditor. Sargent had been wrong before; he was wrong this time too. On Wednesday, August 16, Captain Fullerton met with the governor to explain the financial problem facing the mounted police.[12] Governor Otero was keenly aware of the expense problem under discussion because a few days earlier he had sent a squad of mounted police on a special mission to protect his own son from suspected kidnappers. Ranger Herb McGrath had traveled all the way from Lordsburg to Santa Fe to take up the hunt.[13]

The Legal Opinion Request

Governor Otero asked Captain Fullerton to put his concerns in writing so the problem could be placed before the attorney general for a legal opinion. Miss Olsen took Fullerton's dictation and typed the formal letter to the governor. She next typed Governor Otero's formal request to George W. Prichard. Otero ended his note by saying, "I will be obliged if you will give this matter your early attention."[14] Captain Fullerton had asked the governor to request a legal opinion on two questions.

> 1. Under the act passed by the Legislature creating the Mounted Police force, there was provided the sum of $13,000.00 to pay salaries, etc of officers and men, and in another section it reads "...a sum not exceeding twelve hundred (1,200.00) dollars per annum is hereby appropriated for contingent expense of such company, which shall be paid in the same manner as provided in this act and out of which shall be brought and paid for the arms herein before provided, and such other incidental expenses as shall be necessary for the carrying out of the provisions provided for in this act. All such incidental expenses or contingent expenses shall be accounted for by itemized voucher duly certified by the captain of such Mounted Police and approved by the territorial auditor, but no expense of any kind shall be incurred or allowed in any one year in excess of the sum of twelve hundred dollars." The territorial Auditor holds that the $1,200.00 above mentioned is already included in the $13,000.00 before provided, and in which case the act becomes ambiguous, as it would leave the contingent expense but $1,100.00, providing that all vacancies were filled and the members paid as provided by law.
>
> What I desire is to have a ruling of the Attorney General on this question, for future guidance.

Captain John F. Fullerton's second question dealt with another kind of money problem.

2. In the case of arrest of any prisoner by the Mounted Police outside of the county in which the offense is alleged to have been committed, there seems to be considerable difficulty in having the Boards of County Commissioners approve accounts of members for expenses incurred in conveying prisoners. It would seem that the County to which the prisoner is finally conveyed should pay the expense incurred in so doing, and I would like to have an opinion from the Attorney General for publication on this matter, so that members of the force who have to pay out for railroad fare, guards, etc. shall be able to collect same from the proper county.[15]

Fullerton returned to Socorro that evening, but not before Miss Olsen had reminded him about his overdue annual operational report. Upon his return home he wrote, "In regard to my report, I will get to work on same and get it out as soon as possible."[16]

The Attorney General's Opinion

On Friday August 18, George Prichard sent to the governor a letter containing his requested opinion. The next day the governor sent Fullerton's request letter, the attorney general's opinion and a cover letter to Captain Fullerton. "As these papers must be kept on file in my office I would request that you return them to me, after you have read same and had copies made."[17]

The attorney general's opinion was very good news for the New Mexico Mounted Police.

Attorney General George W. Prichard's opinions were favorable to the operation of the mounted police.

> Yours of the 16th inst., with enclosure from John F. Fullerton, Captain New Mexico Mounted Police, in which my attention is called to Sections 14 and 15 of "An Act to Organize and Equip a Company of Mounted Police for the Territory of New Mexico, Approved February 3rd, 1905," and my opinion asked as to whether the $1200.00 appropriated in the last Section mentioned is embraced in the sum of $13,000.00 in Section 14, has been received....
>
> It will be seen by reference to Section 14 that the $13,000.00 therein named is for the "expense of the organization, equipment and support of said company."
>
> Section 15 provides the sum of $1200.00 "For the contingent expense of said company." The

question presented for my determination is this, is the $1200 meant to be embraced in the $13,000.00 or is it to stand as an independent appropriation? I noticed that Section 14 makes no allusion to "contingent expenses," but refers to the expense of organization, equipment and support of said company. Can the words organization, equipment and support be construed as contingent expenses under this act? I am inclined to think not. Contingent expenses would embrace matters other than the expense of organization, equipment and support; such as telegrams, horse feed, feeding prisoners and expense of arrest, etc. The only exception to this is the expense of purchasing arms for the mounted police, and that is made by express terms of section 15 a contingent expense.

The law is not as clear on the point under consideration as it might be, but construing the two sections together, what was the reasonable intendment of the Legislature? If the Legislature intended to let the $13,000.00 provision cover everything, why did it precede further and appropriate $1200 for contingent expenses, no contingent expenses being mentioned in connection with the $13,000 provision? Did not the Legislature intend the $1200 appropriation as a distinct matter, disconnected from the other provision, and as applying to another subject? Reading the two sections together, bearing on different matters as they do and providing the distinct sums for different purposes, I am of the opinion that it was the intention of that body to make an additional appropriation of $1200.00 for contingent expenses, as shown by Section 15, referred to, and that such is not to be deducted from the $13,000.00. The fact that the Legislature prohibits the incurring of these contingent expenses beyond the sum of $1200 it is a strong fact showing that it was intended as an entirely independent appropriation.[18]

On Wednesday, August 23, Captain Fullerton returned to Governor Otero, as requested, the original attorney general papers for the executive's file. "The decision of the Attorney-General is very favorable and it will be quite a help to us to have this $1,200.00. I wish to thank you for your assistance in this matter." Otero acknowledged receipt of Fullerton's letter with a thank you note for the Mounted Police Department's first annual report.[19]

Fullerton vs. Sergent

Territorial Attorney General George W. Prichard's opinion concerning the expense account landed upon a deaf ear. As late as November 1905 Territorial Auditor W.G. Sargent was still resisting authorization for payments of mounted police bills. John Fullerton wrote him, "Please let me know if you still insist that the $1200.00 is a part of the $13,000.00 that was set aside for our use. I have talked with each member of the [council] committee that drafted the bill and they have all told me that the $1200.00 is separate and distinct from the $13,000.00 ... the Attorney General gave his decision in our favor and [I] should think that you would consider the opinion of the Attorney General." Fullerton once again made his point clear. "I do think that when this money has been set aside by the legislature for our expense that we should have it, and I insist on it."[20]

Governor Otero finally had enough of this feud. He had too many external problems to confront without one of his own appointees giving another one of his department heads unwarranted trouble. Otero's order must have been very direct, because

Sargent immediately stopped his harassment of the mounted police.[21] Will Sargent may have taken note of the fact that a new governor would take office in a couple of months and Will may not have wished to be perceived as troublesome by the new chief executive, since that man would soon have the power to appoint a new territorial auditor.[22] Sergent was also a member of the Republican Party's Territorial Central Committee and needed a good working relationship in that group to maintain his own political base.

In the files of Territorial Treasurer J.H. Vaughn is a list of all the warrants drawn against the Mounted Police Fund during the period of December 20, 1905, through November 10, 1911. Expenses prior to this date were paid from the territory's general accounts and all allocations made after this period are recorded under the new state's first fiscal year.[23]

Two other sets of records can help to develop a picture of how John Fullerton spent ranger funds during the months preceding the establishment of the separate mounted police account. In August 1905, Captain Fullerton prepared his report for Governor Otero detailing his department's first few months of operation. This report contained a financial statement covering March through July 1905. In January 1907, Captain Fred Fornoff presented Governor H.J. Hagerman a department report containing a financial statement covering the 21 month period of April 1905 to December 1906.[24] A side by side comparison of the Fullerton and Fornoff reports with the account sheets made by the territorial treasurer and the territorial auditor uncover a few discrepancies. Most of these differences are minor and some of the disparity seems to be the result of simply recording different data, but at this late date it is difficult to determine all the facts.

The following is a comparison of the reported cost to operate the mounted police during the spring and early summer of 1905.

Fullerton's 1905 Accounting:		*Fornoff's 1907 Recap for 1905:*
54.00	March	.00
1,014.60	April	1,214.76
501.01	May	1,384.29
993.94	June	1,051.21
2,100.75	July	1,120.17
$4,664.30		$4,734.43

The difference between Fullerton's and Fornoff's tally sheets is $124.13, or $70.13 if you disregard the $54 expense Fullerton listed under his recap for March. It may be assumed the March figure represented Captain Fullerton's compensation for that month.[25]

John F. Fullerton was appointed mounted police captain on March 18 and took his oath of office that day. However, Section 24 of the Mounted Police Act of 1905 states, "That no portion of said troops shall become a charge against this territory until organized and placed under orders." It could be argued that the mounted police were not "organized and placed under orders" until the company's muster call on Saturday, April 1, 1905. If that was the situation, Fullerton was not entitled to payment for days prior to April Fool's Day. The opposite point would propose the case that Fullerton was "under orders" from the governor to organize his company thus he was entitled to payment for his services.[26]

If one uses Fullerton's reasoning that his salary was $5.48 per day, one must assume he did not claim payment for a full two weeks in March or he would have received $76.52 instead of the lesser amount.[27] Maybe the $54 was compensation plus expense money for the few select days Fullerton was in Santa Fe prior to the organization meeting on April 1. It should be noted that the mystery $54 appears on no other ledgers accept Fullerton's recap in his 1905 departmental report.

The Appropriation Act of 1907 contains, under Section 15, this single line item, "To reimburse John F. Fullerton for expenses incurred as Captain of the New Mexico Mounted Police, $666.00."[28] No documentation has been located to establish the reason for this payment, but it is interesting to note that this delayed reimbursement equaled Fullerton's salary for four months. Was this some type of belated severance payment; devil's money—$666? Or was this really payment for actual expense Fullerton was perceived to have incurred? Whatever the reason was for the payment, Acting Governor J. Wallace Raynolds approved of it and signed the legislation into law. It can be assumed that Fullerton was happy to receive the money.

When the mounted police operated with a full 11 man staff the total monthly payroll was $991.66. Twice during the first four months Fullerton's Rangers operated short staffed. In April only six privates served the full month and a seventh ranger served only 23 days. April's salary total was $898.47. In July seven privates served the full month and the eighth man served 24 days. The July expenditure was $932.48 for salaries.[29]

During April, the Fullerton report claimed $1,014.60 as the month's total expense. Fornoff's Recap showed $1,214.76. In May, Fullerton recorded $501.01, while Fornoff recorded $1,348.29. In June $993.94 was reported by Fullerton, while $1,051.21 was recorded by Fornoff. And in July the Fullerton expense claim was $2,100.75, while the Fornoff claim was for $1,120.17.

A quick review of the data would seem to indicate an accounting error, yet it is possible that they were both right. John Fullerton had many problems during the months under discussion and one of these problems was his slowness in receiving the mounted police's weekly field reports. These activity reports were often accompanied by reimbursement requests and many times these accounts were delayed for an extended period. Fullerton had to contend with a major difficulty in the reluctance of Territorial Auditor Will Sargent to honor the captain's draft requests.

In the summer of 1906, Herbert J. Hagerman made his only report as a territorial governor to the secretary of the interior. In this statement of conditions in New Mexico Territory, Governor Hagerman included some comments on the rangers. The final sentence said, "The cost of maintaining the department for the first year was $13,284.99." This is the same figure that Captain Fornoff's 1907 report charges to the operation of Fullerton's Rangers. The money was credited thus: "$11,301.63 for salaries and $1,983.36 for contingent expenses."[30]

It would seem that John Fullerton's 1905 accounting, done in August, was the actual accounts due paid during each given month. The information used by Fred Fornoff in his 1907 recap is most likely the adjusted expenditures properly credited

New Mexico Mounted Police Fund
RECORD OF TREASURY WARRANTS 1905–1906

Date	Warrant #	Payee (Purpose)	Amount
20 December 1905	11824	First National Bank, Santa Fe (Unknown)	35.00
03 January 1906	11887	John F. Fullerton, Capt. MP (December 1905 salaries)	949.43
	11888	W. M. Byerts (Unknown)	10.00
	11890	Whitney Company of Albuquerque (Pistol and rifle ammunition)	66.34
08 January 1906	11910	John F. Fullerton, Capt. MP (December 1905 company's expense)	60.25
	11912	Henry Chambon (office rent — December/January)	18.00
03 February 1906	12018	John F. Fullerton, Capt. MP (January 1906 salaries)	864.66
	12019	John F. Fullerton, Capt. MP (January 1906 company's expense)	57.33
01 March 1906	12077	John F. Fullerton, Capt. MP (February 1906 salaries)	916.66
	12078	John F. Fullerton, Capt. MP (February 1906 company's expense)	51.94
	12092	Whitney Company of Albuquerque (Pistol and rifle ammunition)	23.75
23 March 1906	12136	J. W. Raynolds, Terr. Sec. (Filing fee — unknown reason)	3.00
24 March 1906	12137	Socorro Co. Pub(lishing) Co. (Unknown)	13.00
31 March 1906	12167	Henry Chambon (office rent — February/March)	18.00
	12168	John F. Fullerton, Capt MP (March 1906 salaries & expenses)	1128.51

All territorial warrants (checks) were burned, according to law, following the audited report to the governor. There is no warrant record prior to 01 December 1905 for the Mounted Police Fund. (Annual Report, 11 December 1906, Territorial Auditor Records, NMSRCA.)

Beginning in May 1905 Captain Fullerton paid each ranger from a departmental checking account at the Bank of Commerce in Albuquerque. He deposited the monthly territorial warrant(s) and used these funds for salaries and personal expense reimbursements. Prior to December 1905 Captain Fullerton made over 60 voucher requests to the auditor for payment. As of August 1 these requests amounted to $3,614.76. (Misc. Data, Fullerton's letters, NMMP/NMSRCA.)

to the month of their occurrence. Both sets of records seem to show that John Fullerton was a good steward of the public trust.

William G. Sargent's audit report for the 56th Territorial Fiscal Year, ending 30 November 1905, shows that the newly established Mounted Police Fund was credited with $196.54. This tax money had been collected during the fourth quarter of the fiscal year. No treasury warrants had been drawn on the new account.[31]

During the first quarter of the 57th Territorial Fiscal Year, which began 01 December 1905, the territory collected $7,494.22 in direct support for the Mounted Police Department and during this same three months territorial drafts were issued for $2,061.01. Fred Fornoff became ranger chief during the second quarter of the territorial police's first full year to be financed by the Mounted Police Fund. During this period tax collections totaled only $545.49 while expenses were $4,121.81. Tax collections, however, outpaced the rangers' spending by the year's end.[32]

The author of the Mounted Police Act of 1905 had believed that his dedicated tax plan would support the total ranger operation. He said, "At a liberal estimate of the cost we can, I believe, operate a Mounted Police force of twelve men at an expense of less than $1,000 per month."[33] W. H. Greer was almost right. In just three years the special tax had generated enough money for the mounted police operation and had also developed a nice surplus. This surplus fund balance soon became a problem, because the excess revenue had reached $7,948.86 by the time the 60th Territorial Fiscal Year began on December 1, 1908.[34]

When the Territorial Legislative Assembly convened early in 1909, the lawmakers were searching for ways to increase revenue without a general tax increase and the Mounted Police Fund's surplus became an easy target. The problem that the lawmakers faced was that it was a dedicated fund solely for the operation of the mounted police and it was supported by a specific tax. Someone came up with the idea of abolishing the special Mounted Police Fund, but not the special tax. This concept would cause the money held in the special fund to become part of the territory's general account. The special one-half mill tax levy need not be abolished; it was making a sizeable amount of income, but could be absorbed into the overall territorial tax levy. It was reasoned that citizens would continue to pay the same tax amount and would not care how the money was divided in the auditor's financial ledgers.

The 1909 lawmakers not only took away the mounted police's designated fund, but they also cut the force's strength to increase the fund's surplus. However, the lawmakers did not reduce the tax rate accordingly. By the time the new finance law took effect the surplus in the Mounted Police Fund had reached nearly $13,000.[35] It was the lack of an independent tax base that led to the informal disbanding of the state mounted police in December 1913.[36] This nonfunding episode has no relation to the chronicle of Fullerton's Rangers, but it is a vital part of the history of Captain Fred Fornoff's ranger command.

11

Road to Oblivion: The Removal of Capt. John F. Fullerton

> "Facts are stubborn things. Whatever maybe our wishes, our inclinations, or the dictates from passions, they cannot alter the state of facts and evidence."
> John Adams

The governor of New Mexico Territory was provided a $3,000 a year salary by Congress, plus $500 for his office expenses and an additional $500 for a government interpreter. The territorial assembly normally appropriated an additional $4,200 to pay the executive's contingent expenses and the salary of the governor's private secretary. The New Mexico governor was also provided a rent free residence on the Fort Marcy Military Reservation at Santa Fe, worth about $500 per annum. This total compensation package was valued at about $8,700 per year. The man who held the post of New Mexico governor held a lucrative public office at the turn of the century since there was no federal or territorial income tax.[1]

On Saturday, December 23, 1905, Governor Miguel Otero hosted a dinner to honor the new governor-designee. A few days later, before he took office, a newspaper quoted Herbert Hagerman saying that "one of his greatest desires after he has become governor is to heal the breaches in his party and have all work for the good of the territory." This sanctimonious comment soon became Hagerman's albatross. On Monday, January 22, 1906, Herbert James Hagerman became the sixteenth governor (or the 21st if the five interim governors are counted) of New Mexico Territory. It soon became apparent that the new chief executive was not a noticeable fan of his predecessor.[2]

George Curry, who succeeded Hagerman as governor in 1907, wrote in his autobiography, "Many reports had reached the White House, largely from opponents of Governor Otero, of alleged graft and mismanagement of official business. While most of these reports were exaggerated, and some of them untrue, there was so much smoke from the battle among the [territorial] leaders that Roosevelt was convinced there must be fire."[3] Hagerman trusted Roosevelt's viewpoint.

In early March 1906, Otero, acting through a friend, filed a claim with Hagerman for 22 days "expenses" Otero felt was his due from the Governor's Contingent Fund. The territorial legislature had provided $3,000 annually for the governor's expenses and Otero had considered this appropriation as an additional salary to supplement the income paid a territorial governor by Congress. Based upon this belief Otero felt he was due his extra compensation. "In my opinion," Hagerman wrote Otero, "the fund is to be used for legitimate contingent expenses of the office ... and should be accounted for as such." Governor Hagerman sent Otero a territorial warrant for $177.32 with "a voucher for the same, which I would respectfully request you to sign and return to me."[4]

During this time frame Hagerman seems to have viewed Miguel A. Otero as a borderline grafter. However, others believed strongly in Otero's honesty and administrative abilities, so Hagerman's successor appointed him as treasurer of the territory and Otero served in that office for three years. Time has a way of changing a person's point of view and ironic as it seems now, in their later years, the two former governors, Otero and Hagerman, became very close friends.[5]

Hagerman had spent his first day in office attending to his inauguration activities and settling into his self-furnished apartment in the Palace Hotel.[6] On Tuesday and Wednesday he acquainted himself to the office and his duties. On Thursday January 25, 1906, Hagerman formally appointed Clara Olsen as his private secretary "for the time being." She had held the same post under previous governors Thornton and Otero.[7] Among the letters that Miss Olsen typed for Governor Hagerman two days later was one addressed to "Captain J. L. [sic] Fullerton, Socorro, N.M." This was not the first time that Olsen had prepared a letter for the mounted police captain, yet this time she mistyped his name. The "F" and the "L" are typed with different hands. This mistake is almost a foreboding of the relationship that was to develop between Hagerman and Fullerton; one misstep after another that led to total meltdown.

"I enclose herewith copy of a letter to Governor Otero from Mr. Charles Ilfeld of Las Vegas, saying that there is thieving going on near the town of Sunnyside," wrote Hagerman. "Complaints have already come to me in this regard from various other people, and it seems that if some member of the Mounted Police is at present able to make an investigation in that district, he should do so."[8]

Hagerman may not have known that Otero and Ilfeld, a native of Homburg Von der Hobe in Germany, were old friends from their early days together in Las Vegas. Ilfeld had asked Otero to send "a detachment to Sunnyside" to stop the livestock stealing in that area.[9] This was not an unusual request since both Otero and Ilfeld had large livestock holdings in San Miguel and Guadalupe counties.

The new governor replied to Ilfeld's letter saying, "I will investigate the matter in question as soon as it is possible for me to do so." Hagerman did add that he would pass the request on to the mounted police for their action, but then he promised Ilfeld that he would personally undertake an inquiry affair. Three days into office and Hagerman is promising his valuable time to investigate suspected livestock theft in a remote area of central New Mexico? Two days after writing Ilfeld, Hagerman finally forwarded the rancher's request for assistance on to the territorial police with the added comment that he had received the same type of complaint from "various other people about live stock losses near Sunnyside." This is a doubtful claim because Ilfeld's letter is the only correspondence of this nature in the governor's Letters Received File for January 1906. It would seem reasonable to assume that listening to verbal complaints about livestock stealing would not be a top priority for a new governor. In the Hagerman to Fullerton letter concerning Sunnyside, the mounted police captain is treated more like a schoolboy than the leader of a law enforcement agency. "This is merely a suggestion on my part, and I should be glad to know if you have any information about the matter," Hagerman wrote to Fullerton.[10]

Maybe Governor Hagerman didn't read any New Mexico newspapers, or if he did, he somehow seems to have missed the fact that in late January and early February the territorial press was full of headlines extolling the mounted police and how they had closed the "Robbers' Roost" in Guadalupe County and had recovered hundreds of stolen sheep and cattle. Governor Hagerman found that Captain Fullerton was quick to reply to his letter and to inform him that the police were doing their duty. The governor received a copy of Lieutenant Baca's recent field report concerning his squad's actions in Guadalupe County. In his report Baca says he recovered "148 head of sheep, property of Ilfeld, of Las Vegas" on the same day the merchant-rancher wrote to Governor Otero requesting assistance. In his cover letter Fullerton said, "Whenever you receive complaints, from anyone I wish you would kindly forward them to me and all matters will receive our prompt attention." Governor Otero had Miss Olsen to routinely forward all police requests on to Fullerton and the captain was simply requesting the same treatment from the new governor.

Fullerton ended his communication by telling Hagerman, "I have not been able to find the town of Sunnyside on the [postal] map of March 1st, 1905, but [I] think it must be in the district where I now have four men." Sunnyside is not found on today's map of New Mexico either, so where was Sunnyside? In the winter of 1905–1906 Sunnyside was only a crossroads railroad construction camp located near a spring about a mile from present day Fort Sumner. Hagerman had mistakenly referred to Sunnyside as a town, but in early 1906 the site could hardly have been called a settlement, much less a village and certainly not a town.[11]

Even a century later, one can still feel the anger that must have raised Hagerman's blood pressure. First, Fullerton had the nerve to address him in a condescending tone. The general public referred to the president as "Teddy" and even named a toy bear after him, but Roosevelt did not like the nickname and demanded that his friends and family call him Theodore. Herbert James Hagerman was cast from the same mold as the president. Secondly, John had the misfortune to have sounded wishy-washy in his knowledge of the country he was charged with protecting. In Fullerton's defense, few people outside Guadalupe County knew about the camp. Years later, old Fort Sumner residents moved the few miles north to the Sunnyside railroad site, but they brought with them the old fort's name to the new location. The town is now the county seat.

The First Meeting

On Monday morning, February 5, 1906, Governor Hagerman and Captain Fullerton held their first conference.[12] The subject of that meeting is not preserved in official records, but the two men may have discussed the captain's fiscal year end report to Governor Otero. The report had recently been widely published in the newspapers and many editors had used the report to praise the actions of the mounted police. At least one paper, however, had questioned the accurate nature of the financial statement as it was printed in the Santa Fe *New Mexican*.[13]

The unfortunate slant by the *New Mexican* may have been the reason Governor Hagerman asked the territorial auditor to prepare for him "a memorandum showing moneys [sic] that have been paid out for the support of the different members of the Territorial Mounted Police since the formation of that body by the last legislature." Will Sargent was quick to comply.[14]

Captain Fullerton and his chief may also have discussed the personnel problems John was having with some of his men. Three of the mounted police had resigned during December and the suspension and resignation of Dick Huber could have been the focus of this possible agenda item. It would seem that Governor Hagerman was skeptical of the reasons surrounding the Huber suspension and this speculation is supported by the governor's re-appointment of Huber to fill the vacancy caused by the December 31 resignation of Octaviano Perea. The governor made the Huber appointment with the support of Captain Fred Fornoff and an Albuquerque newspaper said that Dick Huber was "a former member of the force and one of the most valuable men in the company."[15] This "most valuable man in the company" was not reappointed to the police in April 1907; it seems that Captain Fornoff may have discovered some of the same problems with Ranger Dick Huber that John Fullerton had experienced.

During their orientation meeting, Governor H.J. Hagerman and Captain John Fullerton may also have discussed their mutual concern for the safety of Sergeant Bob Lewis, plus a general review of fiscal management and general mounted police operating procedures. This conference was most likely a frank business meeting dominated by the commander-in-chief, because Herbert J. Hagerman had come to Santa Fe as "the king's white knight to restore truth and honor and to dispense true justice" in New Mexico Territory.[16] Fullerton left no formal impressions concerning that fateful first meeting with Governor Hagerman, but John did leave some telling remarks in a letter he wrote to an unknown friend. "Politics are badly mixed up here as ever. Every day something new turns up and no man knows where he standeth [sic]."[17]

Fullerton had arrived in Santa Fe on the Monday afternoon train and he gave an interview to a *New Mexican* reporter. These remarks were published the next day under the headline, "Mounted Police Doing Good Work." Monday night, February 5, Fullerton stayed at the Claire Hotel and on Tuesday Fullerton and Hagerman held their conference. Later that day, John was in Albuquerque visiting at the sheriff's office and Tuesday night he was visiting with his son. It would be interesting to know what John told Elmer, if anything, about the new governor. Wednesday evening John was back in Socorro and home with his wife.[18]

The White Knight

Almost three years before Hagerman became governor of New Mexico, President Roosevelt outlined his concept of character to an audience at Claremont, California. "Character has two sides. In addition to decency, morality, virtue, clean living, you must have hardihood, resolution, courage, the power to do, the power to dare, the power to endure, and when you have that combination, then you get the proper type of American citizenship."[19]

Herbert J. Hagerman was a man of stern moral character and he believed himself to be the knight on the white horse ready to champion any just cause. Hagerman was a Cornell University educated lawyer who had practiced his trade in Colorado before becoming the second secretary at the U.S. Embassy in St. Petersburg, Russia. Hagerman recorded his experiences while at the court of the Czar in his book *Letters of a Young Diplomat*. Ambassador Ethan Allen Hitchcock liked his youthful secretary and when Hitchcock was named secretary of the interior under President Roosevelt, he became the moving force behind Hagerman's appointment to succeed Miguel Otero as governor of New Mexico Territory.[20]

A few years before his death, Hagerman began work on his memoirs. In a chapter he called "The Governorship: Rough Riding in New Mexico 1906–1907," he wrote, "My experience as Territorial Governor of New Mexico was brief but hectic. As I look back now on that experience it seems more humorous than tragic, but at the time it was certainly serious enough for me."

The public relations story concerning Hagerman's appointment was that President Roosevelt wanted someone to clean up the political mess within the New Mexico Republican Party and return "sunshine" to the Sunshine Territory. "All that talk about cleaning things up proved to be a mere gesture on his [Roosevelt's] part," Hagerman wrote in his as-yet unpublished autobiography. In fact, as Hagerman learned later the president wanted to be rid of Otero because the governor opposed joint statehood with Arizona, not because the Otero administration was corrupt or ineffective. "The President lost all interest in Secretary Hitchcock's and my attempts to 'bring about good government in New Mexico' as soon as joint statehood with Arizona failed ... in spite of the fact that New Mexico voted for it by a big majority." Roosevelt gave Hagerman no credit for that triumphal victory in New Mexico and Hagerman quickly fell from favor. "In one of the interviews I had

Herbert J. Hagerman, as governor, was the second commander-in-chief of the New Mexico Mounted Police. He chose not to reappoint Fullerton as captain and named his friend Fred Fornoff head of the reorganized ranger force in April 1906 (courtesy of the Fred Fornoff Papers).

with him [Roosevelt] he said to me when an opinion of my Attorney-General which differed from his [opinion on the subject] was mentioned: 'Your Attorney-General ought to have his throat cut; he ought to have his neck wrung.' When I couldn't help smiling at his vociferousness he really looked mad enough to kill me on the spot."[21]

"While Herbert Hagerman had all the qualifications for a foreign diplomatic career, he was wholly without experience in practical politics, especially of the rough-and-ready, and no-holds-barred kind prevalent in the New Mexico of the period," wrote George Curry. "I have always felt that Hagerman's intentions were of the best; that he was largely the victim of bad advice, some of it from politically ambitious men; and that had he proceeded with more deliberation, and only after thorough investigation of men and affairs in the Territory, he could have averted the disaster which befell him."[22] President Roosevelt demanded Governor Hagerman's resignation on April 20, 1907.

The Sheriff Street Controversy

James Alexander Street, a native of Ripley, Mississippi, died in an Albuquerque hospital on August 23, 1937, and the men of the infant New Mexico State Police served as an honor guard for the casket as it was brought home to Tucumcari to rest in Sunnyside Cemetery. Street was eulogized as the organizer of the state police and as a decorated former agent of the Federal Bureau of Investigation. He was 68 years old. Two decades after his death, Jimmy Stewart portrayed a fictional agent based in part upon Street, solving a series of murders on Indian lands in the film *The FBI Story*. Street was an expert on Indian lore and as a young man had ridden the Indian Territory as a deputy U.S. marshal before coming to New Mexico as a cowhand working on the vast Bell Ranch. A few years later, Street and some partners founded the town of Tucumcari and Alex was the town's progressive mayor. When Quay County was formed Street became the first sheriff and served in that office for six terms.[23]

Mounted Policeman Dudley had praised Street to Captain Fullerton. "Mr. Street, sheriff of Quay County, went out [on patrol] with me [and] furnished me a horse [from his livery stable]. The Mt. Police have a friend and helper in Him." The Tucumcari *News* once said that a "more peaceful or law abiding citizenship can not be found in New Mexico than the people of Tucumcari. There have been no bad men in the commonwealth of Quay since Street was sheriff one year." Sheriff Alex Street and District Attorney Merritt C. Mechem, a future state governor, made a worthy set of law enforcement officers.[24]

Alex Street, who believed he was doing an acceptable job as sheriff, must have been stunned when he opened the letters from Governor Hagerman and Attorney General Prichard concerning his poor performance as sheriff of Quay County. "It is my earnest desire," wrote Hagerman, "that the laws of this territory be strictly and properly enforced, and that all officers of the law do their duty fearlessly and unequivocally." The attorney general later laid out the specific charges concerning "thieving and other depredations" being committed within Quay County and how Street and Mechem showed a lack of concern in the performance of their official duties.[25]

It would seem that Captain Fullerton may have brought up the subject of Street and Mechem at his February 5 meeting with Hagerman and then followed up these remarks with a letter. "You will see from these [complaint] letters that this Sheriff, like many others in the Territory, fail to perform the duties of his office; I would suggest that you investigate the matter and if you find he is not capable of filling his office, he, of course, should be removed and a good man appointed to fill his place." Fullerton had planted the seed for his own destruction. He had suggested a standard he himself could not accomplish and may have caused the governor to examine the captain by the measure he had proposed for another; shades of the Biblical Book of Ruth. "Unless we have the cooperation of the County Officers we can not expect to accomplish very much in the way of preserving the law and order in the Territory."[26] Why didn't Fullerton fully investigate these charges before he presented the matter to Hagerman? A few days later, Hagerman wrote to Fullerton, "I shall investigate the matter very thoroughly." He said that he would ask the attorney general to address the complaints with Street and Mechem.

James Alexander Street was longtime sheriff of Quay County, co-founder of Tucumcari, a future territorial policeman and a future FBI special agent (courtesy of Jewel Street Pickerel).

Hagerman also said he would write to both men. "I will write you further about this matter in a day or two." It would appear that the only investigation that Hagerman did was to read Fullerton's letter and the complete letters he sent with it. It is doubtful that the attorney general did any more with his inquiry than the governor had done.[27]

Sheriff Street accepted the challenge and sent Attorney General George Prichard a pointed reply. "I only have warrants against three persons whom I have been unable to get and two of them are in Colorado and the County has no money where with to pay for bring them here." Over the next six paragraphs Street's letter explained each of the three cases in detail. He said the only man still in his jurisdiction was Cage Riley, who lived in the rural hill country along the Texas border and "is too well protected by people who live around him." Street continued, "I have used every thing within my power to get Riley ... every law and order man who lives near Riley has been appointed a [special] deputy by me." Street said he had sent his chief deputy to arrest Riley and even he failed. "I have made three trips to his place to get him ... the people near Riley are his relatives or friends and all of them are either implicated with him or in sympathy with his kind of life." Street ended his letter with a challenge. "I am ready to appear at anytime and answer charges made against me as to my conduct in the office of Sheriff of this County."[28]

Attorney General Prichard soon resigned and entered private practice. He left the Street and Mechem matter for his successor to handle and his successor passed the misconduct investigation on to the mounted police. The new ranger captain tabled the issue and in 1910 he asked that Alex Street be appointed to the mounted police. Street served with distinction for four years.

Enter Fred Fornoff

Within days of taking office, Governor Hagerman received information from Pima County Sheriff James Lowry that he had a man in jail at Prescott who claimed that he had murdered Col. Jose Francisco Chaves. Hagerman quickly requested that United States Marshal Creighton M. Foraker send Fred Fornoff to Arizona to investigate the claim. The deputy marshal traveled to Arizona as the "authorized agent" of Hagerman on a courtesy pass issued over the Santa Fe Railroad system. In Prescott, Fornoff questioned the confessed killer and found him "not of sound mind" and confused as to his own identity. Back in New Mexico, Fred continued his inquiry at Grants, where he confirmed that the Arizona suspect had been employed there on the day that Chaves was murdered hundreds of miles away. On Saturday, February 3, Fornoff visited Hagerman's apartment and gave him his preliminary report, so later that day Hagerman telegraphed Sheriff Lowry that New Mexico had no further interest in his prisoner and that he could release the man from custody. On Tuesday, Fornoff delivered his written report to the governor. It is interesting to speculate if Fullerton and Fornoff saw each other in the governor's office that day.[29]

Later Governor Hagerman wrote Foraker, "The case is so important a one, as you know, that I thought it necessary that an intelligent and honest agent be chosen to make the investigation, and there was no one that filled these requirements that I knew of as well as Mr. Fornoff."[30] Governor Hagerman paid Fred Fornoff $53.40 for his expenses as an "agent" from funds in a special account provided by the Department of the Interior for the governor's use.[31]

On the Saturday before Governor Hagerman met with John F. Fullerton for their first formal encounter, he had held a social visit from the territory's chief federal marshal. Creighton M. Foraker discussed with the governor the projected appointment of a new penitentiary superintendent. Foraker's close friend and deputy, Fred Fornoff, was an open candidate for the post. Hagerman seems to have been impressed with Fornoff's law enforcement abilities, but he might have had some doubt about the deputy U.S. marshal's qualifications and ability to manage a complex business like the territorial prison.[32]

In late February, Governor Hagerman again asked Marshal Foraker to allow Fornoff to undertake a special mission and once again the governor was pleased with Fornoff's conduct.[33] Fornoff went to Taos to deliver the governor's stay of execution for a murderer who was reported to have gone insane. Under investigation, the insanity plea was proved false and the man was hung the same day that he attempted to commit suicide.[34]

It is only conjecture to assume that Hagerman, at some point, had compared Fornoff with his mounted police captain, yet is it significant that Governor Hagerman had not requested that a territorial ranger undertake his two special assignments? Fred Fornoff had been successful with his two special projects for Governor Hagerman and John Fullerton had made a mess of the first case he had to present to the governor. It is doubtful that this unfortunate incident did much to impress Hagerman with Fullerton's knowledge of the law or law enforcement procedures.[35] Deputy U.S. Marshal Fornoff seemed to exemplify a high degree of law enforcement professionalism.

Fullerton and "Graft"

It is conceivable that John Fullerton's real problem with Governor Hagerman was never known by the mounted police leader. W. P. Sanders, of Magdalena, sent Governor Hagerman a two page letter dated February 15, 1906, with an enclosure. Sanders, secretary to the executive committee for the Cattle and Horse Grower's Association of Central New Mexico, had accused Captain Fullerton of charging a local rancher for the services of the mounted police.[36] The white knight governor was shocked at the charge of graft.

A few days later, Hagerman answered Sanders' letter and requested more information: "I assure you I am much interested in your communication, and await with interest your reply."[37] The letter to Sanders would seem to imply that the governor believed the allegation leveled against Fullerton. Is it possible that Hagerman judged his ranger captain guilty of demanding payment from stockmen for the services performed by the rangers without even questioning John Fullerton about the charge? The German philosopher Nietzsche once said, "He who seeks to deceive will always find one willing to be deceived."[38]

Sanders had sent Hagerman a copy of a "bill for service" given to a rancher named W. Z. Redding for the recovery of a stolen steer. The governor did not contact Fullerton concerning any explanation for the "Redding Bill" before making his blunt pronouncement, "The statement shows that Capt. Fullerton charged for his services."[39] The White Knight of Santa Fe was ready to believe that John Fullerton was accepting graft or at the least was guilty of misconduct in office, that Fullerton was just like his former boss. Miguel Otero and John Fullerton were peas in the same pod. A week after his request for additional information Hagerman received a four page letter from Sanders that was a mess of disjointed illusions concerning misconduct by the officials of Socorro County. The letter also contained unfavorable remarks towards former Governor Otero: "He was well probably none to [sic] straight himself," and a few paragraphs of backslapping praise for the new governor's vanity.[40] Buried in this jungle of innuendos is probably the truth behind Sanders' charge against Fullerton. The underlying reason for the Socorro County stockmen's anger and this complaint was simple. They felt rejected by John F. Fullerton and it was payback time. Sanders may not have meant to betray the ranchers' feelings, but he did so, however, when he wrote, "Captain Fullerton, of the N.M.M. Police, was the man chosen [by us] to fill the office of Assessor [for Socorro County]; HE DROPPED THE OFFICE FOR HIS PRESENT POSITION; THUS BETRAYING OUR TRUST [emphasis in original]...."[41]

Fullerton had accepted the ranger post because he felt in this way he could be of greater service to all the stockmen in the territory. Certainly the ranchers knew that John could have made more money at his county job working for a percentage fee than he earned working for the territory, which makes it seem odd that his fellow Socorro County ranchers so misunderstood him.

It would appear that some Socorro County stockmen expected Fullerton to be "fair" when he was making their property value assessments and obviously these same stockmen were disappointed when John served less than three months in office. Even if Fullerton had retained his job in Socorro County there is no evidence to support the idea that John would have been less than honest in his duties. Maybe the real reason for the bitterness was a simple case of racial prejudice. A small time Hispanic machine politico, A.B. Baca, had replaced a respected Anglo rancher, John Fullerton, in a very powerful position of fiscal control. Money and racism had a long history of being strong negative factors in the social and political framework of Socorro County.

Both of W.P. Sanders' letters imply he is speaking on behalf of the executive committee of the Cattle and Horse Growers' Association of Central New Mexico.[42] One of the nine men who composed the association's board was Mounted Police Sergeant Robert W. Lewis. It is doubtful that Lewis had any knowledge of Sanders' efforts against Captain Fullerton because he was on assignment in Old Mexico. If Lewis had no knowledge of Sanders' letters, how many of the other eight members were also in the dark concerning this course of action?

In late February 1906, Fullerton had his second conference with Governor Hagerman at the executive's Santa Fe office.[43] This face-to-face took place at the height of the Sanders-Hagerman letter exchange. The two men discussed the legal requisition for the return of an escaped murderer who was now held in a Mexican jail. No records remain to suggest that Hagerman and Fullerton discussed the "Redding Bill" at this meeting or at any time. Why seek facts when you have already formed a negative opinion and decided on the punishment?

Even if Governor Hagerman did not care to understand the facts behind the "Redding Bill," there does appear to be a simple explanation. Captain Fullerton had ordered Lieutenant Baca, in June 1905, to lead a squad of rangers in search of a gang of cattle rustlers led by Tom Magnum who were operating along the high country between Arizona and New Mexico. A month-long search ended when the rangers captured the gang and recovered well over 100 head of stock.[44] In accordance with the Mounted Police Act the rangers delivered their prisoners to the nearest local peace officer. The Magnums were taken to Aztec, seat of San Juan County, and entrusted to Sheriff Boone Vaughn.[45] The recovered cattle were corralled and the San Juan County sheriff's department began the lengthy task of notifying the proper owners of the animals' recovery.[46]

Socorro County Sheriff Leandro Baca soon arrived in Aztec to take Tom Magnum back to Socorro to stand trial for unlawfully killing cattle in that county. A week later, Baca and his ranger squad returned to their homes. A taxpayer might ask, why didn't Lieutenant Baca just bring Tom Magnum with him when he returned home to Socorro? The answer is simple. Within the territory, prisoner transfer was the lawful duty of a county sheriff and was not the function of the territorial police, because county lawmen earned part of their fees for prisoner transfer and would have resented someone who breached this time-honored duty of a sheriff or his deputy.[47] The Mounted Police where to be used to return extradited prisoners back to New Mexico Territory.

The evidence suggests that Sheriff Vaughn and two of his deputies joined Baca's squad in a search for the stolen stock. Boone Vaughn located a 435-pound steer but could not determine the ownership, so he requested that Captain Fullerton help locate the owner. The brand description was close to one used by W.Z. Redding of Magdalena so Fullerton wrote the rancher asking if he had recently sold or was missing a large steer.[48] Redding's reply was forwarded to Sheriff Vaughn and the San Juan County sheriff sent the rancher an accounting of the cost for the cow's recovery. Vaughn's statement was for two and a half days' work at four dollars a day, plus two days' work for his men at three dollars a day, for a total of $16. To satisfy the expense account statement, Vaughn sold Redding's steer for five cents a pound. The sheriff received $21.70 for the meat minus the butcher's charge of three dollars and fifty cents and the "express charge" for the steer's delivery to slaughter. Sheriff Vaughn then billed the Socorro County rancher for the balance of 80 cents due for the recovery of the stolen cow.[49]

Boone Vaughn was the first sheriff in San Juan County to be re-elected to office. He served a brief term as a territorial policeman before returning to his business interests (courtesy of the San Juan County Sheriff's Office).

The copy of Sheriff Vaughn's statement to Redding that was given to Governor Hagerman claimed to be "an exact copy of Fullerton's statement." The face of the bill says nothing about Fullerton or the mounted police, but it is clearly marked "Copy of Boone C. Vaughn's Statement" at the top of the page. It would appear that for some reason Captain Fullerton had simply supplied Redding with a copy of the accounting done by Sheriff Vaughn and was not seeking to collect any funds for himself or for the mounted police. It is apparent, from the facts, that Governor Hagerman and some association stockmen, each for their own motives, chose to misunderstand the clearly stated intent of the statement sent to the rancher.

The Fake Mountie

One more piece of bad luck came Fullerton's way. Some citizens who lived near Anton Chico, in northwestern Guadalupe County, sent Governor Hagerman a petition complaining about a fence cutter gang and the misconduct of a mounted police. Among the 18 people who had signed the redress was the parish priest, the county clerk, a county commissioner and a justice of the peace.[50]

Hagerman, for some unknown reason, chose to personally investigate these complaints. "I shall look into this matter carefully and adopt such measures as seem advisable and as are within my power."[51] The governor's resulting action so clouded the facts that the truth of all the charges may never be fully understood, and in desperation Hagerman finally ordered the mounted police to take over the investigation. The mounted police quickly broke up the gang of fence cutters and they were also able to arrest a mounted police impersonator.[52] In spite of the rangers' final success in handling the Anton Chico affair, Governor Hagerman appears to have held Captain Fullerton personally responsible for his own messed up handling of the initial investigation.

The public approval of Captain Fullerton and his rangers was summed up in a Santa Fe *New Mexican* editorial. "The record of the police since its organization is very good and so far has justified the passage of the act creating the force. Much [work] has been done towards suppressing cattle rustling and stock depredations generally by its members and the expense incurred in its maintenance so far have been made up several times over by the good work done." The *New Mexican* concluded by saying that each new arrest added "a beautiful feather to those already in their hats for good work done."[53] It would be difficult to surmise from these comments that there was a need to change the leadership of the mounted police, but the governor had a different opinion.

Exactly when Governor Hagerman decided not to re-appoint Fullerton is not known, but on Monday, March 19, 1906, he sent a special messenger to inform John of his intention to appoint a new man to head the territorial police.[54] On Wednesday, the Santa Fe *New Mexican* published a front page scoop that they claimed was based upon "good authority" that Governor Hagerman would replace Fullerton with Deputy U.S. Marshal Fred Fornoff. The story received no public response from John Fullerton, but his brother Will did deny the rumors that John had already resigned or that he planned to resign.[55] A couple of days later, the *New Mexican* reported that Fullerton "has not yet been notified of the contemplated change, but it is said that Fornoff was told he would be given the place when he visited Santa Fe several days ago." Fornoff was then in Las Vegas serving papers for the federal court.[56]

Fornoff's hometown paper, the Albuquerque *Morning Journal*, fanned the rumor mill further on Monday, March 26. "It is now well understood here that Fred Fornoff, of Albuquerque, the popular deputy United States marshal is going to take charge of the mounted police force on the retirement of Captain Fullerton of Socorro." The story went on to say, "It is very probable that Mr. Fullerton will retire about the first of April." It would seem that, for some private reason, the *Journal* wanted to mislead readers into believing that Fullerton was leaving his office voluntarily. The *Journal* concluded with a final backhand slap at Captain Fullerton. "The appointment of Mr. Fornoff will meet with general approval. He is known all over the territory as a fearless and able officer, a man of resourcefulness and executive ability."[57]

In Governor Hagerman's official papers there is a file marked "Special Issues, Reports and Investigations" and contained within that file is an unsigned, cryptic memo. It is dated March 30, 1906, and it is addressed to James G. Fitch, an attorney and influential Republican. "Bursum and Fullerton could not do half the harm [Elfego] Baca is doing. Can nothing be done [about him]?" The nature of this memo suggests that someone was pleading with Fitch to intervene in the proposed removals of the superintendent of the penitentiary and the captain of the territorial police. The argument seems to be that Elfego Baca, a member of the Republican Party Central Committee, was not supportive, if not disloyal, to the new Hagerman administration. Who wrote the memo and how did it get into Hagerman's papers? The answer to those two questions would go a long way toward answering the real question of why Fullerton was not kept in office.[58]

Was there an organized cabal to oust John Fullerton as mounted police captain? There were some Socorro County stockmen who held hard feelings against Fullerton and some well placed political power brokers were unhappy that the popular Dick Huber had been forced out of office directly or indirectly by Fullerton's directives. President Theodore Roosevelt had told the western governors that he would look favorably upon the appointment of any of his former Rough Riders to public office. Fred Fornoff had served as a corporal in Troop G of Roosevelt's First United States Volunteer Cavalry during the Spanish-American War.

In Arizona, President Roosevelt had named his former second-in-command, Alexander O. Brode, as territorial governor and former Rough Rider Ben Daniels as the U.S. marshal. Brode was quick to name First Sergeant Harbo T. "Tom" Rynning as captain of the Arizona Rangers and Harry Wheeler was appointed ranger lieutenant. Rynning, in turn, enlisted nine former Rough Riders into the ranger service. The third territory to furnish recruits to the Rough Riders was Oklahoma. First Lieutenant Frank Frantz was appointed territorial governor in 1906.[59]

In 1907, President Roosevelt would ask Governor Hagerman to find a position for his friend Captain George Curry, who was then serving as a military governor in the Philippines and wished to return to New Mexico. The president suggested that Hagerman might name Curry as the territorial secretary, but Hagerman told Roosevelt he could not help him with that request because he had no job openings. President Roosevelt made a job opening; he fired Hagerman and named Curry as governor of New Mexico.[60] Rough Riders, with a friend in the White House, served at all levels of territorial government in Arizona, Oklahoma and New Mexico.

Captain Fullerton's nonrenewal was not a purely political move and may have been to some degree just personal spite.[61] Governor Hagerman may not have liked John Fullerton, but he did like Fred Fornoff. Cabal or no cabal, there was no other reason needed for Fullerton's dismissal than his disfavor with the territorial governor. In fact, it is doubtful that Hagerman and Fullerton ever talked face to face concerning John's continued leadership of the territorial police.

Governor Hagerman and Fred Fornoff had developed a warm professional and personal friendship.[62] The governor had offered Fornoff the captaincy of the mounted police at a meeting, in the governor's office, that took place on March 19, the same day Hagerman's messenger was to notify Fullerton he would not be reappointed as head of the territorial police.[63] Hagerman had recently removed other top territorial officials including the superintendent of schools, the attorney general and the superintendent of the penitentiary. An editorial in the *San Juan County Index* approved of these changes, saying, "These efforts on the part of Gov. Hagerman seem to indicate that new men and new methods will prevail in graft ridden New Mexico."[64]

A Matter of Principle

Thomas Jefferson is quoted as saying that in matters of principle a person should stand like a rock, but in matters of taste they should swim with the current. John F. Fullerton was a man of principle, so on Sunday, March 26, 1906, he drafted a three-page reply to Governor Hagerman's stated intent to replace him as the mounted police's captain. Fullerton's epistle is a monument to human restraint.

> To His Excellency Herbert J. Hagerman
> Governor of New Mexico,
> Santa Fe, N.M.:
>> Sir: — Replying to your communication dated March 19, 1906[65] stating in effect that you were not satisfied with the service of the Mounted Police, of which I have had the honor of being Captain during the past twelve months, and that you intended making a change in the Captaincy of said Company on the first of April, in this connection permit me to state this Company was organized less than a year ago; that for the first few months the matter of Railroad transportation not being attainable, was a serious handicap to successful administration on account of long distances between points of operation and the extensive area to be covered. This was, however, remedied after a few months and the force equipped and organized for business. It naturally takes some little time for a force of this kind to become thoroughly familiar with conditions and be able to render efficient service. The compensation provided by Law is extremely limited and less than the amount provided by other communities[66] for similar service, yet in spite of all these obstacles, I candidly believe that the Mounted Police have, during the past several months, rendered valuable service to the public and especially have they been of material assistance to the stock interests, namely, sheep, cattle and horses; considerable property has been restored to rightful owners. Many law breakers have been apprehended and many important arrests have been affected; much of the business of the Mounted Police has not been given publicity for the reason that, in the majority of cases, secrecy is absolutely essential to success.
>>
>> I have received words of commendation of the highest character from the various portions of the Territory, representing substantial Live Stock interests, expressing satisfaction of the efficiency of the Mounted Police force. No doubt some mistakes may have been made. However, I have at all times, used every effort to do my duty to

the best of my ability in order to perfect the efficiency of the Company to meet the designs intended by the Legislature.

I recognize that you, perhaps, have the power of removal or substation in my case, if arbitrarily exercised, yet the law creating the office of Captain of the Mounted Police failed to fix any definite period or term of office, but limited the authority of the Executive to sixty days, after passage of the act creating the police force in which to appoint a Captain, (see Section 2, page 3, Laws 1905), the evident intention of the legislature being that no change of officers was contemplated, and the provision of law for enrollment of men being for one year seems to have referred to enlisted men only.

It seems to me that your contemplated action is unfair and will be the means of preventing me from demonstrating the true worth of the force and depriving me of the benefit or credit accruing from my efforts given in good faith towards perfecting the organization to a state of efficiency which, I believe, is an accepted fact by the public most vitally interested, and to which in all justice, I should be entitled. I shall not contest your right to make the change on April 1st, next, as in before stated, although I believe your actions contrary to the intentions of the legislature and not demanded by any public interest, and certainly unfair to the present incumbent.

You kindly offer your good office towards securing for me some other employment in the Territorial service, which are hereby most respectfully declined.

I remain,
    Respectfully,
        John F. Fullerton,
            Captain Mounted Police[67]

On March 29, 1906, Governor Hagerman replied to Fullerton's public comments. The author has been unable to locate a copy of this letter. What did Hagerman say to Fullerton? Did he address Fullerton's well reasoned defense of his territorial service? We may never know the answer to those questions. The original of Fullerton's March 26, 1906, letter is not housed among Hagerman's government papers, nor do the mounted police archives contain a carbon copy. After years of searching for the original Fullerton letter, the author discovered that when he left office Hagerman took a few select official documents with him and among these papers was Fullerton's letter. It is interesting to speculate why Hagerman kept Fullerton's indictment, but didn't also keep a copy of his own response. Today the Fullerton letter is one of a few Herbert Hagerman items housed in a small file of personal papers contained in the larger J.J. Hagerman Family Collection at the Rio Grande Historical Collection at New Mexico State University. The only reason history even knows that the governor responded to Fullerton is because the front page of the captain's letter contains an office stamp noting that it was answered on March 29.

John Fullerton's dispatch was published, at the captain's request, on the front page of the Santa Fe *New Mexican* and in many other papers across the territory. This open letter to Governor Hagerman was the captain's only public comment concerning his dismissal from civil service. The Deming *Graphic* caught the true meaning of the moment when it reported that Captain John F. Fullerton "goes into oblivion April 1."[68]

12

From Fullerton's Rangers to Fornoff's Boys

> "The mounted police department is a new institution in New Mexico. It holds a peculiar position, as we police the entire Territory. In many localities, where the local officers for one reason or another have neglected to enforce the Territorial laws and city ordinances, we have have been called upon, in every case where it was possible to do so have taken into custody the violators."
>
> Captain Fred Fornoff
> *Operations Report of the Mounted Police*
> 1906

John Fullerton's rangers were not larger-than-life heroes. They were just ordinary family men doing a job and time ran out for all of them at midnight on Saturday, March 31, 1906. The final activity report credits Captain John F. Fullerton's Mounted Police troop with making 72 official arrests[1] during their year of active field operation. Fullerton's Rangers held no mustering out ceremony, no order was given to disband the company and no parade was held to celebrate a job well done. There was no good-bye party or even an official notice that the mounted police were to be reorganized. The men just read in their local newspaper that Fullerton was to be replaced and that the new captain would address the rangers at a special meeting to be held in Santa Fe. Like a defeated army, Fullerton's Rangers just melted away and they soon became an almost forgotten footnote in the history of New Mexico Territory.

John Fullerton's former rangers were not sure what to do about the removal of their captain from his command post and they were equally unsure concerning their own fate. Sergeant Bob Lewis expressed this concern best when he was interviewed by a reporter, in Albuquerque, on his way to Santa Fe. He said the rangers were on their way "to see whether they are going to be reinstated or fired."[2] Fred Fornoff called a summit meeting with the former members of Fullerton's Rangers for 2 o'clock on Monday, April 2, 1906. Following a brief discussion led by Fornoff, the former rangers were re-mustered as Company II of the New Mexico Mounted Police.

Julius Meyer seems to have really felt frustrated with his service as one of Fullerton's Rangers. He wrote Fred Fornoff, "I am out here a long way from any where, get no news. Will remain on duty here until I hear from you." Meyer went on to question, "Are we all going to get the G.[reat] B.[oot]? We deserve it."[3]

Governor H.J. Hagerman re-appointed all the officers and privates of Fullerton's Rangers except for the man who had formed the company. The governor added an extra insult to John Fullerton with the re-instatement of Dick Huber as a ranger private. Huber was assigned Octaviano Perea's old badge number.[4] John Brophy's post was filled on May first by Deputy Sheriff John Collier of Silver City, and Robert Burch of Las Cruces replaced Rhea Stewart a few weeks later.[5]

Fullerton's Rangers had fulfilled their mission to establish the New Mexico Mounted Police as a powerful force for law and order. "The force starts out under very favorable auspices and in the *New Mexican[']s* opinion, will prove, within a year a great factor for the preservation of the peace and the protection of the lives and property of the people in the isolated and stock growing sections of the Territory."[6] This editorial comment had been made concerning the formation of John Fullerton's Rangers, but it just as easily could have been made concerning Fred Fornoff's reorganized territorial police force.

This picture of Fred Fornoff was taken while he was serving as a deputy United States marshal, circa 1905. He was appointed the second captain of the mounted police in April 1906 (courtesy of Fred Fornoff, Jr.).

Fred Fornoff was to serve as captain under the territory's last three governors and he would lead the territorial police as they became New Mexico's first state police force. Fornoff's Boys would survive two attempts by territorial lawmakers to abolish the force, a major force reduction, a dwindling state budget and the transition to a new form of police duty during the early years of statehood.

History would repeat itself and in the end Fornoff's Boys, like Fullerton's Rangers, would just fade away. In December 1913, the state legislature refused to allocate funding for a paid state police force, but Fornoff continued to serve as the leader of an unpaid semi-active special mounted police corps, the Phantom Company. It served six month nonsalaried appointments during the period from 1914 until the company was fully funded and reorganized as Company III of the New Mexico Mounted Police during the Mexican border troubles at the height of America's involvement in the Great War in Europe.

Herb McGrath took his oath as the third mounted police captain in May 1918. Two more men served as captain, Apolonio Sena (Company IV during 1919 and 1920) and Lorenzo Delgado (1921), before the state's mounted police law was repealed in mid–February of 1921.

13

John Ferguson Fullerton: The Final Years

> "Capt. John Ferguson Fullerton widely known pioneer cattle and sheep raiser of New Mexico died here [San Diego] yesterday.... [He] organized the New Mexico rangers."
>
> San Diego (Calif.) *Union*
> 27 January 1928

John Fullerton's pride was deeply hurt by his public dismissal as captain of the mounted police and was also displeased that the new captain seemed to go out of his way to distance himself from everything positive that Fullerton had accomplished. The *New Mexican* reported, "Captain Fornoff will put forth an effort from the beginning to improve the force and the organization under him expects to demonstrate to the territorial officials that its members can make their services invaluable."[1]

Following his public dismissal, John Fullerton returned to civilian life and sought refuge at his sheep ranch, but to no avail. Even his private world was in trouble. The major stable force in the former captain's life was his son Elmer, but he was away at school and he was also living his own life. John drew upon his inner strength and managed to keep his public persona upbeat and attended a meeting of the Stockman's Association at the end of April 1906. One can only wonder at the tone of his reception at that meeting.[2]

Hindsight would suggest that John F. Fullerton might have been happier had he remained as the Socorro County assessor, because in that office he may have enjoyed a long and active local political career. He might even have become financially independent and a pillar of Socorro's social structure. He might have been able to save his marriage. He might have....

To say that Fullerton was out of his depth as leader of the New Mexico Mounted Police could be an understatement. Captain Fullerton was a true believer in the mission of the territorial police, but he lacked the practical knowledge of criminal investigation that this type of force demanded. John also lacked the political clout to garner widespread loyalty and support from local law enforcement officials. This said, Fullerton's two shortcomings, to a degree, were compensated for by the high caliber of his officers and the merit of most of his rangers.

John Fullerton's biggest mistake, as ranger captain, seems to have been his unbending determination to conduct the mounted police as a semi-military command.

Yet, to a major degree he cannot be faulted for this style, because the Mounted Police Act had prescribed this method of operation. Even so, Fullerton slowly came to realize that this structure was an operational weakness and he began to disregard the law's directive, but this change in leadership mode came too late to affect John's tenure as commander of the territorial police. History may have chosen another champion, but John never forgot "his rangers" and fought for better compensation for them by the Territorial Legislative Assembly. In 1907, the mounted police were given a pay raise.[3]

Early in the twentieth century, John Fullerton had established a partnership with B.B. Borden to operate a transfer business in Albuquerque. The company had offices at 110 West Gold Avenue and Borden served as the managing agent. John Fullerton sought to divest himself of his stock interest in the Albuquerque Transfer Company when he entered upon the territorial payroll and after a few months he was able to interest his brother-in-law in the venture. John updated Elmer Blinn, the family doctor who had delivered his son Elmer, concerning his outside business ventures. "We have sold the transfer business in Albuquerque, I am happy to say, as it was an elephant on our hands."[4]

John Fullerton's financial difficulties were becoming more manageable by the fall of 1905. Within days, he had received two communiqués concerning the sale of his cattle herd. "We sold our cattle last fall," John told one concerned buyer, "with the exception of about one hundred head, which I still have, and would like to sell them if we can get a fair price." That same day Fullerton also wrote a range neighbor, "I have not decided what disposition we will make of the cattle. Will and I were talking it over sometime ago. We were thinking of selling the cattle as soon as we could get them gathered and putting the money into sheep." John finished the letter by saying that Will would be in Socorro "soon and I will talk the matter over with Him."[5] The Socorro County clerk's office contains the chattel mortgage records for the numerous cattle and sheep transactions consummated by the Fullerton brothers. John and Will were also involved in the acquisition and sale of range properties.

In the summer of 1906, Governor Hagerman issued a proclamation calling for a territorial convention to form a sheep and wool growers association for New Mexico. One of the 13 delegates he invited from Socorro County was Will Fullerton. The delegates assembled at the Elks' Theater, in Albuquerque, in September and debated this quantum leap for economic development.[6] A century later, sheep growing and wool production are still a strong revenue source for the state's ranchers.

Upon leaving the territorial service, Fullerton first worked as a court receiver for a large cattle company. The case centered on ownership rights. During this time it was rumored that John might be appointed as the new superintendent of the territorial penitentiary, but the embittered John Fullerton told Governor Hagerman he was not interested in another government job.[7] Arthur Trelford was appointed to straighten out the penitentiary's management problems, on April 12, 1906, and Hagerman reappointed him for an additional two years on March 19, 1907.[8]

John Fullerton opened an insurance office in Socorro and established his living quarters in a small place behind his office. John was a top salesman for many years and earned numerous company awards before he became the district manager for the Occidental Life Insurance Company in New Mexico. John F. Fullerton and his

Model T Ford, which he nicknamed "Alice," were a common sight on the streets of Socorro and Albuquerque. Once when John was in the Duke City a political cub reporter for a local newspaper mistook Fullerton for the Democratic presidential candidate William J. Bryan. The old lifelong Republican was gentle in his reprimand.[9]

In September 1919, the Fullerton brothers formed a partnership with six other investors to organize a mining company on a 160-acre claim they filed on Torrance County land. They were seeking gas, oil petroleum and asphalt "for the purpose of development to obtain said material from said land and claim." The Hill Oil Placer Mining Claim did not prove to be the great success that the eight member investor group had hoped for, but today asphalt is successfully mined in Torrance County.[10]

Even after he left law enforcement Fullerton was not very far from the center of crime; he was a crime victim twice. Once John was staying at an Albuquerque hotel when a thief climbed into his room, by using the transom over the door, and made off with a diamond stick pin he had received from the Occidental Life Insurance Company. The second robbery was also in a hotel room. On this occasion John Fullerton was at the Magdalena Hotel and he was asleep in the room when he was robbed of his money clip.[11]

John F. Fullerton, Socorro County businessman in the 1920s, photographed in Socorro, N.M. (Irene Fullerton's photograph album).

Home Life

Katharine Lay Sleight, who became John F. Fullerton's second wife on August 6, 1903, had developed into a religious fanatic. She gave her backsliding Presbyterian husband no end of grief as she tried to convert him to her ultra-conservative doctrine. With each passing year the woman became more obsessed with her mission to restore John "to the church," until John finally left home and the couple separated permanently.[12] It is unknown what type of relationship John had with his stepdaughter, Beatrice, before or after the divorce. Present-day family members have no memory of her and have no knowledge of her fate.[13]

John Fullerton sold his beloved ranch to his brother in March 1916 for one dollar. The sale was made so that Katharine could not make a claim to any part of the Fullerton ranch in a divorce settlement. It was verbally agreed between the two brothers that Will would resell the land and holdings to John when all the legal actions were complete. However, something went wrong with this understanding and Fullerton family members have been reluctant to talk about what happened in the misdeal. John's granddaughter has said this feud was one of the few times that John's usually mild-mannered temperament was inflamed to the point that he might have killed his brother had friends not detained him long enough for his anger to subside.[14] "Grandpa could show a temper if he was provoked."[15]

In the end, John Fullerton was unable to regain his 103-acre ranch on the San Augustin Plains and as a result his son Elmer lost his ranching and farming inheritance to his Uncle Will. Will made a large profit when the ranch was sold. John's granddaughter summed up the whole ranch sale deal by saying, "You know it was the rich — and their poor relations."[16]

Will Fullerton married Helen Marie Purdy of Cleveland, Ohio. She was an accomplished oil painter who presented herself as a perfect lady and was loved by members of John's family. Will and Helen had no children. Van R. Purdy, one of her wealthy banker brothers, invested in some New Mexico and Texas oil leases along with the two Fullerton brothers. They all lost their investment money, except for some oil leases in Burnet, Texas.

When Will Fullerton suffered a major business loss he became "weird and unstable" and his wife moved them from Socorro to a very small apartment in downtown Albuquerque. Will would sometimes just wander the streets talking to everyone in sight and became such a disruptive fixture at the First Presbyterian Church that the pastor finally had to ask Helen to keep him at home. Will sometimes became violent and eventually became such a danger to himself and those around him that Helen finally had to have him committed to the New Mexico Insane Asylum at Las Vegas.

Misfortune now dogged Helen Fullerton. Elmer would often drive Helen from Albuquerque to Las Vegas to see her husband. One winter eve Elmer was driving Helen's big Buick touring car when he encountered a patch of black ice and had an accident. Helen was injured and was confined to an Albuquerque hospital for a few days. One day some "family friends" tried to talk a station nurse into giving them Helen's handbag. The nurse refused and told Elmer about the request when he made his next visit. Elmer took charge of his aunt's handbag and her fortune in diamonds.[17]

Helen Fullerton died on April 13, 1947, and was buried in Albuquerque's Fairview Park Cemetery. She left an estate that included a $1,877.50 in stocks and a 1927 Buick valued at $150. Irene LaFont Fullerton received Helen's engagement ring in the bequest. Will Fullerton was never able to return home and he died in the state asylum. He was buried, in an unmarked grave, next to his wife.[18]

Young Elmer

Early in 1905, Elmer Fullerton moved to Albuquerque, living at 605 North Fourth Street. He started working at his father's moving company and continued to work there when his uncle J.C. Kutzner, became the new owner.[19] Before settling in Albuquerque, Elmer had attended the high school section of the School of Mines, present day New Mexico Tech, at Socorro and took some basic freshman work at the

Agriculture and Mechanical College, now New Mexico State University, at Las Cruces.[20]

In the fall of 1906, Elmer Fullerton was living at 635 South Arno Street in Albuquerque. John came to see his son during his dark days of recovery and it was during this visit that he helped Elmer enroll in the Albuquerque Business College. John and his sister Nan were very close so he and Elmer spent a family Christmas at the Kutzners, because the senior Fullertons now lived in San Diego, California, and as always, brother Will chose to travel his own path.

James Fullerton died in 1907. After Nan lost her husband she moved to the West Coast to live with her mother. Amanda Fullerton died in the summer of 1911. Over two decades, John made numerous trips to California to visit with his mother and his sister.[21] He was a lonely man.

Elmer Fullerton once ran his own service business when he formed the Manzano Stage Line between Albuquerque and Mountainair. The motor coach company carried both passengers and merchandise and operated along what is present day New Mexico Highway 10 through the Manzano Mountains. One of Elmer's drivers was a man named Harry Dils, who eventually brought the transportation company from Fullerton and ran it as a family business for many years.[22]

This photograph of John Elmer Fullerton was taken in El Paso, Texas, by Irene La Font during the time she was dating young Elmer in 1912–13. She considered this one of her favorite pictures of her husband (Irene Fullerton's photograph album).

Irene Grace LaFont

Irene LaFont was always an independent woman. She was born on January 26, 1897, in El Paso as the daughter of Adolphe and Claudia LaFont. Her father was a native Frenchman who worked as a miner, while Irene's mother had been born in New Mexico. Irene's two brothers were Earl and Justin. Justin LaFont was good at business and became wealthy as a hotel operator and trading post owner.

Irene's great-grandfather was Col. E.D. Eaton. Eaton was a native New Yorker who came west during the California gold strike and stayed on in New Mexico as a store clerk. A few years later he bought a 200,000 acre land grant and started farming. Eaton became commander of the Union volunteer troops at Fort Craig, New Mexico, during the Civil War battle at Valverde. He later commanded Fort Garland, in Colorado, and finally Fort Wingate, where his command helped to subjugate the Navajos. Later, Ethan Eaton sold his large homestead farm near San Christobal and settled in Socorro to work his mining claims. In 1884, Eaton led the Socorro vigilante committee that hung Joel Fowler and a few other hardcases.[23]

Irene LaFont became an excellent horsewoman and even wanted to become a jockey before her father's untimely death forced her to help her mother support the family by taking in sewing. She did, however, follow horse racing the rest of her life. Claudia LaFont moved her family to live with her brother in the Pacific Northwest country for a short time following her husband's death, but she soon returned to the Sunshine Territory. Irene, now a pretty socialite, attended the high school section of the New Mexico School of Mines at Socorro where she "dated" Sergeant Bob Lewis' son Pat until she met Elmer Fullerton.[24]

This meeting between Irene and Elmer seems to have been a classic love-at-first-sight encounter. Even twenty years after Elmer's death Irene's face still glowed when she talked about the man she called "Daddy." Mrs. LaFont helped Elmer find a clerk's job in El Paso so he could earn enough money for the young couple to have a proper courtship.

Irene Fullerton and Susan Leverett in the fall of 1984, in a photograph taken by the author in the front yard of the Leverett home in Albuquerque.

The 25-year-old John Elmer Fullerton married 16-year-old Irene Grace LaFont in St. Clement's Episcopal Church in El Paso on Saturday, September 6, 1913. A daughter, Susan, was born in 1914.[25] A short time later, Elmer moved his wife and young daughter to Socorro, then Los Lunas, and finally up to Albuquerque where he was employed as a salesman by the Charles Ilfeld Mercantile Company.

In later years, Irene became a postmaster and she and Elmer worked in an Indian trading post at Prewitt, owned by her brother Justin. Irene, Elmer and Susan loved the life at the settlement on the edge of the Navajo country. Once Irene was looking for some clean linens in a bedroom closet when she came face to face with a diamondback rattlesnake and she never forgot that close up look at death. Elmer was happy to sell boots to truck drivers and Indian jewelry to the tourists who stopped for gas along the old Route 66.[26] However, fate had a different plan and in 1963 Elmer suffered an aneurysm in the aorta near his heart. A major operation saved his life, but he could no longer live the active life at the old trading post. After a few years more at Prewitt, Irene and Elmer were forced to settle for a tamer life on the LaFont family farm located south of Albuquerque.

Elmer Fullerton had been drinking heavily the night he died and this may have contributed to his accident when he slipped and fell in the bathroom and hit his head on a wooden box. This head injury resulted in his death early on the morning of June 18, 1976, at the LaFont farm near Albuquerque. Irene had the body cremated and she scattered Elmer's ashes over the mountains near the old Fullerton Ranch were he had loved to ride his horse, Indio.[27]

Irene LaFont Fullerton celebrated her hundredth birthday on January 26, 1997, with a big party at her daughter's home. Susan recalled, "It was a grand time. We relived old days, ate cake and ice cream, and had fun. That's what life is all about. Fun. Even the president sent a [birthday] card."[28] Irene joined her beloved Elmer for the eternal rest on February 9, 2002. She had been confined to a nursing home after breaking her hip and never recovered her mobility. Family and friends remembered this lovely lady in an Episcopal Church service. Her 105-year-old body was cremated and her ashes now rest in a special place in the mountains of Socorro County.[29]

The Final Journey

John Fullerton made his last trip to California in mid–January 1928. The 71-year-old Fullerton caught a chest cold which deepened into pneumonia and caused his death on the afternoon of Thursday, January 26. John's death certificate said he was a livestock raiser, a widower, and lived in Socorro, New Mexico. The official form listed his wife's name as Susan.[30]

New Mexico's first mounted police captain is buried in the Elks Rest section of Greenwood Memorial Park in San Diego. John F. Fullerton's forever love, Susan, and his infant son Raymond were sent to California to share the eternal sleep with him.[31] It has been said that in the game of life, heredity deals the hand, society makes the rules, but you still play your own cards. John Fullerton played his cards with style.

"My grandfather had a generous lap for a little girl to sit on and he always smelled so good," remembered Susan Fullerton Leverett about John F. Fullerton. "He would come for Sunday dinner and he loved my mother's cooking. When he really liked something he would say, 'That was larruping good.' Grandpa seemed to always love sweets and so do I. He really liked whipped cream, not the store-bought kind like you see today, but the real thing. He would say, 'I love whipped cream so much I could eat it on saw dust.' I was named after his first wife and we had fun together. When I was older he would take me to the Saturday afternoon movies and vaudeville show at the Sunshine Theater or the Kimo Theater in downtown Albuquerque. That was a real treat for a little girl to see a motion picture and the stage acts with her grandfather. He was such an even mannered and loveable person just like my father."[32]

The Next Generations

"There will not be no [sic] more Fullertons of this branch [of the family tree]," remembered Irene Fullerton. "Elmer and I had just one daughter, no sons. Susan, our daughter, is married to William J. Leverett. They had one daughter, Sheila F. Leverett."[33]

Susan Fullerton married a combat hero of the Second World War. Bill Leverett had grown up in Albuquerque and had helped out around the office of the family real estate business. During his youth, Bill often had long conversations with Elfego Baca. The former gunman turned lawyer-newspaperman had his office near the Leveretts' real estate office. Baca would often walk to a nearby lunch counter and on his return trip he would stop and rest on the awning-covered wooden bench in front of the real estate office. Bill became a government consultant after leaving the Corps of Engineers and enjoyed oil painting as a hobby, while Susan played golf. They love their two cats and old white dog and these pets are true members of the family. Old age may have slowed the Leveretts' movements and dimmed their hearing, but it has not dimmed their spirit and their zest for life. Bill loves to discuss baseball and a good book.

The Leveretts' daughter survived the misadventures of her youth to become a highly respected schoolteacher. John Fullerton's great-granddaughter is a hotel sales executive and his great-grandson is employed in the entertainment business.

Epilogue

"It is not the critic who counts; not the man who points out how the strong man stumbles, or where the doer of deeds could have done them better. The credit belongs to the man who is actually in the arena, whose face is marred by dust and sweat and blood; who strives valiantly; who errs, and comes short again and again; because there is not effort without error and shortcoming; but who does actually strive to do the deeds; who knows the great enthusiasms, the great devotions; who spends himself in a worthy cause, who at the best knows in the end the triumphs of high achievement and who at the worst, if he fails, at least fails while daring greatly, so that his place shall never be with those cold and timid souls who know neither victory nor defeat."

Theodore Roosevelt
23 April 1910

Our tale of John Fullerton and his territorial rangers is finished and the ghost parade now passes for a final review by two commanders-in-chief, Miguel Otero and Herbert Hagerman. Captain John F. Fullerton sits tall in his saddle as he leads his column of ghost rangers along the frontier of forever.

We say goodbye to Lieutenant Cipriano Baca and Sergeant Robert "Stuttering Bob" Lewis. Next comes Dick Huber, carrying the mounted police flag, and with him Julius Meyer. Both deserve a solemn salute. Goodbye to Will Dudley and John Brophy; a tip of the hat to fast-shooting Fate Avant and the deadly Herb McGrath. Rafael Gomez and Bob Putman earned respect. Honors also go to Octiviano Perea, Rhea Stewart and George Elkins. They too rode as New Mexico Territorial Mounted Police.

None of Fullerton's Rangers backed down under fire or threat of danger. Their work for honor and justice was followed by the deeds of other New Mexico Mounted Police for another 15 years before this pioneering territorial/state police force was abolished by an act of the Fourth State Legislature in early February 1921.

The mounted police legend continues today with a new breed of state law enforcement professionals. Since 1935, 30 years after Fullerton had quoted from the eighth chapter of the *Book of Proverbs* ("I follow the course of righteousness along the paths of justice") to his men as their reason for public service, the guardians of justice in the Land of Enchantment have been the men and women of the New Mexico State Police.

*"**Pro Bono Publico**—For The Public Good"*
The New Mexico State Police Motto

Appendix: Cover Route Sheet and Text of the Greer Mounted Police Bill

Amended C.B 26
in lieu [illegible]

36th LEGISLATIVE ASSEMBLY.

Council Bill No. 26

Introduced by W. H. Greer
26 day of January, 1905.
An Act entitled an Act to organize and equip a Company of Mounted Police for the Territory of New Mexico.

Read first time in full, and under suspension of rules, read second time and [illegible] ordered translated, and printed and referred to Committee on Finance

Delivered to Translator 1/26 1905.
Returned by Translator 1/27 1905.
Delivered to Printer 1/27 1905.
Returned by Printer 2/1 1905.
Delivered to Committee 2/1 1905.
Reported to ~~House~~ Committee by Committee on the 9 day of February 1905, with recommendation that it do pass with amendments offered by Committee. Report of Committee adopted: Amendments adopted.

Taken up for consideration Read this time in full as amended, ~~read third time~~

preparatory to its passage, placed on its passage and duly passed as amended

A. P. O'Neill
Chief Clerk Council.

(Duplicate entry made on "Amended Council Bill no 26, as reported to House")

2/9-05 Rec'd from Council as having been passed.
2/10-05 Taken up under suspension of rules. Read first and second time by title. Under further suspension of rules, considered referred. Read third time in full preparatory to its passage. Placed upon its passage and duly passed.
Del'd to Council.

Geo. W. Armijo
Chief Clerk House.

2/14/05 –
Received from House of Representatives as having been duly concurred in. Delivered to Enr. & Eng. Clerk. Returned by Enr. & Eng. Clerk. 2/15/05. Delivered to Com. on Enr. & Eng. Bills with engrossed copy thereof. Returned from Com. on Enr. & Eng. Bills as properly enrolled & engrossed. Delivered to Chairman of Com. on Enr. & Eng. Bills.

Chas. P. Orr
Chief Clerk Council.

FILED IN OFFICE OF
SECRETARY OF NEW MEXICO
FEB 15 1905 — 3:17 pm
J. W. Raynolds
SECRETARY

AN ACT TO ORGANIZE AND EQUIP A COMPANY OF MOUNTED POLICE FOR THE TERRITORY OF NEW MEXICO.

---oOo---

Be it Enacted by the Legislative Assembly of the Territory of New Mexico.

Section 1. That the Governor of this Territory is hereby authorized to raise and muster into service of this Territory, for the protection of the frontier of this Territory, and for the preservation of the peace and the capture of persons charged with crime, one Company of New Mexico Mounted Police, to be raised as hereinafter prescribed, and to consist of one captain, one sergeant and not more than ~~ten~~ eight privates, each entitled to pay as follows: Captain to receive one hundred and twenty dollars ($120.00) per month; sergeant to receive seventy-five dollars ($75.00) per month; and privates fifty-five dollars ($55.00) per month, each; and the pay herein provided shall be full compensation in lieu of all other pay and compensation for clothing for both officers and men.

Section 2. That the Governor is authorized and empowered, Within Sixty days ~~when in its opinion the public emergency shall require it,~~ after the passage of this Act, to appoint competent persons as captain and sergeant, and to enroll, as set forth in this Act, the requisite number of men for the company; the captain shall return to the Governor the muster roll and the report of the condition of the company, and the Governor shall thereupon commission the said officers of said company, supply said company as under the provisions of this Act he may deem proper and necessary, and order them upon duty in accordance with the provisions of this Act.

Section 3. Said men shall be furnished by the Territory with the most effective and approved breech-loading rifles, and for this purpose the Governor is hereby authorized to contract in behalf of the Territory for ~~twelve~~ *five* stands of arms, together with a full supply of ammunition, the same to be all of the same make and calibre, and each member of the company to be furnished with the arms to be used by him at the price the same shall cost the Territory, which sum shall be retained out of the first money due him.

Section 4. That each member of said company shall be required to furnish himself with a suitable horse, six shooting pistol (army size) and all necessary accoutrements and camp equipage, the same to be passed upon and approved by the enrolling officer before enlisted, and should any member fail to keep himself furnished as above required, then the officer in command shall be authorized and required to purchase the articles of which he may be deficient, and charge the cost of the same to the person for whom the same shall be provided: PROVIDED, That all horses killed in action shall be replaced by the Territory, and the cost of horses so killed in action shall be determined by the captain.

Section 5. That said officers and men shall be furnished by the Territory with provisions, ammunition, and forage for horses when necessary and when on duty.

Section 6. That the men shall be enrolled for twelve months, unless sooner discharged, and at the expiration of their term of service they shall be again enrolled, or others shall be enrolled to supply their places, ~~in case the Governor deems such action necessary for the protection of the frontier, or for the preservation of the peace, or the capture of persons charged with crime~~.

Section 7. That no enlisted men shall be discharged from the service without special order from the Governor, nor shall any mem-

-2-

er os said company dispose of or exchange their horses or arms without the consent of the commanding officer of the company while in service of the Territory.

Section 8. That the captain of the company shall use his own discretion as to the manner of operations, selecting as his base the most unprotected and exposed settlement of the ~~frontier~~ territory.

Section 9. That the troops raised under and by virtue of this Act shall be governed by the rules and regulations of the army of the United States, as far as the same may be applicable, but shall always be and remain subject to the authority of the Territory of New Mexico for frontier service.

Section 10. The captain of such company shall have authority to concentrate all of such company, or divide it into squads for the purpose of following and capturing any outlaws, law breakers, marauding Indians, or bands of hostile Indians, or for the purpose of carrying out any measure that may contribute to the better security of the frontier; but the entire force raised under the provisions of this Act shall be at all times during their employment, as aforesaid, under and subject to the orders of the Governor, and shall be exempt from all military, jury and other service, except that for which they shall be appointed or controlled, as aforesaid; and that the Governor shall direct all the arrangements necessary to carry out the intention of this Act, with full power to remove any officer or man thereof for incompetency, neglect of duty or disobedience of orders.

Section 11. Members of said company shall have full power to make arrests of criminals in any part of the Territory, and upon the arrest of any criminal, shall deliver the same over to some peace officer in the county where the crime is committed.

Section 12. It shall be the duty of the auditor of this Territory to draw his warrant on the Territorial Treasurer at the end of each month for the pay of each officer and man in said company, and to forward the same to the captain of said company, and also a warrant for the amount of provisions, ammunition and forage; but the food of each officer or man in said ~~company~~ shall not exceed in price the sum of one dollar per day and such forage shall not exceed the sum of fifty cents per day for each horse; the same shall be forwarded upon the receipt by said officer of an itemized account from the captain of said company, to be signed by such captain and certified by him, and which shall be carefully scrutinized by such auditor, and should the same or any item therein be found unlawful or unreasonable, he shall suspend payment of the same and refer the same to the Governor, who shall pass thereon and certify the same for the payment in such sum as he shall find correct and reasonable; and it shall be the duty of the Territorial treasurer to pay such warrants out of the fund for Mounted Police, as other warrants are paid.

Section 13. That the captain shall be authorized to purchase all necessary pack animals to be furnished said company for transportation purposes, but not exceeding four in number; to purchase all necessary supplies to be delivered by contractors at the place to be designated by the captain of the company; and all accounts and certificates of such agent shall be examined and allowed by the captain of the company and certified by him, as the accounts for the payment of men, food or forage.

~~Section 14. The Governor shall have power to disband said company or any portion thereof when in his opinion their services shall no longer be necessary for frontier protection.~~

Section 1~~5~~4. There shall be annually levied and collected in addition to all other taxes authorized by law, a tax of *one half mill* ~~of each one hundred dollars~~ of taxable property in this Territory, to be placed in a fund by the Territorial treasurer, to be known as the New Mexico Mounted Police Fund, and upon which fund all warrants and payments made under any of the provisions of this Act, shall be drawn and made. Said tax shall be levied and collected in the same manner, and at the same time and by the same officers as other Territorial taxes.

Section 16. That no portion of said troops shall become a charge against this Territory until organized and placed under orders, and the total cost and expense of the organization, equipment and support of said company shall not exceed the sum of fifteen thousand dollars ($15,000.00) for any one year.

Section 16. The captain of said company shall provide and issue to each member of said company a badge, uniform in size and shape, with the words "New Mexico Mounted Police" inscribed thereon in plain, legible letters, which said badge shall belong to, and be returned to, this Territory, and be returned to it by the possessor thereof when any member of said company shall cease to be a member thereof; and the cost of said badge shall be paid by the Territory in the same manner as hereinbefore provided for the payment of other incidental expenses of said company.

Section 17. This Act shall take effect and be in full force from and after its passage.

AMEND PRINTED BILL AS FOLLOWS: in line One, Section one, after the word "captain" insert the word "one lieutenant"; line two, after the word "receive" strike out all of said line, also strike out all of line three, all of line four, five and six, and insert in lieu thereof the following: "Two Thousand Dollars per annum, lieutenant to receive fifteen hundred Dollars per annum, sargeant to receive twelve hundred Dollars per annum, and privates to receive nine hundred Dollars per annum each, and the pay herein provided for shall be full compensation in lieu of all other pay and compensation, including clothing and other all other expenses for officers and men."

Section 2. At the end of line eight insert the word "lieutenant".

Section 3 line one, strike out the word ten, insert in lieu thereof the word "eleven".

Strike out all of Section 5.

Section 12 strike out all after the word "company" in line four strike out all of line five, six, seven eight, nine, ten, eleven, twelve, thirteen and all in line fourteen up to and including the word "reasonable".

Strike out all of section thirteen. Add the following amendment at the end of section 14: " Provided, that until collections shall have been made under the provision of the levy herein authorized for the payment of such mounted police that the territorial treasurer shall pay the same out of any funds except the interest funds in the territorial treasury.

In section 15 line three, strike out the words fifteen thousand and insert in lieu thereof the sum "Thirteen Thousand".

In section 16, strike out all in line 10 after the word "thereof strike out all of line eleven, line twelve, of said section, and insert in lieu thereof the following": A sum not exceeding twelve hundred dollars per annum is hereby appropriated for the contingent expense of said Company, which shall be paid in the same manner as heretofore provided in this Act, and out of which shall be bought and paid for the arms hereinbeforeprovided for and such other incidental expenses

shall be necessary for the carrying out of the provisions provideed r in this Act." All such incidental expenses or contingent expense all be accounted for by itemized voucher duly certified by the ptain of such mounted police, and approved by the Territorial Auditor, t no expense of any kind shall be incurred or allowed in any one year in excess the sum of twelve hundred dollars."

o amend by inserting section 6 as follows: "Section 6. The Cap- n of such company has authority to suspend any member for cause and ll immediately report his action in writing to the Governor for his sideration.

~~Sectixxxxxxx~~ Amend , by striking out all of section 7 and insert lieu thereof, the following: "Section 7. No member of said com- y shall dispose of or exchange his or their horses or arms without consent of the commanding officer of the company while in the ser- e of the Territory.

COUNCIL BILL NO. 26.

AS AMENDED BY COMMITTEE.

AN ACT TO ORGANIZE AND EQUIP A COMPANY OF MOUNTED POLICE FOR TH
TERRITORY OF NEW MEXICO.

BE IT ENACTED BY THE LEGISLATIVE ASSEMBLY OF THE TERRITORY OF NEW MEXICO:

Section 1. That the Governor of this Territory is hereby authorized to raise and muster into service of this Territory, for the protection of the fontier of this Territory, and for the preservation of the peace and the capture of persons charged with crime, one company of New Mexico Mounted Police, to be raised as hereinafter prescribed, and to consist of one captain, one lieutenant, one sergeant, and not more than eight privates, each entitled to pay as follows: captain to receive two thousand ($2,000.00) Dollars per annum, lieutenant to receive Fifteen Hundred ($1,500.00) Dollars per annum, sergeant to receive twelve hundred ($1,200.00) Dollars per annum and privates to receive Nine Hundred ($900.00) Dollars each per annum, and the pay herein provided shall be full compensation in lieu of all other pay and compensation, including clothing and all other expenses for officers and men.

Section 2. That the Governor is authorized and empowered, within sixty days after the passage of this act, to appoint competent persons as captain, lieutenant and sergeant, and to enroll, as set forth in this act, the requisite number of men for the company; the captain shall return to the Governor the muster roll and the report of the condition of the company, and the Governor shall thereupon commission the officers of the said company, supply said company, as under the provisions of this act he may deem proper and necessary, and order them upon duty in accordance with the provisions of this Act.

Section 3. Said men shall be furnished by the territory with the most effective and approved breech-loading rifles, and for this purpose the Governor is hereby authorized to contract in behalf of the Territory for eleven stands of arms, together with a full supply of ammunition, the same to be all of the same make and calibre, and each member of the company to be furnished with the arms to be used by him

-2-

at the price, the same shall cost the territory, which sum shall be retained out of the first money due him.

Section 4. Each member of said company shall be required to furnish himself with a suitable horse, six-shooting pistol (army size) and all necessary accoutrements and camp equippage, the same to be passed upon and approved by the enrolling officer before enlisted; and should any member fail to keep himself/as above furnished required, then the officer in command shall be authorized and required to purchase the articles of which he may be deficient, and charge the cost of the same to the person for whom the same shall be provided; PROVIDED, that all horses killed in action shall be replaced by the Territory, and the cost of horses so killed in action shall be determined by the captain.

Section 5. The men shall be enrolled for twelve months, unless sooner dishcarged and at the expiration of their term of service they shall be again enrolled, or others shall be enrolled to supply their places.

Section 6. The captain of such company has authority to suspend any member for cause and/shall immediately report his action in writing to the Governor for his consideration;

Section 7. No member of said company shall dispose of or exchange his or their horses or arms without the consent of the commanding officer of the company while in the service of the territory.

Section 8. That the captain of the company shall use his own discretion as to the manner of operations, selecting as his base the most unprotected and exposed settlement of the territory.

Section 9. That the troops raised under and by virtue of this act shall be governed by the rules and regulations of the army of the United States, as far as the same may be applicable, but shall always be and remain subject to the authority of the territory of New Mexico for frontier service.

Section 10. The captain of such company shall have authority to comentrate all of such company, or divide it into squads for the purpose of following and capturing any out-laws, law breakers, marauding Indians, or bands of hostile Indians or for the purpose of carrying

-3-

out any measure that may contribute to the better security of the frontier; but the entire force raised under the provisions of this Act shall be at all times during their employment, as aforesaid, under and subject to the orders of the Governor, and shall be exempt from all military, jury and other service, except that for which they shall be appointed or controlled as aforesaid, and that the Governor shall direct all the arrangements necessary to carry out the intentions of this Act, with full power to remove any officer or man thereof for incompetency, neglect of duty or disobedience of orders.

Section 11. Members of said company shall have full power to make arrests of criminals in any part of the territory, and upon the arrest of any criminal, shall deliver the same over to some peace officer in the county where the crime is committed.

Section 12. It shall be the duty of the Auditor of this Territory to draw his warrant on the Territorial Treasurer at the end of each month for the pay of each officer and man in said company, and to forward the same to the Captain of said Company; and it shall be the duty of the Territorial Treasurer to pay such warrants out of the fund for mounted police, as other warrants are paid.

Section 13. There shall be annually levied and collected in addition to all other taxes authorized by law, a tax of one-half mill on taxable property in this territory, to be placed in a fund by the Territorial Treasurer, to be known as the New Mexico Mounted Police Fund, and upon which fund all warrants and payments made under any of the provions of this Act, shall be drawn and made. Said tax shall be levied and collected in the same manner, and at the same time and by the same officers as other territorial taxes; Provided, that until collections shall have been made under the provision of the levy herein authorized for the payment of such mounted police that the territorial treausrer shall pay the same out of any funds, except the interest and sinking funds, in the territorial treasury.

-4-

Section 14. That no portion of said troops shall become a charge against this territory until organized and placed under orders, and the total cost and expense of the organization, equipment and support of said company shall not exceed the sum of Thirteen Thous and $13,000.00)Dollars for any one year.

Section 15. The captain of said company shall provide and issue to each member of said company, a badge, uniform in size and shape, with the words" New Mexico Mounted Police" inscribed thereon in plain, legible letters, which said badge shall belong to, and be returned to this territory, and be returned to it by the possessor thereof, when any member of such company shall cease to be a member thereof; a sum not exceeding twelve hundred dollars ($1,200.00) Dollars per annum, is hereby appropriated for the contingent expense of such company, which shall be paid in the same manner as heretofore provided in this Act, and out of which shall be bought and paid for the arms hereinbefore provided and such other incidental expenses as shall be necessary for the carrying out of the provisions provided for in this Act. All such incidental expenses or contingent expense shall be accounted for by itemized voucher duly certified to by the captain of such mounted police and approved by the territorial auditor, but no expense of any kind shall be incurred or allowed in any one year in excess of the sum of twelve hundred ($1,200.00) Dollars.

Section 16. This Act shall take effect and be in full force from and after its passage.

Notes

Abbreviations

NMMP/NMSRCA: The official New Mexico Mounted Police records are in the New Mexico State Records Center and Archives, Santa Fe. These are recorded on three Territorial Archives Record Microfilm Rolls. Roll 91 contains letters received (1905–1911), Roll 92 is composed of letter-books of communications sent (1905–1911) and the appointment files. Roll 93 contains Captain Fred Fornoff's Arrest Book, special investigation files and a scrapbook of wanted posters. The author was able to consult and copy the original documents.

NMMP/AC: The author's collection of New Mexico Mounted Police documents, police equipment, family remembrances, photographs and personal memorabilia. The collection includes the Fred Lambert Archives and the personal papers of many of the mounted police.

NMSRCA: The New Mexico State Records Center and Archives at Santa Fe has microfilmed most of the territorial archives, by department or public office, on 189 rolls. The author was able to consult and copy many of these original documents before they were microfilmed.

CSR/UNM: Center for Southwest Research, Zimmerman Library, University of New Mexico, Albuquerque.

RGH/NMSU: Rio Grande Historical Collection, Branson Library, New Mexico State University, Las Cruces.

AZ Archives: Archives Division, Department of Library, Archives and Public Records, Phoenix, Ariz.

TX Archives: Archives and Information Services Division, Texas State Library and Archives Commission, Austin.

NARC: National Archives and Record Center, Washington, D.C.

Introduction

1. Miguel A. Otero, *My Nine Years as Governor of the Territory of New Mexico 1897–1906* (Albuquerque: The University of New Mexico, 1940), p. 40.
2. Gilson Willets, "Most Un-American Part of the United States," *New York Times,* 20 August 1905, Magazine Section, p. 5. Willets also worked as a contract writer for *Leslie's Illustrated Weekly* magazine. On this 1905 trip he was the guest of the Southern Pacific Railroad.
3. Edwin Walters, "Sunny New Mexico: A Land That is Bright in Future Prospects," El Paso *Evening News,* 07 April 1905.
4. New Mexico data is taken from a fact sheet published by the secretary of state's office.
5. In his book, *Seeds of Discord: New Mexico in the Aftermath of the American Conquest 1846–1861* (Chicago: Nelson-Hall, 1979), Alvin R. Sunseri presents the case for Anglo exploitation of the Hispanic people living in New Mexico. He asked, "Why was it not before a full century of inequality had passed that the rebellion of Chicanos took place?"

Chapter 1

1. William Holmes McGuffey (1800–1873) was considered the "schoolmaster of the nation" and published his first reader in 1836. This series of books was the mainstay of public education until the 1920s and sold over 125 million copies.
2. Comparative Data, Twelfth U.S. Census, New Mexico Territory, NA; Era data from Hannah Campbell's *Why Did They Name It...?: The Story Behind the Stories of the Brand Names That Have Become Household Words Throughout the World* (New York: Ace Books, 1964).
3. Each year New Mexico's territorial governor was required to make a "state of the territory" report to the secretary of the interior. These voluminous annual reports contain a wealth of data concerning all facets of life in the territory. Printed copies of these reports are in NMSRCA.
4. Miguel A. Otero, *Report of the Governor of New Mexico to the Secretary of the Interior,* (Washington: Government Printing Office, 1905) p. 2. A typed copy of this report, dated 15 September 1905, is in the Gov. M.A. Otero Papers, NMSRCA.

Chapter 2

1. "New Mexico Mounted Police," *The* (Socorro) *Chieftain*, 03 February 1899.
2. Contemporary newspaper accounts and data file, NMMP/AC.
3. See Larry Ball's *The United States Marshals of New Mexico and Arizona Territories 1846–1912* (Albuquerque: The University of New Mexico Press, 1978) for the function of federal marshals, and Frank Richard Prassel's *The Western Peace Officer: A Legacy of Law and Order* (Norman: University of Oklahoma Press, 1972) for a discussion of the Posse Comitatus Law in the western territories.
4. The Cattle and Horse Protective Association of Central New Mexico was chartered with nearly 100 members. The association was formed with "the purpose of protecting stock raisers from the depredations of the many cattle rustlers operating in New Mexico." The San Marcial *Bee*, 23 June 1901. Background information: Gerald Baydo, "Cattlemen's Associations in New Mexico Territory," *Journal of the West*, July 1975.
5. Phoenix *Gazette* quoted by the Nogales *Border Vidette*, 27 October 1898.
6. Howard Bryan, "Guns Governed N.M. at Turn of the Century," Albuquerque *Tribune*, 17 July 1984. It would seem that both Catron and Ancheta supported the concept of a territorial police force. Six years later Catron voted against a similar measure to once again embarrass his political rival, Governor Otero.
7. Roswell *Register*, 10 February 1899.
8. Richardson Avenue in Roswell is named in honor of Granville H. Richardson. The city police department's headquarters is located on this street. Family information from I.J. Richardson.
9. *Journal of the Council 1899,* 30 January 1899, Secretary of the Territory Records, Microfilm Roll 13, NMSRCA.
10. "New Mexico Mounted Police," *The* (Socorro) *Chieftain*, 03 February 1899.
11. Albuquerque *Morning Journal*, 17 January 1899.
12. Scarborough was a Louisiana native who had been the first elected sheriff of Jones County, Texas; a deputy U.S. marshal; the killer of John Selman, the man who killed John Wesley Hardin; and the man who captured female stage robber Pearl Hart. See Robert K. DeArment's *George Scarborough: The Life and Death of a Lawman on the Closing Frontier* (Norman: The University of Oklahoma Press, 1992) for a well researched biography.
13. Santa Fe *New Mexican*, 19 January 1899.
14. Foraker wrote Scarborough, "I will be more than pleased to do all I can for you when the matter comes up." Letter: Foraker to Scarborough, 05 January 1899, U.S. Marshal Papers, CSR/UNM.
15. The (Socorro) *Chieftain*, 10 February 1899.
16. *Journal of the Council 1899*, 14 March 1899, NMSRCA.
17. *Journal of the Council 1899*, 14 March 1899, NMSRCA.
18. *Journal of the Council 1899*, 16 March 1899, NMSRCA.
19. Otero, *My Nine Years As Governor*, pp. 78–80.
20. Defeated and Vetoed Bills, Council 1899, NMSRCA.
21. *The Pecos Valley Argus* (Carlsbad), 10 February 1899.
22. *New Mexico Coded Laws 1899*, NMSRCA.
23. Governor's Message, Thirty-third Legislative Assembly, 16 January 1899, NMSRCA.
A new territorial Capitol had burned down in May 1892 in a mysterious fire, so arrangements had been made for the Legislative Assembly to meet in one of the buildings of St. Michael's College. Four assemblies used the college before a new Capitol was finally dedicated in June 1900.
24. J. Marvin Hunter, *The Story of Lottie Deno: Her Life and Times* (Bandera, Texas: The 4 Hunters, 1959) pp. 99, 100 and 171.
25. Silver City *Independent*, 09 October 1900.
26. J. Marvin Hunter claimed that he had been given a commission as a "special officer" by Gov. Otero dated September 10, 1900. The author has been unable to locate any official documentation to support Hunter's claim concerning a territorial commission or a territorial badge issued by Gov. M.A. Otero. Hunter became the founder of *Frontier Times* and the *True West* family of historical publications.
27. George Edger Scarborough, Jr., had first ridden in a posse when he was 18. He soon developed a reputation for high-handed arrest techniques and a quick trigger-finger. Ed was an excellent marksman and didn't seem to know fear. He became an Arizona Ranger in 1901, but was discharged after nine months of service because of his general disorderly and overbearing attitude. At different times, Ed was charged with murder, carrying a concealed weapon, and robbery, but none of these charges ever came before a judge and jury. In 1909, the mounted police wanted Ed for "larceny of a horse" in Socorro County. Ed fled to California and did not return to the southwest until 1915 and then he worked on a ranch in Arizona. Within months, he shot a neighbor rancher, was arrested for murder, tried and convicted and was sentenced to the Arizona State Prison. A year later, Ed escaped and fled to Mexico. He was never recaptured and died about 1945. Letters: Robert K. DeArment to the author, 12 January 1985, NMMP/AC; Socorro County District Attorney John Griffin to Captain Fred Fornoff, 18 June 1909, Letters Received, NMMP/NMSRCA.
28. This Collier may have been John W. Collier who lived in Silver City at the turn of the century. If they are the same man then Collier rode with both Scarborough's Rangers and later became a mounted police under Captain Fornoff. Twice John W. Collier served as second-in-command of the territorial/state rangers led by Fornoff.
29. Conversations: Robert K. DeArment and the author, NOLA Rendezvous, El Paso, Texas, 24–27 July 1991; WOLA Convention, Deadwood, S.D., 20–23 July 1994; NOLA Rendezvous, Roswell, N.M., 26–29 July 1995; WOLA Convention, Crag, Colo., 17–20 July 1996. DeArment believes that the Scarborough posse was the "grandfather" of the New Mexico Mounted Police.
30. The Arizona Ranger laws are contained in *The Revised Statutes of Arizona Territory 1901*; *Acts, Resolutions and Memorials of the Twenty-Second Legislative Assembly of the Territory of Arizona 1903* and *Acts, Resolutions and Memorials of the Twenty-Fifth Legislative*

Assembly of the Territory of Arizona 1909, AZ Archives.
See Bill O'Neal's very readable *The Arizona Rangers* (Austin, Texas: Eakin Press, 1987) for a well developed history of the ranger era and *The Arizona Rangers* (New York: Hastings House, 1972) for contemporary newspaper accounts skillfully edited by Joseph Miller. Both books contain classic photographs and informative appendices.

Chapter 3

1. Captain Thomas H. Rynning, as told to Al Cohn and Joe Chisholm, *Gun Notches: The Life of a Cowboy-Soldier* (New York: Fredrick A. Stokes Co., 1931), p. 200.
2. Rynning, *Gun Notches*, p. 201.
3. Rynning, *Gun Notches*, pp. 201 and 202.
4. "Arizona Rangers Reviewed," Tucson (Arizona) *Citizen*, 06 January 1902.
5. Interview: Burton C. Mossman and J. Evetts Haley, 25 February 1945, Roswell, N.M., J. Evetts Haley Collection, Box II, File B, Haley Memorial Library and History Center, Midland, Texas.
6. *House Journal 1901*, Twenty-first Legislative Assembly Records, AZ Archives.
7. *Council Journal 1901*, Twenty-first Legislative Assembly Records, AZ Archives.
8. General Mabry's remarks, *Bi-annual Report of the Adjutant General, 1891–1892*, p. 8; General Order No. 24, *Bi-annual Report of the Adjutant General, 1900–1901*, Texas Adjutant General Records, TX State Archives, Austin.
9. General Order No. 62, *Bi-annual Report of the Adjutant General, 1901–1902*, Texas Adjutant General Records, Texas State Archives, Austin.
10. Solomonville (Arizona) *Bulletin*, August 1901.
11. Margin Notes: Harry Sexon comment recorded with the interview of Burton C. Mossman and J. Evetts Haley, 25 February 1945, Roswell, N.M., J. Evetts Haley Collection, Box II, File B, Haley Memorial Library and History Center, Midland, Texas.
12. Bill O'Neal, *The Arizona Rangers* (Austin, Texas: Eakin Press, 1987), Footnote 9, p. 189.
13. Interview: Burton C. Mossman and J. Evetts Haley, 25 February 1945, Roswell, N.M., J. Evetts Haley Papers, Box II, File B, Haley Memorial Library and History Center, Midland, Texas.
14. Letter: N.O. Murphy to M.A. Otero, 19 August 1901, Western History Collection of Anthony Sapienza, Paramus, N.J. The contents of this letter are quoted with the permission of the owner.
15. Letter: Gov. Otero to Gov. Murphy, 01 October 1901, Gov. Otero Papers, Letters Sent, NMSRCA.
16. Rynning, *Gun Notches*, p. 200.
17. Record Group 42: Arizona Rangers, Box 4: Requisition Requests, AZ Archives.
18. Interview: Burton C. Mossman and J. Evetts Haley, 25 July 1945, Roswell, N.M., J. Evetts Haley Collection, Box II, File B, Haley Memorial Library and History Center, Midland, Texas.
19. Letter: Gov. Otero to Walter H. Cole, Editor of the Tombstone (Arizona) *Epitaph*, 10 August 1936, Box 6, Folder 37, O-SC/CSR/UNM.
20. Otero, *My Nine Years As Governor*, p. 207.
21. *The Coconino Sun* (Flagstaff, Ariz.), 03 October 1903.
22. Letter: Burton C. Mossman to Arizona historian Will C. Barnes, as quoted by Joseph Miller (Ed.) in the Foreword to *The Arizona Rangers* (New York: Hastings House, Publishers, 1972), x.
23. "Cowboy Star 'Lucky' Hayden Dies at 70," Lubbock (Texas) *Avalanche-Journal*, 13 June 1981.
24. Harris M. Lentz III, *Television Westerns Episode Guide*, (Jefferson, N.C.: McFarland & Co., Inc., Publishers, 1997), pp. 421–424; "Why 26 Men?" *TV Guide*, week unknown, 1958, pp. 28–30.
25. Tucson (Arizona) *Citizen*, 05 May 1982.
26. Paul L. Allen, "Ranger Roundup," Tucson *Citizen*, 29 July 2002. The new Arizona Rangers became an official state law enforcement support unit on 01 August 2002.
27. "Arizona Rangers Reviewed," Tucson (Arizona) *Citizen*, 06 January 1902.

Chapter 4

1. "Editorial," Nogal *Republican*, 22 May 1902.
2. "What is Necessary for Good Times," Santa Fe *New Mexican*, 16 January 1905. The paper said, "All signs indicate that the record of the present assembly will be good and wholesome. Times will be improved as much as they can be by the legislation of the Thirty-Sixth Legislative Assembly. Good laws alone, however, can not make good times. Energy, thrift, and business capacity on the part of the people are necessary to do so in addition all should work in union for the development of the great natural resources of New Mexico." The *New Mexican* felt that the legislature would "do everything in its power for the advancement and progress of the people."
3. "Rangers Wanted," Santa Fe *New Mexican*, 19 January 1905.
4. Report: Capt. Rynning to Gov. A.O. Brodie, Record Group 42—Arizona Rangers, AZ Archives.
5. "Mr. Greer Proposes Relief From Outlaws," Santa Fe *New Mexican*, 26 January 1905.
6. Holm O. Bursum Papers, SRC/UNM.
7. Miguel A. Otero, *Report of the Governor of New Mexico*, September 15, 1904 (Washington, D.C.: Government Printing Office, 1904) p. 428.
8. Compiled from contemporary newspapers accounts, NMMP/AC.
9. "Mr. Greer Proposes Relief From Outlaws," Santa Fe *New Mexican*, 26 January 1905.
10. "Mounted Police Bill Appears," The Las Vegas *Daily Optic*, 27 January 1905.
11. "A Ranger Service Demanded by Stockmen," Santa Fe *New Mexican*, 16 January 1905; "Rangers Wanted," Santa Fe *New Mexican*, 19 January 1905.
12. Col. Greer's biographical data was compiled from numerous contemporary newspaper accounts, NMMP/AC; "Greer's Good Plan Goes Into Effect," Santa Fe *New Mexican*, 11 February 1905.
13. Santa Fe *New Mexican*, 08 February 1905.
14. Albuquerque *Morning Journal*, 26 January 1907; Portales *Herald*, undated news clip, NMMP/AC.
15. "For Sale at a Bargain," Deming *Headlight*, 11 May 1905; *Albuquerque City Directory* 1907, NP; Deming *Headlight*, 30 September 1910.

16. *Journal of the Council 1905*, 26 January 1905, p. 69, NMSRCA.
17. Otero, *My Eight Years As Governor*, pp. 147–149.
18. Prisoner 131, *Book of Convicts 1884–1904* (Roll 1); Prisoner 131, *Punishment Record Book 1885–1913* (Roll 3), Territorial Prison Records, NMSRCA. Martin served as a clerk-bookkeeper and assistant to the warden at this same prison from May 1899 to February 1904.
19. The committee assignments and member biographies were compiled from the *Journal of the Council* 1905 and biographical items from the Santa Fe *New Mexican*. Some members of the Cattle Sanitary Board were prepared to offer an alternative ranger plan to the lawmakers if the Greer Mounted Police Bill was unable to generate enough legislative support. Alamogordo *News*, 11 February 1905.
20. Joseph H. Kibbey, *Reports of the Department of the Interior, Governor of Arizona 1905* (Washington, D.C.: Government Printing Office, 1905) p. 192.
21. Council Bill 26 and Amended Council Bill 26 as presented to the council by the finance committee, copies in NMMP/AC. (See Appendix)
22. *Journal of the Council 1905*, 09 February 1905, pp. 116–118, NMSRCA.
23. *Journal of the House 1905*, 09 February 1905, p. 77; 10 February 1905, pp. 139–140; 15 February 1905, p. 215, NMSRCA. The Santa Fe paper reported that the second House vote was 18 to 4. This would have meant that two representatives had not voted. Santa Fe *New Mexican*, 11 February 1905.
24. "I have the honor to inform your honorable body that I have this day signed the following; Amended Council Bill No. 26, Providing for Mounted Police." Gov. Otero's Message No. 11, 15 February 1905, to the House of Representatives and the Legislative Council of the 36th Legislative Assembly, Gov. Otero Papers, NMSRCA.

The Mounted Police Act was officially filed in the office of the Secretary of Territory at 3:15 p.m. on 15 February 1905. This action made the act an enforceable law in the Sunshine Territory. J.W. Raynolds, secretary of the territory, provided John F. Fullerton a certified copy of this act on 18 March 1905 when he took his oath as captain of the mounted police. Photocopy in NMMP/AC.
25. "New Mexico's Rangers," Denver *Republican*, as it was reprinted in the Socorro *Chieftain*, 08 April 1905.

Chapter 5

1. Virgil D. White (Abstractor), *Genealogical Abstracts of Revolutionary War Pension Files, Vol. II F-M* (Waynesboro, Tenn.: National Historical Publishing Co., 1991) p. 1291.
2. James S. Fullerton, Civil War Pension Record 753990, Bureau of Pension, Department of the Interior Records, National Archives and Records Service, Washington, D.C. (JSF Pensions/NA).
3. James S. Fullerton, Civil War Service Record, Military Service Branch, National Archives and Records Service, Washington, D.C. (JSF Service Record/NA).
4. Ira Berlin, et al., editors, "Testimony of the Superintendent of Contrabands," *Freedom: A Documentary History of Emancipation, 1862–1867, Series I, Vol. I: The Destruction of Slavery* (New York: Cambridge University Press, 1985) p. 90.
5. The Socorro *Chieftain*, 12 November 1897.
6. See Gary W. Callagher, editor, *The Richmond Campaign of 1862: The Peninsula & the Seven Days* (Chapel Hill, N.C.: The University of North Carolina Press, 2000) for a thoughtful discussion of these fateful battlefield events.
7. JSF Pension Records/NA.
8. Duty Record, 1st Lt. James S. Fullerton, War Department Records, JSF Service Record/NA.
9. General Affidavit, Walter Fullerton, 25 November 1890, and Theodore P. McWilliams, 30 August 1890, JSF Pension Records/NA.
10. *History of Lewis, Clark, Knox and Scotland Counties, Missouri* (NP: 1887) p. 408.
11. *Scotland County, Missouri: In Retrospect* (Scotland County Bicentennial Committee and Scotland County Historical Society, 1977) pp. 1074–1075.
12. *National Democrat* (Memphis, Mo.), 07 July 1860.
13. *Journal of the Congress of the Confederate States of America 1861–1865*, Vol. 1 (Records of the Third Session, 20 July to 31 August 1861, and the Fifth Session, 18 November 1861 to 17 February 1862), pp. 362–363, 366, 368–370, 377, 479–483, Records of the War of the Rebellion, NARC; "Missouri Admitted Into The Rebel Government," New York *Herald*, 02 December 1861 (The news report was taken from the Richmond [Va.] *Dispatch*); Capt. Thomas Speed, *The Union Cause in Kentucky 1860–1865* (New York: G.P. Putnam & Sons, 1907) pp. 200–211.
14. *History*, p. 433.
15. *History*, p. 499; JSF Pension Records/NA.
16. *Record of Membership*, Book 1, First Presbyterian Church, Memphis, Mo.
17. Southern Presbyterians, meeting in convention at Augusta, Georgia, on December 4, 1861, organized the Assembly of the Presbyterian Church in the Confederate States of America. After the war this assembly was called the Presbyterian Church — South. The Methodist Church did a similar type of sectional split.
18. *Scotland County, Missouri: In Retrospect*, p. 30.
19. The Ninth Federal Census (1870), Town of Memphis, Scotland County, Mo., p. 30, NA.
20. *History*, p. 503.
21. *Illinois Executive Record 1837–1843*, p. 233, Gov. Carlin Papers, Illinois State Archives, Springfield, Ill.
22. Letter: Mrs. Elmer (Irene) Fullerton to the author, 28 July 1984, NMMP/AC.
23. Memphis Business Directory 1875, as reported in *History*, p. 503; Fullerton Family Records, NMMP/AC.
24. Conversation Notes: Irene Fullerton and Susan Leverett and the author, Albuquerque, N.M., 28 July 1984, NMMP/AC; Letters: Irene Fullerton to author, 01 August 1984; Susan Leverett to author, 14 August and 04 September 1997, NMMP/AC.
25. Fullerton Family Records, NMMP/AC.
26. The Socorro *Chieftain*, 28 April 1900.
27. In early July 1947, five members a Socorro County ranch family were rock hunting on the Plains when they discovered an aircraft crash site. They were soon joined by a college professor and his five archaeology students and a short time later a government

mapmaker also joined the group. These dozen people are now part of the UFO mystique that is the "Roswell Incident" and its aftermath. See Stanton T. Friedman and Don Berliner, *Crash at Corona* (New York: Marlowe & Company, 1992, updated 1995) for a detailed discussion of this event.
In 2003, New Mexico lawmakers authorized the second Tuesday of February as "Extraterrestrial Culture Day" in the state. "Space Aliens Get A Day Of Their Own," Midland (Texas) *Reporter-Telegram,* 23 March 2003.

28. *Deed Record Books* 31, 38, 39, 54, County Clerk's Office, Socorro County Courthouse, Socorro, N.M.; The (Socorro) *Chieftain,* 20 January 1899.

29. *Brand Book of the Territory of New Mexico* (Santa Fe, N.M.: New Mexico Printing Company, 1900) pp. 61, 72, 76 and 93.

30. General Affidavit, Benjamin McClure and Henry Myers, 05 May 1897, JSF Pension Papers, NA.

31. Magdalena *Mountain Mail,* 25 October 1888; The (Socorro) *Chieftain,* 12 November 1897.

32. General Affidavit, Milton Fullerton, 30 August 1890; General Pension Application 1897 and 1907, JSF Pension Records/ NA.

33. John Elmer Fullerton, named in honor of his father and Dr. Elmer Blinn, was born 18 December 1888. Conversation Notes: Mrs. Irene Fullerton and daughter, Mrs. Susan Leverett, 24 July 1995, NMMP/AC.

34. Conversation Notes: Irene Fullerton and the author, Albuquerque, N.M., 28 July 1984; Letter: Irene Fullerton to author, 22 June 1984, NMMP/AC. Irene Fullerton told the author that she had heard family tales that the Indian raiders at the Fullerton ranch had been led by Geronimo. This does not seem likely since Geronimo and his small band of followers had surrendered to the U.S. Army in August 1886 and had been sent, via the railroad, to Fort Pickens, on Santa Rosa Island in Pensacola Bay, Florida.

35. Conversation Notes: Irene Fullerton and the author, Albuquerque, N.M., 28 July 1984, NMMP/AC. Tombstone Data: Susan Baker Fullerton was born 15 January 1864 and died 29 December 1893. Raymond Parish Fullerton was born 16 July 1892 and died 10 January 1894, Fullerton family tombstone, Greenwood Memorial Park, San Diego, Calif.

36. The Socorro *Chieftain,* 14 July 1899 and 08 June 1901.

37. The Socorro *Chieftain,* 08 June 1901.

38. John lost interest in the trading post business after the death of his wife and son. The general area was still called Fullerton for many years after John finally sold the place.

39. The Socorro *Chieftain,* 13 September 1902.

40. Conversation Notes: Irene Fullerton and the author, Albuquerque, N.M., 28 July 1984, NMMP/AC. Will Fullerton's temperament was discussed by Mrs. Fullerton and she felt that Will was an anti-social nut. His conduct was suspect even among other family members.

41. The Socorro *Chieftain,* 28 December 1901 and 06 October 1899.

42. *Deed Books* 54 and 84, County Clerk's Office, Socorro County Courthouse, Socorro, N.M.; Mortgage Records, Bank of Magdalena, private collection, copy NMMP/AC.

43. Letter: W.S. Fullerton to H.O. Bursum, 15 August 1902, H.O. Bursum Papers, Box 1, File 3, CSR/UNM.

44. Albuquerque *Evening Citizen,* 24 July 1905.

45. The Socorro *Chieftain,* 17 August 1901.

46. The Socorro *Chieftain,* 02 November 1901; 24 February 1900; 16 November 1900.

47. *Marriage Record 1885–,* County Clerk's Office, Courthouse, Socorro, N.M., p. 240. The Rev. C.F. Taylor performed the wedding and filed the record on 21 August 1903.

48. The Socorro *Chieftain,* 25 May 1901.

49. The Socorro *Chieftain,* 15 October 1901.

50. Copy of Gov. Otero's speech, 16 October 1901, M.A. Otero Papers, CSR/UNM.

51. *Deed Book* 54, County Clerk's Office, Socorro County Courthouse, Socorro, N.M.

52. Oaths of Office and *Bond Record Book,* County Clerk's Office, Socorro County, Courthouse, Socorro, N.M.

53. Letter: Capt. Fullerton to Frank Clancy, 25 October 1905, Letters Sent, NMMP/NMSRCA.

54. The Socorro *Chieftain,* 25 March 1905; *Executive Record Book* #5, 17 March 1905, Gov. M.A. Otero Papers, NMSRCA; Oaths of Office 1905, NMMP/NMSRCA.

55. John Fullerton's "dark eyes" were in fact a light blue.

56. "Are Sworn Into Office," Santa Fe *New Mexican,* 01 April 1905.

57. Letter: Gov. Otero to W.H. Byerts, 11 November 1905, Letters Sent, Gov. M.A. Otero Papers, NMSRC.

Chapter 6

1. Personal and family data provided to the author by relatives and friends of Fullerton's Rangers, Notes in NMMP/AC.

2. "Veteran Officer Dead," Albuquerque *Journal,* 23 September 1936; Certificate of Death, Vital Records, New Mexico Health and Social Services Department, Santa Fe, N.M.; Burial records, Sunset Memorial Park, Albuquerque, N.M.

3. Letters: Cipriana Baca Randolph to author, 08 September 1982 and 10 October 1982, NMMP/AC. Mrs. Randolph provided the author with Baca family history, letters, photographs and interviews for use in a full length biography of her father.

4. Letter: Cipriana Randolph to author, 30 October 1985, NMMP/AC.; "Sheriff Baca," Deming *Herald,* 07 May 1901.

5. "Bronco's Break," Silver City *Enterprise,* 13 March 1891.

6. Baca worked for Socorro County Sheriff Leopoldo Contreras (1893–94) and Sheriff Holm Olaf Bursum (1895–96).

7. The Socorro *Chieftain,* 23 October and 06 November 1896, 22 January and 02 April 1897. Baca's deputy assessor was in the office Monday through Saturday, 9 a.m. to 4 p.m., during the months of March and April. Baca received 4 percent of the taxes collected in 1897 and 2 percent of the collection in 1898. He charged 33 percent interest on all late taxes. The Socorro *Chieftain,* 30 April 1897.

8. The Socorro *Chieftain*, 30 July and 23 July 1897. In mid-1897 Grant County rancher Creighton M. Foraker was appointed federal marshal for New Mexico Territory. The new lawman had known Baca from his deputy sheriff days in Grant County and Foraker needed good men on his staff. Federal deputies, at this time, were not paid a yearly salary, but were paid a fee for service rendered.

9. Baca-Berry family records from Cipriana Randolph, NMMP/AC.

10. The (Socorro) *Chieftain*, 27 January and 03 February 1899.

11. The Socorro *Chieftain*, 16 February 1901.

12. The Santa Fe *New Mexican*, 02 April 1901.

13. Deming *Herald* reprinted in Socorro *Chieftain*, 30 August 1902. When the new Luna County officials were named by Gov. Otero, the *Western Liberal* (Lordsburg), 05 April 1901, editorialized by saying, "It will probably be a long time before all the officers of Luna county are again republican." The area around Deming was heavily Democratic. The Luna County Commissioners canvassed the general election votes on 10 November 1902. There were 504 votes cast in the sheriff's race. Foster received 281 and Baca 223.

When Baca left office in January 1903 the county owed him hundreds of dollars for arrest fees, mileage, feeding jail prisoners, providing water for the jail and a two dollar bounty for "1 coyote killed." The county had trouble collecting tax money, thus it had no money to pay its bills. Official records seem to support the fact that Baca was finally paid most of the money due him. *Proceedings of Board of County Commissioners — Luna County, Book 1*, County Clerk's Office, Luna County Courthouse, Deming, N.M.

14. See Walter Hovey, "Black Jack Ketchum Tried to Give Me a Break!," *True West* (April 1972, p 48) for an example of this idea.

15. *Executive Record Book #6*, 07 January 1907, Gov. H.J. Hagerman Papers, NMSRCA; "Lieutenant Cipriano Baca Has Resigned," Albuquerque *Morning Journal*, 08 January 1907.

16. Socorro *Chieftain*, 07 December 1907, 12 January and 19 January 1908.

17. "Cipriano Baca to be Deputy at Mogollon," Socorro *Chieftain*, 10 September 1910.

18. The words and music to *Stand By Me* was written by Charles Albert Tindley in 1906.

19. Letter: Cipriana Randolph to author, 13 December 1982, NMMP/AC.

20. Letter: Louise Baca to author, 12 August 1982, NMMP/AC.

21. Appointment notice and oath of office, 1918 file, NMMP/NMSRCA.

22. *Albuquerque City Directory* 1925–1936, Southwest Collection, Albuquerque Public Library.

23. Letter: Cipriano Baca to Cipriana Randolph, 22 August 1936, Copy in NMMP/AC.

24. Conversation Notes: Persey Sickles and author, spring-fall 1968, NMMP/AC. Sickles was a Socorro County native who, as a young man, had known both John Fullerton and Bob Lewis.

25. Certificate of Death, New Mexico Health and Social Services Department, Santa Fe, N.M.; Howard Bryan, "Lost Adams Diggings Gold Sold Here, Pioneer Says," The Albuquerque *Tribune*, 23 May 1949.

26. Howard Bryan, "NM Pioneer Stores His Gun and Spurs," The Albuquerque *Tribune*, 26 May 1949.

27. Conversation Notes, Howard Bryan and Author, 16 January 1971, Albuquerque, N.M., NMMP/AC.

28. Santa Fe *New Mexican*, 27 April 1905.

29. Grant Maxwell, "Cow Town," *New Mexico Magazine*, October 1935; Howard Bryan, "Billy the Kid Alive, Bob Lewis Believes," The Albuquerque *Tribune*, 25 May 1949.

30. "Famed Law Officer, Robert Lewis, Dies," Albuquerque *Tribune*, 19 August 1950. The Lewis family plot is enclosed with a fence made by the Stewart Iron Works of Cincinnati, Ohio. The two youngest daughters have engraved stone markers for their grave sites. The Flora Lewis grave is marked by a large stone. Three other sites are marked by wooden planks and one of these may be Bob's final resting place. There were no site records kept for the old Socorro Cemetery.

31. Socorro *Chieftain*, 11 January 1902; "Cattle and Horse Protective Association," Socorro *Chieftain*, 25 March 1905.

32. Socorro *Chieftain*, 21 August 1909.

33. Socorro *Chieftain*, 23 July 1910 and 26 August 1911.

34. Socorro *Chieftain*, 18 May 1912.

35. Grant Maxwell, "Cow Town," *New Mexico Magazine*, October 1935, p. 12; "Bob Lewis Does Wholesale Arrest," Magdalena *News*, 26 June 1937.

36. Howard Bryan, "Lost Adams Diggings Gold Sold Here, Pioneer Says," Albuquerque *Tribune*, 23 May 1949.

37. Howard Bryan, "NM Pioneer Stores His Gun and Spurs," The Albuquerque *Tribune*, 26 May 1949.

38. Grant Maxwell, "Cow Town," *New Mexico Magazine*, October 1935, p. 12.

39. Howard Bryan, "Billy the Kid Alive, Bob Lewis Believes," Albuquerque *Tribune*, 25 May 1949.

40 (Howard Bryan), "Famed Law Officer, Robert Lewis, Dies," Albuquerque *Tribune*, 19 August 1950.

41. Files of the Bursum-Luna Committee and George Elkins' mounted police oath of office form, NMMP/NMSRCA.; Deming *Graphic*, 18 April 1905.

42. Letter: Chandler Elkins to author, 30 September 1970, NMMP/AC.

43. Silver City *Independent*, 09 January 1906; Letter: Elkins to M.T. Everhart, 25 December 1909, The Hatchet Ranch archives, Hachita, N.M.

44. The Hatchet Ranch headquarters was originally built as a straight line adobe. When George Elkins moved his family to the place a new wing was added to the building to form an "L" shape. Letter: M.T. Everhart to author, 13 July 1984, NMMP/AC.

45. Letter: Elkins to M.T. Everhart, 20 March 1916, the Hatchet Ranch archives, Hachita, N.M. Howard Bryan, in his column for the Albuquerque *Tribune* (11 April 1957), recounted an interview with Elkins' son George concerning life along the Mexico border during the Villa era.

46. Letter: M.T. Everhart to author, 18 May 1985, NMMP/AC.

47. Letter: Chandler Elkins to author, 30 September 1970, NMMP/AC.

48. During the 1980s the author corresponded with Meyer's grandchildren Jesse B. Meyer, Mrs. I.B.

Singer and Steve Meyer. They all lived in Albuquerque.

49. *Marriage Record Book A-1*, License 445, County Clerk's Office, Torrance County Courthouse, Estancia, N.M.

50. Conversation Notes: Mrs. I.B. Singer and author, Mountainair, N.M., 24 June 1984, NMMP/AC; Librada S. Meyer's tombstone, Catholic Cemetery, Willard, N.M.; Thirteenth United States Census (1910), Microfilm Roll 919, Estancia, Torrance County, N.M., NA.

51. Many of the early business records of the New Mexico Salt Company were destroyed in the Estancia fire of 1911. Copies of some of the remaining company records are among Fred Fornoff's personal papers. Fred Fornoff Papers, NMMP/NMSRCA.

52. Letter: Earl Scott to Fornoff, 09 August 1911, Fred Fornoff Papers, NMMP/NMSRCA.

53. *Marriage Record Book A-1*, Torrance County, N.M.

54. Meyer family descendants/author correspondence, NMMP/AC.

55. "Local Briefs," The Clayton *Enterprise*, 03 March 1905.

56. Brophy's Mounted Police Oath of Office, NMMP/NMSRCA; *The Quay County Democrat* (Tucumcari), 23 April 1904; John J. Brophy File, NMMP/AC.

57. *The Quay County Democrat* (Tucumcari), 23 April 1904; *Tucumcari News and Tucumcari Times*, 24 December 1910 and 16 November 1911.

58. "Assaults Kindly Disposed Officer," Santa Fe *New Mexican*, 10 August 1905. John Brophy first became a lawman in April 1894 when he was appointed by the county commissioners as a constable in Union County. He won election to that office in January 1895. *Record of Official Bonds — Union County Book A*, County Clerk's Office, Union County Courthouse, Clayton, N.M.

59. Brophy's 1905 Mounted Police Oath of Office lists his age as 42 and his occupation as a cowman. The 1910 federal census list John's age as 45 and his occupation as a Union County deputy sheriff. The job change is understandable, but aging only three years in a five year period is a neat trick.

60. Brophy wrote, "My object in this matter is to better my own interest. I will be at home with my family." Letter: Brophy to Capt. Fullerton, 20 March 1906, Letters Received, NMMP/NMSRCA. The duties of the Clayton marshal were listed in the city ordinances published in the 29 June 1906 Clayton *Enterprise*.

61. Letter: Capt. Fornoff to Brophy, 16 July 1906, Letters Sent, NMMP/NMSRCA; Following the attempted lynching at Clayton, it would seem that Marshal Brophy transferred his prisoner to a stronger jail at Raton. Prisoner Listings, *Colfax County Jail Calendar 1895–1915*, Sheriff's Office, Courthouse, Raton, N.M.; "Local and Personal," The Clayton *Citizen*, 07 December 1906; "Local and Personal," The Clayton *News*, 24 April 1915.

62. Brophy family history was provided the author by former Harding County Sheriff J.B. McNeil, Interview Notes: McNeil and the author, Roy, N.M., Summer 1971, NMMP/AC; Clara Toombs Harvey, *Not So Wild, The Old West* (Denver: Golden Bell Press, 1961), p. 116.

63. The Clayton *News*, 10 June 1916. Rosa Brophy was a 40 year old widow in 1920, and living with her mother and a young boarder. Fourteenth United States Census (1920), Clayton, Union County, New Mexico, NA. The 1910 Census had misstated Mrs. Brophy's age as being 32 years old.

When Rosa Duran Brophy died she left her remaining son, John of Fort Sill, Okla., 60 percent of her estate ($88.25), plus the household furniture. The remainder of her estate went to her mother, brother and two sisters at 10 percent or $20.58 each. Her estate was valued at $170.57, while her funeral expenses totaled $206. Mrs. Brophy's will was executed eight days before her 04 April 1925 death. She had been born on 13 April 1879. *Probate Records — Union County*, County Clerk's Office, Union County Courthouse, Clayton, N.M. Record and Bill of Items, Rosaria D. Brophy funeral, Hass Funeral Home, Clayton, N.M.

64. "Dudley's Birthday," The Alamogordo *News*, 17 February 1906; *Deed Book 27 — Crosby County, Marriage License Book 1 — Crosby County*, County Clerk's Office, Crosby County Courthouse, Crosbyton, Texas.

65. The Capitan *News*, 21 August 1903; The Alamogordo *Daily Journal*, 08 August 1904.

66. *Otero County Advertiser* (Alamogordo), 09 September 1905; The Alamogordo *News*, 07 October 1905; The Tucumcari *News*, 02 December 1905; Raton *Reporter*, 28 August 1913; Knights of Pythias information booklet, ND/NP.

67. Will Dudley resigned effective 30 September 1910, NMMP/NMSRCA; "W.E. Dudley, formerly mounted policeman, was in the city Tuesday," Carrizozo *Outlook*, 03 March 1911. *Colfax County Jail Calendar 1895–1915*, Sheriff's Office, Courthouse, Raton, N.M. Deputy Sheriff/Marshal Will Dudley's first arrest was recorded on 13 December 1911 and the last arrest entry was made for 03 March 1914.

68. Conversation Notes: Frank Shofner, Dudley's grandson, and author, 24 May 1986, Albuquerque, N.M., NMMP/AC. Dudley's son Lenon was born 24 August 1906. He lived four days and was buried in Alamogordo's Monte Vista Cemetery.

69. "Rev. Dudley Is Arrested," Herington (Kan.) *Times*, 18 July 1918. J.W. Kelso, a federal revenue officer in Arizona, supported the head wound story and the undercover service of Will Dudley. Gladys Johnson remembered Dudley as her pastor when she was a schoolgirl. "He had a head injury — like a plate in his head." Letter: Virginia Brunner, Director, Tri-County Historical Society, Herington, Kan., to author, 16 September 1992, NMMP/AC. Frank Shofner said family tradition is that his grandfather migrated to Canada and became a red-coated lawman. Shofner's mother, Lois Ann Dudley, remembered that her father was dead when she and her mother and sister moved back to Alamogordo in 1919. They had been living in a small town in Union County were Josie Dudley had taught school. Conversation Notes: Frank Shofner and author, 24 May 1986, NMMP/AC.

70. "Rev. Dudley Is Arrested," Herington (Kan.) *Times*, 18 July 1918; "Dudley Had Reason to Forget Past in New Mexico, Say Capitol Officials," Santa Fe *New Mexican*, 02 August 1918; Church Board

Records: First Baptist Church, Herington, Kan., provided to the author by Sally Cathin, 04 December 1992, copies in NMMP/AC.

71. In Case #39022 Will Dudley was charged with wife desertion. In Case #40274 Will was charged with bond forfeiture for Case #39022. In Case #41517 Mildred Dudley was granted a divorce. District Court Records, District Court Clerk's Office, Sedgwick County Courthouse, Wichita, KS.; Herington (KS) *Times*, 14 February, 21 February, 17 March, 18 April, 16 May and 23 May 1918.

72. Letter: Joyce Caughron, administrator, Landsun Homes, to author, 07 June 1986. When Josie Dudley came to live at the Methodist Church retirement home in Carlsbad, N.M., her records listed her husband as dead and his burial place as Italy. At the time of his arrest in Kansas, Dudley told authorities that he was planning to go to Italy as a government interpreter. "Rev. Dudley Is Arrested," Herington (Kan.) *Times*, 18 July 1918.

73. When the brick building at 6th and Maryland was built it had the name Dudley cut in stone above the main doorway. By the late 1990s the building was no longer being used as a public school, but was a drug treatment center called Maryland House. Mary Josephine Dudley was born 11 February 1877 at Kosse, Texas. She was the daughter of John and Fannie Kidd Burleson. She died on 19 April 1978 and was survived by two daughters, two grandsons, two great-grandsons, four great-granddaughters, and one great-great-grandson. Burial Records, Hamilton Funeral Home, Alamogordo, N.M.

74. Mounted Police Oath of Office, NMMP/NMSRCA.; Twelfth U.S. Census, Lincoln County, New Mexico Territory, NA.; *The* (Socorro) *Chieftain*, 04 September 1896.

75. Santa Fe *New Mexican*, 01 March 1905.

76. The Socorro *Chieftain*, 04 September 1896.

77. The Capitan *Progress*, 28 March 1902.

78. In 1896, Demetrio Perea, Octaviano's father, was captain of the Territorial Militia Company in Lincoln County and county clerk. He was Lincoln County sheriff for 1899 and 1900. Following his law enforcement job, Demetrio was postmaster at Lincoln. In November 1901, he embezzled $2,000 and fled to Mexico. Postal Inspector C.L. Doran captured Perea in February 1902 at Santa Eulatia, Chihuahua. Perea pleaded guilty to embezzlement and received a two year and two day penitentiary sentence plus a fine. This crime ended Octaviano's hope of ever being elected Lincoln County sheriff himself. The son may have felt that citizens were punishing him for his father's misdeeds. The Capitan *Progress*, 15 August 1902.

79. The Capitan *Progress*, 11 January 1901.

80. Socorro *Chieftain*, 17 June 1905.

81. Santa Fe *New Mexican*, 30 October 1911; *The Outlook* (Carrizozo), 20 November 1908.

82. *Western Liberal* (Lordsburg), 22 February 1901. McGrath had also worked with his father and brother in a mercantile and hotel business at Lordsburg.

83. "Two Robbers Killed," *Western Liberal* (Lordsburg), 24 March 1905; "Sheriff Kills Man," Carrizozo *Outlook*, 24 February 1911.

84. McGrath, a Democrat, was appointed by the Republican governor as a show of bi-partisan support for the new ranger corps. Herb took his oath of office on 16 April 1918, NMMP/War Time/ NMSRCA. McGrath had his headquarters at Silver City. His secretary was Miss Grace Ilgner. She and Herb married in 1923. They had no children. McGrath and his first wife, Nancy Baird, who died in 1911, raised a daughter, who died when she was eleven, a son and Herb's two orphaned nieces. Letter and Family Data: Tom McGrath to author, 09 June 1971, NMMP/AC.

85. "Herbert J. McGrath, Stockman, Famous Former Sheriff, Grant County, Died Here Wednesday," Silver City *Enterprise*, 06 October 1933.

86. Markers, McGrath-Baird family plot, Concordia Cemetery, El Paso, Texas. The cemetery is also the final resting place for the gunman John Wesley Hardin and his killer, John Selman.

87. Huber's Mounted Police Oath of Office listed his birthplace as St. Paul, Minnesota. The 1900 census for Santa Fe, N.M. and Huber's death certificate list his state of birth as Minnesota, however his obituary in the Santa Fe *New Mexican* (30 March 1929) said he was a "native of Quincy, Illinois."

88. "Dick Huber, Veteran Stage Driver, Law Officer, Crosses the Divide," Santa Fe *New Mexican*, 30 March 1929. In 1890, a C.R. Huber was referred to as "Windy Dick" and was held to be "a notorious character of very unenviable reputation" by the Silver City *Enterprise* (18 April 1890).

89. In 1882, a C.R. Huber had come to New Mexico to work for Lew Fifer at Hanover Gulch. Two years later he was in Pinos Altos, then the Mangas and finally back to Pinos Altos as a store clerk. Silver City *Enterprise*, 23 May 1890.

In 1888, a C.R. Huber was the constable at Pinos Altos in Grant County. He wounded one Mexican and killed another while making an arrest. The local paper said, "The general opinion is that the officer was too anxious to kill some one and make a reputation." (Silver City *Enterprise*, 08 June 1888). Huber was found not guilty of murder, but was convicted of assault with intent to kill.

In the spring of 1890, a C.R. Huber was called "the terror of The Mangas" by the *Enterprise* (18 April 1890). He and two other men were caught robbing the mine payroll at Pinos Altos; Huber was wounded in the attempt. At his trial Huber, pleaded guilty and was sentenced to the territorial penitentiary. In August 1891, Huber escaped. Silver City *Enterprise*, 29 August 1890 and 21 August 1891.

In 1899, Dick Huber was a deputy sheriff in Santa Fe County. He held this position when he was appointed to Fullerton's Rangers. Santa Fe *New Mexican*, 27 May 1905.

90. Huber's obituary in the Santa Fe *New Mexican* (30 March 1929) said, "Mr. Huber leaves a widow and an adopted daughter." Dick's death certificate listed him as being divorced. The *New Mexican* (01 April 1929) and his death certificate say that Huber was buried in the Rosario Catholic Cemetery in Santa Fe. The cemetery has no record of his burial.

91. Letters: Jettie Avant Sullenger, Fate's granddaughter, to author, 1981–1984, NMMP/AC.; The Capitan *Progress*, 06 February 1903.

92. In the fall of 1909, the Avant family was hard hit by four cases of typhoid fever. Fate's youngest son, three year old Fred, named in honor of Fred Fornoff,

was among the ill. All four survived, but Avant was now determined to spend more time near his family. *Southwestern Outlook* (Carrizozo), 29 October 1909.

93. Letter: Jettie Sullenger to author, 27 August 1984, NMMP/AC.

94. Mounted police appointment notices and oaths of office, NMMP/NMSRCA.

95. Letter: Jettie Sullenger to author, 20 February 1983, NMMP/AC; "Funeral Rites Set For Jess. L. Avant," El Paso *Times*, 15 July 1940.

96. Cemetery Records, City Clerk's Office, Deming, N.M.; Thirteenth United States Census (1910), Microfilm Roll 915, Silver City, Grant County, New Mexico Territory, NA.

97. Putman was told he would accompany Sergeant Lewis for "some *very important* work." Letter: Capt. Fullerton to Putman, 02 July 1905, Letters Sent, NMMP/NMSRCA.

98. The Socorro *Chieftain*, 12 August 1905.

99. Bob Putman was in charge of the investigation team that Dick Huber deserted, thus ending his service with Fullerton's Rangers. At the turn of the century, Socorro was a very segregated community. The Anglo and Hispanic children might play together, but the adults kept their social and business dealings separated. Cipriana Baca Randolph told the author that the Lewis and Baca children did, however, often play together. She didn't remember Fullerton's son as a child or even recall Putman or his family.

100. *New Mexico Mounted Police Arrest Book 1906–1912*, NMMP/NMSRCA.

101. Misc. Data, Bob Putman File, NMMP/AC.

102. Much valuable information concerning the Mogollon shootout is contained in the Collier Report and the records of the Beal-Putman murder trial. Report: Sgt. John Collier to Capt. Fornoff, 23 September 1910, Letters Received, NMMP/NMSRCA; Cases #3467, #3468 and #3469, *Criminal Docket Book C*, District Court Clerk's Office, Socorro County Courthouse, Socorro, N.M.

103. Howard Bryan, "Off the Beaten Path," Albuquerque *Tribune*, 12 April 1954.

104. Enlistment Records, NMMP/War Time/NMSRCA; Fourteenth United States Census (1920), Microfilm Roll 1076, Hachita, Luna County, New Mexico, NA; "Obituaries," Deming *Graphic*, 09 October 1947.

105. Mounted police oath of office form, NMMP/NMSRCA.

106. "Mounted Police," The Estancia *News*, 01 September 1905.

107. Farmington *Enterprise*, 01 June 1906, El Paso *Times*, 25 May 1906; Mounted Police arrest records, NMMP/NMSRCA.

108. Twelfth United States Census (1900), Microfilm Roll 1002, Precinct 4, Santa Fe County, New Mexico Territory, NA.; 1905 Mounted Police Oath of Office, NMMP/NMSRCA.

109. Mounted police appointment notices and oath of office forms, NMMP/NMSRCA. Holm Bursum had recommended Gomez to Capt. Fullerton.

110. 1918 Mounted Police Arrest Records, NMMP/War Time/NMSRCA.

111. Twelfth United States Census (1900), Microfilm Roll 1002, Precinct 5, Sierra County, New Mexico Territory, NA.; "Mounted Police Force," *The Socorro Chieftain*, 25 March 1905.

112. "Two horses and two mules were stolen from W.M. Taylor on the Mimbres a few days since." The Silver City *Enterprise*, 20 April 1888. This incident may have been a reason why Bill Taylor considered becoming a New Mexico Mounted Police.

113. 1901 Luna County Appointments, Gov. M.A. Otero Papers, NMSRCA; Deming *Graphic*, 24 March 1905.

114. Letters: Taylor to Gov. Otero, 16 May 1905; Miss. C.H. Olson to Taylor, 19 May 1905, Letters Received/ Letters Sent, Gov. M.A. Otero Papers, NMSRCA.

115. Deming *Graphic*, 19 May 1905 and 21 March 1906.

Chapter 7

1. Letter: H.A. Jastro to Gov. Otero, 17 February 1905, Letters Received, Gov. M.A. Otero Papers, NMSRCA.

2. Contemporary newspaper stories provided the background data on Bursum and Luna.

3. Only a few memos and letters remain to attest to the function of the Bursum-Luna Selection Committee. A partial list of Mounted Police candidates can be compiled from newspapers and scattered references in Governor Otero's correspondence. Most of the candidates were from the Sunshine Territory, but there were office seekers from neighboring Colorado and Oklahoma. Even, T.H. Tucker, the Socorro gunman who had led the notorious and ill-fated cattlemen's protection group called the New Mexico Rangers, wanted to serve with the new territorial police. In a letter to a candidate from Tularosa the governor explained the function of the search committee and mentioned the number of applicants. Letter: Gov. Otero to A.B. Homan, 04 March 1905, Gov. M.A. Otero Papers, NMSRCA.

4. Santa Fe *New Mexican*, 27 February 1905.

5. Santa Fe *New Mexican*, 01 March 1905.

6. This visit was listed as "Mr. Perea from Otero County" while a subsequent visit was listed as "Mounted Police Perea." *Executive Ticker, Territory of New Mexico 1903–1905*, 13 February 1905, 18 November 1905, O-S/CSR/UNM.

7. "O. Perea Accepts," The Alamogordo *News*, 25 March 1905.

8. *New Mexico Mounted Police Regulations* (1918), NMMP/AC. This small booklet contains the operational guidelines for the reorganized Mounted Police under Capt. Herb McGrath.

9. Santa Fe *New Mexican,* 01 March 1905.

10. *Executive Ticker,* 01 March 1905, O-S/CSR/UNM.

11. Letters: Baca to Foraker, 14 March and 22 March 1905, Letters Received, United States Marshal's Office Papers (USMP), CSR/UNM.

12. *Executive Ticker,* 07 March 1905, O-S/CSR/UNM.

13. Dudley and his wife were both excellent schoolteachers and administrators. In the last half of the 1900s an elementary school in Alamogordo honored the Dudley name.

14. Will Dudley had an 11:30 a.m. "personal-social" visit with Governor Otero on Saturday, 25 February 1905. *Executive Ticker,* S-O/SRC/UNM; Appointment Letters, NMMP/NMSRCA.
15. In 1910, Dudley was appointed the rangers' second-in-command by Gov. William J. Mills.
16. "Dudley Praises Native Children," Santa Fe *New Mexican,* 24 February 1905; "Prof. Dudley Visits Santa Fe," The Alamogordo *News,* 04 March 1905.
17. John Brophy may not have known Gov. Otero personally because his name was misspelled as "Prophy" in the appointment logbook. *Executive Ticker,* 18 March 1905, O-S/CSR/ UNM. A "J.J. Brophy, Clayton" was listed as a guest at the Palace Hotel on 18 March 1905, Santa Fe *New Mexican,* 18 March 1905; Appointment Requests, NMMP/NMSRCA; Miscellaneous Notes, John J. Brophy File, NMMP/AC.
18. Miscellaneous Notes, Herbert J. McGrath File, NMMP/AC.
19. *Executive Ticker,* 17 March 1905, O-S/CSR/ UNM.
20. Letter: Bursum and Luna to Gov. Otero, 17 March 1905, NMMP/NMSRCA.
21. "The Governor this day accepted the resignation of John F. Fullerton as Assessor of Socorro County." *Executive Record Book* #6, 17 March 1905, Secretary of the Territory Records, NMSRCA. This notation would seem to be misdated because Otero and Fullerton didn't have their first face-to-face meeting until 18 March 1905.
22. Letters: John Fullerton to Gov. Otero, 17 March 1905; Holm Bursum to Gov. Otero, 17 March 1905, Letters Received, Gov. M.A. Otero Papers, NMSRCA; *Executive Record Book* #6, 18 March 1905, Secretary of the Territory Records, NMSRCA.

Fullerton's and Bursum's letters were both typed on stationary of the Republican Central Committee of New Mexico and both letters were misdated. Even Governor Otero's handwritten acceptance of John Fullerton's resignation was misdated.

Abednago B. Baca was a deputy sheriff at San Marcial. The *New Mexican* reported that Baca was in the capital "on business" during these days in mid–March 1905. Baca had served as marshal at Socorro, 1893–1895, and had been county jailor under Sheriff Holm Bursum. Baca was the eldest brother of Elfego Baca, but was not related in any way to Cipriano Baca. The Socorro Chamber of Commence publishes a *Socorro County Guidebook* to help visitors appreciate the area's history. The booklet lists the A.B. Baca house as a fine example of the Emborregado style of exterior plastering that makes the plaster have a wood grain effect. The rectangular structure, built in 1910, has a metal roof and four gables.

23. Otero devoted a full chapter, "New Mexico Proves Her Loyalty," to the Spanish-American War effort in his book about his nine years as New Mexico governor.
24. *Executive Ticker,* 20, 21, 22 March 1905, O-S/CSR/UNM. Otero left for his vacation on 28 March 1905 and did not return to his office until 19 April 1905. He left the territory again on 22 September 1905 and returned on 23 October 1905. Gov. Otero and Capt. Fullerton met again in May (13) for one visit. They later conferred three times in July (18, 28, 29), four times in August (08, 09, 12, 16), once in September (02) and twice in December (06, 14). The governor and his territorial police chief held 15 face-to-face meetings over a ten month period.
25. John F. Fullerton's Mounted Police Commission, Fullerton Family, Copy in NMMP/AC.
26. Fullerton's certified, typed copy of the Mounted Police Act is dated 18 March 1905, signed by J.W. Raynolds and embossed with the territorial seal. This document is five legal size pages, including the cover sheet that depicts the territorial capitol building, bound to a heavy sheet of black paper. The mounted police law was so new that there were no printed copies generally available. A copy of Fullerton's document is in NMMP/AC.
27. *New Mexico Coded Law 1905*, Chapter 9 Mounted Police.
28. Elkins lived in the far southwestern "boot-heel" section of the territory, Brophy lived up in the far northeastern corner, Meyer was stationed in the remote north central area, while Dudley lived on the edge of the White Sands and eastern mountains. Baca's new home was at Socorro on the Rio Grande.
29. Bob Lewis was settled in Socorro. His patrol unit was a little more concentrated than that led by Cipriano Baca. Taylor and McGrath lived along the Mexico border, Apodaca was stationed along the western edge of the eastern mountains, while Perea lived along the east side of the eastern mountains. Taylor and Apodaca never served with the rangers. Their replacements lived along the east side of the eastern mountains and in Santa Fe.
30. "Personals," Las Vegas *Daily Optic,* 27 March 1905.
31. Conversation Notes: Cipriana Randolph and author, via telephone, 21 June 1984, NMMP/AC.
32. Copies of the 1905 Mounted Police Oath of Office forms and the Fullerton's Rangers' Muster Roll, NMMP/NMSRCA.
33. This was the only time Captain Fornoff held a gathering of his police. He did, however, have a large number of them at the territorial fair in 1908. They made camp at the home of U.S. Marshal Creighton Foraker. Albuquerque *Morning Journal,* 30 September 1908.
34. "Are Sworn into Office," Santa Fe *New Mexican,* 01 April 1905.
35. Socorro boosted a population of about 1,500 persons, while Deming had 2,500 and Alamogordo had nearly 4,000 people. Fairview and Estancia contained about 100 inhabitants each. These are a few of the community areas where Fullerton's Rangers lived.
36. The Mounted Police received the set of brand books from the Cattle Sanitary Board. Letter: Capt. Fullerton to W.O. Barnes, secretary of the board, 24 June 1905, NMMP/NMSRCA. The three brass cuspidors were purchased from the Whitney Company of Albuquerque. Fullerton paid $7.20 for the spittoons on 09 October 1905 with check #62. John Fullerton Papers, NMMP/NMSRCA.
37. "Headquarters at Socorro," Socorro *Chieftain,* 25 March 1905. *The New Mexico Business Directory 1905–06* (Denver: Gazetteer Publishing Co., 1905) listed the mounted police office at Socorro. Elfego Baca was appointed district attorney for Socorro and Sierra counties on 16 March 1905. Appointment

Notice, Gov. M.A. Otero Papers, NMSRCA. Baca and his son also ran a barber shop in Socorro.

38. Fullerton's vouchers and inventory records, NMMP/NMSRCA.

39. Office inventory and Fullerton's purchase offer, NMMP/NMSRCA. Baca made the observation, "Mr. Fullerton [is] very pleasant." The record book was ordered from the territory's public printer on 01 May 1905 and was delivered to the mounted police on 06 June 1905. The cost was $17.50. This ledger is not among the mounted police records in the state archives.
The Public Printing Office report contained numerous sections. The first part was a monthly breakdown of all the print job orders and their charges per month. Another section contained a total recap, by department, of all orders and their costs. The Public Printing Office claimed they did $30 worth of printing work for the mounted police during the period of 01 March 1905 to 01 December 1906. However, when you add Fullerton's $17.50 charge with the $7 charge made by Captain Fornoff, that still leaves an unaccounted for charge of $5.50. What service was provided for this fee? Could it have been the charge for printing Fullerton's Weekly Report forms? Report of Public Printer, 01 March 1905 to 01 December 1906, Gov. H.J. Hagerman Papers, NMSRCA.
Fullerton paid $105.00 to George S. Ramsey, of Albuquerque, "for the machine." The make and model are unknown. Letter: Capt. Fullerton to Ramsey, 12 September 1905, NMMP/NMSRCA.

40. Mounted Police Voucher, 03 June 1905, NMMP/NMSRCA.

41. One of these postal maps is in NMMP/AC.

42. J.W. Raynolds (compiler), *Acts of the Legislative Assembly of the Territory of New Mexico, Thirty-Sixth Session, 1905* (Santa Fe: Government Printer, 1905).

43. "Are Sworn Into Office," Santa Fe *New Mexican*, 01 April 1905; "Headquarters at Socorro," Las Cruces *Citizen*, 01 April 1905.

44. This may have been James Williamson's 1896 war remembrances called *Mosby's Rangers*. The present location of the Fullerton/Baca book is unknown.

45. Sam Moore, *Through The Shadow: A Boy's Memories* (Clark County Historical Association Museum, ND), p. 114

46. "Uniformed The Boys," Las Vegas *Daily Optic*, 17 April 1905, p. 6; Nathan Salomon Letterhead, NMMP/AC

47. Letter: Capt. Fullerton to his rangers, 24 April 1905, NMMP/NMSRCA.

48. Letter: Capt. Fullerton to Will Dudley, 24 April 1905, NMMP/NMSRCA.

49. Mounted Police Voucher #22, 01 May 1905, Fullerton's Voucher Report, NMMP/NMSRCA.

50. Mounted Police Voucher #37, 00 June 1905, Fullerton's Voucher Report, NMMP/NMSRCA.

51. Letter: Capt. Fullerton to Elkins, 11 July 1905, NMMP/NMSRCA.

52. Mounted Police Department Report, August 1905, Gov. M.A. Otero Papers, NMMP/NMSRCA; "First Report of Mounted Police," Santa Fe *New Mexican*, 18 December 1905.

53. *Sears, Roebuck & Co. Catalogue #104* (1897), *Catalogue #111* (1902) and *Catalogue #117* (1908), Copies in NMMP/AC.

54. Monty McCord, *Law Enforcement Memorabilia* (Iola, Wis.: Krause Publications, 1999), "Basic Body Types and Styles" pp. 19–28, "Hallmarks," pp. 29–56.

55. "Mounted Police Begin Their Work," Albuquerque *Morning Journal*, 02 April 1905. Mounted Police Voucher #4 was written for $23. This was $22 for the badges and one dollar for the shipping. Fullerton's Voucher Report, 01 August 1905, NMMP/NMSRCA.

56. The only known authentic Fornoff era mounted police star is in the author's collection. A few documented "special ranger" shields are known to be in private badge collections.

57. *Western Liberal* (Lordsburg), 12 May 1905; *Otero County Advertiser* (Alamogordo), 20 May 1905; Letter: Elkins Report, 07 May 1905, Letters Received, NMMP/NMSRCA.

58. Attorney General Opinion #252, 19 May 1905, Attorney General Records, NMSRCA.

59. *New Mexico Coded Law 1905*, Chapter 9 Mounted Police.

60. Letter: Capt. Fullerton to Whitney Co., 10 July 1905, NMMP/NMSRCA.

61. Letter: Capt. Fullerton to his rangers, 17 April 1905, NMMP/NMSRCA.

62. The author's mounted police hardware collection contains many of these weapons, plus handcuffs, ranger trail gear and badges.

63. *Sears, Roebuck & Co. Catalogues*, 1897, 1900, 1902, 1908.

64. Dudley Report, 07 May 1905, Letters Received, NMMP/NMSRCA.

65. Letters Sent; the April 1906 inventory of the mounted police office, NMMP/NMSRCA. Mounted Police Voucher #40 was issued to R.C. Garret, assistant superintendent of the territorial penitentiary. The $78.00 authorization was payment for extra sets of handcuffs. Letter: Capt. Fullerton to Garret, 24 July 1905, Letters Sent, NMMP/NMSRCA.

66. *New Mexico Coded Laws 1905*, Chapter 9 Mounted Police. A special ranger's horse was killed in 1917, but the lawman was not compensated for the animal. "Ranger's Horse Shot Through The Nose," Albuquerque *Herald*, 04 April 1917.

67. Letters: Capt. Fullerton to W.E. Dudley, 11 June 1905, and Capt. Fullerton to Charles Closson, 29 April 1905, Letters Sent, NMMP/NMSRCA.

68. Council Bill #26 "An Act to Organize and Equip a Company of Mounted Police for the Territory of New Mexico," Miscellaneous File, NMMP/NMSRCA.

69. *Western Liberal* (Lordsburg), 14 April 1905.

70. *Western Liberal* (Lordsburg), 14 April 1905.

71. Letter: Capt. Fullerton to W.M. Borrowdale, 09 November 1905, Letters Sent, NMMP/NMSRCA.

72. Clayton *Enterprise*, 27 April 1906.

73. *New Mexico Coded Laws 1907*, Appropriation Act, Section 20 — Mounted Police; *New Mexico Coded Laws 1909*, Chapter 27 — Appropriations, Section A — Mounted Police; *Laws of New Mexico 1912*, Chapter 83 — Appropriations, Section 13 — Mounted Police.

74. Chuck Hornung, "The Motor Pony," *The West*, August 1970, pp. 28–29, 61–62; Letters: J.C. Allen Co. to Charles Springer, chairman of the State Council of Defense, 28 April 1919; Herbert J. McGrath to W.M. Danberg, secretary of the State Council of Defense,

17 April 1919, Records of the Council of Defense, 1917–1919, NMSRCA.

75. In 1903, the safety razor company sold only 51 of their new razor kits at $5 each. Within three years, they sold over 300,000 razor kits and 500,000 replacement blades. Much of Fred Lambert's camp gear is part of the author's New Mexico Mounted Police collection.

76. Conversation Notes: Fred Lambert and the author, 18 June 1967, Cimarron, N.M., NMMP/AC.

77. Pine tar soap is still formulated and marketed by Grandpa's Soap Company of Erlanger, Ky. They have produced this specialty type of soap since 1878.

78. Comparison cost data from the Department of Commerce, Bureau of the Census Data Sheet for the year 2000, NA.

79. The weather records kept by the New Mexico School of Mines at Socorro show that from 01 August 1904 to 01 May 1905, sixteen inches of rain fell in the area. This moisture record didn't include the massive amount of snow that also fell in the area. During these months the average temperature was four degrees below normal. In the territory's southern mountain area 18 April 1905 marked the 46th straight day of rain. The Rio Grande was near flood level from El Paso north to Las Cruces.

80. Letter: Capt. Fullerton to Gov. Otero, 03 May 1905, Letters Sent, NMMP/NMSRCA.

81. Letter: Capt. Fullerton to Gov. Otero, 03 May 1905, Letters Sent, NMMP/NMSRCA.

82. Harold J. Weiss, Jr. "Organized Constabularies: The Texas Rangers and the Early State Police Movement in the American Southwest," *Journal of the West*, V 24 #1, January 1995, pp. 27–33.

83. The history of the Hawkins Act is contained in the journals of the 35th, 36th, 37th and 38th Territorial Legislative Assembly for the House and the Council, Records of the Secretary of the Territory, NMSRCA.

84. Otero, *My Nine Years As Governor*, p. 72.

85. Telegrams: Gov. Otero to Capt. Fullerton, 10 July 1905; Capt. Fullerton to Gov. Otero, 10 July 1905; Letter: Gov. Otero to Capt. Fullerton, 11 July 1905, Gov. M.A. Otero Papers, Letters Sent/Letters Received, NMSRCA.

86. Telegrams: Gov. Otero to Capt. Fullerton, 10 July 1905; Fullerton to Otero, 11 July 1905. Letters: Otero to Fullerton, 11 July 1905; J.E. Hurley, GM/ATSF-RR, to Otero, 02 October 1905; Otero to Fullerton, 10 November 1905 and Fullerton to Otero, 16 November 1905, NMMP/NMSRCA.

87. Letter: J.B. Grimshaw to Capt. Fullerton, 14 April 1905, NMMP/NMSRCA.

88. White Oaks *Outlook*, reprinted in the Tucumcari *News*, 14 April 1906.

89. Bruce Ashcroft, *The Territorial History of Socorro, New Mexico* (El Paso: Texas Western Press, 1988) p. 47; "Telephone Line for New Mexico," *The Outlook* (White Oaks), 23 March 1905.

90. Mounted police stationery samples, NMMP/AC.

91. Report of Public Printer, 01 March 1905 to 01 December 1906, Gov. Hagerman Papers, NMSRCA.

92. Lt. Baca's Field Report, 08 July 1905, Letters Received, NMMP/NMSRCA.

93. Letter: Meyer to Fred Fornoff, 31 March 1906, Letters Received, NMMP/NMSRCA.

94. "Looking For His Wife," *The Weekly Optic & Stock Grower* (Las Vegas), 28 October 1905, reprinted from the Estancia *News*.

95. Letters: Capt. Fullerton to Capt. Rynning, 21April 1905; Capt. Fullerton to Capt. McDonald, 01 June 1905, Letters Sent, NMMP/NMSRCA.

96. A copy of the 1905–06 Report Form is in NMMP/AC.

97. Elkins Report, 03 June 1905, Letters Received, NMMP/NMSRCA.

98. Mounted Police General Order #3, 01 June 1905; Letter: Capt. Fullerton to Meyer, 01 June 1905, Letters Sent, NMMP/NMSRCA.

99. Jill Lawless, "After 100 Years, Fingerprints Still Vital Tool for Scotland Yard," Midland (Texas) *Reporter Telegram*, 28 June 2001.

100. *Executive Ticker*, O-S/CSR/UNM.

101. Mounted Police Voucher and Check Files, NMMP/NMSRCA.

102. Conversation Notes: Irene Fullerton and author, Albuquerque, N.M., 28 July 1984, NMMP/AC.

103. Letter: Capt. Fullerton to M.C. O'Donnel, 03 November 1905, Letters Sent, NMMP/NMSRCA.

104. "Indians Troublesome," Santa Fe *New Mexican*, 16 December 1905.

105. Albuquerque *Morning Journal*, 26 April 1905.

106. Albuquerque *Morning Journal*, 22 April 1905.

107. *Western Liberal* (Lordsburg), 14 April 1905.

108. Dudley Report, 23 July 1905, Letters Received, NMMP/NMSRCA.

109. A couple of weeks before his appointment to the mounted police, Deputy Game Warden Dick Huber had arrested a man in Torrance County for selling illegal venison. The justice who heard the case dismissed the charge because Huber lived in Santa Fe County and could not legally make a game law arrest out of his home county. Santa Fe *New Mexican*, 27 February 1905.

In May 1905, Territorial Game Warden Page Otero appointed each of the mounted police as a deputy game warden. The legality of these appointments was later upheld in an opinion issued by the territorial attorney general. *Otero County Advertiser*, 20 May 1905; Attorney General Opinion 252, 19 May 1905, Attorney General Records 1905, NMSRCA.

110. Clayton *Enterprise*, 23 February 1906.

Chapter 8

1. The El Paso *Times*, 17 April 1905.
2. The Las Cruces *Citizen*, 01 April 1905; the El Paso *Evening News*, 04 April 1905.
3. Albuquerque *Evening Citizen*, 06 April 1905.
4. The Socorro *Chieftain*, 08 April 1905.
5. El Paso *Times*, 31 March 1905.
6. Albuquerque *Morning Journal*, 02 April 1905.
7. *Pocket Map and Shippers' Guide of New Mexico* (Chicago: Rand McNally & Co., 1905). This pocket book was the standard reference used by Globe Express, United States Express and Wells, Fargo Express companies during the era of Fullerton's Rangers. See also the daily train schedule in and out of El Paso published in the El Paso *Evening News*; "News from Alamogordo," The El Paso *Evening News*, 03 April 1905.

8. It should be remembered that both John Brophy and Julius Meyer were assigned to the patrol squad commanded by Lt. Cipriano Baca.
9. Silver City *Independent*, 04 April 1905.
10. Silver City *Independent*, 04 April 1905.
11. The Socorro *Chieftain*, 08 April 1905.
12. "The 'Bad Men' Will Be Forced To Vacate," Santa Fe *New Mexican*, 18 April 1905.
13. *The Outlook* (White Oaks), 13 April and 06 April 1905.
14. Letter: Capt. Fullerton to Will Dudley, May 1905, Letters Sent, NMMP/NMSRCA.
15. Bundy Avant as told to Arthur Clements, "The Bundy Avant Story, Part 1," *True West* (May–June 1978), p. 12.
16. Letter: Avant Report, 10 May 1905, Letters Received, NMMP/NMSRCA.
17. Letter: Capt. Fullerton to B.F. Knight of Ancho, N.M., 05 May 1905, Letters Sent, NMMP/ NMSRCA.
18. Albert J. Fountain Murder Case File, Roll 93, Frames 126–160, NMMP/NMSRCA.
19. Howard Bryan, "Fountains Slain By Ketchum, Pioneer NM Officer Asserts," *Albuquerque Tribune*, 24 May 1949.
20. Chuck Hornung, "Surprising New Information on Pat Garrett's Death: Details From The Fornoff Report," *The Journal, Western Outlaw-Lawmen History Association,* Spring/Summer 1997, pp. 20–24 and 40–43.
21. Col. J. Francisco Chaves Murder Case File, Roll 93, Frames 161–240, NMMP/NMSRCA.
22. Chaves Investigation File, Roll 162, Frames 1182–1227, Gov H.J. Hagerman Papers, NMSRCA.
23. Letter: Cipriano Baca to Gov. Hagerman, 12 January 1907, Letters Received, Gov. H.J. Hagerman Papers, NMSRCA.
24. *Acts of the Legislative Assembly of the Territory of New Mexico, Thirty-Sixth Session 1905* (Santa Fe: New Mexican Printing Co., 1905) Chapter 9 Mounted Police, pp 31–34.
25. Albuquerque *Morning Journal*, 02 April 1905.
26. Silver City *Independent*, 11 April 1905; Elkins Report, 13 April 1905, Letters Received, NMMP/NMSRCA.
27. Letter: Capt. Fullerton to Elkins, 17 April 1905, Letters Sent, NMMP/NMSRCA.
28. Silver City *Independent*, 25 April 1905.
29. *Otero County Advertiser* (Alamogordo), 22 April 1905.
30. "Wants New Mexico Rangers," The Alamogordo *News*, 04 February 1905.
31. Silver City *Independent*, 25 April 1905.
32. Albuquerque *Morning Journal*, 02 April 1905.
33. Letter: Elkins Report, 07 May 1905, Letters Received, NMMP/NMSRCA.
34. Letter: Annual Report of the Cattle Sanitary Board to the Governor, Boards and Commission Reports 1906, Gov. H.J. Hagerman Papers, NMSRCA; El Paso *Times*, 11, 17, 25 and 26 May 1905.
35. Letter: Elkins Report, 14 May 1905, Letters Received, NMMP/NMSRCA.
36. Letter: Elkins Report, 22 May 1905, Letters Received, NMMP/NMSRCA.
37. Susan Montoya Bryan, "High Hope for Bighorn Sheep," Dallas (Texas) *Morning News*, 20 April 2003.
38. "Wants New Mexico Rangers," The Alamogordo *News*, 04 February 1905.
39. Letter: Capt. Fullerton to Elkins, 22 May 1905, Letters Sent, NMMP/NMSRCA.
40. Letters: Elkins Report, 23 May 1905, Letters Received; Capt. Fullerton to Elkins, 26 May 1905, Letters Sent, NMMP/NMSRCA.
41. Letter: Capt. Fullerton to Elkins, 02 June 1905, Letters Sent, NMMP/NMSRCA.
42. Letter: Capt. Fullerton to Elkins, 02 June 1905, Letters Sent, NMMP/NMSRCA.
43. Randall Hackley (AP), "Mexican Bandits Spark Threat Of Range War," Lubbock (Texas) *Avalanche-Journal*, 30 January 1983. Two border ranchers were killed in 1980 by drug smugglers. Other Mexicans cut fences and steal cattle and equipment because of lax border law enforcement. Ranchers go armed and one said, "This is the wild, wooly West. Anything can happen."; "Smaller Towns Deal With Gangs," Lubbock (Texas) *Avalanche-Journal*, 18 December 1995. Youth gang violence is spreading into rural remote southwestern New Mexico.
44. Letters: Elkins Reports, 02 June and 10 June 1905, Letters Received, NMMP/NMSRCA.
45. Letter: Elkins Report, 17 June 1905, Letters Received, NMMP/NMSRCA.
46. Letter: Capt. Fullerton to Putman, 02 July 1905, Letters Sent, NMMP/NMSRCA.
47. Letter: McGrath Report, 21 July 1905, Letters Received, NMMP/NMSRCA.
48. Records of Prisoner 1926, *Book of Convicts 05 April 1905–13 February 1915*, Territorial Prison Records, NMSRCA. Littleton had a "knife wound in palm of both hands" which he most likely had received while doing fence work or cow castrations.
49. Silver City *Independent*, 25 April 1905.
50. Socorro *Chieftain*, 30 April 1905; Santa Fe *New Mexican*, 27 April 1905.
51. Letter: Capt. Fullerton to Meyer, 07 June 1905, Letters Sent, NMMP/NMSRCA.
52. Letter: Capt. Fullerton to Perea, 24 April 1905, Letters Sent, NMMP/NMSRCA.
53. Letter: Capt. Fullerton to Dudley, 28 April 1905, Letters Sent, NMMP/NMSRCA.
54. Letter: Dudley Report, 01 May 1905, Letters Received, NMMP/NMSRCA.
55. Letter: Huber-Meyer Joint Report, 03 May 1905, Letters Received, NMMP/NMSRCA.
56. Letter: Capt. Fullerton to H.A. Scott, 05 May 1905, Letters Sent, NMMP/NMSRCA.
57. Letter: Lewis Report, 07 May 1905; McGrath Report, 07 May 1905, Letters Received, NMMP/NMSRCA.
58. Letter: McGrath Report, 14 May 1905, Letters Received, NMMP/NMSRCA.
59. Letter: McGrath Report, 21 May 1905, NMMP/NMSRCA.
60. Santa Fe *New Mexican*, 06 June 1905.
61. Tombstone (Arizona) *Prospector*, 22 June 1905.
62. El Paso *Times*, 30 June 1905; "Train Delays," Las Vegas *Daily Optic*, 14 June 1905.
63. Letter: McGrath to Capt. Fullerton, 18 June 1905, Letters Received, NMMP/NMSRCA.
64. *Western Liberal* (Lordsburg), 30 June, 21 July and 28 July 1905.
65. Letter: Capt. Fullerton to Putman, 02 July 1905, Letters Sent, NMMP/NMSRCA.
66. Alamogordo *News*, 13 May 1905.

67. Letter: Capt. Fullerton to Elkins, 24 May 1905, Letters Received, NMMP/NMSRCA.
68. Letter: Capt. Fullerton to Avant, 03 August 1905, Letters Sent, NMMP/NMSRCA.
69. *Daily Journal*, Welch and Titsworth Store, Capitan, Lincoln County Records AC 134, Box 9, File 2, Fray Angelico Chavez Library, Museum of New Mexico; Alamogordo *News*, 20 May 1905.
70. *Otero County Advertiser* (Alamogordo), 20 May 1905.
71. Capitan *News*, 12 May, 19 May and 28 July 1905.
72. Letter: Dudley Report, 05 August 1905, NMMP/NMSRCA.
73. Letter: Perea Report, 20 May 1905, Letters Received, NMMP/NMSRCA.
74. Letters: Capt. Fullerton to L.F. Avant, 24 June 1905; Capt. Fullerton to W.H. Greer, 23 October 1905, Letters Sent, NMMP/NMSRCA.
75. Letter: Capt. Fullerton to Baca, 14 July 1905, Letters Sent, NMMP/NMSRCA.
76. Nogal *Republican*, 26 June 1902.
77. Santa Fe *New Mexican*, 16 January 1900.
78. Letter: Dudley Report, 24 May 1905, Letters Received, NMMP/NMSRCA.
79. Alamogordo *News*, 13 May 1905; *Otero County Advertiser* (Alamogordo), 20 May 1905.
80. Alamogordo *News*, 13 May 1905.
81. Letters: Perea Report, 01 June 1905; Avant Report, 28 May 1905, Letters Received, NMMP/NMSRCA.
82. Conversation Notes: Jettie Avant Sullenger and the author, 09 June 1984, Mountainair, N.M., NMMP/AC.
83. The Socorro *Chieftain*, 17 June 1905.
84. The Capitan *Progress*, 28 March 1902.
85. Letter: C.E. MacConnell to the author, 01 September 1972, NMMP/AC.
86. Santa Fe *New Mexican*, 27 May 1905; Letter: Meyer-Huber Joint Report, 03 May 1905, Letters Received, NMMP/NMSRCA.
87. Santa Fe *New Mexican*, 27 May 1905; Escaped prisoner notice, NMMP/NMSRCA.
88. Letter: Capt. Fullerton to Page B. Otero, 03 June 1905, Letters Sent, NMMP/NMSRCA.
89. Letter: Meyer-Huber Joint Report, 28 May 1905, Letters Received, NMMP/NMSRCA.
90. Letter: Capt. Fullerton to Meyer, 01 June 1905, Letters Sent, NMMP/NMSRCA.
91. Letter: Meyer-Huber Joint Report, 03 May 1905, Letters Received, NMMP/NMSRCA.
92. Letter: Huber Report, 10 June 1905, Letters Received, NMMP/NMSRCA.
93. Letter: Meyer Report, 11 June 1905, Letters Received, NMMP/NMSRCA.
94. Letter: Meyer Report, 18 June 1905, Letters Received, NMMP/NMSRCA; *Santa Fe New Mexican*, 16 June 1905. The 'smoker' invitations were printed on high quality card stock and carried a fancy engraved formal request to attend the soiree. One of these cards is among Otero's personal papers. CSR/UNM.
95. "Fine Conditions," Las Vegas *Daily Optic*, 14 June 1905.
96. Letter: Meyer Report, 18 June 1905, Letters Received, NMMP/NMSRCA.
97. "New Mexico News," El Paso *Times*, 04 and 08 June 1905.
98. "Mounted Police Recover Herd of Stolen Cattle," Albuquerque *Evening Citizen*, 20 June 1905. "New Mexico News," El Paso *Times*, 23 June 1905; Letter: Huber Report, 24 June 1905, Letters Received, NMMP/NMSRCA.
99. "New Mexico News," El Paso *Times*, 03 June 1905.
100. "New Mexico News," El Paso *Times*, 23 June 1905.
101. Letter: Dudley Report, 17 July 1905, Letters Received, NMMP/NMSRCA.
102. Conversation Notes: Mrs. Jettie Avant Sullenger and the author, Mountainair, N.M., 07 July 1984, NMMP/AC.
103. Letter: Dudley Report, 23 July 1905, Letters Received, NMMP/NMSRCA; "Captured By Mounted Police," Santa Fe *New Mexican*, 31 July 1905.
104. Letter: Capt. Fullerton to Brophy, 09 July 1905, Letters Sent, NMMP/NMSRCA.
105. "Local Briefs," The Clayton *Enterprise*, 16 June and 07 July 1905.
106. "Local Briefs," The Clayton *Enterprise*, 16 June and 07 July 1905; "Assault Kindly Disposed Officer," Santa Fe *New Mexican*, 10 August 1905.
107. Letter: Avant Report, 22 July 1905, Letters Received, NMMP/NMSRCA.
108. "Left the Beef," Capitan *News*, 25 August 1905. Courtesy of the W.A. Keleher Collection.
109. Santa Fe *New Mexican*, 16 January 1900.
110. Letter: Avant Report, 07 August 1905, Letters Received, NMMP/NMSRCA.
111. Letter: Avant Report, 19 August 1905, Letters Received, NMMP/NMSRCA.
112. Capitan *News*, 25 August 1905. Courtesy of the W.A. Keleher Collection.
113. Conversation Notes: Mrs. Merlinda Trujillo, Capitan, N.M., 13 July 2002, NMMP/AC.
114. "First Report of Mounted Police," Santa Fe *New Mexican*, 18 December 1905.
115. "Left the Beef," Capitan *News*, 25 August 1905. Courtesy of the W.A. Keleher Collection.
116. Bundy Avant as told to Arthur Clements, "The Bundy Avant Story, Part 2," *True West* (July–August 1978), p. 27.
117. "Left the Beef," Capitan *News*, 25 August 1905. Courtesy of the W.A. Keleher Collection.
118. Santa Fe *New Mexican*, 30 August 1905.
119. Letter: Avant Report, 19 August 1905, Letters Received, NMMP/NMSRCA.
120. The Alamogordo *News*, 02 September 1905.
121. Capitan *News*, 25 August 1905. Courtesy of the W.A. Keleher Collection.
122. "Good Work of Territorial Ranger in Lincoln County," Las Vegas *Daily Optic*, 31 August 1905.
123. Letter: Capt. Fullerton to Will Dudley, 08 July 1905, Letters Received, NMMP/NMSRCA; Attorney General Opinion 252, 19 May 1905, *Biennial Report of Attorney General of New Mexico 1905–1906* (Santa Fe: New Mexico Printing Company, 1907).
124. Capitan *News*, 25 August 1905. Courtesy of the W.A. Keleher Collection.
125. Capitan *News*, 25 August 1905. Courtesy of the W.A. Keleher Collection.
126. Alice Blakestad (compiled by), *Gravesite Directory of Cemeteries in Lincoln County* (Hondo, N.M.: Lincoln County Historical Society Publications, 2001) No listing for Rusher.

127. Editorial, Santa Fe *New Mexican*, 01 September 1905.
128. Capitan *News*, 25 August 1905. Courtesy of the W.A. Keleher Collection.
129. John Fullerton, *Report of the Operations of the Mounted Police April 1, 1905 to June 30, 1905*, Departments, Boards and Commissions Annual Reports, Gov. Otero Papers, NMSRCA.
130. "New Mexico Item" column from the Associated Press during the summer of 1905, Newspaper Clip File, NMMP/AC.
131. Letter: Capt. Fullerton to Avant, 08 July 1905, Letters Sent, NMMP/NMSRCA.
132. *Otero County Advertiser* (Alamogordo), 05 August 1905. A Socorro jeweler had quoted Capt. Fullerton a $4.00 price to make a replacement badge for Dudley.
133. Socorro *Chieftain*, 09 June 1906.
134. Letter: Dudley Report, 05 August 1905, Letters Received, NMMP/NMSRCA.
135. Letter: Capt. Fullerton to Avant and Dudley, 14 July 1905, NMMP/NMSRCA.
136. "New Mexico News," El Paso *Times*, 26 May 1905.
137. Conversation Notes: Mrs. Jettie Avant Sullenger and the author, Mountainair, N.M., 07 July 1984, NMMP/AC.
138. Letter: Dudley Report, 05 August 1905, Letters Received, NMMP/NMSRCA.
139. Capt. Fullerton and Will Dudley met in Santa Fe on 11 August 1905. Santa Fe *New Mexican*, 12 August 1905. The captain had also conferred with Gov. Otero. *Executive Ticker*, O/S, CSR/UNM.
140. Albuquerque *Evening Citizen*, reprinted in the Socorro *Chieftain*, 19 August 1905.
141. Socorro *Chieftain*, 26 August 1905.
142. "Territorial Mounted Police Force," Socorro *Chieftain*, 01 April 1905.
143. Letter: Capt. Fullerton to W.C. Barnes, 26 July 1905, Letters Sent, NMMP/NMSRCA.
144. Letter: Capt. Fullerton to W.C. Barnes, 27 July 1905, Letters Sent, NMMP/NMSRCA.
145. Letter: Capt. Fullerton to Whitney Company, 10 July 1905, Letters Sent, NMMP/NMSRCA; Reconstructed NMMP Voucher Records, NMMP/AC (See chapter on the Mounted Police Fund).
146. Letter: Baca to his wife, ND, Cipriano Baca Papers, Baca Family Collection.
147. Zelie Pollon, "Goodbye, Route 666: A Road by Any Other Name is Less Sinister," Dallas *Morning News*, 27 July 2003.
148. Socorro *Chieftain*, 12 August 1905; Albuquerque *Evening Citizen*, 09 August 1905.
149. Silver City *Independent*, 15 August 1905; *San Juan Index*, 25 August 1905. Vaughn was the first San Juan County sheriff to be elected to two consecutive terms of office.
150. Durango (Colo.) *Evening Herald*, 29 August 1905; *San Juan Index*, reprinted in the Estancia *News*, 01 September 1905.
151. Letters: Capt. Fullerton to Lt. Baca and the three wives, June–August 1905, Letters Sent, NMMP/NMSRCA.
152. "Horse Thieves Make A Raid," Las Vegas *Daily Optic*, 01 July 1905; "Claude Doane Is Still At Large In The Valley," Albuquerque *Morning Journal*, 02 July 1905; Letter: Capt. Fullerton to Dudley, 08 July 1905, Letters Sent, NMMP/NMSRCA.
153. "Doane And Baca Safely Lodged In The County Jail." Albuquerque *Morning Journal*, 09 July 1905; Las Vegas *Daily Optic*, 10 July 1905.
154. Letters: Huber Reports, 15 July and 22 July 1905, Letters Received, NMMP/NMSRCA; Albuquerque *Morning Journal*, 22 August 1905.
155. Penitentiary Record Book of Convicts, 05 April 1904 to 13 February 1915, Convict 1960, Territorial Prison Records, Microfilm Roll 1, NMSRCA.
156. Socorro *Chieftain*, 02 September 1905; "Escaped Convict Returned," Socorro *Chieftain*, 23 September 1905.
157. Penitentiary Record Book of Convicts, 05 April 1904 to 13 February 1915, Convict 1969, Territorial Prison Records, Microfilm Roll 1, NMSRCA.
158. H.B. Hening (Ed.), *George Curry, 1861–1947: An Autobiography* (Albuquerque: University of New Mexico Press, 1958), p. 191.
159. The Hubbell and Vigil Hearing Files and the countercharges against Frank Clancy compose Frames 950–1311, Roll 51, Territorial Archives of New Mexico, NMSRCA.
160. Letter: Capt. Fullerton to Lt. Baca, 12 September 1905, Letters Sent, NMMP/NMSRCA.
161. Letter: Capt. Fullerton to Will Dudley, 12 September 1905, Letters Sent, NMMP/NMSRCA.
162. Letter: Capt. Fullerton to William Huntington, 25 September 1905, Letters Sent, NMMP/NMSRCA. Elmer Fullerton lived at 110 West Gold Ave. in Albuquerque. The younger Fullerton and his friend Clyde Stauder worked at the transfer company. When John sold the business in July 1905, the two young friends remained and worked for the new owner. Stauder was Cipriano Baca's brother-in-law and also the brother-in-law of the territorial auditor, William Sergent.
163. John Fullerton Personal Papers, NMMP/NMSRCA.
164. "The Governor Actually Fears Abduction Of Son," Albuquerque *Morning Journal*, 13 July 1905.
165. "Local and Personal," Albuquerque *Morning Journal*, 31 July 1905; "Personals," Las Vegas *Daily Optic*, 10 August 1905.
166. Miguel Otero, *My Nine Years as Governor of the Territory of New Mexico 1897–1906* (Albuquerque: The University of New Mexico Press, 1940), p. 101.
167. Miguel A. Otero, Jr. (IV), would grow up and serve a year as a New Mexico Mounted Police sergeant (December 1919–December 1920) while his Uncle Page Otero served as a ranger under Captain Fornoff from 1908–1910. The nephew and uncle spent much time together when Miguel was a youth. In later years, when Page was an ailing old man and needed some financial assistance with medical bills, his wife asked Miguel for a loan. Miguel refused the request by claiming he was not well off at the time himself. Otero, a former state auditor and former state attorney general, was never a man without some means. Letters: The Otero-Stinson Collection (506), Box 3, Folder 15, CSR/UNM.
168. Letter: Miguel Otero to Mrs. Lottie Otero, 13 September 1933, The Otero-Stinson Collection (506), Box 3, Folder 15, CSR/UNM.
169. "Would Be Kidnappers," Santa Fe *New Mexi-

can, 08 August 1905; *Western Liberal* (Lordsburg), 11 August 1905; "Armed Band After Governor," Las Vegas *Daily Optic,* 11 August 1905; Otero, *My Nine Years as Governor,* p. 100.

170. Gov. Hagerman fired Page Otero as the territorial fish and game warden because he felt him "unfortunately unfit for the position on account of his excessive intemperance." Letter: Herbert J. Hagerman to William Loeb, Jr., secretary to President Roosevelt, 02 April 1906, John James Hagerman Family Papers MS104, Box 4, RGHC/NMSU.

171. "Don't Kidnap the Governor," Albuquerque *Morning Journal*, 23 August 1905.

172. *Executive Ticker*, 16 August 1905; Santa Fe *New Mexican*, 17 August 1905.

173. Otero, *My Nine Years as Governor*, p. 101; Letter: Huber Report, 12 August 1905, Letters Received, NMMP/NMSRCA.

174. Farmington *Enterprise,* 21 July 1905.

175. Letters: W.H. Greer to Gov. Otero, 08 September 1905, Letters Received; Otero to Greer, 12 September 1905, Letters Sent, Gov. Otero Papers, NMSRCA.

176. Letter: Capt. Fullerton to Will Dudley, 12 September 1905, Letters Sent, NMMP/NMSRCA; "Mounted Police Here For Parade," Albuquerque *Morning Journal*, 20 September 1905; "Stolen Sheep Found," Santa Fe *New Mexican*, 19 September 1905.

177. "Mounted Police In Fair Parade," Albuquerque *Evening Citizen*, 20 September 1905.

178. Letter: Capt. Fullerton to Dr. B.H. Briggs, 10 October 1905, Letters Sent, NMMP/NMSRCA.

179. Albuquerque *Morning Journal*, 23 September 1905.

180. Letter: Capt. Fullerton to William Huntington, 24 August 1905, Letters Sent, NMMP/NMSRCA.

181. Northeastern New Mexico was in a boom stage. The miners at Dawson had a new schoolhouse under construction and the citizens of Las Vegas Town were building a YMCA. Businessmen at Folsom had formed a brass band to play at community functions.

182. Letters: R.E. Twichell to Gov. Otero, 23 August 1905, Letters Received; Otero to Twichell, 30 August and 02 September 1905, Letters Sent, Gov. Otero Papers, NMSRCA.

183. The Alamogordo *News*, 07 October 1905; The Tucumcari *News,* 02 December 1905.

184. "Most Magnificent Floral & Industrial Parade in Territorial Annals," Las Vegas *Daily Optic,* 28 September 1905.

185. Albuquerque's Simon Stern's Company supplied the new head gear at $3.00 per hat. On 25 October 1905 Fullerton issued Mounted Police Voucher #57 for $30. The territory paid the bill with warrant #11728 on 05 November 1905. Interestingly enough, Fullerton next deducted $3.00 from each of the ranger's paychecks to pay for their hat. No record has been located as to the dispossession Fullerton made of this $30. Letters: Fullerton to Stern's Co., 25 October 1905; Fullerton to rangers with paycheck, 14 November 1905, Letters Sent, NMMP; Mounted Police Voucher Records, NMMP/ NMSRCA.

186. Santa Fe *New Mexican*, 21 September 1905; "Mounted Police Here For Parade," Albuquerque *Morning Journal*, 20 September 1905. The present location of the Mounted Police flag is uncertain.

187. Socorro *Chieftain*, 23 September 1905.

188. Telegrams: Rio Arriba County Sheriff B.C. Hernandez to Gov. Otero, 26 September 1905; C.M. O'Donell to Gov. Otero, 27 September 1905; J.W. Raynolds, Acting Governor, to Capt. Fullerton, 27 September 1905; Fullerton to Raynolds, 27 September 1905; C.M. O'Donell to Otero, 29 September 1905, Raynolds to Fullerton, 29 September 1905 and Fullerton to Raynolds, 29 September 1905, Letters Sent/Letters Received, NMMP/NMSRCA.

189. Telegrams: Capt. Fullerton to Acting Governor Raynolds, 27 September and 02 October 1905, Letters Sent, NMMP/NMSRCA.

190. "New Mexico News," El Paso *Times*, 06 June 1905.

191. "Work For The Mounted Police," Deming *Graphic,* 18 August 1905.

192. The first *Gorras Blancos* (White Cap) era took place during the early 1890s. The San Miguel County gang had members and friends among the local political leadership, including the sheriff's office, and they were very popular among the Hispanic population. The gang was finally broken up with the help of a Pinkerton private detective, employed by the governor, and the timely killing of one of the gang's principal leaders.

193. See Peter Nabokov's *Tijerina and the Courthouse Raid* (Albuquerque: University of New Mexico Press, 1969) for an insightful account of Reies Lopez Tijerina and this struggle for land.

194. "Territorial Mounted Police Arrest Alleged Whitecaps," Albuquerque *Evening Citizen*, 01 November 1905; "Some Good Work by the Mounted Police," Santa Fe *New Mexican*, 06 November 1905.

195. Letter: Capt. Fullerton to Avant and Dudley, 14 July 1905, Letters Sent, NMMP/NMSRCA.

196. Letter: Capt. Fullerton to Avant and Dudley, 14 July 1905, Letters Sent, NMMP/NMSRCA.

197. Letters: Gov. Hagerman to Capt. Fullerton, 09 February 1906, Letters Sent, Gov. Hagerman Papers, NMSRCA; Capt. Fullerton to Gov. Hagerman, 10 February 1906, Letters Sent, NMMP/ NMSRCA.

198. Alamogordo *News*, 07 October and 04 November 1905.

199. Telegram: C.M. O'Donell to Gov. Otero, 29 September 1905, Letters Received, Gov. Otero Papers, NMSRCA. See David Remley, *Bell Ranch, Cattle Ranching in the Southwest 1824–1947* (Las Cruces, N.M.: Yucca Tree Press, 2000) for a history of this vast empire.

200. "Territorial Mounted Police Arrest Alleged Whitecaps," Albuquerque *Evening Citizen*, 01 November 1905; "White Caps Terrorize New Mexico," Tombstone (Ariz.) *Prospector*, 04 November 1905.

201. The El Paso *Times*, 06 October 1905.

202. Letter: Capt. Fullerton to Will Dudley, 14 November 1905, Letters Sent, NMMP/NMSRCA.

203. Letter: Capt. Fullerton to Sergeant Lewis, 06 October 1905, Letters Sent, NMMP/NMSRCA.

204. Conversation Notes: Fred Lambert and author, Cimarron, N.M., 14 September 1968; Lambert's White Cap Case File, NMMP/AC.

205. B.C. Hernandez twice represented New Mexico in the U.S. House of Representatives, 1915–1916 and 1919–1920.

206. *Western Liberal* (Lordsburg), 27 October 1905.
207. *Western Liberal* (Lordsburg), 27 October 1905; "Huber Lands Horse Thief," The Las Vegas *Weekly Optic & Stock Grower*, 28 October 1905.
208. Conversation Notes: Mrs. Ethel Stockard, Perry Stockard and author, 28 July 1995, Roswell, N.M., NMMP/AC. The motor coach started to carry the U.S. Mail in January 1906.
209. Herbert J. Hagerman, *Report of the Governor of New Mexico to the Secretary of the Interior for the Year Ending June 30, 1906* (Washington: Government Printing Office, 1906), p. 3.
210. "Report of an Attempted Holdup on Santa Fe," Santa Fe *New Mexican*, 04 October 1905.
211. Capitan *News*, 01 September and 08 September 1905. Courtesy of the W.A. Keleher Collection.
212. Santa Fe *New Mexican*, 01 September 1905.
213. Miscellaneous Associated Press accounts, Newspaper Clip File, NMMP/AC.
214. "First Report of Mounted Police," Santa Fe *New Mexican*, 18 December 1905.
215. Letter: Capt. Fullerton to W.M. Barrowdale, 09 November 1905, Letters Sent, NMMP/NSMRCA. Barrowdale served as postmaster at Magdalena from 1888 to 1898.
216. Letter: Capt. Fullerton to Will Dudley, 12 September 1905, Letter Sent, NMMP/NMSRCA. This sentence is not contained in the copy published in Miguel A. Otero's *Report of the Governor of New Mexico to the Secretary of the Interior for the Year Ending June 30, 1905* (Washington: Government Printing Office, 1905) pp. 179 and 180. Copy in NMSRCA.
217. Socorro *Chieftain*, 09 September 1905.
218. Socorro *Chieftain*, 16 December 1905.
219. Letter: Gov. Otero to Mrs. Corbin, 28 October 1905, Letters Sent, Gov. Otero Papers, NMSRCA.
220. Associated Press news clip dated 08 November 1905, Newspaper Clip File, NMMP/AC.
221. "Arrested at Carrizozo Wanted in Texas," Santa Fe *New Mexican*, 16 October 1905.
222. Capitan *News*, 13 October and 10 November 1905. Courtesy of the W.A. Keleher Collection.
223. Letter: Capt. Fullerton to Avant, 14 November 1905, Letters Sent, NMMP/NMSRCA.
224. Letter: Capt. Fullerton to Ed Armijo, 14 November 1905, Letters Sent, NMMP/NMSRCA.
225. "Mounted Police Will Go After Them," Denver *Republican*, 18 August 1905; "Mounted Police Chase Apache Kid And His Squaw," Albuquerque *Morning Journal*, 18 August 1905. The Denver datelined Associated Press story implied that the Mounted Police headquarters was in Santa Fe.
226. The Socorro *Chieftain*, 23 September 1905.
227. Mrs. Tom Charles, *Tales of the Tularosa* (Alamogordo, N.M.: Private, 1953) p. 28; Marc Simmons, "Hunting Expedition Came Back With Bigger Game Than Expected," New Mexican Scrapbook column, El Paso *Times*, 02 February 1986.
228. McGrath's athletic career was covered in the college newspaper *The Collagist*, RCHC/NMSU.
229. *New Mexico Coded Laws 1905*, Chapter 9 Mounted Police; "Red Men Are Lawless," Socorro *Chieftain*, 16 December 1905.
230. Letter: Capt. Fullerton to Page B. Otero, 03 November 1905, Letters Sent, NMMP/NMSRCA.
231. Letter: Page B. Otero to Capt. Fullerton, 08 November 1905, Letters Sent, Fish and Game Warden Records, NMSRCA.
232. Letter: Page B. Otero to R. Perry, 11 November 1905, Letters Sent, Fish and Game Warden Records, NMSRCA.
233. Letter: Capt. Fullerton to W.M. Barrowdale, 09 November 1905, Letters Sent, NMMP/ NMSRCA.
234. Letter: U.S. Marshal Creighton Foraker to the U.S. Attorney General, 26 October 1897, Letter Book 1897, USMP/UNM.
235. Letter: Capt. Fullerton to James Patterson, 15 November 1905, Letters Sent, NMMP/NMSRCA.
236. Letter: Page B. Otero to Capt. Fullerton, 18 November 1905, Letters Sent, Fish and Game Warden Records, NMSRCA.
237. Judge A.J. Abbott's report is published on pages 59–61 of Governor Hagerman's *Report of the Governor of New Mexico to the Secretary of the Interior for the Year Ending June 30, 1906* (Washington: Government Printing Office, 1906). The author's copy was once owned by former territorial governor L. Bradford Prince (1889–1893) and contains his comments written on the inside cover sheet and in the margins. One of the Prince notes says, "The volume was printed during the enforcement of Pres Roosevelt's order as to spelling. The Governor was not responsible for the spelling." TR tried to standardize phonetic spelling in government documents; "althou" and "thoro" are some examples.
238. El Paso *Times*, 02 December 1905.
239. "Red Men Are Lawless," Socorro *Chieftain*, 16 December 1905; "Trouble With Pueblos," Portales *Herald*, 22 October 1904.
240. Letters: Lt. Baca to Game Warden Page Otero, 17 October 1905, Otero to Baca, 30 October 1905, Letter Book, Fish and Game Warden Records, NMSRCA; "Indians Troublesome," Santa Fe *New Mexican*, 16 December 1905; Roswell *Register*, 26 January 1906.
241. Letter: Page B. Otero to Capt. Fullerton, 27 November 1905, Letters Sent, Fish and Game Warden Records, NMSRCA.
242. Letter: Capt. Fullerton to S.B. Grimshaw, 03 November 1905, Letters Sent, NMMP/NMSRCA.
243. *New Mexico Mounted Police Arrest Book 1907–1912*, Roll 93, NMMP/NMSRCA.
244. "Wholesale Thief Arrested," *Otero County Advertiser* (Alamogordo), 23 December 1905.
245. Santa Fe *New Mexican*, 12 December 1905; El Paso *Times*, 16 December 1905; "Negro Convict Sanders Caught At La Junta," Albuquerque *Morning Journal*, 28 December 1905.
246. El Paso *Times*, 30 December 1905.
247. El Paso *Times*, undated, News-clip File, NMMP/AC.
248. The Clayton *Enterprise*, 16 February 1906.
249. Letter: A.B. Harris to Capt. Fullerton, 07 February 1906, Letters Received, NMMP/NMSRCA.
250. "About Town," The El Paso *Evening News*, 04–06 January 1906; "Native Thugs Robbing and Burning Stores in Alamogordo," Albuquerque *Morning Journal*.
251. "Convict Flees to Border," Albuquerque *Morning Journal*, 28 December 1905. Grant County Deputy Sheriff John Collier became a mounted police in May 1906. He would twice serve as second-in-command of the rangers under Captain Fred Fornoff.

252. The Alpine (Texas) *Times*, 27 December 1905. In his notice rancher G.W. Beakley also said, "My pastures are posted according to law and all persons hunting or trespassing will be prosecuted."
253. Company B Duty Report, January 1906; Company C Duty Report and Scout Report, January 1906, Ranger Force Records, Ranger Records, Texas Adjutant General's Department, TX Archives.
254. "Officer Killed?" Santa Fe *New Mexican*, 22 February 1906.
255. Socorro *Chieftain*, 17 February 1906.
256. "Little Girl Badly Burned," Socorro *Chieftain*, 03 February 1906.
257. "Perhaps Slain By Outlaw Band," El Paso *Times*, 23 February 1906.
258. "Little Una Lewis Dead," Socorro *Chieftain*, 17 February 1906.
259. The Clayton *Enterprise*, 23 February 1906.
260. "Sergeant Lewis Very Much Alive," Santa Fe *New Mexican*, 23 February 1906. Only two rangers died while on duty during the 15 year history of the mounted police. A special ranger was murdered in 1910 and a year later a regular ranger died of pneumonia resulting from a cold he caught while bringing a prisoner through a winter storm.
261. The telegram exchange between Capt. Fullerton and Sgt. Lewis is not preserved in the official records contained in NMMP/NMSRCA.
262. Socorro *Chieftain*, 24 February 1906.
263. "Officer Killed?" Santa Fe *New Mexican*, 22 February 1906.
264. "Little Una Lewis Dead," Socorro *Chieftain*, 17 February 1906.
265. If Sgt. Lewis made a written report of his trip into Mexico it has not survived as part of the official records contained in NMMP/NMSRCA.
266. "Little Una Lewis Dead," Socorro *Chieftain*, 17 February 1905.
267. *Western Liberal* (Lordsburg), 29 December 1905.
268. Telegram: Gov. Hagerman to Fullerton, 24 February 1906, Letters Received, NMMP/NMSRCA.
269. Santa Fe *New Mexican*, 23 February 1906.
270. The Fullerton to Lewis telegram is not part of the official Mounted Police records.
271. "Requisition, To the Governor of Sonora [Mexico]: For Claude Barbee charged with murder. Approved Feb. 28, 1906," *Biennial Report of Attorney General of New Mexico 1905–1906*, Gov. H.J. Hagerman Papers, NMSRCA.
272. The Clayton *Enterprise*, 23 February 1906.
273. Socorro *Chieftain*, 03 March 1906.
274. "New Mexico," The El Paso *Evening News*, 04 and 18 January 1906.
275. "New Mexico," The El Paso *Evening News*, 07 January 1906.
276. Letter: Baca Report, 26 January 1906, Letters Received, NMMP/NMSRCA.
The Guadalupe County prisoners had been sent to the Quay County Jail for safekeeping during the repair work on the jail. Three men were able to escape custody while being held at Tucumcari. "New Mexico," The El Paso *Evening News*, 06 January 1906.
277. "New Mexico News," El Paso *Times*, 08 January 1906; "New Mexico," The El Paso *Evening News*, 17 January 1906.
278. Letter: Baca to Capt. Fullerton, 26 January 1906, Letters Received, NMMP/NMSRCA.
279. "No Trains For Two Weeks," Roswell *Register*, 19 January and 02 February 1906.
280. "Lieutenant Baca of Rangers Raids Robbers' Roost," Albuquerque *Morning Journal*, 28 January 1906.
281. Tucumcari *News*, 10 February 1906.
282. The Clayton *Enterprise*, 16 February 1906.
283. Socorro *Chieftain*, 17 February 1906.
284. "Lieutenant Cipriano Baca," Socorro *Chieftain*, 03 March 1906.
285. Santa Fe *New Mexican*, 10 March 1906.
286. "Car Thieves Arrested," Santa Fe *New Mexican*, 12 March 1906; "Ranger Captures Thieves," El Paso *Times*, 12 March 1906.
287. "Ranger Lands Five Car Thieves," Albuquerque *Morning Journal*, 12 March 1906; "Freight Thieves Work On Rock Island," *Otero County Advertiser* (Alamogordo), 31 March 1906.
288. Socorro *Chieftain*, 10 February 1906.
289. "Fornoff For Captain Of Mounted Police," Santa Fe *New Mexican*, 21 March 1906.
290. Letter: Putman Report, 31 March 1905, Letters Received, NMMP/NMSRCA.
291. Grant Maxwell, "Cow Town," *New Mexico Magazine*, October 1935, pp. 11–13 and 44.
292. Hagerman, *Report of the Governor 1906*, p. 5.

Chapter 9

1. Letter: Capt. Fornoff to Gov. Hagerman, 02 January 1907, Letters Received, Gov. H.J. Hagerman Papers, NMSRCA. The report was included as an appendix in the printed copy of Gov. Herbert J Hagerman's address to the 37th Legislative Assembly.
2. Fred Fornoff, *Operation's Report of the Mounted Police, April 1, 1905 to December 31, 1906*, NMMP/NMSRCA.
3. These estimates are based upon information contained in the annual reports Gov. Otero sent to the secretary of the interior concerning the conditions within the Territory.
4. "Lincoln County Policeman," Capitan *News*, 07 April 1905; "Rangers Appointed," *The Outlook* (White Oaks), 23 March 1905.
5. "Lincoln County Policeman," Capitan *News*, 07 April 1905.
6. Letters: Appointment notice, resignation letter of William Taylor; Telegrams: Acting Gov. Raynolds to Capt. Fullerton, Fullerton to Raynolds, 06 April 1905, Letters Sent/Letters Received, NMMP/NMSRCA.
7. Letters: Elkins Report, 17 June 1905, Letters Received; Capt. Fullerton to Elkins, 19 June 1905, Letters Sent, NMMP/NMSRCA.
8. Letters: Capt. Fullerton to Putman, 24 June and 28 June 1905, Letters Sent, NMMP/NMSRCA.
9. Letters: Capt. Fullerton to McGrath, 24 June 1905; Capt. Fullerton to Elkins, 02 June 1905. Letters Sent, NMMP/NMSRCA.
10. *Executive Record Book #6*, Secretary of the Territory Records, NMSRCA.
11. *Executive Record Book #6*, Secretary of the Ter-

ritory Records; Mounted Police appointment notice and oath of office, NMMP/NMSRCA; "Appointment to the Mounted Police," Santa Fe *New Mexican*, 03 July 1905; Letter: Capt. Fullerton to Elkins, 19 June 1905, Letters Sent, NMMP/ NMSRCA.

12. Letter: Capt. Fullerton to Elkins, 11 July 1905, Letters Sent, NMMP/NMSRCA.

13. Letter: Perea to Capt. Fullerton, 20 December 1905, Letters Received, NMMP/NMSRCA; *Executive Ticker*, 18 November 1905, CSR/UNM; Santa Fe *New Mexican*, 17 November 1905.

14. Letter: Capt. Fullerton to Huber, 17 June 1905, Letters Sent, NMMP/NMSRCA.

15. Letter: Capt. Fullerton to Huber, 11 July 1905, Letters Sent, NMMP/NMSRCA.

16. Miguel A. Otero, *My Life on the Frontier II 1882–1897: Death Knell of a Territory and Birth of a State* (Albuquerque, the University of New Mexico Press, 1939), pp. 215–216, 288–292.

17. Letter: Gov. Otero to Capt. Fullerton, 11 July 1905, Letters Received, NMMP/NMSRCA.

18. Letter: Gov. Otero to Capt. Fullerton, 14 July 1905, Letters Received, NMMP/NMSRCA.

19. Letter: Lt. Baca to Huber, 21 October 1905, Letters Sent, NMMP/NMSRCA.

20. "Dick Huber, Veteran Stage Driver, Law Officer, Crosses the Divide," Santa Fe *New Mexican*, 30 March 1929.

21. Otero, *My Nine Years As Governor*, pp. 335 and 336; pp. 302 and 340.

22. Letter: Gov. Otero to Capt. Fullerton, 15 November 1905, Letter Book, Gov. Otero Papers, NMSRCA.

23. Letter: Capt. Fullerton to Gov. Otero, 24 November 1905, Letters Sent, NMMP/NMSRCA.

24. Letter: Capt. Fullerton to Frank W. Clancy, 15 November 1905, Letters Sent, NMMP/NMSRCA.

25. "Hunt For The Willard Robbers Is Abandoned," Santa Fe *New Mexican*, 20 November 1905; Albuquerque *Morning Journal* and Albuquerque *Evening Citizen*, 20 November 1905; Socorro *Chieftain*, 11 November 1905.

26. Socorro *Chieftain*, 26 November 1905.

27. Letter: Capt. Fullerton to Gov. Otero, 04 December 1905, Letters Sent, NMMP/NMSRCA; Santa Fe *New Mexican*, 06 December 1905; *Executive Ticker*, 06 December 1905, CSR/UNM.

28. *Western Liberal* (Lordsburg), 08 December 1905.

29. Letters: Dick Huber to Capt. Fullerton, 07 December 1905, Letters Received; Fullerton to Huber, 09 December 1905, Letters Sent, NMMP/NMSRCA.

30. Record Group 42 — Arizona Rangers, General Orders 1907, AZ Archives.

31. Letter: Capt. Fullerton to McGrath, 09 December 1905, Letters Sent, NMMP/NMSRCA; *Western Liberal* (Lordsburg), 31 March 1905.

32. Letter: McGrath to Capt. Fullerton, 05 December 1905, Letters Received, NMMP/NMSRCA.

33. Letters: Capt. Fullerton to Deputy Sheriff, Clifton, Ariz., 07 June 1905: Capt. Fullerton to Thiel Detective Service, NYC/NY, 05 October 1905, Letters Sent, NMMP/NMSRCA.

34. Contemporary newspaper accounts of McGrath's arrests and McGrath's mounted police field reports.

35. Letter: Capt. Fullerton to Gov. Otero, 13 December 1905, Letters Sent, NMMP/NMSRCA.

36. Prison Records, Holm O. Bursum Papers, Box 1, File 9, SCR/UNM.

37. *Executive Ticker*, 14 December 1905; "Called On Gov. Otero," Santa Fe *New Mexican*, 16 December 1905; Appointment Notice, Oaths of Office, NMMP/NMSRCA.

38. "Good Men," Las Vegas *Weekly Optic & Stock Grower*, 23 December 1905.

39. "Called On Gov. Otero," Santa Fe *New Mexican*, 16 December 1905.

40. The Las Vegas *Weekly Optic & Stock Grower*, 23 December 1905.

41. Letter: Brophy to Capt. Fullerton, 20 March 1906, Letters Received, NMMP/NMSRCA.

Chapter 10

1. Letter: Miss Clara H. Olsen to Capt. Fullerton, 31 July 1905, Letters Sent, Gov. M.A. Otero Papers, NMSRCA.

2. List of the territorial warrants drawn on the Mounted Police Fund, Territorial Auditor's Records 1905, NMSRCA.

3. The mill, equal to one-tenth of a cent, was declared the lowest money of account by Congress in 1786, but the coin was never minted. The mounted police tax was half of the lowest legal currency.

4. *New Mexico Coded Laws 1905*, Chapter 9 Mounted Police, NMSRCA.

5. Military Code of Arizona (Title 46), Chapter 2 (Arizona Rangers), Section 17 (Tax), *The Revised Statutes of Arizona Territory* (Columbia, Mo.: Press of E.W. Stephens, 1901), p. 836.

6. *New Mexico Coded Laws 1905*, Chapter 9 Mounted Police, NMSRCA.

7. This data was compiled from the known mounted police vouchers issued by Capt. Fullerton and the known payments approved by the territorial auditor and paid by the territorial treasurer.

8. *New Mexico Coded Laws 1905*, Chapter 9 Mounted Police, NMSRCA.

9. "Record Breaking Day In Territorial Legislature," The Las Vegas *Daily Optic*, 10 February 1905. The *Daily Optic* had pointed out the difference between the $13,000 operating account and the $1,200 contingency account. The discussion was part of the paper's story about the debate in the council over the amendments to the Greer Mounted Police Bill.

10. This assumption is based upon reasons that will become clearer later. The author could find no paper trail to support this idea.

11. Letter: Capt. Fullerton to Territorial Auditor W.G. Sargent, Letters Sent, 26 April 1905, NMMP/NMSRCA.

12. It is possible that Gov. Otero and Capt. Fullerton had previously discussed the funding issue. They may have talked over the troubles while visiting during their train trip between Albuquerque and Santa Fe. Charles V. Safford, the territorial traveling auditor, and J.W. Raynolds, territorial secretary, were also on the same train with the governor. Albuquerque *Morning Journal*, 16 August 1905; Santa Fe *New Mexican*, 17 August 1905. Capt. Fullerton and Gov. Otero

held their scheduled meeting at 3:00 p.m. They had also met at noon four days earlier. *Executive Ticker*, 12 and 16 August 1905, O-S/CSR/UNM.
13. Silver City *Independent*, 22 August 1905.
14. Letter: Gov. Otero to George Prichard, 16 August 1905, Letters Sent, Gov. M.A. Otero Papers, NMSRCA.
15. Letter: Capt. Fullerton to Gov. Otero, 16 August 1905, Letters Received, Gov. M.A. Otero Papers, NMSRCA.
16. Letter: Capt. Fullerton to Gov. Otero, 23 August 1905, Letters Received, Gov. M.A. Otero Papers, NMSRCA.
17. Letter: Gov. Otero to Capt. Fullerton, 19 August 1905, Letters Sent, Gov. M.A. Otero Papers, NMSRCA.
18. Letter: Attorney General George W. Prichard to Gov. Otero, 18 August 1905, Letters Received, Gov. M.A. Otero Papers, NMSRCA. The main part of Prichard's letter was issued as Attorney General Opinion No. 269. *Opinions 1905*, Attorney General Records, NMSRCA.
19. Letters: Capt. Fullerton to Gov. Otero, 23 August 1905; Miss C.H. Olsen to Capt. Fullerton, 30 August 1905, Letters Received/ Letters Sent, Gov. M.A. Otero Papers, NMSRCA.
20. Letter: Capt. Fullerton to W.D. [sic] Sargent, 16 November 1905, Letters Sent, NMMP/NMSRCA.
21. Captain Fullerton's troubles with Will Sargent are mentioned in the correspondence between him and Governor Otero. Letters: Fullerton/Otero, August 1905–December 1905, Letters Sent/Letters Received, NMMP and Gov. M.A. Otero Papers, NMSRCA. Will Sargent remained as territorial auditor until New Mexico statehood in 1912. He won election as the first state auditor and was re-elected four more times, serving into January 1921. Sargent worked with four of the five mounted police captains. Miguel A. Otero, Jr., son of the former territorial governor, served as state auditor, 1927–1928, before being elected to a two-year term as attorney general in November 1928.
22. Sargent did impress Governor Hagerman. Shortly before he left office Hagerman gave Sargent a two year extension to his appointment as auditor. Appointments, 19 March 1907, Gov. H.J. Hagerman Papers, NMSRCA.
23. N.M.M.P. Warrants, 20 December 1905 to 10 November 1911, Territorial Treasurer Records, NMSRCA.
24. Mounted Police Department Report 1905 and 1907, NMMP/NMSRCA.
25. N.M.M.P. Warrants, 20 December 1905 to 10 November 1911, Territorial Treasurer Records, NMSRCA.
26. *New Mexico Coded Laws 1905*, Chapter 9 Mounted Police, NMSRCA.
27. Letter: Capt. Fullerton to Territorial Auditor W.G. Sargent, Letters Sent, 26 April 1905, NMMP/NMSRCA.
28. *New Mexico Coded Law 1907*, Section 15 — Appropriations, NMSRCA.
29. These figures are compiled from computation of each Mounted Police's paycheck based upon his oath taking date and his authorized salary.
30. Reports: Gov. Hagerman to Secretary of the Interior E.A. Hitchcock; Capt. Fornoff to Gov. Hagerman, Letters Sent/ Letters Received, Gov. H.J. Hagerman Papers, NMSRCA.
31. Report: Territorial Auditor — 56th Fiscal Year, Auditor Records, NMSRCA.
32. Report: Territorial Auditor — 57th Fiscal Year, Auditor Records, NMSRCA.
33. "Mr Greer Proposes Relief From Outlaws," Santa Fe *New Mexican*, 26 January 1905.
34. Report: Territorial Auditor — 59th Fiscal Year, Auditor Records, NMSRCA.
35. *New Mexico Coded Laws 1909*, Chapter 127 Appropriations, NMSRCA. The Mounted Police Fund levy for the 60th Fiscal Year was $.00050 per $100 of real property valuation. Report: Territorial Auditor — 60th Fiscal Year, Auditor Records, NMSRCA.
36. "State ex rel.-V- Sargent, N.M. 272," *Journal Supreme Court of New Mexico,* January Term 1913, pp. 271–281.

Chapter 11

1. Otero, *My Nine Years As Governor*, p. 382.
2. "New Mexico," El Paso *Evening News*, 02 January 1906. Deputy U.S. Marshal Fred Fornoff was among the many citizens who attended Hagerman's inauguration ceremony. Santa Fe *New Mexican*, 23 January 1906.
3. H.B. Hening (Ed.), *George Curry, 1861–1947: An Autobiography* (Albuquerque: University of New Mexico Press, 1958) p. 193.
4. Letter: Gov. Hagerman to M.A. Otero, 06 March 1906, Letters Sent, Gov. H.J. Hagerman Papers, NMSRCA.
5. Hagerman had been born in Milwaukee on 15 December 1871 and he died in Santa Fe on 28 January 1935. Otero lived another nine years and died in Santa Fe on 07 August 1944. He had been born in St. Louis on 17 October 1859.
6. Hagerman soon leased and remodeled one of the former officers' quarters at old Fort Marcy and furnished it in luxurious style, hired a staff of servants and entertained in the manner of the European royalty. The new governor even established a first for Santa Fe; he employed a Negro butler for his home. Hening, *George Curry,* p. 193.
7. Appointments, Gov. H.J. Hagerman Papers, NMSRCA.
8. Letter: Gov. Hagerman to Capt. Fullerton, 27 January 1906, Letters Sent, Gov. H.J. Hagerman Papers, NMSRCA.
9. Letter: Charles Ilfeld to Gov. Otero, 18 January 1906, Letters Received, Gov. Otero Papers, NMSRCA.
10. Letters: Gov. Hagerman to Charles Ilfeld, 25 January 1906; Gov. Hagerman to Capt. Fullerton, 27 January 1906, Letters Sent, Gov. H.J. Hagerman Papers, NMSRCA.
11. Letter: Capt. Fullerton to Gov. Hagerman, 29 January 1906, Letters Received, Gov. H.J. Hagerman Papers, NMSRCA; Baca Report, 26 January 1906, Letters Received, NMMP/NMSRCA.
12. "Mounted Police Doing Good Work," Santa Fe *New Mexican*, 06 February 1906.
13. *Western Liberal* (Lordsburg), 22 December 1905. The *Liberal* took issue with the *New Mexican*

story, "First Report of Mounted Police" of 18 December 1905.

14. Letter: Gov. Hagerman to Territorial Auditor Will Sargent, 29 January 1906, Letters Sent, Gov. H.J. Hagerman Papers, NMSRCA.

15. "Reorganization of the Mounted Police Effected," Albuquerque *Morning Journal*, 03 April 1906.

16. President Theodore Roosevelt had appointed Herbert J. Hagerman governor on 24 November 1905. It was almost two months before Hagerman was able to take office. "In 1906 Roosevelt appointed him governor of the Territory and told him to clean house, an order Hagerman had every intention of following religiously." Robert W. Larson, "New Mexico Progressives," *New Mexico Historical Review*, XLV: 3, 1970, p. 237.

17. Unaddressed and undated letter, NMMP/NMSRCA.

18. Santa Fe *New Mexican*, 06 February 1906; Albuquerque *Morning Journal*, 08 February 1906; "Mounted Police Doing Good Work," Santa Fe *New Mexican*, 06 February 1906; Socorro *Chieftain*, 10 February 1906.

19. Theodore Roosevelt, *California Addresses*, (San Francisco: NP, 1903), pp. 22–23.

20. Ralph Emerson Twitchell, *Leading Facts of New Mexican History, Vol. II*, (Cedar Rapids, Iowa: The Torch Press, 1912), pp. 549–562; Herbert J. Hagerman, *Letters of a Young Diplomat* (Santa Fe: Rydal Press, 1937). This book was published two years after Hagerman's death.
President Theodore Roosevelt was an enthusiastic disciple of astrology. He had his natal horoscope mounted on a chessboard and studied it daily. He may even have made his administrative actions and appointments based upon the stars.

21. *Herbert. J. Hagerman Memoirs* manuscript, James John Hagerman Family Papers (MS 104), Box 5, RGHC/ NMSU.

22. Hening, *George Curry*, pp. 193 and 199.

23. Alex Street Data File, NMMP/AC.

24. Letter: Will Dudley to Capt. Fullerton, 23 July 1905, Letters Received, NMMP/NMSRCA; The Tucumcari *News*, 17 February 1906.

25. Letter: Gov. Hagerman to Alex Street, 12 February 1906, Gov. H.J. Hagerman Papers, NMSRCA.

26. The Socorro *Chieftain*, 10 February 1906; Letter: Capt. Fullerton to Gov. Hagerman, 09 February 1906, Letters Received, Gov. H.J. Hagerman Papers, NMSRCA.

27. Letter: Gov. Hagerman to Capt. Fullerton, 12 February 1906, Letters Received, NMMP/NMSRCA.

28. Letter: J.A. Street to Attorney General Prichard, 14 February 1906, Letters Received, Attorney General Records, NMSRCA.

29. Letters: Gov. Hagerman to Sheriff J.R. Lowry, 26 January 1906; Gov. Hagerman to A.G. Wells, general manager, AT&SF RR, 29 January 1906; Gov. Hagerman and Fred Fornoff to Sheriff Lowry, 03 February 1906, Letters Sent, NMMP/NMSRCA; "Alleged Confession Of Murder," Santa Fe *New Mexican*, 26 January 1906; "Rumors Say That Bell Now Denies," Santa Fe *New Mexican*, 27 January 1906; "Frank Bell Has Made Confession," Santa Fe *New Mexican*, 29 January 1906; "Governor Puzzled," Santa Fe *New Mexican*, 02 February 1906; "New Mexico Does Not Desire Bell," Santa Fe *New Mexican*, 06 February 1906.

30. Letter: Gov. Hagerman to U.S. Marshal Foraker, 29 January 1906, Letters Sent, Gov. H.J. Hagerman Papers, NMSRCA.

31. Federal Contingent Expense Account of the Office of the Governor of New Mexico, 1st Quarter ending 31 March 1905, Gov. H.J. Hagerman Papers, NMSRCA.

32. "The Governor intimated that there might be some question as to Mr. Fornoff's experience, although he did it in such a way as to convey no information or intimation of the status of his own mind on that point." Letter: Chief Deputy U.S. Marshal George Kaseman to W.C. Reid, 05 February 1906, Letters Sent, USMP/CSR/UNM.

33. Letter: Gov. Hagerman to Fornoff, 17 February 1906, Letters Sent, Gov. H.J. Hagerman Papers, NMSRCA.

34. "Conley Cut Throat To Cheat Gallows," Santa Fe *New Mexican*, 26 February 1906.

35. This idea is discussed in a previous chapter. Fred Fornoff and Ben Williams had captured Claude Doane, New Mexico's "most wanted outlaw," in July 1905.

36. Letter: W.P. Sanders to Gov. Hagerman, 15 February 1906, Letters Received, Gov. H.J. Hagerman Papers, NMSRCA.

37. Letter: Gov. Hagerman to W.P. Sanders, 20 February 1906, Letters Sent, Gov. H.J. Hagerman Papers, NMSRCA.

38. Friedrich Wilhelm Nietzshe (1844–1900) proclaimed that men must use ruthless self-assertion to achieve human perfection and that force was morally justified to reach that goal of perfection.

39. Letter: W.P. Sanders to Gov. Hagerman, 15 February 1906, Letters Received, Gov. H.J. Hagerman Papers, NMSRCA.

40. Letter: W.P. Sanders to Gov. Hagerman, 26 February 1906, Letters Received, Gov. H.J. Hagerman Papers, NMSRCA.

41. Letter: W.P. Sanders to Gov. Hagerman, 15 February 1906, Letters Received, Gov. H.J. Hagerman Papers, NMSRCA.

42. The two letters written by Sanders to the governor were on the Cattle and Horse Protective Association of Central New Mexico letterhead, copies in NMMP/AC. The Cattle and Horse Protective Association of Central New Mexico was formed for "the purpose of protecting stock raisers from the depredations of many cattle rustlers operating in New Mexico." The association had 100 members in the summer of 1901. San Marcial *Bee*, 27 June 1901.

43. Santa Fe *New Mexican*, 23 February 1905.

44. Letter: Baca's Report, 08 July 1905, Letters Received, NMMP/NMSRCA; "Captures Cattle Thieves And Stolen Stock," Santa Fe *New Mexican*, 09 August 1905; "Mounted Police Corral Notorious Cattle Rustlers," Albuquerque *Morning Journal*, 10 August 1905.

45. *New Mexico Coded Law 1905*, Chapter 9 Mounted Police.

46. "Mounted Police," The Estancia *News*, 01 September 1905, reprinted from the *San Juan Index*.

47. Socorro *Chieftain*, 16 September and 23 September 1905. One of the charges leveled against

Sheriff Leandro Baca, when Gov. Hagerman removed him from office, was that he kept loose records and was overbilling Socorro County for his services. Another charge was that the sheriff was running a gambling table in a Socorro saloon. Interestingly, a few years later Leandro Baca was appointed a mounted police under Captain Fred Fornoff.

48. Letter: Captain Fullerton to W.Z. Redding, 25 August 1905, Letter Sent, NMMP/NMSRCA.

49. Letter: Sanders to Governor Hagerman (with a copy of Sheriff Boone Vaughn's statement), 15 February 1906, Letters Received, Gov. H.J. Hagerman Papers, NMSRCA.

50. Letter: Eduardo Martinez to Gov. Hagerman, 08 February 1906, Letters Received, NMMP/NMSRCA.

51. Letter: Gov. Hagerman to Eduardo Martinez, 09 February 1906, Letters Sent, Gov. H.J. Hagerman Papers, NMSRCA.

52. Letters: Gov. Hagerman to Capt. Fullerton, 09 February 1906; Capt. Fullerton to Gov. Hagerman, 10 February 1906, Gov. Hagerman to Capt. Fullerton, 12 February 1906, Letters Received/Letters Sent, Gov. H.J. Hagerman Papers, NMSRCA; "Mounted Police Good Work," Socorro *Chieftain*, 17 February 1906.

53. "After The Desperadoes In The Mogollons" (editorial), Santa Fe *New Mexican*, 24 February 1906.

54. On the same day that Fullerton was sent a 'bad-news' messenger, Penitentiary Warden Holm Bursum also had a visitor. "I hereby acknowledge receipt of you verbal message, conveyed by special messenger, stating your desire to obtain my resignation." Letter: H.O. Bursum to Gov. Hagerman, 19 March 1906, James John Hagerman Papers MS104, RGHC/NMSU. The author has found no proof to prove that Fullerton actually received Hagerman's message on 19 March.

55. Will Fullerton's remarks concerning his brother were published in the Albuquerque *Evening Citizen*, 19 March 1906; "Fornoff For Captain Of Mounted Police," Santa Fe *New Mexican*, 21 March 1906.

56. "Fornoff For Captain Of Mounted Police," Santa Fe *New Mexican,* 21 March 1906.

57. "Fornoff Gets The Job," Albuquerque *Morning Journal,* 26 March 1906.

58. Letter: Unknown to James G. Fitch, 30 March 1906, Letters Sent, Gov. H.J. Hagerman Papers, NMSRCA.

59. There many excellent books dealing with the Spanish-American War. Read Theodore Roosevelt's *The Rough Riders* (New York: Signet Classics, 1961, reprint of the 1899 edition) for a personal account of his life within the Rough Rider regiment.

60. When newspaper publisher Alfred Henry Lewis asked President Roosevelt for some information about George Curry the president replied, "You can find out all about him from Bat Masterson [a columnist for Lewis' newspaper] as he was one of Bat's deputies in the old days at Dodge City [Kansas]." Letter: President Roosevelt to Lewis, 27 July 1907, Letters Sent, Theodore Roosevelt Papers, NA. Masterson served one term as Ford County (Kan.) sheriff in the late 1870s. Curry was only a teenager at the time and no official records show that he ever worked for Masterson.

61. In 1908 Hagerman wrote and "Printed for Private Circulation" a small booklet entitled *Matters Relating to the Administration and Removal of Herbert J. Hagerman Governor of New Mexico 1906–1907* to explain his conduct as chief executive. Fullerton is only mentioned once, on page 11, among a list of administrative changes authorized by Hagerman.

62. Former Gov. Hagerman sent Captain Fornoff a warm personal letter and a signed photograph at the time of Fred's wedding in 1910. At another time, Hagerman gave Fred a special engraved presentation pearl handle, silver plated Colt .45 as a gift. This pistol was stolen from Fornoff's home, most likely by a next door neighbor kid, in January 1926. Conversation Notes: Fred Fornoff, Jr., and author, 28 March 1991, NMMP/AC. Lost for decades, Fornoff's Colt revolver was located in the late 1990s and is now part of a private western history collection along with the captain's NMMP lapel badge and beaded watch fob.

63. Santa Fe *New Mexican*, 20 March 1906.

64. "Governor Requests Resignations," *San Juan County Index,* 30 March 1905. This editorial was written by owner/editor E.P. Wilson.

65. When Fullerton's letter was published in some newspapers the date was misprinted as the 16th.

Maybe this was the final omen. Among the first was the misdating of the official stamp on the muster roll filed in the Secretary of the Territory's Office. The year was stamped "1900" not "1905" as it should have been. Was this some kind of 'spirit prank' suggesting that the police should have been formed five years earlier?

66. When Fullerton's letter was published some newspapers used the word 'commonwealth' here.

67. Letter: Capt. Fullerton to Gov. Hagerman, 26 March 1906, James John Hagerman Papers (MS 104), Box 4, File 4, RGHC/NMSU.

68. "Mounted Police Captain Resigns," Santa Fe *New Mexican,* 27 March 1906; "Changes Unlooked For," Deming *Graphic,* 30 March 1906. Historians of territorial law enforcement will note the similarities between John Fullerton's removal as mounted police captain and that of Burton C. Mossman as Arizona ranger captain. Both men were the founder and first leader of their territory's ranger force, both were businessmen and ranchers, both men left office after only one year of public service, both men left office amidst controversy about the way they had conducted their office and managed their ranger command, and both men were overshadowed by their successors.

Chapter 12

1. Fred Fornoff, *Operations Report of the Mounted Police,* July 1906, NMMP/NMSRCA.

2. Albuquerque *Evening Citizen*, 02 April 1906.

3. Letter: Meyer to Fred Fornoff, 31 March 1906, Letters Received, NMMP/NMSRCA.

4. "Reorganization Mounted Police Effected Today," Santa Fe *New Mexican*, 02 April 1906.

5. Mounted Police Appointment Notices, Oaths of Office, NMMP/NMSRCA.

6. "Are Sworn Into Office," Santa Fe *New Mexican*, 01 April 1905.

Chapter 13

1. "Reorganization Mounted Police Effected Today," Santa Fe *New Mexican*, 02 April 1906.
2. The Socorro *Chieftain*, 21 April 1906.
3. Albuquerque *Evening Citizen*, 12 April 1905; The Clayton *Enterprise*, 27 April 1905; "Mounted Police Want Raise," The Tucumcari *News*, 21 April 1905.
4. Letter: Captain Fullerton to Messrs. Boulware & Eno, Silver City, N.M., 14 September 1905, Letters Sent, NMMP/NMSRCA.
5. Letter: Captain Fullerton to James Patterson, Patterson, N.M., 14 September 1905, Letters Sent, NMMP/NMSRCA.
6. Proclamations, Gov. H.J. Hagerman Papers, NMSRCA.
7. Letter: Captain Fullerton to Gov. Hagerman, 26 March 1906, Letters Sent, NMMP/NMSRCA.
8. Appointments, Gov. H.J. Hagerman Papers, NMSRCA.
9. Conversation Notes: Irene Fullerton and author, Albuquerque, N.M., 28 July 1984, NMMP/AC. The Bryan mistake information is taken from an Associated Press news clip from December 1907, News Clip File, NMMP/AC.
10. *Mining Claims Book A-1*, County Clerk's Office, Torrance County Courthouse, Estancia, N.M.; Conversation Notes, Susan Leverett and author, Albuquerque, N.M., 13 July 1995, NMMP/AC.
11. Conversation Notes: Irene Fullerton, Susan Leverett and author, Albuquerque, N.M., 24 July 1984, NMMP/AC; "Robbed Captain Fullerton," Magdalena *News* reprinted in Santa Fe *New Mexican*, 13 April 1912.
12. Conversation notes: Irene Fullerton and author, Albuquerque, NM, 28 July 1984, NMMP/AC; *Marriage Record Book 1885–(ND)*, County Clerk's Office, Socorro County Courthouse, Socorro.
13. The Socorro *Chieftain*, of 22 June 1901, mentions Mrs. Sleight and her daughter.
14. Conversation Notes: Susan Leverett and author, Albuquerque, N.M., 25 August 1997, NMMP/AC.
15. Conversation Notes: Susan Leverett and author, Albuquerque, N.M., 25 August 1997, NMMP/AC.
16. John Fullerton also lost his third interest in his father's 160 acre homestead ranch. Conversation Notes: Irene Fullerton, Susan Leverett and author, Albuquerque, N.M., 13 July and 28 July 1984, NMMP/AC; *Deed Book 84*, County Clerk's Office, Socorro County Courthouse, Socorro, N.M. Today, the San Agustin Plain is home to the 27 dish antennas of the National Radio Astronomy Observatory. The Very Large Array (VLA) is used to probe the universe and reaches trillions of miles into space seeking proof of extraterrestrial life. Nancy Plevin, "Gigantic Radio Telescope to Peer at Universe's Edge," San Angelo (Texas) *Standard Times*, 09 August 1992.
17. Conversation Notes: Irene Fullerton, Susan Leverett and author, Albuquerque, N.M., 13 July and 24 July 1995, 25 August 1997, NMMP/AC.
18. Helen Marie Purdy Fullerton Probate Records (1947), Probate Court Clerk's Office, Bernalillo County Courthouse, Albuquerque, N.M.
19. Letter: Captain Fullerton to E.P. Blinn, 27 July 1905, Letters Sent, NMMP/NMSRCA. John Fullerton was no stranger to the Duke City. As early as 1898, he was reported doing business in the town. One local newspaper even refereed to him as "Captain Fullerton", but the author has found no explanation for this title. Albuquerque *Morning Democrat*, 02 January 1898.
20. "Roll of Students," *New Mexico School of Mines Annual Bulletin 1902–1903,1903–1904*, and *1904–1905*; Socorro *Chieftain*, 29 December 1906 and 10 January 1907.
21. Conversation Notes: Irene Fullerton and author, Albuquerque, N.M., 28 July 1984, NMMP/AC; *Socorro Chieftain*, 09 December 1906 and 26 August 1911.
22. History of Torrance County, N.M.
23. See Bob L'Aloge's *The Incident of New Mexico's Nightriders, A True Account of the Socorro Vigilantes* (Sunnyside, Wash.: Box BJS Brand Books, 1992) for a brief account of Col. Eaton's life and the actions of the citizen lawmen of Socorro.
24. Conversation Notes: Irene Fullerton and Susan Leverett and the author, Albuquerque, N.M., 24 July 1984 and 21 July 1997, NMMP/AC.
25. Letter: Irene Fullerton to author, 22 June 1984, NMMP/AC.
26. It is interesting to note that both the son of John Fullerton and the eldest son of Fred Fornoff enjoyed careers as shoe salesmen.
27. Conversation Notes: Irene Fullerton, Susan Leverett and the author, Albuquerque, N.M., 24 July 1995 and 21 July 1997, NMMP/AC. In 1920, the Elmer Fullerton family was living at 511 West Mountain Street in Albuquerque. Later they moved to 314 North 10th Street. Justin LaFont, Irene's 13-year-old brother, was living with the couple while he attended school. Fourteenth Census of the United States (1920), Albuquerque, Bernalillo County, New Mexico, Microfilm T 625, Roll 04, NA.
28. Conversation Notes: Susan Leverett and the author, Albuquerque, N.M., 21 July 1997 and 24 July 1995, NMMP/AC.
29. Conversation Notes: Susan and Bill Leverett and author, Albuquerque, N.M., 08–09 July 2002, NMMP/AC.
30. John F. Fullerton Death Certificate, California Department of Health Service, State Registrar of Vital Statistics, Sacramento, Calif. John Fullerton died intestate and his son filed a petition to be administrator of his father's estate. Elmer had to post a $400 performance bond to dispose of his father's estate that amounted to only $200 in personal property. In court documents Elmer testified that he did not know if his father owned any real estate at the time of his death. Estate of John F. Fullerton, Case No. 390, Probate Court Records, Socorro County Courthouse, Socorro, N.M.
31. Burial records and location map, Greenwood Memorial Park, San Diego, Calif.; "Pioneer Ranger Dies in San Diego, Capt. J.F. Fullerton, Cattleman of New Mexico, Had Come to See Daughter," San Diego *Union*, 27 January 1928; "Former Ranger Dies at Daughter's Home, Pioneer Cattleman of New Mexico is Dead," San Diego *Sun*, 27 January 1928.

The necrology references to Mrs. Nannie Kutzner as John's daughter are incorrect. She was his older sister. The west coast press also reported that John Fullerton's body would "be sent by the Johnson-Saum Company to Socorro, N.M. for funeral service and interment." Elmer had him buried with his family in California.

32. Conversation Notes: Susan Leverett and author, Albuquerque, N.M., 25 August 1997, NMMP/AC.

33. Letter: Irene Fullerton to author, 24 July 1984, NMMP/AC

Bibliography

Primary Published Sources

BOOKS AND ARTICLES

Adams, Clarence S., ed. *Little Town West of the Pecos 1909*. Roswell: New Mexico Pioneer Printing, 1983.
Albuquerque City Directory. NP: 1907.
Avant, Bundy (as told to Arthur Clements). "The Bundy Avant Story." *True West*, Part I, May-June 1978, and Part II, July-August 1978.
Berlin, Ira, et al. (editors). "Testimony of the Superintendent of Contraband," *Freedom: A Documentary History of Emancipation 1862–1867, Series I, Vol. I: The Destruction of Slavery*. New York: Cambridge University Press, 1985.
Bryan, Howard. "Guns Governed NM at Turn of the Century." Albuquerque *Tribune*, 17 July 1984.
_____. "Off the Beaten Path." Albuquerque *Tribune*, 12 April 1954, 11 April 1957, 09 February 1967 and 21 June 1984.
Frost, Max, and Paul A.F. Walter (editors). *The Land of Sunshine*. Santa Fe: Bureau of Immigration, Territory of New Mexico, 1906.
Hagerman, Herbert J. *Letters of a Young Diplomat*. Santa Fe: Rydal Press, 1937.
_____. *Memoirs*. Unpublished manuscript.
_____. *Report of the Governor of New Mexico to the Secretary of the Interior, 1906*. Washington: Government Printing Office, 1906.
History of Lewis, Clark, Knox and Scotland Counties, Missouri. NP: 1887.
Hovey, Walters. "Black Jack Ketchum Tried to Give Me a Break!" *True West*, April 1972.
Moore, Sam. *Through The Shadow: A Boy's Memories*. Clark County (Va.) Historical Society, ND.
Otero, Miguel A. *My Nine Years as Governor of the Territory of New Mexico 1897–1906*. Albuquerque: University of New Mexico Press, 1940.
_____. *Report of the Governor of New Mexico to the Secretary of the Interior 1904*. Washington: Government Printing Office, 1904.
_____. *Report of the Governor of New Mexico to the Secretary of the Interior 1905*. Washington: Government Printing Office, 1905.
Pocket Map and Shippers' Guide of New Mexico. Chicago: Rand McNally, 1905.
Sears, Roebuck & Co. Catalogue. Chicago: Sears, Roebuck & Co., Vol. 104 (1897), Vol. 111 (1902) and Vol. 117 (1908).
Twitchell, Ralph Emerson. *Leading Facts of New Mexican History, Vol. II*. Cedar Rapids, Iowa: Torch Press, 1912.
White, Virgil D. (abstractor). *Genealogical Abstracts of Revolutionary War Pension Files*, Vol. VII F-M. Waynesboro, Tenn.: National Historical Publishing, 1991.

Published Interviews with Sgt./Lt. Robert W. "Stuttering Bob" Lewis

Bryan, Howard. "Billy the Kid Alive, Bob Lewis Believes." Albuquerque *Tribune*, 25 May 1949.
_____. "Fountain Slain by Ketchum, Pioneer NM Officer Asserts." Albuquerque *Tribune*, 24 May 1949.
_____. "Lost Adams Diggings Gold Sold Here, Pioneer Says." Albuquerque *Tribune*, 23 May 1949
_____. "NM Pioneer Stores His Guns and Spurs." Albuquerque *Tribune*, 26 May 1949.
Maxwell, Grant. "Cow Town." *New Mexico Magazine*, October 1935.

Secondary Published Sources

Ashcroft, Bruce. *The Territorial History of Socorro, New Mexico*. El Paso: Texas Western Press, 1988.
Ball, Larry D. *Desert Lawmen: The High Sheriffs of New Mexico and Arizona 1846–1912*. Albuquerque: University of New Mexico Press, 1992.
_____. *The United States Marshals of New Mexico and Arizona Territories 1846–1912*. Albuquerque: University of New Mexico Press, 1978.
Baydo, Gerald. "Cattlemen's Associations in New Mexico Territory," *Journal of the West*, V13 #3, July 1975.
Blakested, Alice (complied by). *Gravesite Directory of Cemeteries in Lincoln County*. Hondo, N.M.: Lincoln County Historical Society Publication, 2001.
Campbell, Hannah. *Why Did They Name It…?: The Story Behind the Stories of the Brand Names That Have Become Household Words Throughout the World*. New York: Ace Books, 1964.
Charles, Mrs. Tom. *Tales of the Tularosa*. Alamogordo, N.M.: Private, 1953.
DeArment, Robert K. *George Scarborough: The Life and Death of a Lawman on the Changing Frontier*. Norman: University of Oklahoma Press, 1992.
Friedman, Stanton T., and Don Berliner. *Crash at Corona*. New York: Marlowe & Company, 1992.
Grove, Pearce S., Barnett, Beck J., and Hansen, Sandra J. (editors). *New Mexico Newspapers, A Comprehensive Guide to Bibliographical Entries and Locations*. Albuquerque: University of New Mexico, 1965.
Harvey, Clara Toombs. *Not So Wild, The Old West*. Denver: Golden Bell Press, 1961.
Hening, H.B. (editor). *George Curry, 1861–1947: An Autobiography*. Albuquerque: University of New Mexico Press, 1958.
Hornung, Chuck. "Cipriano Baca, New Mexico Lawman." *Real West*, December 1981.
_____. "Cipriano Baca, New Mexico Peace Officer." *The Journal* (Western Outlaw-Lawman History Association), Spring/Summer 1996.
_____. "The Fornoff Report: New Light on the Death of Pat Garrett." *True West*, March 1998.
_____. "Fred Lambert, The Dean of New Mexico Lawmen." Raton (N.M.) *Daily Range* (Associated Press) 23 January 1971.
_____. "Fred Lambert Was The Youngest Member Of Famed Territorial Mounted Police." Raton (N.M.) *Daily Range* (Associated Press) 06 February 1972.
_____. "Fullerton's Rangers." *Tombstone Epitaph National Edition*, VIII: 1, January 1981.
_____. "George M. Elkins, The Cowboy Ranger." *Real West*, October 1984.
_____. "John Collier and the Ghost Girl." *The Roadrunner* (New Mexico State Police Association), Summer 1989.
_____. "Law Enforcement in the Land of Enchantment: Territorial Mounted Police to State Police." *The Journal* (Western Outlaw-Lawmen History Association), Winter 1999.
_____. "Lawmen Were People, Too." *Real West*, November 1979.
_____. "The Motor Pony: Fred Lambert and the Mounted Police's First Motorcycle Patrol." *The West*, August 1970.
_____. "The New Mexico Territorial Mounted Police." *The English Westerner's Tally Sheet*, Part 1, XXV: 2, January 1979; Part 2, XXV: 3, April 1979.
_____. "Surprising New Information on Pat Garrett's Death: Details from the Fornoff Report."

The Journal (Western Outlaw-Lawman History Association), Spring/Summer 1997.

_____. "They Called Him 'Stuttering Bob': Robert W. Lewis, New Mexico Lawman." *Quarterly of the National Association and Center for Outlaw and Lawmen History,* October–December 1998.

_____. *The Thin Gray Line: The New Mexico Mounted Police.* Fort Worth: Western Heritage Press, 1971.

_____. "Wind Jammer John: The Ghost Girl and the Bruja." *Real West*, March 1982.

Hunter, J. Marvin. *The Story of Lottie Deno: Her Life and Times.* Bandera, Texas: The 4 Hunters, 1959.

Julyan, Robert. *The Place Names of New Mexico.* Albuquerque: University of New Mexico Press, 1996.

Knights of Pythias Fact Booklet, No publisher, no date.

L'Aloge, Bob. *The Incident of New Mexico's Nightriders.* Sunnyside, Wash.: Box BJS Brand Books, 1992.

Larson, Robert W. "New Mexico Progressives." *New Mexico Historical Review* XLV: 3, 1970.

_____. *New Mexico's Quest For Statehood 1846–1912.* Albuquerque: University of New Mexico Press, 1986.

Lentz, Harris M., III. *Television Westerns Episode Guide.* Jefferson, N.C.: McFarland, 1997.

McCord, Monty. *Law Enforcement Memorabilia.* Iola, Wis.: Krause Publications, 1999.

Miller, Joseph. *The Arizona Rangers.* New York: Hastings House, 1972.

Myrick, David F. *New Mexico Railroads, An Historical Survey.* Golden: Colorado Railroad Museum, 1970.

O'Neal, Bill. *The Arizona Rangers.* Austin, Texas: Eakin Press, 1987.

Pearce, T.M. (editor). *New Mexico Place Names, A Geographical Dictionary.* Albuquerque: University of New Mexico Press, 1965.

Plevin, Nancy. "Gigantic Radio Telescope to Peer at Universe's Edge." San Angelo (Texas) *Standard Times*, 09 August 1992.

Prassel, Frank Richard. *The Western Peace Officer, A Legacy of Law and Order.* Norman: University of Oklahoma Press, 1972.

Remley, David. *Bell Ranch, Cattle Ranching in the Southwest 1824–1947.* Las Cruces, N.M.: Yucca Tree Press, 2000.

Rynning, Thomas H. (as told to Al Cohn and Joe Chisholm). *Gun Notches: The Life of a Cowboy-Soldier.* New York: Fredrick A. Stokes Co., 1931.

Scotland County, Missouri: In Retrospect. Memphis, Mo.: Scotland County Bicentennial Committee and Scotland County Historical Society, 1977.

Simmons, Marc. "Hunting Expedition Came Back With Bigger Game Than Expected." New Mexican Scrapbook, El Paso *Times*, 02 February 1986.

Speed, Capt. Thomas. *The Union Cause in Kentucky 1860–1865.* New York: G.P. Putman & Sons, 1907.

Spellman, Paul N. *Captain John H. Rogers, Texas Ranger.* Denton, Texas: University of North Texas Press, 2003.

Sunseri, Alvin R. *Seeds Of Discord, New Mexico in the Aftermath of the American Conquest 1846–1861.* Chicago: Nelson-Hall, 1979.

Weiss, Harold J., Jr. "Organized Constabularies: The Texas Rangers and the Early State Police Movement in the American West." *Journal of the West*, XXXIV: 1, January 1995.

Government Record Centers and Archives

NEW MEXICO STATE RECORDS CENTER AND ARCHIVES, SANTA FE (NMSRCA)

Attorney General: Biennial Report 1905–1906
Attorney General Records and Opinions (Roll 54)
Gov. Herbert J. Hagerman Papers (Rolls 156–163)
Gov. Miguel A. Otero Papers (Rolls 128–155)

Health and Social Services Department Records
Journal of the Council 1899 (Roll 13) and 1905 (Roll 17)
Journal of the House of Representatives 1899 (Roll 13) and 1905 (Roll 17)
Journal of the Supreme Court of New Mexico 1913
Laws of New Mexico 1912
New Mexico Coded Laws 1897, 1899, 1905, 1907 and 1909
New Mexico Mounted Police Records (Rolls 91–93)
Records of the Council of Defense (1917–1919): New Mexico Mounted Police File
Records of the Secretary of the Territory: Executive Record Book (Rolls 23– 24)
Territorial Auditor Records (Rolls 47–52)
Territorial Fish and Game Warden Records
Territorial Prison Records (Rolls 01–03)
Territorial Treasurer Records (Roll 44–46)

ARIZONA DEPARTMENT OF LIBRARY, ARCHIVES AND PUBLIC RECORDS, PHOENIX (AZ ARCHIVES)

Acts, Resolutions and Memorials ... Territory of Arizona 1903
Arizona Ranger Records (Records Group 42)
Council Journal 1901
Gov. J. H. Kibby 1905 Annual Report
House of Representative Journal 1901
Revised Statutes of Arizona Territory 1901

TEXAS STATE LIBRARY AND ARCHIVES COMMISSION, AUSTIN (TX ARCHIVES)

Bi-annual Report of the Adjutant General 1891–1892 and 1900–1901
Ranger Force Records, Ranger Records, Texas Adjutant General Department Records

NATIONAL ARCHIVES AND RECORDS CENTER, WASHINGTON, D.C. (NARC)

Civil War Service Records, Duty Records, Pension Records: James S. Fullerton
Journal of the Congress of the Confederate States of America, Vol. I (1861)
1870 U.S. Census, Scotland County, Missouri
1880 U.S. Census, Pima County, Arizona Territory
1900 U.S. Census, Santa Fe County, New Mexico Territory
1900 U.S. Census, Sierra County, New Mexico Territory
1910 U.S. Census, Torrance County, New Mexico Territory
1920 U.S. Census, Bernalillo County, New Mexico
1920 U.S. Census, Luna County, New Mexico
1920 U.S. Census, Torrance County, New Mexico
1920 U.S. Census, Union County, New Mexico

NEW MEXICO COUNTY RECORDS, COUNTY COURTHOUSES

Bernalillo County: Probate Court Records
Catron County: Deed Records
Colfax County: Jail Calendar
Luna County: Oaths of Office File, Deed Records, Birth Records, Death Records, and Commissioner Proceedings
Socorro County: District Court Criminal Docket, Oaths of Office File, Bond Records, Deed Records, Mining Claim Records, Probate Court Records and Marriage Records
Torrance County: Mining Claim Records, Marriage Records and Bounty Records
Union County: Probate Court Records, Oaths of Office File, and Bond Records

Center for Southwest Research, University of New Mexico, Albuquerque (CSR/UNM)

Holm O. Bursum Papers
Otero-Stinson Collection and Papers (506)
United States Marshal Records, Territory of New Mexico

Rio Grande Historical Collection, New Mexico State University, Las Cruces

The Colligate, New Mexico State University newspaper
James John Hagerman Family Papers (MS 104)

Fray Angelico Chavez Library, Museum of New Mexico, Sante Fe

Welch and Titsworth Store (Captain) Business Records
Atchison Topeka and Santa Fe Railroad—New Mexico Division Records

New Mexico Tech University Library, Socorro, N.M.

New Mexico School of Mines Annual Bulletin
Roll of Students, New Mexico School of Mines 1900–1907

Miscellaneous Public Records

Burial Records, Concordia Cemetery, El Paso, Texas
Burial Records, Deming Cemetery, Deming, N.M.
Burial Records, Evergreen Cemetery, El Paso, Texas
Burial Records, Fairview Park Cemetery, Albuquerque, N.M.
Burial Records, Greenwood Memorial Park, San Diego, Calif.
Burial Records, Kilburn Cemetery, Clayton, N.M.
Burial Records, Rosario Catholic Cemetery, Santa Fe, N.M.
Burial Records, Socorro Cemetery, Socorro, N.M.
Burial Records, Sunset Memorial Park, Albuquerque, N.M.
City Directory Collection 1925–1980, Southwest Collection, Albuquerque Public Library
Death Records, State of California, Sacramento, Calif.
Deed Book 27, Marriage License Book I, County Clerk's Office, Crosby County Courthouse, Crosbyton, Texas
District Court Records (1918), Sedgwick County Courthouse, Wichita, Kan.
Genealogy Collection, Midland County Public Library, Midland, Texas.
Illinois Executive Record Book 1837–1843, Gov. Carlin Papers, Illinois State Library and Archives, Springfield, Ill.
Southwest Collection, Ector Couty Public Library, Odessa, Texas.
Tombstone Marker, Willard Cemetery, Willard, N.M.

Private Records, Family Papers and Collections

Private Records

Marriage Records, Church of the Epiphany, Socorro, N.M.
Minute Book, First Baptist Church, Herington, Kan.
Record of Membership, Book I, First Presbyterian Church, Memphis, Mo.

Family Papers and Memorabilia

Fate Avant Papers, Jettie Sullenger, Mountainair, N.M.
Cipriano Baca Papers, Cipriana Baca Randolph, Long Beach, Calif.
Will Dudley Papers, Frank Shofner, Albuquerque, N.M.
George Elkins Papers, Hatchet Ranch Archives, Hachita, N.M.
Fred Fornoff Papers, Fred Fornoff, Jr., Los Lunas, N.M.
John F. Fullerton Papers, Susan Leverett, Albuquerque, N.M.
Herbert J. McGrath Papers, Tom McGrath, Las Vegas, N.M.
Julius Meyer Papers, The Meyer Families, Albuquerque, N.M.

The Haley Memorial Library and History Center, Midland, Texas

Brand Book of the Territory of New Mexico 1900
Robert N. Mullin Interview Collection

Private Collections

Chuck Hornung Mounted Police Collection (NMMP/AC)
New Mexico Territorial Newspapers, W.A. Kelleher Collection, Albuquerque
Anthony Sapienza Western History Collection, Paramus, N.J.

Newspaper Collections and Archives

New Mexico Newspapers

Albuquerque *Evening Citizen*
Albuquerque *Herald*
Albuquerque *Morning Journal*
Albuquerque *Tribune*
Alamogordo *Daily Journal*
Alamogordo *News*
(Alamogordo) *Otero County Advertiser*
(Aztec) *San Juan County Index*
Capitan *News*
Capitan *Progress*
(Carlsbad) *The Pecos Valley Argus*
Carrizozo *Outlook/Southwestern Outlook*
Clayton *Citizen*
Clayton *Enterprise*
Clayton *News*
Deming *Graphic*
Deming *Headlight*
Estancia *News*
Farmington *Enterprise*
Las Cruces *Citizen*
Las Vegas *Daily Optic*
Las Vegas *Weekly Optic & Live Stock Grower*
(Lordsburg) *Western Liberal*
Magdalena *Mountain Mail*
Magdalena *News*
Nogal *Republican*
Portales *Herald*
Roswell *Register*
San Marcial *Bee*

Santa Fe *New Mexican*
Silver City *Enterprise*
Silver City *Independent*
Socorro *Chieftain*
Tucumcari *News and Tucumcari Times*
(Tucumcari) *Quay County Democrat*
White Oaks *Outlook*

OTHER NEWSPAPERS

Alpine (Texas) *Times*
Dallas (Texas) *Morning News*
Denver (Colo.) *Republican*
Durango (Colo.) *Evening Herald*
El Paso (Texas) *Evening News*
El Paso (Texas) *Times*
(Flagstaff, Ariz.) *The Coconino Sun*
The Herington (Kan.) *Times*
Lubbock (Texas) *Avalanche-Journal*
Memphis (Mo.) *National Democrat*
Midland (Texas) *Reporter-Telegram*
The New York (N.Y.) *Herald*
The New York (N.Y.) *Times*
Nogales (Ariz.) *Border Vidette*
Odessa (Texas) *American*
San Angelo (Texas) *Standard Times*
San Diego (Calif.) *Sun*
San Diego (Calif.) *Union*
Solomonville (Ariz.)*Bulletin*
Tombstone (Ariz.) *Epitaph*
Tombstone (Ariz.) *Prospector*
Tucson (Ariz.) *Citizen*

Index

Abbott, A.J. 147
Abo Pass 115, 149
Adams, John (president) 181
Adams Cattle Company 54
Aken, W.B. 109
Alamo City *see* Alamogordo, NM
Alamogordo, NM 55, 59, 60, 94, 99, 108, 111, 113, 119, 124, 126, 150, 151
Alamogordo News 59, 104, 122, 139
Albuquerque, NM 12, 15, 31, 32, 56, 84, 89, 94, 99, 116, 117, 119, 124, 126, 129, 131, 132, 135, 136, 139, 145, 146, 155, 157, 166, 168, 184, 186, 196, 199–202, 204, 205
Albuquerque Business College 202
Albuquerque Evening Citizen 98, 99, 116, 125, 126, 136, 139, 196
Albuquerque Morning Journal 31, 52, 61, 64, 93, 99, 130, 131, 134, 184, 192, 193
Albuquerque Transfer Company 199, 201
Alice, TX 152
Alma, NM 130
Alpine, TX 152
American Red Cross 59
Anasazi Indians 127
Ancheta, J.H. (councilman) 15, 18
Ancho, NM 101
Angel Peak 127
Angora goats 163
Animas River 127
Animas Valley 105, 106
Anthony, NM 33
Anti-Saloon League of America 11
Anton Chico, NM 139, 192
Apache Indian raid 46, 147
Apache Kid (Zenogalache) 30, 144, 145
Apache Peak 144
Apodaca, Francisco 65, 72, 73, 89, 163, 164
Arbuckle's Ariosa Coffee 10, 84

Arizona and New Mexico Railroad 107
Arizona Rangers 15, 21, 22–28, 29–30, 34, 72, 86, 95, 99, 113, 131, 163, 167, 173, 193
Arizona Territory 23, 27, 29, 30, 32, 34, 51, 101, 104, 107, 117, 132, 144, 146, 185, 188, 190, 193
Arkansas River 105
Armijo, Perfecto 131
Artesia, NM 13
Aspencades 142
Atchison, Topeka & Santa Fe Railroad 66, 84, 88, 149, 157, 188
Aunt Jemima Pancake Mix 10
Automobiles and roads 1, 12
Avant, Ella 62
Avant, Howard 62
Avant, Jessie LaFettie (L.F. or Fate) 62, 101, 110, 111, 113, 118–126, photo 120, 138, 139, 143, 144, 164, 165, 206
Axtell, Samuel B. (governor) 14
Aztec, NM 64, 127, 170, 190

Baca, Abdenago (A.B.) 49, 70, 190
Baca, Cipriana *see* Randolph, Cipriana Baca
Baca, Cipriano (lieutenant) 51–53, 62, 64, 66–69, 72, 73, 76, 79, 82, 90, 93, 99, 101–103, 106, 112, 114, 119, 124, 126–129, photo 128, 137, 139, 141, 144–146, 148, 155, 157–159, photo 158, 166, 170, 173, 183, 190, 191, 206
Baca, Don Celso 158
Baca, Elfego 49, 75, 193, 205
Baca, Florentino 52, 53, 156, 190
Baca, Jose 129, 132, 133
Baca, Jose Sosteno 139
Baca, Leandro 54, 95
Baca, Louis Nazareth 52
Baca, Mary Berry 51–52, 127, 129
Baca Land Grant 116
Bado de Juan Pais 139

Baker, Frank 44
Baker, Halle 44
Baker, the Rev. 44
Baker, Susan Grayson *see* Fullerton, Susan Baker
Bakersfield, CA 31
Baldanero, Pedro 150
Ballard, Charles (councilman) 34
Baptist Church 42, 121
Bar N Ranch 55
Barbee, Claude 154–156
Barelas, NM 131
Barnes, W.C. 126
Bass, Ike 119, 120
Beal, John Alexander 63, 81
Beaty, Clarence (Arizona Ranger) 28
Belen, NM 101, 115, 141, 149
Bell Ranch 94, 138, 139, 186
Bernalillo County, NM 32, 53, 130–133, 166
Bible 10, 127, 143, 187, 206
Big Bend country 152
Big Hatchet Mountains 56
Birchfield, Walt 20
Bisbee, AZ 104
Black River 26
Blackington, Dr. C.F. 153
Blanchard, Phil 120
Blinn, Dr. Elmer 199
Block Ranch 109
Bloomfield, NM 128
Bluewater, NM 145, 146
Bonito River (Rio Bonito) 113, 118, 120
Bootheel section 55, 103–107, 118, 126
Borden, B.B. 199
Brockton, MS 125
Brodie, Alexander Oakes (Arizona governor) 22, 29, 193
Brophy, Frank George 58
Brophy, John Duran 58
Brophy, John James 57–58, 69, 72, 73, 79, 99, 119, 120, 125, 126, 133, 136, 138, 150, 158, 159, 171, 197, 206
Brophy, Rosaria Duran 58
Brownsville, TX 59

253

Index

Bryan, William, Jr. 200
Bull Durham tobacco 11
Burleson, Fannie R. "Grandmother" 113
Burleson, Mary Josephine *see* Dudley, Josie
Burley, NM 157
Burnet, TX 201
Burns, T.D. (councilman) 17
Bursum, Holm (councilman) 30, 67, photo 68, 132–134, 170, 193

Cabbage snake 113, 114
California 31, 32, 57, 60, 73, 86, 204
Canadian Mounted Police 16, 73, 76, 123
Canadian River 138, 140
Capitan, NM 27, 62, 101, 111, 120, 122–125
Capitan Mountains 106, 108, 110, 113, 143, 151
Capitan News 111, 120–122, 141, 163, 164
Capitan Progress 114
Carrizozo, NM 111
Carrizozo Malpais 132
Carthage Coal Camp, NM 63
Catron, Thomas Benton (Councilman) 15, 18, 34, 131
Catron County, NM 54, 130
Cattle and Horse Growers Association of Central New Mexico 189–190
Cerrillos, NM 115
Chaco Canyon 127
Chadbourne, TX 62
Chalk Hills 102
Chambon, Henry 74
Chambon Building, Socorro 74–75, photo 75, 132
Charles Ilfeld Mercantile Company 151, 204
Chaves, Jacobo (councilman) 33
Chaves, James W. "Jimmie" 115, 116
Chaves, Jose Francisco (councilman) 18, 30, 102, 103, 115, 188
Chaves County, NM 18, 141
Chaves Ranch 116, 117
Chenoworth, Howard 151–154
Chesterfield cigarettes 11
Chicago, Rock Island Railroad 99
Christmas 28, 142, 143, 151
Cimarron, NM 3, 142
Cimarron County, OK 58
City of Holy Faith *see* Santa Fe
Claire Hotel, Albuquerque 165, 184
Clancy, Frank W. 167
Claremont, CA 184
Claremore, OK 56
Clark, Ann *see* Fullerton, Ann
Clark, John S. (councilman) 33

Clarke, John R. (Arizona Ranger) 28
Clayton, NM 57, 58, 69, 99, 102, 120, 142, 150, 171
Clayton Enterprise 57, 150, 156, 158
Clear Creek, NM 130
Cleveland, OH 201
Closson, Charles C. 82, 134
Coalora, NM 62, 111, 121, 164
Coca-Cola 10
Cochise County, AZ 109
Cockburn, Thomas 135
Cockfighting 118–119
Coffin, Tris (actor) 28
Colfax County, NM 1, 105
Collier, John Wesley (lieutenant) 20, 81, 150, 151, 197
Colorado 76, 86, 141, 142, 146, 185, 187
Colorado City, TX 152
Columbus, NM 56
Comanche County, TX 53
Coming Men of America 2
Conchas River 140
Congress, United States 18, 125
Connecticut 6, 86
Continental Divide 140
Corbin, A.B. 143
Cornell University 185
Cotulla, TX 62
Cox, Frank 24
Coyote, NM 114
Cream of Wheat 10
Crest Eundo— It Grows As It Goes 6
Crockett County, TX 115
Crosby County, TX 59, 113
Cuchillo Negro 65
Curry, George (governor) 131, 181, 186, 193
Cyanide 11

Dalhart, TX 99
Datil, NM 130, 145, 146
Dawson Coal Camp 2, 52, 59
DeBaca, Ezequiel Cabeza (governor) 1
Delaware 6
Delgado, Lorenzo (captain) 62, 197, 206
Delling, M.G. (Texas Ranger) 152
Deming, NM 32, 51, 63–65, 99, 103, 105
Deming Graphic 101, 138, 195
Deming Headlight 32
Deming Herald 52
Denver, CO 149
Denver & Rio Grande Railroad 141, 145, 146
Denver Republican 93, 144
Department of Indian Affairs 147
Department of the Interior 188
Detroit, MI 143
Diamond A Cattle Company 55

Dils, Harry 202
Doak 20
Doane, Claude 129, 130, 132, 133, 139
Dona Ana County, NM 18, 33
Douglas, AZ 66
Dow, Les 15
Dudley, Josie 59–60, 113, 124
Dudley, Lenon 59
Dudley, Lois Ann *see* Shofner, Lois Ann
Dudley, William E. 2, 59–60, 69, 72, 73, 77, photo 78, 79, 81, 93, 99, 100, 101, 108, 110–113, photo 117, 118, 119, 124, 126, 137–140, 150, 151, 159, 164, 165, 186, 206
Duke City *see* Albuquerque
Dulce, NM 140, 141
Dunaway, J.D. (Texas Ranger) 152
Durango Evening Herald 60, 12

Eagle Brand condensed milk 11
Earp, Wyatt 51
Eaton, Ethan D. 202, 203
Eddy County, NM 18
El Comino Real 115
El Paso, TX 2, 61, 62, 64, 94, 99, 117, 120, 125, 142, 149, 151–154, 165
El Paso and Northeastern Railroad 11, 99, 141
El Paso and Southwestern Railroad 52, 99
El Paso Evening News 98, 151, 157
El Paso, Rock Island Railroad 99, 119, 159
El Paso Times 56, 93, 98, 139, 157, 159
Elephant Butte Lake 27, 63
Elk Mountains 144
Elkins, Chandler 56
Elkins, George M. 6, 55–56, 65, 72, 73, 79, 91, 99, 103, photo 104, 104–107, 155, 164, 165, 170, 206
Embudo, NM 129
Emmett, Caroline Virginia *see* Otero, Caroline
Engle, NM 27, 150
Episcopal Church 204
Epler, Geneva *see* Meyer, Geneva
Estancia, NM 91, 99, 101, 108, 115–117
Estancia News 116
Everheart, M.T. 56

Fall, Albert Bacon 25
Farm Journal 11
Farmington, NM 127, 145
Farnesworth, Charles 99
Faywood Station, NM 65, 110
The FBI Story (motion picture) 186

Index

Federal Bureau of Investigation 186
Ferguson, Amanda J. *see* Fullerton, Amanda
Fernandez, Miguel 115
Fierra, Miguel 109
Fire extinguisher 12
Firearms 12
First Baptist Church, Herington, KS 59
Fitch, James G. 193
Folsom, NM 119, 150
Foraker, Creighton M. (U.S. Marshal) 17, 69, 146, 188
Fornoff, Fred, Jr. 197
Fornoff, Frederick (captain) 1, 2, 48, 56, 63–65, 73, 74, 76, 79, 81, 89, 90, 91, 93, 102, 103, 129, 130, 139, 148, 163, 177–180, 185, 188, 189, 192, 196–198, photo 197, 206
Fornoff Report 102
Fort Craig, NM 202
Fort Defiance, AZ 145
Fort Garland, CO 22
Fort Marcy, NM 181
Fort Stanton, NM 60
Fort Sumner, NM 183
Fort Wingate, NM 203
Fort Worth, TX 113
Fort Worth & Denver City Railroad 99
Fountain, Albert Jennings 15, 30
Fowler, Dr. D.B. 42
Fowler, Joel 203
Frantz, Frank 193
Frisco, NM 130, 144
Fullerton, Amanda J. 38, 42, 202
Fullerton, Ann C. 38
Fullerton, Frank 44
Fullerton, Helen 201
Fullerton, Irene ii, 45, 70, 202–205, photo 203
Fullerton, James M. 38
Fullerton, James S. 38, 41–43, 46, 202
Fullerton, John Elmer 45–46, photo 100, 132, 184, 198, 199, 201–205, photo 202
Fullerton, John Ferguson (captain): agent of the court 199; appointment to NMMP 68–72; boyhood in northeastern Missouri 41–43; Col. Greer's pistol 35; death 204; dismissal from the NMMP 181–195; family heritage 37–38; family life after the rangers 200–205; insurance agent 199; life in Socorro County, NM 44; life in St. Louis 43–44; life on the AJF Ranch 45–49; mining venture at Chloride, NM 45; Mounted Police captain 67–195; oil lease speculations 200–201; photographs ii, 70, 100, 200; separation/ divorce 200
Fullerton, Katharine Lay 48, 49
Fullerton, Milton 168
Fullerton, Nannie Amanda *see* Katzner, Nannie
Fullerton, Raymond Parish 45–46, photo 100
Fullerton, Susan *see* Leverett, Susan
Fullerton, Susan Baker 44, photo 45, 46, photo 100, 204
Fullerton, Walter 39, 41
Fullerton, William Sharpe 43, 47, 49, 192, 199–201

Galisteo, NM 115
Gallinas Cut 99
Gallinas Mountains 159
Gallup, NM 116, 124, 126, 150
Gambling 13
Garrett, Patrick Floyd 15, 102
Gaylord, M.D. 151
Gila River National Forrest Reserve 148
Gillette, King C., safety razor 11, 84
Globe, AZ 159
Glorieta, NM 133–135
Goddard, J. 109
Golden, NM 30
Gomez, Rafael 2, 64–65, 114, 157, 158, 170, 171, 206
Good Housekeeping 10
Gorras Blancas see White Caps fence cutters
Gorrin, M.G., Rev. 42
Graham County, AZ 26
Grant County, NM 2, 18, 30, 33, 51, 52, 62, 63, 69, 99, 103, 104, 109, 110, 151, 152, 155, 159, 169, 170
Greer, A.J. 31
Greer, George 31
Greer, Mary 31
Greer, William H. (councilman) 31–32, picture 31, 38, 55, 98, 104, 107, 112, 135, 136, 180
Guadalupe Canyon 104, 107
Guadalupe County, NM 115, 138, 139, 149, 150, 157, 158, 182, 183

Hachita Junction, NM 99, 103–105, 107, 165, 170
Hacienda de Agua Negra Land Grant 158
Hagerman, Herbert James (governor) 103, 139, 141, 143, 155, 156, 159, 160, 163, 177, 178, 181, 182, 184–195, photo 185, 197, 199, 206
Hagerman, James J. 195
Haley, J.A. 122
Hampstead Act 95

Hataway, Dan (Texas Ranger) 20
Hatchet Mountains 106
Hatchet Ranch 55, 56, 104
Hawkins Act 87–88
Hayden, Russell (actor) 28
Henderson, Kelo (actor) 28
Hepburn Act 88
Herington, KS 59
Hernandez, Benigno Cardenas 14, 138
Heroin 10
Hitchcock, Ethan Allen 185
Higgins, Flora *see* Lewis, Flora
Higgins, Fred 53
Higgins, Pat 54, 144
Hill Oil Placer Mining Claim 200
Hillsboro, NM 30, 65
Homburg Von der Hobe, Germany 182
Hondo Valley 113
Hopalong Cassidy (TV show) 28
Hornung, Chuck 3, 4
Hornung, Scott: photo 3
Hornung, V.J.: photo 3
Horse racing 114, 115
Hot Springs, AK 135
Hot Springs (Truth or Consequences), NM 65
Howell, A.N. 109
Hubbell, Frank 131, 132
Hubbell, Thomas S. 129, 131–134
Huber, Charles Richard "Dick" 2, 61, 65, 78, 82, 93, 101, 107–109, 115–117, 130, 134, 135, 137, 138, 140, 164–169, 184, 193, 197, 206
Huerta, Victoriano (Mexican president) 62
Hunt, Stewart 109
Hunter, J. Marvin 19

Ilfeld, Charles 182, 183
Indian Territory 186
Isleta Pueblo Indians 124
Ivory soap 11

Japan 125
Jarilla (present day Brice), NM 119
Jastro, H.A. 67
Jastro, Mary *see* Greer, Mary
Jaycees 2
Jefferson, Thomas (president) 194
Jell-O 11
Jemez Pueblo Indians 148, 149
Jemez Springs 32
Jesuit School Act 14
Johnson Mesa 105
Johnson-Flynn world heavyweight boxing match 2
Jornada del Muerta 101
Juarez, Mexico 151

Justice Department, special agent 53, 59

Kansas 63, 119
Kansas City Stock Commission 1
Kelly, NM 59, 114, 159
Kenton, OK 58
Kentucky 39, 41, 42, 84, 114
Keresan Indian language 148
Ketchum, Sam 102
Ketchum, Tom "Black Jack" 102
Kibbey, Joseph H. (Arizona governor) 34, 168
Kichne, August 49, 144
Kilburn, W.H. 151
Kimo Theater, Albuquerque 205
Knight, B.F. 101, 102
Knights of Pythias 2, 59, 76, 136, 137
Kutzner, J.C. 38, 47, 201, 202
Kutzner, Nannie 38, 132, 202

La Gran Quivera, NM 143
La Plata River 127
Ladies' Home Journal 10
LaFont, Adophe 202
LaFont, Claudia 202–203
LaFont, Earl 202
LaFont, Irene Grace *see* Fullerton, Irene
LaFont, Justin 202, 204
LaFont farm 204
Laguna Pueblo Indians 157
Lambert, Charles Fredrick "Fred" 2–4, photo 3, 50, 81, 83–85, photo 85, 127, 128
Lambert, Henry 1
Lambert, Katie 1, 4
Lambert, William 1
Las Cruces, NM 28, 84, 108, 145
Las Cruces Citizen 98
Las Lunas, NM 12, 204
Las Vegas, NM 12, 15, 89, 94, 115, 133, 134, 136, 138, 151, 157, 182, 192, 201
Las Vegas Daily Optic 30, 64, 77, 118, 122, 129, 137
Law against carrying arms 12
Law against gambling 13, 149
Law against "red light" district 14
Law against selling alcohol on Sunday 12, 150
Leboron, Ala 53
Letters of a Young Diplomat 185
Leverett, Sheila F. 205
Leverett, Susan 71, 201, photo 203, 204, 205
Leverett, William J. 205
Lewis, Ben 53
Lewis, Ben II 55
Lewis, Carlyne 53
Lewis, Carrie 55
Lewis, Flora 54, 55, 154, 156
Lewis, Patrick 55, 203
Lewis, Robert W. (sergeant) 1, 53–55, 63, 69, 72, 73, 76, 79, 98, 99, 102, 107, 109, 111, 117, 125, 126, 130, 133, 134, 138–140, 142–144, 150–156, photo 153, 160, 170, 184, 206
Lewis, Robert W., Jr. 55
Lewis, Una Jane 54, 153, 154, 156
Lewis, Velma 55
Lewis, W.T. 55
Liberty, NM 58
Lincoln, NM 114, 120, 122
Lincoln County, NM 59, 101, 106, 111–114, 116–118, 120, 122, 123, 125, 132, 139, 143, 148, 149, 164
Lindsey, Washington E. (governor) 1
Little Hatchet Mountains 104
Littleton, Harris L. "Lod" 107
Lockhart, James A. 51
Log Cabin syrup 10
Lordsburg, NM 60, 99, 107, 109, 110, 170, 174
Lordsburg Western Liberal 82
Los Angeles, CA 32
Lost Adams Mine 55
Louisiana 118
Lowry, James 188
Lozano, Jose 130
Luna, Solomon (councilman) 68, photo 68
Luna County, NM 33, 52, 106, 155, 158

Mabry, Woodford 23
MacConnell, C.E. "XIT Buck" 114
MacDonald, John H. (Canadian prime minister) 16
Magdalena, NM 1, 30, 54, 55, 101, 157, 159, 160, 189, 191, 200
Magdalena Cattle Drive Trial 130
Magnum brothers photo 128, 129, 133, 170, 190, 191
Maine 6
Manzano Mountains 115, 116
Manzano Stage Line 202
Marijuana 10
Martin, William E. "Billie" (councilman) 33
Martinez, Malaquies (councilman) 18, 33–34
Martinez, Romudo (United States Marshal) 166
Massachusetts 6, 84
Maxwell House coffee 10
Mayberry, H.T. 49
McCulloch County, TX 55
McDonald, William C. (governor) 1
McDonald, William J. (Texas Ranger captain) 91, 152
McGrath, Herbert James (captain) 2, 53, 60–61, 63–65, 69, 72, 73, 78, 79, 84, 95, 99, 107, 109, 110, 117, 133, 141, 144, 145, 152, 155, 163–165, 169, photo 169, 170, 174, 197, 206
McGuffey's Eclectic Readers 10
McHughes, James H. 81
McKinley, William (president) 26, 166
McKinley County, NM 32, 126, 128, 129, 150
McMahan, Frank M. 20
McMarters, the Rev. Dr. Aljorman S. 38
Meadow City *see* Las Vegas
Mechem, Merritt C. 186–188
Memphis, MO 41
Mesilla Valley 105
Mexico 30, 34, 102, 104, 109, 117, 154, 156, 190
Meyer, Charles 57
Meyer, Geneva 57
Meyer, Julius 2, 56–57, 72, 73, 79, 89, 90, 92, 93, 99, 100, 101, 107, photo 108, 109, 115–117, 126–129, photo 128, 138, 140, 144–146, 148, 157–159, 196, 206
Meyer, Librada "Libby" 56, 90, 129
Michigan 30
Mileage fees 18–21
Miller, Abran 122
Millican, W.A. (Texas Ranger) 152
Mills, William J. (governor) 1
Mining 12
Minute Tapioca 11
Mississippi River 41
Missouri 37, 41
Mogollon, NM 52, 63, 130
Mogollon Mountains 130, 144
Monero, NM 138, 140
Mongdon, Albert 150
Montoya, Nestor (councilman) 30, 32
Moonshine Canyon 130
Mora, NM 84
Mormon (Church of Jesus Christ of Later Day Saints) 127
Morrison, the Rev. A.P. 116
Mossman, Burton C. (Arizona Ranger captain) 23–26, 27–28, 94
Motorcycle 1, 84
Mount Taylor 145
Mountainair, NM 115, 202
Murphy, Frank 27
Murphy, Nathan Oakes (Arizona governor) 23–27, 48
Murphy, Sarah 27

Nacimiento badlands 127
National Democrat (Memphis, MO) 41
National Police Gazette 11
Navajo Indians 127, 145, 203, 204

Negrito River 144
Nelson, Charles 63
New Hampshire 6
New Jersey 6
New Mexico Cattle Protective Association 19
New Mexico Cattle Sanitary Board 18, 30, 32, 53, 54, 61, 63, 105, 126, 170
New Mexico Insane Asylum 201
New Mexico Mounted Police Fund: abolishment 180, 197; attorney general opinion 174–176; auditor problems 176–180; contingency expense 173–174; deficit financing 172; mill levy 173–180; purpose 180; record of warrants issued against 179
New Mexico National Guard 31, 136, 137
New Mexico Sheep Sanitary Board 58
New Mexico State Legislature 1, 197, 206
New Mexico State Police 197, 206
New Mexico State University 14, 16, 145, 195, 202
New Mexico Tech (School of Mines) 201, 203
New Mexico Territorial Legislative Assembly 1, 13–20, 29–35, 102, 147, 163, 176, 180, 195, 197, 199
New Mexico Territorial Mounted Police: annual report to the governor 172, 175, 176; appointment list 96–97; appointment of Stewart and Gomez 170–171; badge 79, 124, 165; bootheel raids 103–104; CB 26: Greer Mounted Police Bill (1905) 33–36, 82, 172–180, 190, 195, 198; CB 54: Richardson Mounted Police Bill (1899) 16–18, 24, 79; command structure 94–95, 199; communications 89–90; deputy territorial fish and game warden 79, 115; Dudley's June Scout 117–118; epilogue of Fullerton's Rangers 206; expense account 83; field reports 90–91, 172; first killing, shootout at Capitan 120–124; first territorial police patrol 98–106; flags 137, photo 137; fountain and Chaves murder cases 102–103; Fullerton-Hagerman-Fornoff triangle 181–195; general orders 91–92, 168–169; headquarters 74; Hicks brothers' case 101–102; horse and camp gear 82–85, 110, 115; Huber's suspension/ resignation 165–168; hunt for Apache Kid 144, 145; hunt for Chaves Ranch cattle 115–117; hunt for Doan and Baca 129, 130, 132; hunt for Indian poachers 145–149; hunt for the Magnum brothers 126–129, 190, 191; illness among the rangers 143, 144; inter-agency co-operative 95–96, 110; Lincoln County roundup 110–114; list of arrests made by the rangers 161–162; list of Council vote for Greer Mounted Police Bill 35; list of Fullerton's Rangers' oath of office 96, 97; list of House vote for Greer Mounted Police Bill 35; list of NM county sheriffs, 1905–1906 97; Luna-Bursum Selection Committee 67–70, 89; modus operandi 92–93; muster ceremony 72–74; need for the territorial police 163; Otero kidnapping plot 132–135, 174; patrol duty 84; patrol squads 72; police equipment 81–82, photo 82, 194; purchase orders/ payroll vouchers 75, 77, 172, 174; railroad passes 86–89, photo 87, 103, 106, 124, 194; recommendation for more rangers, better compensation 163, 194, 199; resignation of Brophy 171; resignation of Elkins 164, 165; resignation of McGrath 169–170; resignation of Perea 170–171; secondary appointments 163–164; Sgt. Lewis' Long Hunt 151–156; Sheriff Street controversy 186–188; Territorial fair, Albuquerque 135, 136, 141, 170; Territorial fair, Las Vegas 136, 137, 141, 170; transition of ranger command 196; uniform 76–78, 106; weapons 79–81, photos 80, 103, 105, 110, 121, 126, 165; White Caps fence cutters 15, 30, 138–140, 192
New Mexico Territorial Penitentiary 52, 169, 188, 199
New Mexico Territory 5, 6, 9, 30, 32, 53, 55, 56, 63, 76, 100, 104–106, 118, 124, 125, 129, 132, 138, 142, 143 146, 147, 149, 150, 156, 157, 159, 163, 166, 170, 172–180, 181, 184, 185, 187, 188, 190, 191, 193, 194, 196, 197, 199, 201, 203
New Mexico Volunteer Infantry 102
New York 6
New York Stock Exchange 157
New York Times 5, 9

Nietzsche 189
Nogal, NM 59, 151
Nogal Republican 29, 100
Nuevomexicano 6, 65, 111, 112, 138

Occidental Life Insurance Company 199, 200
Oconto, WS 57
Odd Fellows fraternity 136
O'Donel, Charles M. 94
Oklahoma 193
Old Mission Trail 117
Olsen, Clara 70, 88, 89, 165, 172, 174, 175, 182, 183
Otero, Caroline 133
Otero, Elizabeth 133
Otero, Lottie 133
Otero, Miguel Antonio (governor) 2, 5, 12, 19, 24–27, photo 26, 30, 32–36, 48, 49, 52, 57, 61, 64–71, 76, 84, 87, 88, 93, 116, 125, 131–137, 139, 143, 155, 164–168, 170, 172, 174, 176, 181–183, 189, 206
Otero, Miguel Antonio III 133
Otero, Miguel Antonio IV 132–135
Otero, Page 79, 133, 134, 145–149, photo 146
Otero, Page, Jr. 133
Otero County, NM 18, 27, 33, 60, 106, 108, 111, 124, 164
Otero County Advertiser 67, 103, 111, 150
Otero Guards 76
Otero Ranch 133
Ozona Kicker 115

Palace Hotel, Santa Fe 32, 182
Palace of the Governors 116
Palomas, Mexico 56
Paris, MO 56
Park House Hotel, Socorro 54
Parker, Arch 143
Parker, Judge Frank W. 107, 130
Parker County, TX 59
Parmer, Oliver (Arizona Ranger) 28
Pass City *see* El Paso, TX
Patterson, Dr. 41
Patterson, NM 130, 146
Pecos River 133–135, 141, 148
Pennsylvania 41, 84
Perea, Octaviano 60, 67, 68, 72, 73, 79, 93, 99, 108, 111, photo 112, 112–114, 117, 126–129, photo 127, 164, 165, 170, 171, 184, 197, 206
Perea, Pedro 49
Perez, Severo 122
Pershing, Gen. John J. 56
Philippines 193
Phoenix, AZ 109
Pickerel, Jewel Street 187
Pierce, William 139

Pinos Wells, NM 115
Pittsburg, PA 11
Popular Mechanics 11
Posse Comitatus law 15
Post Toasties (Elijah's Manna) 11
Postum coffee substitute 11
Postura, NM 151, 157
Presbyterian Church 42, 44, 200, 201
Prescott, AZ 188
Prewitt, NM 204
Price Brothers' Store 129
Prichard, George W. 123, 174–176, photo 175, 186–188
Progresso, NM 109
Public schools 14
Pueblo Indians 147, 148
Purdy, Helen Marie *see* Fullerton, Helen
Purdy, Van R. 201
Putman, Rhody 63
Putman, Robert G. 63–64, 76, 107, 110, 117, 130, 134, 140, 141, 150, 159, 160, 164, 167, 168, 206

Quaker Oats 10
Quay County, NM 58, 118
Quemado, NM 130

Railroads 12, 149, 150
Ramah, NM 128, 145
Randolph, Cipriana Baca 51–53, 73, 77
Raton, NM 15, 84, 105, 142
Raynolds, J. Wallace (acting-governor) 70, 73, 163, 164, 178
Red Cliff House Lodge, Pecos River 133
Redding, W.Z. 189–191
Redmond, John McK (Arizona Ranger) 28
Regan, Jim 56
Republican Party 32–34, 67–69, 75, 114
Reserve, NM 130
Rhode Island 6
Richardson, Granville A. (councilman) 16–17, photo 16
Richardson, NM 109
Riley, Cage 187
Rincon, NM 99
Rio Arriba County, NM 17, 33, 138, 140, 141
Rio Grande 27, 101, 108, 116, 117, 114, 129, 141, 146, 149, 152
Ripley, Miss 186
robbers' roost 21, 158, 183
Rodgers, John H. (Texas Ranger captain) 152
Rodreguez, Perfecto 151
Roosevelt, Anna Eleanor 70
Roosevelt, Franklin Delano 70
Roosevelt, Theodore (president) 10, 70, 87, 144, 167, 181, 183–186, 193, 206

Rosemead, CA 6
Ross, Betsey 5
Ross, Edmund G. (governor) 33
Roswell, NM 16, 34, 141
Rough Rider regiment 17, 87, 193
Ruidoso, NM 111, 118, 142
Rurales (Mexican federal police) 30, 152
Rusher, Robert 120, 122, 123
Rusk, J.B. "Slim" 81
Russia 125
Russie, Robert 120
Rynning, Thomas Harbro (Arizona Ranger captain) 22, 26, 28, 30, 72, 91, 94

Sacramento Mountains 118
St. Louis, MO 102
St. Louis, Rocky Mountain & Pacific Railroad 142
St. Petersburg, Russia 185
Salado Pastura 111, 151
Salado River 118
Salmon, NM 127
San Antonio, NM 101
San Antonio, TX 62
San Antonio Hot Springs, NM 32
San Augustin Plains 45, 46
San Cristobal, NM 203
San Diego, CA 198, 204
San Diego Union 32
San Felipe Pueblo Indians 148
San Juan County, NM 33, 64, 127–129, 145, 164, 170, 190, 191
San Juan Index 128, 129
San Juan River 127
San Marcial, NM 108, 124
San Mateo Mountains 144
San Miguel County, NM 105, 115, 138, 157, 182, 192
Sanchez, G.E. (sheriff) 52
Sanchez, Librada *see* Meyer, Libby
Sanchez y Baca, Felipe 157
Sanders, W.P. 189–191
Sandia Park, NM 55
Sandoval, Don Antonio 158
Sandoval County, NM 32
Sandoval Land Grant 116
Sanka coffee substitute 11
Santa Ana, CA 57
Santa Fe, NM 2, 17, 29, 32, 61, 64, 69, 72, 74, 76, 84, 89, 94, 98, 99, 116, 119, 125, 130, 133–136, 138, 141, 146, 150, 155, 166, 170, 174, 178, 181, 184, 189, 196
Santa Fe Central Railroad 88, 99
Santa Fe County, NM 61, 64, 114, 116, 148, 164
Santa Fe New Mexican 29, 32, 37, 63, 69, 74, 93, 98–100, 113, 120, 122, 123, 139, 142, 155, 159, 165, 184, 192, 195, 197, 198
Santa Fe Pacific Railroad 86, 99

Santa Rosa, NM 99, 115, 151, 155, 157, 158
Santa Rosa Sun 157
Sargent, William G. 173–180, photo 173, 184
Scarborough, George 17, 19–20, photo 19
Scarborough, George Edward "Ed" (Arizona Ranger) 20, 26–27
Scarborough's Rangers 18–20
Scott, Earl 56
Scott, H.A. 109
Scott County, MO 41
Sellers, D.K.B. 31, 38, 135
Sena, Apolonio A. (captain) 62, 84, 197, 206
Shaffer, Pop 115
Sherman, Gen. William Tecumseh 5
Shofner, Frank 78, 117
Shofner, Lois Ann 59, 113
Sierra Blanca, TX 152
Sierra County, NM 18, 27, 30, 63, 65, 141, 164
Sierra Oscura 117
Silver City, NM 2, 12, 15, 52, 61, 63, 99, 109, 110, 124, 151, 197
Silver City Enterprise 60
Silver City Independent 99, 103, 128
Simons, Ella *see* Avant, Ella
Singer, I.B. 108
Six-Shooter Siding *see* Tucumcari
Sleight, Beatrice 48, 200
Sleight, Katharine Lay *see* Fullerton, Katharine
Smith, Bill gang 26
Smith, H.B. (Texas Ranger) 152
Smith, Thomas S. 24
Smith, W.H. "Hudson" 119
Smith Brothers' Cough Drops 10
Snyder, OK 125
Socorro, NM 12, 53, 54, 84, 98, 99, 101, 106, 110, 114, 117, 121, 124, 129, 130, 132, 141, 153–155, 160, 166, 182, 190, 193, 203, 204
Socorro Chieftain 13, 17, 98, 100, 108, 114, 124, 126, 145, 154–156, 159, 168
Socorro County, NM 18, 27, 51, 53, 54, 63, 64, 69, 75, 109, 117, 130, 144–149, 156, 160, 189–191, 193, 198, 200, 204
Socorro vigilantes 203
Solomon, Nathan 77, 78
Sonora, AZ 99
South Africa 125
Southern Pacific Railroad 24, 99, 151
Springer Lake 119
Steamboat race 43
Stewart, E. Rhea 64, 206, 128, 170, 171, 197

Index

Stewart, Jimmy (actor) 186
Stewart, Miles Cicero 95
Stock detective law 19
Street, James Alexander 58, 95, 159, 160, 186–188, 186, photo 187
Sullenger, Jettie Avant 120
Sunnyside, NM 182, 183
Sunshine Territory *see* New Mexico Territory
Sunshine Theater, Albuquerque 205

Tabasco Coal Camp, NM 150
Tafolla, Carlos (Arizona Ranger) 26–27
Taos, NM
Taos County, NM 17, 30, 33–34
Taos Pueblo Indians 148
Taylor, William M. 65, 66, 72, 73, 79, 89, 164
Teec Nos Pos, NM 127
Territorial fair 32, 170
Texas 29, 34, 62, 76, 115, 142, 143, 149, 150, 152, 187, 201
Texas Pacific Railroad 152
Texas Rangers 1, 21, 23–24, 28, 95, 99, 131, 152, 153, 163, 167
Texico, NM 149
Thornton, William T. (governor) 182
Tierra Amarilla, NM 12
Titsworth, George 120–122
Tiwa Indian language 148
Tombstone, AZ 109
Tome, NM 108
Torrance, NM 99
Torrance County, NM 2, 33, 56, 108, 109, 115, 116, 141, 149, 200
Torreon, NM 60, 117
Towa Indian language 148
Trelford, Arthur 199

Tres Piedras, NM 157
Trinidad, CO 136
Tucumcari, NM 30, 119, 138, 171, 186
Tucumcari News 158, 186
Tularosa, NM 30
Turkey Track Bars Ranch 114
Turquoise State *see* New Mexico Territory
20 Mule Team Borax 11
26 Men (TV show) 28
Tyler, TX 59

Union County, NM 57, 58, 105, 119, 150, 171
United States Indian Service 1–2
University of Chicago 31
University of New Mexico 14, 145
Utah 76

Valencia County, NM 33, 60, 64, 102, 145
Valley of Fire 101, 132
Valley of Playas 107
Valverde, battle of 202
Van Camp's Pork and Beans 11
Vaseline Petroleum Jelly 10
Vaughn, Boone C. 95, 128, 190, 191, photo 191
Vaughn, J.H. 177
Vaughn, NM 128, 150, 157
Vermejo Park, NM 54
Vermejo River 1
Vick's Vapo Rub 10
Victor Land and Cattle Company 31
Vigil, Eslanio 131
Villa, Francisco "Poncho" 2, 56
The Virginian 126
VV Ranch 121, 122

Waldon, Henry, Judge 133
Waldrip, TX 55
Wall Street Stock Exchange 157
Walters, William "Bronco Bill" 51
War Between the States 38–41, 53, 70, 102
Waterloo, Iowa 31
Watrous, NM 105
Welch, E.B. 120
Welch & Titsworth Store 120, 122
Wells, Fargo Express Company 30
Wheeler, Henry (Arizona Ranger captain) 94, 168, 193
Whirlwind 135
White Caps fence cutters 15, 30, 138–140, 192
White Mountains 108, 113
White Oaks, NM 56, 59, 101
White Oaks Outlook 88, 100, 164
Wichita, KS 59
Willard, NM 56, 115–117, 167, 168
Williams, Ben 129, 130, 139
Williams, Vancouver 150
Windsor Hotel, Socorro 132
Winters, David C. (councilman) 33
Winton automobile 141
Wise, C.A. 109
Wister, Owen 126
Woman's Home Companion 10
Women's Christian Temperance Union 13
Woodbury's women's products 11
World War I (The Great War) 197

Y & E Quick Copier Machine 11

www.ingramcontent.com/pod-product-compliance
Ingram Content Group UK Ltd.
Pitfield, Milton Keynes, MK11 3LW, UK
UKHW050537150426
5217IPUK00026B/1976